THE CHANCE OF A LIFETIME ?

The Chance of a Lifetime ?

A study of boys' and coeducational
boarding schools in England and Wales

ROYSTON LAMBERT
with Roger Bullock and Spencer Millham

Weidenfeld and Nicolson
London

Weidenfeld and Nicolson
11 St John's Hill   London SW11

ISBN 0 297 76862 X

Printed and bound in Great Britain by
REDWOOD BURN LIMITED
Trowbridge & Esher

Contents

Acknowledgements

The research from which this book derives was made possible by grants from the Department of Education and Science and King's College, Cambridge, which also provided space in its Research Centre. I owe thanks to both institutions for their support.

To many boys and girls, teachers, housestaff and headmasters (and their wives) who helped us not only with information but with warmth and hospitality, I offer most grateful thanks. In particular I am indebted to those who were open-minded and generous enough to help the research in its most precarious, tentative stages: especially John Dancy, Harry Edwards and John Underwood.

Encouragement came from many academic colleagues but I received particular help at various stages from the following: Noel Annan, David Donnison, Liam Hudson, the late Richard Titmuss, Peter Townsend and Michael Young.

Members of the group who at one time or another contributed to the work in this book were: Gay Boehm, Penny Fitzgerald, John Hipkin, Penny Mellor, Susan Moody, Philip Powell, Mallory Wober and Raymond Woolfe. Spencer Millham and Roger Bullock have been involved throughout and substantially contributed to the preparation of this report.

To Carol Haine, Mrs Pullen, Aileen Stein, Penny Hardwicke, Lee Mosedale, Betty Paull and Marilyn Coles thanks are also due for typing the various drafts.

ROYSTON LAMBERT
Dartington Hall School
Devon
May 1973

Introduction

This book is not the one which I had in mind when the research which it discusses started in 1964. Circumstances changed so markedly during and after the work in the field, and partly because of it, that the final outcome of the research has had to change as well.

When the study of the nature and effects of boarding education began, there was very little evidence available on the subject. Admittedly, the shelves of the University Library at Cambridge concerned with residential education groaned under a mass of published works. But they were all memoirs, or manifestos, or polemics, and not objective studies of the issue. They were also entirely about the public schools, as though these particular schools were the only residential ones for normal children in the country. My inquiry therefore had three aims: first, to find out what kinds of boarding schools there were in England and Wales and to compare them in terms of objectives, operation and effect; secondly, to assess, in so far as it was possible, the general effects on children of residential education compared with day education; and thirdly, to develop an objective framework for studying and comparing schools as societies.

Soon after the research began the situation began to change. Partly in response to the election late in 1964 of a Labour Government pledged to alter the public school system, partly because of the unexpected interest generated by the research itself and partly because other independent scholars began to report, general concern about the issue mounted rapidly and so did the information available. Two academic sociologists produced valuable studies of the public schools, Ian Weinberg in 1967 and John Wakeford in 1969. The Headmasters' Conference commissioned a statistician, Graham Kalton, to survey the boys' public schools and the first thorough statistics on them appeared in 1966. In the same year a useful factual survey was published on behalf of the boys' preparatory schools. Another more general study of residential education, not based on empirical inquiry, was produced by W.R. Fraser in

1968, and excellent historical accounts of the public school style of boarding by T. Bamford and by Bishop and Wilkinson appeared in 1967.

While my main research was proceeding, confined by the terms of the original grant to boys, and coeducational schools of secondary-age range, we were invited to undertake some special further investigation for the Public Schools Commission which was set up in 1965 and to publish some byproducts of our work to help inform the lively discussion. We therefore published reports on conferences and seminars on boarding education, studies on the alleged 'need' for boarding education and the policies of local authorities with regard to it, on state maintained boarding schools, on different schemes of social integration then operating in public schools, on religious education in a residential context, on coeducation, on the informal systems in schools. The separate study of girls' boarding schools undertaken from my unit by Mallory Wober was published in 1971. Yet other studies were made on the 'progressive' style of education and on need and demand for boarding education but those are not yet fully published. A selection from the large mass of illustrative data which we had gathered on the main inquiry appeared in a separate book in 1968 as the children's view of their experience. Later we published the first results of our effort to develop an objective methodology of studying the school as a society. Meanwhile we had been submitting confidential reports to the Public Schools Commission which itself reported in 1968 in two substantial volumes containing some results of the surveys it had sponsored. And, as soon as our fieldwork was completed on the original investigation, we were invited to make a further study, this time for the Home Office, of residential schools for delinquent and deprived boys based on our earlier methodology. A full report on this was presented to the government in 1972 and a shorter version is shortly to appear in print. A list of all these studies deriving from the research is given in Appendix 1.

Thus in 1964 there had been a scarcity of evidence on boarding education but by 1969, when this book was first drafted, there was a plethora of material. By the latter date general interest in the matter had also begun to wane as it became clear that no government action was likely in response to the policies advocated by the Commission.

The research however then underwent an even more unexpected development. Having spent the years 1964-8 teaching, interviewing, discussing and recording in schools all over the country, I was inevitably concerned that the results of research to which so many people had contributed should be widely disseminated. I had therefore already organized seminars and conferences at which the issues raised could be debated by those involved in the schools and out of this came the formation of a Boarding Schools Association in 1966 as a forum for people working in this area of education. The research group had also advised several government departments, local authorities, the governing bodies of some state and independent schools on practical plans for schools in their care. In other words, though I believed the process of research to be objective, I had been prepared, indeed thought it morally imperative when so requested, to help translate the findings of research into practical action and even to enter controversial situations as a result. In 1967, suddenly and unexpectedly, I was invited by the trustees of Dartington Hall to become head of their 'progressive' boarding school in Devon and to put some of the ideas produced by my research into practice there. Accordingly a year later I moved to Dartington as headmaster and my research unit moved with me, concentrating its field-work on the study of approved schools for the Home Office. Now in 1973, having initiated and seen through a range of experiments at the school, I am hoping to move Dartington to one of its experimental outposts which has been established from there but I am also continuing to work with the research unit on its studies of residential special education.

My original aim in 1964 had been to produce an extensive and detailed report giving the results of our studies on the nature and effects of boarding and the first draft of 1969 ran to twenty-six chapters. In view of the large amount of diffuse material which was still appearing it seemed advisable to wait until the spate of publication and debate was exhausted and then to produce a more succinct work: one which attempted to sum up the present state of our knowledge about the aims, structures, styles and effects of boarding education for ordinary children. Moreover it seemed sensible also to wait too for the outcome of some of the initiatives being tried at Dartington so that some of the practical consequences of the research could receive discussion if not final objective evaluation. The original draft has therefore been scrapped. The book has been rewritten in less elaborate form, cutting out picturesque illustrative quotations, fine points of sociological analysis, and reducing the supporting mass of statistical tables. Those who want to see such data can do so at the Research Office at Dartington. I have also included a more personal chapter on the developments undertaken at Dartington in the light of the research. I hope that this presentation of findings will serve as both the general conclusion of the original research and a general review of boarding education in boys' and coeducational schools as it is now in the mid 1970s. Readers who wish to pursue themes in greater depth can turn to the specialist monographs mentioned above and listed in the bibliographies.

One personal point. As a direct result of this research I have been for five years head of a school which is independent, 'progressive' and largely boarding. This does not mean that this book is biased in favour of schools which are independent or 'progressive' or boarding as described in this book or, indeed, that I believe that school structures as we know them are universally necessary for the development of the young. It certainly does not mean that this book favours one kind of boarding against another or boarding in general as opposed to day education. This book reports fairly on the findings of research which was as objective as I and my colleagues could make it. And it gives my view, and my view alone, of what has happened at Dartington since the research ended. I could not know when I first stepped out of my panelled rooms at King's College, Cambridge in 1964 to make the first stay of my life in a boarding school at Clifton in Bristol that my inquiries would change my own work from academic sociology to practical construction and lead me to an experimental centre in a mining town in Yorkshire.

I in no way regret my present combination of roles but I hope that this book will not be rendered suspect because of it.

II

When it started in 1964 our main research programme was con-

fined by time, money and other considerations to a study of
sixty-six boarding schools, their staff and pupils, some
comparison day schools and the families of boarders.

As the research proceeded we were able to undertake further
investigations of other topics. Thus we completed a survey of
the attitudes of parents, pupils and staff of state day schools
towards boarding and the policies of all the English local
authorities on the matter. We covered by research the special
project of integration by which in 1966-8 pupils from state day
schools in Swindon were taken in as boarders to the public
school at Marlborough. We made studies for the Public Schools
Commission of boys' preparatory schools and girls' boarding
schools, of various schemes of integration, of criteria of 'need'
for boarding, and problems of need and demand. Since these
researches ended we have undertaken and completed a survey of
residential schools for deprived and delinquent children and,
though this book does not present the findings of this research,
it has benefited from the perspective which this special area of
boarding offers to a study of the ordinary kind. A fuller
account of the research programme and its methodology is
given in Appendix II.

The main research of 1964-8 covered a sample of sixty-six
schools in England and Wales, all for boys, or coeducational, all
of secondary-age range, all of which had half or more of their
pupils as boarders and all of which were recognized by the
Ministry of Education as efficient. The terms of the original
grant towards our research, quite apart from the attitudes of the
schools, did not enable us to include preparatory or girls'
schools or those which were not recognized by the Ministry.
To ensure that important minorities in our defined field were
fully represented, we varied the sampling from the lists of
schools. We studied one in every three of all the boarding
schools on the list of boys' public schools (the Headmasters'
Conference list), one in three of schools of the 'progressive'
variety (as listed in the *Independent Progressive School*), and
one in five of all the other recognized independent boarding
schools in the published government handbook. Some of these
schools - direct grant or independent - had half or more of
their pupils supported financially either by state agencies or
charitable funds and they are described as 'integrated' schools in

this book. In view of the interest of the small and developing state maintained sector of boarding we took a sample of one in every 1·5 of the mainly boarding schools directly run by local education authorities. We also visited three boarding schools run by the Ministry of Defence abroad for British children and half a dozen small boarding hostels attached to day schools, but we are not using statistical material from any of these in this book.

To give the research depth as well as breadth and to gain the confidence of the schools, most of which had never encountered researchers before, we started work in a sub-sample of seven of the sixty-six schools and studied them minutely during a period of continuous observation and survey lasting in each at least half a term or more. These seven schools we shall call the *intensive sample*. They comprised four public schools, three integrated or maintained ones and were carefully selected by region, size, fee structure and boarding/day pupil composition, though obviously they are not a scientifically valid sub-sample. In six of them (one refused) all of the pupils aged sixteen to eighteen, 1,238 in all or ninety-seven per cent of the age group, completed a searching three and a half hour questionnaire under controlled conditions. For various practical and sensible reasons put forward by staff and discussed in Appendix II it was not possible to sample among pupils in the schools we visited, and we therefore surveyed, census-like, all the age group concerned.

The other fifty-nine schools were visited, sometimes by two or three of the research team together, for shorter periods most usually of two weeks or more. These schools we shall call *the extensive sample*.

Length of stay at sixty-six schools

	No. of schools
Three nights to one week	25
Up to two weeks	27
Up to three weeks	6
Over three weeks	8
	66

In all the schools on the extensive as well as the intensive sample, the researchers lived and slept on the premises, went through the ordinary pattern of life and tried to experience all aspects of the school: classroom, chapel, games, social service, corps, the pupil world, the staff common room, meetings and social life. Subsequent visits were made to about a quarter of the schools and contact maintained with them over some years. In all the schools the headmaster was interviewed at length, and a sample from careers masters, deputy headmasters and chaplains was also interviewed. One in 1·4 of the housemasters of public schools and 1 in 2·5 of housestaff in other schools were interviewed, one in six of other staff, one in four of the matrons and one in seven of the school doctors. Every head boy was also interviewed. Besides much individual and group discussion with pupils of all ages, several standard questionnaires and tests were completed by pupils in classroom situations under the supervision of the researchers. Over fifty-three per cent of all the pupils in the fifty-nine schools completed such tests, but the response was always over seventy-five per cent of the age groups concerned in each school. Once again these sampling ratios are considerably greater than needed for statistical validity but were imposed on us by the conditions in which research was done in the schools.

Many pupils wrote diaries or special accounts of their experiences for us. In addition much documentary information was made available by headmasters, their staff and the pupils, consisting of files, reports, school papers, minutes, housebooks and numerous records and memoranda of one kind or another.

We wished to assess the effects of boarding as compared with day education and decided, given our budget and the scale of our survey, that the best practicable method was to contrast boarders and day pupils within *the same schools*, thereby holding as constant as possible the varieties of school setting and, to a lesser degree, those of social class and background culture. Therefore we compared boarders and day pupils in two public schools on the intensive sample and in ten other schools on the extensive sample consisting of two other public schools, one integrated, two progressive and five state boarding schools. To make yet broader comparisons we chose four completely day schools and compared their pupils on certain criteria with

those from boarding schools similar in status, structure, composition and background. Details are given in Chapter 8. In all
these schools the boarders and day pupils completed tests and
questionnaires containing questions from our initial hypotheses
on the effects of residential or non-residential experience.

The following table sums up on the data on the sixty-six
schools:

No.	Type of school	Completed interviews:		No. of children answering question-naires	Total nos. in school	Percentage of pupils interviewed and answering
		Staff	Pupils			
15	Maintained	145	165	2148	3090	69·5
18	Independent	186	244	2414	4014	60·1
7	Progressive	86	71	1336	1855	72·0
26	Public schools	333	349	4283	10204	42·0
66	Total	750	829	10181	19163	53·1

It was important to examine the family life of the boarder
about which nothing was known. Once again financial
stringency made us look deeply rather than extensively. We
took three contrasting kinds of boarder and examined their
family lives: those at a large and famous public school with
conventional and long-established patterns of residence; those at
an old established state boarding school well known to be run
on public school lines, who had mixed grounds for boarding and
backgrounds of residence; those from a maintained secondary
modern school with no background of residential experience at
all. We interviewed parents of a stratified random sample of
boy boarders who had been at each of these schools for four or
more years, our sampling ranging from one in two to one in
four according to the size of the school. Over ninety-five per
cent of the parents eligible agreed to be interviewed in their
homes for three hours, 179 parents in all. We also had their
sons' questionnaires completed independently at school to
compare with their own answers, with fascinating results.

So much for the main research, further details of which
appear in Appendix II, and in the separate chapters also. This

book also refers to some material gathered in the other, later and supplementary, studies undertaken by my unit. In 1966-8 a survey was made of a sample of twenty-five independent recognized preparatory schools for boys, and we occasionally use data from this. In discussing effects of boarding we also refer to findings in Dr Wober's separate study of recognized girls' boarding schools of which he studied a sample of twenty-three. Information is also used on boarding policies gathered from 136 local education authorities in England and Wales, and also on attitudes towards boarding, the actual or potential 'need' for residence, gathered from a special study done in five different areas of the country, 124 state day schools, 11,047 pupils, 9,953 parents as well as teachers, social workers and others.

All this then is the basis for our review of the nature and effects of boarding education.

1 Boarding in society

Educational institutions serve three basic functions for the society in which they are placed. First, they can be one means by which society *allocates* its human resources: to various kinds or levels of occupation, to different statuses or roles or to different social classes. The process of education is thus one of stratification and can operate to promote or to obstruct social mobility. Secondly, all educational institutions act as a means of *integration* within society. They integrate instrumentally by transmitting those basic skills - intellectual, physical, social and practical - without which society could not function efficiently. They integrate expressively by communicating those common values without which the society could not cohere and continue: norms of morality, belief and behaviour, history, tradition and the accepted culture of the society. Thirdly, educational institutions can perform *administrative* tasks for the society, acting as agents of social welfare, shelter or custody and, in various degrees, taking over some of the functions of the family.

All schools have these three kinds of function, but boarding schools, those where boys and girls reside as well as learn under the control of adults other than their families, can exercise some of them more effectively than can day schools. There is no evidence that allocative functions are more adequately served by boarding as opposed to day schools; indeed, day school systems preponderate in most societies as the main means of stratification by education. However, when it comes to the *integrative* functions, the two kinds of schooling differ in their effectiveness. There is little evidence that boarding education is a more effective means of transmitting instrumental skills than day education, though most societies, primitive, ancient and modern, have used some form of boarding as a means of transmitting certain 'mysteries', as in the training of warriors, military castes and religious elites. But in attaining *expressive* integration - the communication of values, norms and cultural patterns - the more embracing and sustained experience of the boarding school can be more effective than the limited one provided by the day school. In this respect, boarding

education is one of the most powerful methods known for
influencing the young. As we shall see, it is the greater
potential of residential education for achieving expressive
integration that has led some societies to cherish it, others
deliberately to adopt it, and subcultures within them all to use
it as a means of their own self-perpetuation. Finally, the
administrative functions of boarding schools for society
are clearly more extensive than those of day schools, even those
with patterns of extended day education. For meeting social
dislocation - taking over some of the functions of the family,
acting as an agent of social welfare or custody - the boarding
school is more appropriately equipped and structured than its
counterpart.

Though these comparisons apply to boarding and day schools
in general, the precise functions of residential education vary
from society to society and even from country to country; this
book cannot explore them all. Nevertheless, a review of the
role of boarding in different parts of our contemporary world is
essential if we are to understand the unique part it plays in
Britain.

II

Something akin to boarding, in practice and function, can be
found among many primitive societies where adolescent boys
are removed from their families to live under adult control in
order to be initiated into the lore, responsibilities and roles of
adulthood.[1] Among the members of the Poro society of West
Africa, for example, boys might go away to a 'bush school' for a
year or more to learn tribal lore and customs, skills of hunting,
warfare, trades and sexual knowledge. Among other tribes - the
Mbuti pigmies, the Suku of the Congo, the Bantu of East
Central Africa - similar periods of adolescent seclusion, training,
mortification and toughening are followed by a ritual initiation
into adulthood. Among the Moslem people of the Zanzibar
coast some girls spend up to six months away from their home
under instruction, while girls belonging to the Poro society may
retreat into the bush for up to a year to be instructed in the
wifely, maternal and domestic roles which they will assume on
return to the adult world. Basuto boys in South Africa leave

their herds at puberty and build their own school, where they spend three months being instructed in law, tradition, sex and hunting. These initiation rituals culminate in the ceremonial burning down of the school - a school-leaving celebration found among other tribes but denied to more sophisticated boarders of advanced societies. Many other primitive societies in Africa and elsewhere have similar practices.[2]

Though the analogy cannot be pushed too far and the duration of the period away from home is nearly always short, there are remarkable similarities between boarding in primitive and in some advanced societies. It is supervised by elders, it affects mainly adolescent boys, it prepares for the transition from childhood to adult roles, it transmits adult culture and it is accompanied by rituals symbolizing the discarding of the juvenile past, the hardening to manhood and the adoption of adult stature. Though in some cases there are signs that the processes in these tribes occasionally have allocative functions such as the marking out of particularly hardy elites and the elimination of weaklings and deviants,[3] the main functions of this kind of boarding are clearly integrative in both the instrumental and expressive senses: it hands on the necessary skills, roles and culture of the tribe. In primitive societies boarding outside the family is not used as an administrative or welfare device.

In two advanced societies outside western Europe boarding is used as an educational method on a larger scale than anywhere else in the world including Britain. These are Israel and the Soviet Union.

In Israel there are a variety of boarding schools: agricultural schools within the state system containing some 7,500 boys and girls over the age of fourteen; Yeshivot schools which are independent religious schools for boys containing some 5,000 boarders; and the 150 schools run by the Youth Aliyah Organization, catering for 10,000 children of all ages, mainly immigrants or those from unsettled homes.[4] In addition there are the kibbutzim settlements where over five per cent of Israeli children live and are educated alongside their families, but not sufficiently apart to come within the definition of boarding used in this book. Excluding these children, it seems that children boarding at school in Israel are five per cent of the whole school population and about fifteen per cent of the secondary school population. In no other country in the world is such a large proportion of school children experiencing residential education. There seems to be no special allocative role played by boarding in Israeli society: boarding (as distinct from kibbutz life) is not connected with the rearing of an elite of any kind. Instead, its integrative and administrative functions are paramount. Though the schools provide training in skills of all kinds, especially rural skills, Youth Aliyah has been concerned to integrate newcomers to Israeli values and culture, and the Yeshivot exists substantially to pass on and sustain religious learning and practice. Thus the stress is on expressive values in all the schools. Likewise, in all schools, and particularly those of the Youth Aliyah, administrative functions are of great importance: many children in them have no proper home and the school acts as their family substitute as well as the agent of the State's welfare policy.

In the Soviet Union boarding has been adopted deliberately as an educational policy of the State.[5] Beginning under the Kruschev regime, the numbers boarding in state schools rose from 56,000 in 1956 to about 900,000 boys and girls in over two thousand schools by 1966. No other country in the world has so many children boarding in schools and though these children are only two per cent of the total school population, this is a higher proportion than that of any other country except Israel. Originally, it was intended to have still more boarders - three million by 1970 - but in the mid-1960s economic pressures, the fall of Kruschev, an enforced reduction in the length of schooling from eleven to ten years, and problems raised by the haste of the development led to an abandonment of this grandiose aim. Instead, effort is now being put into the development of schools with extended day programmes: there were about four million children in extended day schools in 1970. Soviet boarding schools have unique features: they are state maintained and are used by all social groups; many are urban, located close to the home and to industry, with a weekly boarding pattern, distinctive methods of pastoral care and extra curricula activity. Their main function is administrative - they were founded chiefly to meet the needs of children deprived of normal parental care, and to enable the parents of others to go out to work. There are also integrative functions - to encourage children to stay longer at school, to enable manual, social and industrial work to be fully brought into the experience of scholars, and to inculcate communist values and mores more deeply than could be done in the day school. The schools seem to have been set up with no particular allocative purpose *as a system*. True, there are some special boarding schools for music, ballet and the arts, and more recent ones for physics, mathematics and chemistry, but this residential element seems incidental rather than deliberate as there are similar day schools. Boarding is not seen as a favoured means of rearing elites or of disposing of human resources in the Soviet Union.

Elsewhere in the world - apart from England - residential education is of much less significance. Many European countries have boarding schools of various kinds. Many have them serving the administrative function of bringing together children who, living in scattered rural communities, would otherwise not be able to go to a secondary school. Others meet the needs of those with defective home situations. In Denmark there is a system of 107 junior high schools containing about 10,000 boys and girls aged fourteen to eighteen, providing non-academic secondary education for children from rural areas.[6] In Spain a similar system of rural boarding schools is now being developed: twenty-three had been opened by 1970 catering for 2,500 children.[7] In Germany and France similar schools exist, and boarding departments are sometimes attached to mainly day schools, as in some French *lycées*. Most countries have boarding schools which serve integrative functions of an instrumental kind: vocational schools for farmwork in Greece and elsewhere, schools for those going into the merchant marine in Italy and so on. All countries also use residential methods for selecting and training potential officers in the forces or recruits for religious orders. These institutions obviously integrate expressively. Different countries often contain other boarding schools or clusters of them which recruit and integrate young people into the norms and patterns of various distinct subcultures. The boarding schools attached to religious orders, mainly Catholic ones, in France, Germany and Italy are examples of this kind. Others serve the interests of minorities or remain citadels of expressive ideas in education: schools like the fifteen remaining *Landerziehungsheime* in Germany, the last, and now increasingly academic, remains of a 'get-back-to-nature', non-academic, family-relations movement of the early century; schools like the *Ecole des Roches* in France, a mixture of the English public school and progressive idioms, or the International School in Holland and Salem in Germany.[8]

In Germany private education possibly carries some prestige, but in the other countries there is none attached to boarding in particular. Indeed, in some - France for example - the boarder is more likely to be an object of pity than envy. Individual boarding schools have been influential, and some are sought after by certain social groups, but they fulfil no particular allocative role in society. They do not function as a channel by which children are routed to predictable destinations.

It is only when we turn to those countries which have been influenced by the English way of life that we see boarding playing this role in society. Countries which were formerly part of the empire - Canada, Australia, South Africa and India among them - have not only the usual residential schools for preparing military and religious elites, and charity-based schools meeting the needs of children with abnormal backgrounds, but also a system of private boarding schools for fee-paying children. These schools often have a higher academic standard than those of the state system and a distinctive religious adherence that confers high social status. They are conspicuously linked with the governing group and other elite groups in society. Canadian public schools, for example, which are rapidly increasing, contain a small fraction of the total school population, but have a disproportionately large number of their former students in positions of economic power.[9] In India the public boarding schools seem more connected with the social, educational, administrative and military elites than the many missionary boarding schools.[10] Unlike the other countries we have so far mentioned, in these ones boarding has important and recognized allocative functions: it is a well-known and, in some, an increasingly sought-after route by which high social status and entry into some form of elite can be gained or preserved. As an integrative mechanism it inculcates, instrumentally and expressively, the attributes necessary in the social groups for which it provides.

Even in the United States there are indications that boarding
has a perceptible allocative function. Private education seems
to be on the increase, catering for a demand for more intensive
academic education and more articulated social education than
is thought to be provided by the state system. Many boarding
schools are connected with religious subcultures, but a group of
them, in the north east in particular, seem to prepare for high
status positions, high status universities, and certain social or
military elites.

These schools may or may not be important in recruiting the
power groups in the USA - there is controversy and little
evidence on the matter. There is some evidence, however, that
they are important in forming certain social elites. It is relevant
that boarding definitely has some recognized allocative
functions related to social stratification in that country.[11]

These then are the functions of boarding outside England. It
is only in England that the allocative role of boarding is both
important and established, even to the point of being
exaggerated.

III

Before discussing the functions of boarding in England it is
necessary to know the facts about it.

In England and Wales boarding is confined to a small minority
of school children. The facts come from the last full government survey in 1967 but are substantially accurate for the mid
1970s. There are about 152,585 boarders and they comprise
1·9 per cent of the total school population. As most children
start boarding at puberty, they constitute 3·4 per cent of all
children of secondary school age. There are more than twice as
many boys boarding as girls. Just under a third of the boys
(29,302), start boarding before the age of thirteen, usually
around the age of eight or nine years, but only an eighth of girls
start boarding before the secondary age.

In all, there are 853 schools which have a majority of their
pupils as boarders; 407 secondary schools and 446 primary or
preparatory ones - and there are 372 others which are mainly
day schools which provide also for boarders. Most full boarding

TABLE 1:1

Boarding in England and Wales 1967

School	Total day pupils	Boarders: Boys	Girls	Total boarders
Maintained	7,316,866	8,610	2,634	11,244
Direct grant	106,927	8,487	2,153	10,640
Recognized independent	140,044	38,993	18,877	57,870
Non-recognized independent	120,019	6,809	3,038	9,847
Public	44,281	41,349	21,635	62,984
Totals	7,728,137	104,248	48,337	152,585

Source: Public Schools Commission, *First Report*, 1968, p 33 adapted.
'Public Schools' in this table means schools in membership of the Headmasters' Conference, the Governing Bodies' Association and the Association of Governing Bodies of Girls' Public Schools.

schools belong to the independent fee-paying sector of education; indeed, there are more boarding schools in the independent sector than day ones and boarders constitute a third of all those in this sector. By contrast in the state-maintained or state-supported (direct grant) sectors of education there are only nineteen and fifteen full boarding schools respectively, compared with 5,874 day schools, and the boarders in these sectors are an infinitessimal 0·3 per cent of all the school children in them. 167 maintained and direct grant day schools have some residential accommodation. Most English boarding schools are single sex ones - there are relatively few (fifty-one) mixed boarding schools,[12] and the maintained sector contains a disproportionate number of them.

The independent boarding schools are not a homegeneous group. Certain among them have a group character, a common tradition and status which is designated by the term 'public school'. Definitions of this term vary but for most people and throughout this book the term refers, as far as boys boarding is concerned, to the eighty-eight mainly boarding schools in membership of the Headmasters' Conference. For girls'

TABLE 1:2

Mainly boarding secondary schools in England and Wales 1967

Schools	Boarding:			Total	Day or mainly day	Total
	Boys	Girls	Mixed			
Public	103	80	3	186	87	273
Other recognized independent	73	76	41	190	287	464
Direct grant	14	1	–	15	164	179
Maintained	12	1	6	19	5,710	5,730
	202	158	50	407	6,248	6,656

Source: Public Schools Commission, *First Report*, p.31, adapted.
'Mainly boarding' means with a majority of pupils as boarders.

schools - which have much less of a tradition, less corporate identity, status and influence - the term 'public schools' may be taken to mean those eighty in membership of the Governing Bodies' Association of Girls' Public Schools. The girls' public schools contain some 20,000 boarders - nearly two-thirds of the girls of secondary age in the independent sector. The boys' public schools are linked in ethos and character to a group of preparatory schools for boys aged seven to thirteen: they contain 30,000 boarders, virtually the whole number of boys boarding in this age group in the country. The public schools and these feeding schools constitute the largest coherent block of schools and pupils in the English boarding system. Nevertheless, outside this block there are still another 197 independent secondary boarding schools with over 26,500 boarders in them. These schools contain a wide variety of approaches to education and to residence and are by no means all, or even mainly, similar to the public schools.

In all, then, there are 130,701 boarders in independent schools. By contrast there are only 21,884 boarders in direct grant and maintained schools in this country. They are scattered over thirty-five schools which are mainly boarding and

167 others which are mainly day. Among these schools are
secondary modern as well as state-maintained grammar and
direct grant schools. The small numbers of state boarders in
this country and their widespread dispersal does not mean they
are insignificant. Once again, within this small sector there are
wide divergences of approach to residential education and some
important continuities which are distinctive in the general
picture of this education method.

Four other characteristics of boarding schools should be
mentioned. First, they are on average smaller than comparable
day schools, and girls' boarding schools are usually smaller than
boys' ones. Secondly, they are mainly concentrated in the south
of England, whereas thirty-one per cent of the population lives
north of a line drawn between Chester and Lincoln. Third,
they all have a more favourable staff ratio per pupil than do
comparable day schools in their own sector. Finally, they are
all fee paying: even parents with children supported by the local
education authorities contribute to the residential costs
according to means.

IV

Boarding schools, or one group of them, exercise functions for
English society much more basic than numerical importance
would indicate. The public schools provide one major route by
which the English governing elite of most kinds - political,
administrative, educational, military, legal, religious - is
recruited. As allocative mechanisms for filling positions of
power in English society, these boarding schools are still of
crucial importance.[13] Their integrative functions correspond:
they train their pupils instrumentally with suitable skills and set
out to impart the norms, values, culture and style of life
appropriate to those who will later be at the apex of English
society and who wield power over others.[14] Round them
operate other feeding or satellite schools, and others which,
though less securely established in allocating power, cater for
those who see in boarding of this kind a means to preserve or
gain status or access to certain social groups or privileges.

This function of the English boarding school overshadows all
others. The public school, with its important role and its very

distinctive style, has become synonomous with 'boarding'. It
dominates the literature, public attention, political policy and
educational debate about residential education in this country.
This obsession is not entirely justified. As we have seen, the
public schools and those like them by no means represent the
whole boarding sector of English education. The allocative
function, about which there has been so much controversy, is
not the only important function of even the public schools: for
example, their administrative role is not unimportant, for about
a third of their pupils are cases of 'need' for residential
education.[15] Besides them there are a whole cluster of other
schools which provide for children from abnormal or deprived
homes: but this administrative function is not, as in the cases of
the public schools, part of a process of upward social allocation.
There are schools with primary integrative functions such as
those serving vocational purposes and those serving various subcultures - religious ones such as Catholic or Quaker or Methodist
schools and educational ones such as the self-styled 'progressive'
schools. In each of these cases there may or may not be
upward social allocation. Outside the usual definition of
'boarding' are the other maintained or independent schools
which meet by residential methods the needs of special populations such as the delinquent, the maladjusted, the delicate and
the handicapped. These cater for a much greater social range
than other boarding schools; they perform a purely administrative function and also seek to integrate children into the social
patterns of widely differing strata of society. Unlike all other
English boarding schools they are not associated with upward
social mobility. Their experience, as we shall see, might be
important if the ordinary boarding system were to develop
further along the lines outlined by recent public policy. Even
within ordinary boarding schools, however, the diversity of
social functions and thus of education provided is in reality
much greater than the dominance of the public school issue and
the public school stereotype would make it seem.

The social functions of boarding have crystallized over a long
period, during which the various strands were, at times, interwoven. Thus in the Middle Ages boarding schools were
administrative in the sense that younger sons often had to go
away to live if they were to be educated at all and integrative in

the sense that they prepared boys to be gentlemen, scholars, administrators and clerics. Some were integrative due to their attachment to religious orders; some were allocative in the sense that they developed special reputations - Winchester for civil servants, Eton for the aristocracy and gentry - or possessed a cachet through royal or other connections. After the Reformation the patterns became more distinct as the sub-cultural education of the monastic church dropped away. For the most part, boarding education was administrative in its main function - providing beds for the sons of the reasonably well-to-do or more, in schools which had the same social function and educational patterns as the day grammar schools. Some special charity schools were founded to cater for special needs: for example, the Bluecoat Schools such as Christ's Hospital, Cheetham's Hospital and Queen Elizabeth's Hospital, Bristol. At the same time some boarding schools still had special characteristics or prestige or patronage that gave them a special status: Eton, Winchester, Charterhouse, Westminster and Harrow.

The nineteenth century saw a major change in the role of boarding in English society. The pressure of newly powerful social groups and changing national needs brought about by the advent of the empire created out of the old boarding grammar and newly created residential schools, a system known as the 'public schools'. This mid and late Victorian creation differed essentially from what had gone before. The schools, all independent boarding ones, formed a consciously sustained system, which aimed to inculcate established religion, conventional scholarship, manliness and skills of responsible leadership and good administration. To attain these ends the old, open, uncontrolled way of life was adandoned in favour of a method by which the whole of a pupil's existence was controlled by the institution in pursuit of these aims. A system of satellite preparatory schools developed, enlarging the total scope of the system. Later some boarding schools for girls grew up on similar lines, though residence has never become as important to the education of girls as it is to that of boys from the English governing classes. By the end of the century these schools had developed as the means by which a large proportion of all the governing, financial, cultural and social elites were

selected - the one exception was the industrial elite. The
schools' unique allocative position was established.[16]

The nineteenth century and the early part of this one saw,
too, an efflorescence of boarding schools serving special subcultural groups. Catholic schools were refounded; Quaker,
Methodist and Congregational ones set up. Various vocational
schools - naval, military, agricultural - also appeared. Some of
these schools were absorbed into the public school system
because they recruited from and allocated to a high social
status, for example, schools like Downside or Ampleforth
among the Catholic refoundations. Other subcultural schools
which pursued their aim regardless of social class remained outside the public school system, like the Catholic schools run by
the de la Salle brothers and the Mill Hill Fathers. Between 1890
and 1925 a set of 'progressive' boarding schools was founded to
serve broader educational aims than the public schools, and
pursued them by ostensibly more liberal, less total and non-
authoritarian methods. Most of these schools were coeducational, unlike any of the public schools at the time.
Though set up in conscious opposition to the traditional
public schools, they drew from roughly the same socio-
economic groups and performed a similar allocative and
integrative function, but in their case for an elite of nonconformist, professional, creative intelligentsia.

The administrative role of boarding was also transformed in
the last century. Some of the ancient schools originally founded
to cater for social need were incorporated into the public school
system, because they had come to cater for needs mainly
within the middle-class social groups. This happened at Christ's
Hospital and the Royal Masonic School; they acted either as a
safety net to preserve or as a springboard to enhance the status
of people from groups who might otherwise be disadvantaged.
More broadly based foundation schools were set up to cater for
the needs of working-class children and, beginning in the late
nineteenth century, a whole galaxy of boarding schools maintained, subsidized, or supervised by the State came into being to
cater for the special needs of the delinquent, the maladjusted,
and the physically handicapped.

The old administrative functions of boarding, in the shape of
beds attached to grammar schools, tended to decline as the state

began to provide a national network of secondary day schools available to all. The small boarding houses attached to such grammar schools became less necessary and much more educationally problematic because of their lack of definite function, status or philosophy as adjuncts to day education. More recently, and especially since the Second World War, the maintained sector has had a policy of helping children from abnormal backgrounds to have a boarding education irrespective of parental means. Many children (over 35,000) are now helped in independent schools, in boarding departments attached either to day schools or to the nineteen mainly boarding schools which have been developed since 1944 and which are run by local education authorities.[17]

V

The functions which boarding performs for society in the 1970s affects the aims and nature of the schools.

As far as allocation goes, the public schools and their dependent preparatory and other satellite schools still act as a main source of recruitment to the governing, administrative and cultural elites, and nowadays to the commercial and industrial ones. Some elites are no longer exclusively recruited from such schools as in the past, but the number of public school boarders in their recruitment is still disproportionately high. These functions are recognized by the schools and by the parents who use them to perpetuate or enhance their own social status. In most of these schools the idea of elite preparation is explicitly used to justify and frame a distinctive set of goals and methods. Most other boarding schools reflect the elitist functions of this archetypal group, and either maintain or are believed to maintain high social position and to increase life chances of their members. In this, boarding education in England differs markedly from day education. The fact that boarding schools are always selective whereas state day schools are increasingly non-selective gives the former enhanced prestige. Thus, whilst most secondary modern day schools ensure low social status and, for some, downward social mobility, some secondary modern boarding schools are much sought after because their selective character is thought to secure upward social access.

Some parents who would otherwise send their children to minor public schools get them into state boarding schools with similar attributes.[18] Some other schools outside the orbit of the public schools, including most independent ones and the boarding sides of direct grant schools, often model the values and ethics they instil on those found in public schools and thus transmit the culture of elite groups to pupils who may neither aspire to nor reach such status.

On the other hand, there are a few schools, mainly state ones, which attempt by their selection process to discourage their use as vehicles of upward and social mobility. But there are very few English boarding schools which do not serve and are recognized as not serving the maintenance or acquisition of social status; among this minority are some smaller independent schools, a couple of the coeducational 'progressive' schools, half a dozen state or vocational schools, some charitable ones, and a few service schools.

The integrative functions also influence the schools' aims. It may be thought that the fundamental ends of *all* schools, the transmission of basic academic, social and physical skills, would not differ markedly. But, as we shall see, the need to integrate for different sectors of society influences even instrumental aims: schools with the function of elite preparation view the training of intelligence, the pursuit of qualifications, of vocational or manual skills in a basically different manner from schools without such a function. Obviously the integrative functions impinge most powerfully in the area of values, social norms and cultural patterns. The values, style of life and social norms of the English governing classes are distinctive, and homogeneous, and schools which prepare for this elite faithfully reflect them in their goals, stressing them as the *one* absolutely worthwhile culture. Other schools, less tied to elite preparation reflect in their styles the more diverse social attributes of their staff and pupils. In them there may be less stress on values altogether, and certainly less attempt to present or enforce one cultural style as absolute. Progressive schools are more diverse. Some follow the latter pattern, while others stress values which prepare pupils for the intellectual, nonconformist elite; others propagate values which are *sui generis* and which may, if deeply imbibed, render their former pupils, especially boys, normless in wider society and dependent on the artificial perpetuation in later life of the separate culture of the school. Cutting across these integrative functions are patterns of denomination and coeducation: these may, as in some Quaker and Free Church Schools (not so much in Catholic or Anglican ones) modify the value system which might otherwise result from the assured social destinations of the pupils.

All English boarding schools have administrative functions. A third of the children in public schools need to live away from home; preparatory and progressive schools have as many and more. However, most of these children and their backgrounds fit into the allocative pattern of these schools. In some of the charitable or independent schools with public school aims there are considerable numbers of 'need' children who neither have nor aspire to high social status, and this causes problems which we shall analyse later. All maintained schools have a considerable proportion of children who need to board, usually about sixty per cent, the other children being from normal families and there by choice.[19] Though all schools take over the functions of the family there is an important distinction in the way schools react to their administrative role. In some - all public, most integrated and independent, and a few state schools - the function of meeting social dislocation is conceived as incidental to others which have higher priority. In other schools, however - most state, some progressive, some independent and some integrated ones - the position is reversed: their function of meeting need, their administrative role is their raison d'être, and the goals by which this purpose is expressed are central, transcending other expressive ones and on a par with the instrumental ones which all schools as schools must pursue. These opposed interpretations of the common administrative function produce some of the major differences in boarding structures and style which we shall explore.

So much for the functions of boarding at the present day. It deserves notice that the public school style of boarding has influenced almost all the other kinds to some degree, even the progressive schools set up in opposition to them in the early twentieth century. The public schools, however, have been remarkably little influenced by any of the other boarding styles elaborated in this country. The general public still associates

'boarding' with the major public schools as a method of preparation for elite roles within a total, single-sex kind of institution.
Even teachers and others working in schools of quite a different
style from this often seem not to realize how different their
styles and methods are. The Public Schools' Commission of
1968 proposed a change in the basic functions of the public
boarding schools in our society away from allocation to the
elite and towards the administrative function of meeting social
need. The Commissioners themselves failed to realize that such
a fundamental change in function would involve a radical
change of ends and means in these schools and, like most other
people transfixed by the public school problem, also failed to
examine those other boarding schools which already exist to
serve the administrative functions of meeting need without
preparing for elite status, schools which have evolved styles of
boarding significantly different from the public school model.
If there were to be a tendency for boarding education to be less
associated with preparation for high social status in the future,
the experience of these latter schools, indeed of special schools,
would be of great practical consequence.

2   The schools surveyed

Boarding schools differ in hosts of ways: there is probably more variety and are certainly greater extremes in this kind of education than in the day system. But which of all these differences are the most important? We need to find out the most important differentiating factors between the sixty-six schools in our sample so that we can group them for analysis and comparison later. This chapter examines those differences which arise from the social, educational, physical and sexual structures of schools: these we shall call the empirical variables to distinguish them from less statistically obvious but sometimes more important sociological differences which arise within the nature of the school society and which are discussed later.

Obviously a fundamental variable between the schools is their constitutional status in the educational system. According to the degree to which they are independent or state controlled, they fall into the following groups.

TABLE 2:1

Constitutional status of sample

Independent	47
Direct grant	4
Maintained or voluntary aided or controlled	15

Far more important, however, are the constitutional varieties of schools within the large independent sector.

TABLE 2:2

Constitutional groupings of the schools

Independent public on HMC	26
Independent schools, non-integrated	7
Independent schools, integrated	11
Independent progressive	7
Maintained	15

For the purpose of this study 'integrated' independent schools are those which have half or more of their pupils aided by public or charitable funds but which retain independent governing bodies. Independent 'progressive' schools are those listing themselves as progressive in the handbook of 1962 and are members of the coeducational conference.[1]

The differences of sector are fundamental: they correspond as we know to the different functions the schools serve for society, to the differences in clientele and background that we shall discuss in the next chapter. We shall find that goals and structures, styles and effects also differ according to these variables.

Nevertheless it would be wrong to group the schools solely in these terms, for each constitutional group is not homogeneous: within each there are further important differences. The maintained and independent integrated or non-integrated sectors are not homogeneous at all: they contain schools varying fundamentally in aims, operation and effect. More homogeneous are the progressive group, for the differences between them are scarcely fundamental. Very few differences of importance occur among the public schools on our sample, except for two with fairly large intakes of assisted pupils and two other 'progressive' public schools which are closer on most of our indices to schools of the progressive group to which in the past both formerly adhered rather than to those of the Headmasters' Conference to which they now belong. It is therefore dangerous to discuss boarding schools solely according to constitutional groupings.

One other difference is the *sexual* composition of the schools, remembering that this study concerns boys' and coeducational schools only.

TABLE 2:3

Single sex or coeducational composition of the schools

	Boys	Coeducational
Independent public	26	0
Independent non-integrated	7	0
Independent integrated	7	4
Independent progressive	0	7
Maintained	10	5

Coeducation, a minority aspect of boarding, very much follows constitutional factors: it arises in schools which are socially integrated, or state controlled, or those which adopt the progressive philosophy. It is noticeably absent from the public school sector, though it has in the 1970s slowly gained some footholds there.[2] Clearly the sex composition of the school profoundly influences the aims, structure, style, staffing and problems of schools. It will, therefore, be treated in the book as a variable independent in its own right.

What then of the denominational status of the schools, for many of them have cherished links with particular branches of religion?

TABLE 2:4

Denominational adherence of schools

	Anglican	Roman Catholic	Methodist	Quaker	Jewish	Non-denominational
Public	20	2	3	1		
Independent non-integrated	3	1			1	2
Independent integrated	8					3
Progressive				3		4
Maintained	1					14

The denominational character of the school is somewhat less important than is often publicly proclaimed. We found that the denominational schools had a more pronounced stress on expressive aims than the others, and sometimes the religious character of schools clearly influenced specific goals, control, pastoral care and routine. Once again, however, within each category there was a great deal of variety, least in the Anglican kind and most among the non-denominational. The three Catholic schools varied considerably. One more homogeneous group was the Quaker progressive schools which have common characteristics which will lead us to single them out in our discussion of boarding styles.

Does the geographical situation of the schools have any effect?

TABLE 2:5

Region of schools

	South west	Wales/ west midlands	South/ south/ east	London/ home counties	East	Mid-lands	North
Public	5		7	5	1	5	3
Independent non-integrated	1		3		1		2
Independent integrated	2	2	1	4	2		
Progressive	1		1	2		1	2
Maintained	3	3	1	3	1	2	2

Most boarding schools of all kinds are in the south. When we examined the schools by region we found no significant differences emerging as far as their aims, structures and effects went. It is true that the northern public and independent schools have a more heavily localized or regional intake of pupils, seem to be less prone to change and are more instrumental in their pupils' orientation to goals. These effects are so slight that we can state that region is an unimportant differentiating factor between our schools.

More important is the location of schools whether in urban, mixed, or isolated environments. Attempting to distinguish between kinds of location, we found our schools were distributed as shown in Table 2:6

Most boarding schools are rural, many completely isolated from other communities or in smallish villages. Relatively more public and integrated schools are found in large towns or in their suburbs - in most cases ancient charity foundations which have developed in different constitutional directions. Once more, however, the dramatic contrasts in location produced no consistent and predictable effects on the schools in each situation. Obviously the problems and underlife of isolated and urban schools varied in some respects as did educational opportunities but, for example, we found urban schools which because of their system of control isolated their inmates as much as physical factors did elsewhere, whereas schools in remoter areas used the resources of regional centres as much or more than schools actually in such centres.

TABLE 2:6

Location of schools

	Large town	Suburb	Country town	Village	Isolated
Public	4	8	4	5	5
Independent non-integrated		1	1	4	1
Independent integrated	1	3		1	6
Progressive			2	2	3
Maintained	1	1	5	4	4

Perhaps more influential is the local, regional, national and international catchment area of the schools.

TABLE 2:7

Catchment of schools

	Majority of pupils live within one hour's travelling distance of school	Majority of pupils live in same region (Table 2:5)	Majority of pupils live outside the region
Public	2	12	12
Independent non-integrated		5	2
Independent integrated	2	7	4
Progressive		4	3
Maintained	9	5	1

Maintained schools are more heavily local or regional in their recruitment than all others which tend to be regional or national. This factor obviously affects the character and opportunity of maintained schools in terms of boarding policy, relations with home, in other goals, and pastoral care. In some of these schools it does, though not invariably, condition much of the style of boarding adopted, as we shall see.

What then of the size of the school? How is our sample divided according to this factor?

TABLE 2:8

Numbers of pupils in schools

	150	151-300	301-450	451-500	501-700	Over 700
Public		4	13	3	4	2
Independent non-integrated	2	4	1			
Independent integrated	4	4	2			1
Maintained	2	8	3	1	2	
Progressive	2	3	2			

Public schools tend to be larger than the other schools, often with a two or three form entry. State schools are somewhat varied but the majority are small, like all other kinds of boarding schools which are smaller than the corresponding secondary day schools of their type. Though size at first seems important, it is less so than in day education, as residential communities of all sizes are subdivided for living and organizational purposes. Thus we found some of the smaller public schools with structures as federal and fragmented as those of the larger ones, though, no doubt, the generally larger size of public schools enhances the tendency to federal subdivisions within them and schools of smaller size contain more centralized living and authority systems. Perhaps the most noticeable consequences of size which we found were on the schools' ability to change, on communication within them and on the roles and conflicts of role which are induced.

Does the fee-paying nature of much of boarding education seem to correlate with provision within the schools? Obviously it correlates to some degree with the **social** class and economic background of pupils as we shall see **in C**hapter 10.

TABLE 2:9

Size of fees of schools in 1967

	1 Over £600	2 551- 600	3 501- 550	4 451- 500	5 401- 450	6 351- 400	7 301- 350	8 251- 300	9 201- 250	10 151- 200	11 101- 150
Public	1	3	11	4	3	1	1	1			
Independent non- integrated	1	1		2	1	1					1
Independent integrated					4	2	2	2			1
Progressive			3		3		1				
Maintained			3		1	1	1	3	4	1	1

Public and independent schools are obviously more expensive than others. But more relevant to social background and the above table is the proportion of parents in the schools who are assisted in some way with the full fees set out in the table below. As that table shows by definition, maintained and integrated schools contain pupils virtually all of whom are assisted, whereas the other schools contain only small numbers so assisted.

TABLE 2:10

Help with fees for boarding and/or tuition
(in percentages of numbers of pupils)

	Less than 25	25-50	51-75	76-all
Public	21	5		
Independent non- integrated	6	1		
Independent integrated			3	8
Progressive	5	2		
Maintained				15

Differences in fee-paying structures correspond substantially with constitutional status and with functions for society and are therefore fundamental to differences between schools. But does the level of fees affect the provision which boarding schools offer? For example, does the cost of a school correlate with the generosity or otherwise of the staff-pupil ratio, as calculated by standard government procedures? The following table shows that it is only in the very extremes of fees charged that staff-pupil ratios do seem to be affected in the independent schools.

TABLE 2:11

Fees charged in 1967 related to staff-pupil ratios (weighted*)
Independent schools only

Staff-pupil ratio (weighted)	Over £601	501-600	401-500	301-400	201-300	Under 201
Under 1:10·9	1	1				
1:11-12·9		1	2			
1:13-14·9		1	7	3		
1:15-16·9		5	2	1	1	1
1:17-18·9		5	1	1	1	
1:19 and above		1	1		1	

* Weighted ratios are those in which pupils following sixth form courses are counted twice for purposes of computation.

Similarly, we tried to correlate size of fees with physical provision; again there was relatively little correlation in independent schools except at the obvious extremes. Size of fees bore little relation to the kind of living accommodation, for example, though more to scientific and academic equipment. It certainly correlates with the size of allowances paid to staff, and, though this is only a subjective guess, also to the quality of staff. The physical plant varied in schools from the lavish to the most impoverished and makeshift. In terms of the school's effectiveness in achieving its aims or pupil commitment, however, the nature of the plant was irrelevant: one of the most lavishly equipped schools had a pupil society basically alienated from its ends and, on the other hand, a poor school housed in makeshift huts and an old Victorian secondary school had one of the most committed groups of students and was one of the most effective of all those on our sample. Physical provision by no means determines the success of a school in achieving its aims, though it conditions its opportunity and life style.

One of the most profoundly important determinants of style and effects of boarding, as we shall frequently find, is the age structure of boarding in the schools concerned. The rest of the book will spell out the consequences of the information in the following table taken from a subsample of pupils in sixty-six schools:

TABLE 2:12

Age of first boarding
(in percentages of numbers of pupils)

	Before 8	8-11	Over 11	Schools	Number of sixth-form pupils answering
Public	37	42	21	14	1929
Independent non-integrated	32	35	33	4	243
Independent integrated	14	31	55	6	622
Progressive	5	41	56	4	215
Maintained	1	15	84	11	537

Source: general sample.

A majority of all children at independent and public schools have boarded before eleven years of age and a third or more before eight, whereas in integrated and maintained schools the decided majority are late boarders. The progressive schools fall between the two extremes. The age of first boarding, as we shall find, correlates with some of the more distinct effects of boarding on pupils, on family styles and relates also to the ethos of schools and to the presenting culture of each group.

The pre-socialization which early boarding affords is in some schools accentuated by the existence of a junior school attached to the secondary one, so that from the ages of eight to ten young pupils are brought up in the same general atmosphere and according to the aims of the secondary school. Twenty schools on our sample had junior departments attached of which five were integrated with the secondary school and the head was the same for both and the staff interchanged.

TABLE 2:13

Secondary schools with junior schools

Public	9
Independent non-integrated	4
Independent integrated	3
Progressive	1
Maintained	3

Such pre-socialization into the life of some schools conditioned the commitment of pupils and, in the case of the 'radical' progressive schools, the successful implementation of their philosophy. Virtually all boarders at public schools have, however, been pre-socialized because their prep schools, even if constitutionally independent of the main school, seek to prepare for the ethos and values of the secondary ones.

The longitudinal age structures of schools apart from those possessing junior units seem less important, with the exception of the presence or otherwise of an age group of pupils aged fifteen and over. Nine of our schools, chiefly maintained or small independent ones, had no such group. Clearly the presence or otherwise of a group of pupils aged between sixteen and eighteen affects levels of control, the system of authority and order adopted by pupils and staff. It is one reason why some state schools seem to have a higher level of control than other kinds: the age structure of the one ends at fifteen, of the others at eighteen.

Academic character obviously differentiates schools. The definitions used in state day education scarcely apply to the idiosyncratic and diverse independent boarding sector. We found our sample of schools fell into four broad categories.

The first were those schools which provided academic courses for all their pupils on the assumption that all of them could undertake such courses, though many of them would never have qualified for entry to a state grammar school. These courses are those which lead direct to university entry requirements: GCE at O and A levels. In at least three of the independent non-integrated schools the majority of the pupils seemed well below the ability to cope with such courses which were provided to suit the aspirations of parents rather than the needs of their sons. The schools with only academic courses were:

TABLE 2:14

Schools offering academic courses only

Public	26
Independent non-integrated	4
Independent integrated	2
Progressive	6
Maintained	5

The actual numbers doing A level or work to that level in the schools was as follows:

TABLE 2:15

Percentage of pupils doing A level work in schools

	0-10	11-20	21-30	31-40	41-50	51-
Public	1		9	6	8	2
Independent integrated	4	2	2			
Independent non-integrated	2	1	3	1		
Maintained	2	7	2			
Progressive	1	2	3	1		

It will be seen that public schools have more pupils at this higher academic and age level than the others.

The next group of schools did not aim to provide qualifications for entry to the universities or the higher professions. Though their pupils were sometimes no less able than those in some of the schools in the first group, these schools offered a CSE type of approach with a few GCE O levels but no higher academic work leading to A level. Most are maintained 'secondary modern' types of school:

TABLE 2:16

Schools offering non-academic courses

Independent non-integrated	4
Independent integrated	4
Progressive	1
Maintained	7

Schools which set out with courses and styles of teaching developed for a wide range of ability both academic and non-academic, that is, comprehensive schools, were few.

TABLE 2:17

Schools offering courses for academic/non-academic

Independent integrated	1
Maintained	3

Finally there was a unique group of schools not found at all in the day system which trained boys between eleven and fifteen and beyond for a specific job or vocation. Of these four vocational schools, two were state maintained, one for agriculture, the other for building, and two were independent but integrated in social composition, one preparing for the merchant navy, the other for potential entry to the Catholic priesthood. We shall discuss the special styles of boarding which resulted from their functions in Chapter 7.

It is conventional to classify and discuss schools in English education according to their academic type and, doubtless, in day education such differences are crucial. It is one of the most important features of boarding education that differences in academic structure or standing are less important. As we shall see, many schools pursue broad aims which, in some cases, are given more priority than the narrowly academic ones which must obviously be paramount in day education. The academic sub-systems of the schools do vary widely, and inevitably this conditions the ethos of the school, but a state bilateral boarding school might still have more in common in terms of goals, structure and effects, with a public school than with its day counterpart. Boarding also cuts across and diminishes the

importance of fundamental structural features common in the
day school, such as streaming by ability, or horizontal age
groups, or the form system. Thus, for example, academic
streaming is rendered less important by the availability of other
diverse and often more prestigious channels of achievement
open to the child; the horizontal age group or the form unit can
be cut across by the vertical age grouping and pastoral unit of
the house which seems to so many pupils and staff more
important. In other words, in boarding education academic
goals and organization are only part of a much broader set of
goals and sub-systems created to pursue them. In fact only a
few of the features which contribute to the basic differences
between boarding schools derive from their academic nature.
Other related matters - such as age structure and the degree of
selectivity of the entry - are more important.

Unlike many day schools almost all boarding schools for
ordinary children are selective in the sense that, providing there
is demand for places, they can choose the pupils who enter them
according to criteria set by the school. Even when academic
factors exist in selection they are seldom the only ones: most
schools accept a minimum academic performance as qualifying
and then go on to select between candidates on other criteria
such as suitability for boarding, for the school or house in
question. This is another key difference with day education
where selection, when it exists, is always on 'objective'
academic criteria. We examined the entry patterns of our
schools and found that the majority fell into the kind described
above, with a smaller group where there was a substantial competitive entry on academic grounds and a few others where
academic criteria did not operate at all - integrated schools
catering for cases of 'need', or some of the maintained secondary modern schools.

Though all our schools were theoretically empowered to
select for entry there were some in practice which could or did
not: either demand for their places was so low that they took
every applicant, or their charitable purpose meant that they
took virtually all applicants of a certain kind (e.g. naval ratings'
sons) or even had them assigned to them by an external,
mediating authority. There were four schools with a low
application which precluded selection: two independent and

two maintained secondary modern schools. Three other charitable schools took an entry of need or other kinds of children not on a selective basis.

TABLE 2:18

Academic selectivity of schools

	Competitive entry	Minimum qualifying standards	Non-selective
Public	4	22	
Independent non-integrated		7	
Independent integrated	3	5	3
Progressive		7	
Maintained		10	5

The degree of selectivity can crucially affect the boarding school: the goals of the school may be affected, as also the demands on roles, the pupils' informal world and adaptations to the school. Significantly, the three schools where goals concerning the schools' organization dominated other educational aims were low in selectivity. Also those schools where a majority of pupils seemed to be alienated from official goals were chiefly of this type. But again one cannot uniformly predict from the selective character of schools: some of the non-selective ones seem to produce structures and effects much like those of more selective schools.

One other feature which affected our schools was the proportion of day boys in them, which according to our definition of boarding school was less than half. Boarders as a percentage of all pupils varied in our schools, as shown in Table 2:19

The presence of substantial quantities of day pupils can be a differentiating factor between schools but, once again, not uniformly so. It all depends on the policy of the school toward its day members. In some schools they are treated as boarders who simply sleep at home and when at home are expected to keep to the rules and regulations which apply to boarders at school. In others they exist as a somewhat inferior caste playing significantly less part in the school outside the classroom or sports field. In some others boarders and days were so integrated that it was very difficult to tell the difference between them. The presence of large numbers of day pupils usually increases the emphasis on instrumental ends and may affect the system of control, the pupils' informal world and adaptation to the school. Again, however, boarding schools with day pupils need not differ substantially from those without; the majority of schools have very few day pupils anyway. Later chapters will explore some of the differences between day pupils and boarders in the same school.

TABLE 2:19

Percentage of pupils as boarders

	51-60	61-70	71-80	81-90	91-100
Public	1	2	3	4	16
Independent non-integrated		1		1	5
Independent integrated			1	1	9
Progressive	1	1		1	4
Maintained	4			1	10

Another feature of the entry can bear powerfully on the character of schools: the proportion of pupils in them who 'need' to live away from home. It is difficult to establish an objective criterion for such need cases since children of busy or mobile professional parents may have as much 'need' to live away at school as the more obvious cases of children from homes which are structurally defective, such as the children of widowers. For the present, however, we take as 'need' cases only those who come within the accepted local authority

TABLE 2:20

Percentage of pupils with 'need' (LEA criteria only)

	Less than 25	26-50	50-75	75-100
Public	25	1		
Independent non-integrated	2	1	2	2
Independent integrated	1	3	4	3
Progressive	1	5	1	
Maintained		2	9	4

definitions of children who might be supported by the state
for boarding education in ordinary schools on grounds of
'need'.[3] The proportions are estimated by the heads, and
checked with estimates from house staff.

For reasons already discussed 'need' children are heavily concentrated in maintained and integrated schools, but are also
prominent in the less important (non-HMC) kind of independent schools. Their presence in large proportions inevitably
affects the goals and structures and such areas of the school as
pastoral care, roles taken up by the staff and pupils and the
informal world of the pupils. In some cases the function of the
school in meeting need is formally recognized by the aims and
organization; in some others the function is not so recognized
and the school pursues goals, operates a structure and promotes
an ethos like that of an ordinary boarding school of its kind.
We found that in such cases severe problems could ensue,
caused by the school's inability to acknowledge and adapt to
the function it was actually serving. Either way the need composition of schools is an important variable in explaining
differences in their nature and working.

That factors concerning staff differentiate schools we shall
see in the next chapter. The educational, boarding or day background of staff, the degree of mobility between schools and
within them, obviously profoundly affect the aims and
operation, the nature of roles and the schools' capacity for
change as well as their relation to society. We shall find important distinctions emerging between schools in this area, the
consequences of which will emerge as this book proceeds.

One notable feature of boarding schools is the greater
number of staff per pupil found in them compared with day
schools; a superiority which results from their residential
nature and the more continuous and extensive care provided by
adults. When we examine the actual teaching staff-pupil ratio in
our schools, however, a surprising variety emerges among them.
To calculate the ratio, we have adopted the standard procedures
used by the Department of Education and Science, including
double weighting pupils in the sixth form in acknowledgment of
the more intensive use of teachers at this level in all schools, day
or boarding.

TABLE 2:21

Weighted teacher-pupil ratios

One teacher to:	8-9·9	10-11·9	12-13·9	14-15·9	16-17·9	18-19·9	20-
Public			4	5	8	6	1
Independent non-integrated		2	3	2			
Independent integrated		3	2	3	1	2	
Progressive	2	2	1	1	1		1
Maintained		1	4	5	4	1	

In terms of these academic kinds of ratio it will be seen that the progressive and independent sectors are the most heavily staffed: a feature which arises from their small size of schools in these sectors and the absence of large sixth forms. In academic terms the staff-pupil ratio in public and some maintained schools is more varied, approaching that of a day school in some cases. Perhaps the significant figures are not the weighted ratios but the *unweighted* ones: the simple ratio of qualified teachers in the community to the pupils. For it is on the number of staff per pupil *out of class*, irrespective of double weighting for sixth form pupils, that some important features and styles of boarding depend.

TABLE 2:22

Teacher-pupil ratio unweighted

One teacher to:	8-9·9	10-11·9	12-13·9	14-15·9	16-17·9	18-19·9	20-
Public	6	12	17	1			
Independent non-integrated	1	3	3				
Independent integrated		3	3	2	2	1	
Progressive	2	2	3				
Maintained		2	3	5	4	1	

We see immediately that the ratios of public schools change. Once their large sixth forms are counted as no more than other forms then staff-pupil ratios become about as favourable as the progressive schools. In terms of sheer numbers of trained adults per pupil available in the community, these two kinds of school are more favourably situated than others. It clearly helps to account for their active extra-curricular patterns, the high degree of involvement of staff and the multiple roles they play, the absence of defined 'contractual' roles imposed on staff, their performance of them as a socially accepted obligation not a formal compulsion, the effective pastoral care provided, and the penetration of the pupil society and its activities by the staff. By contrast the integrated and maintained schools have a wide, indeed extreme, variety of staff-pupil ratios. In some of these schools the numbers of staff available per pupil (the crude unweighted ratios) in the boarding situation is scarcely much greater than in comparable day schools, and significantly worse than is the case in the public and progressive or purely independent sector. This, too, has important consequences for such schools: where staff-pupil ratios are low, roles may be limited, performance of them may be exacted by contract, commitment to them may be low, the pupil society may be unpenetrated by the staff and pastoral care may be less effective. When, as we shall see later, public and progressive schools attain a higher and more homogeneous commitment to their ends than the other schools, their favourable ratings in terms of adult-pupil must be taken into account along with the other factors then discussed. Here then is the last variable of importance.

So much for our introduction of some main features of schools which may affect their aims, structures and effects and differentiate between groups of them. Some will recur frequently as major independent variables by which schools will be discussed: constitution, sex composition, academic structure, degree of selectivity, crude staff-pupil ratios. Some others are dependent on these factors, such as age of first boarding, pre-socialization of pupils and staff, 'need' composition and so on. Other variables which may be independent seem of relatively little consistent effect, including those of denomination, location and region, cost and even size.

By themselves these empirical factors are inadequate as a framework for discussing boarding schools: there are others external and internal. All schools are interwoven with their context and are profoundly affected by the background experience of their staff, pupils and governors, by the other bodies with which they interact and other external forces. Internally too there are other features which, though sometimes related to the empirical variables discussed in this chapter, may count for much more in determining the nature and working of school life and society: these are sociological differences. We turn next to the background context of our schools and then to the differences between them.

3   The presenting culture

Schools - even boarding ones which are often remote and cut
off from the outside world - do not exist in isolation. They are
profoundly influenced by and always interact with their human
context. Unless newly founded (and even then only partially)
schools cannot, by themselves, choose the whole range of ends
they serve and the structures and practices they employ to gain
them. Schools already existing are so conditioned by factors
external and internal to the society that they may be unable
substantially to alter the aims and methods which they have
inherited. Inside the school, as later chapters show, factors of
social structure and operation and patterns of response by staff
and pupils help to determine the setting of aims, the shaping of
means, the scope for change and the school's effectiveness in
gaining its ends. Outside the school, other factors bear equally
powerfully on its aims, means and effectiveness; the forces of
history or tradition, the influences of organizations in its
environment, and the expectations, experience and culture of
its staff, parents and pupils. Together these external elements
define the relationship between the school and the immediate
society or section of society it serves. These relationships differ
fundamentally and are crucial determinants of the differences
we shall find in the aims, nature and effectiveness of boarding
schools.

II

Historical forces have left a distinct and variable impress upon
the schools.
   Residential education in this country is still much used as a
means of sustaining various kinds of religious faith. The large
majority of boarding schools are linked to the particular
denominations which helped to fertilize education in the
nineteenth century. The numerous Anglican schools and the
several Quaker, Methodist and Congregationalist ones are now
less sectarian in intake or in their preparation for specific

Christian sub-cultures but their association gives them pronounced expressive aims and practices and distinctive traditions.
The denominations which are heavily represented on their
governing bodies and staff still see these schools as important
training grounds. Some other schools - the fair number of
Catholic schools, the few for Jews or Christian Scientists - are
less open in their catchment.[1] Catholic schools are often linked
in organization, routine and place to resident monastic or
teaching orders, who act as the governing body and the key
members of staff: the schools are thus impregnated with a
religious way of life. This pronounced, and for many schools,
central religious character distinguishes boarding from day
education, which for the vast majority of children in state and
even independent schools is non-denominational or but
nominally religious in context.[2] Public boarding schools are
nearly all denominational (eighty-one out of eighty-eight) and
mainly Church of England; independent schools contain a wider
variety of denominational schools; progressive schools tend to
be secular or inter-denominational and state ones are non-
denominational.

History has also embedded certain strands of educational
philosophy firmly in some areas of the boarding system. What
has been called the 'Arnold tradition' of preparing boys to
become responsible, tolerant, intellectually competent,
physically healthy and Christian leaders or administrators
developed in the nineteenth-century public school. Re-
interpreted and modified in contemporary terms as we shall see,
it still finds its greatest stronghold in the public schools and
those which follow their model, but it has also profoundly
affected the whole of English education, contributing to day
schooling in these islands an expressive breadth - a concern with
character, physical well-being, extra-curricular life and pastoral
care - not usually found elsewhere in Europe. Most boarding
schools have been influenced by this tradition, either consciously in aims or in methods (such as the house system)
derived from the public schools. More recently a 'progressive'
tradition, which emphasizes the free development of personality,
emotional and creative growth and democratic involvement, has
also been widely influential. Under external and internal
pressures - the stress on public examinations and the recognition

of the child's psychological need for a framework of authority - the pure progressive ethic of the utopian experiments of the 1920s has been modified. Originated and still in its complete form confined to a few boarding schools, this tradition has influenced other independent and maintained ones but especially the state primary day school.[3] In some Quaker schools the usually separate strands of denomination and progressivism meet. Though, in general, public and preparatory schools have only been slightly affected by the 'progressive' approach, two HMC schools on our sample subscribe partly to this tradition and their measurable effects on their pupils are nearer to those of self-styled 'progressive schools' outside the HMC than to those of other schools within that organization.[4]

Traditions of a specialized nature remain surprisingly tenacious. Schools founded as charitable institutions for the poor in the last two centuries find that elements of their original purpose, their rescuing functions or even buildings - sometimes bleak and unsympathetic elements - still affect features of their approach to children, or to parents of children with 'need' for boarding, to physical comfort and provision. In some of these 'integrated' schools such lingering features can affect the pupils' response to boarding. Similarly some schools which stem from that ancient 'administrative' stream of boarding - grammar schools with beds in them for convenience - or which have as their historical source the state day school tradition, elementary or grammar, often possess priorities and scope different from other boarding schools even when, as in the case of some maintained or direct grant schools, they have adopted features from the public school tradition. Aspects of the expressive aims and life of the public schools have not always been successfully transplanted to schools from a tradition which has tended to ignore them. The older values embodied in structure, patterns of living, expectations and norms remain surprisingly persistent in these boarding communities. We found that this was true too of those schools which once functioned as recruiting and training schools for the services but which are now ordinary schools sending only a small minority of pupils into the forces. In these schools some aims - instrumental ones concerning the kinds of skills taught - have changed but others, expressive traditions in particular, remain resistant to change, linger stubbornly on in crucial areas, in systems of control, in definitions of roles, in norms about relations between staff and pupils or among the pupils.

All boarding schools face an uncomfortable paradox in respect of their history. Because the boarding society is closed and total in its scope, the goals and values of the school can deeply impregnate and shape the structure of the institution and its way of life such that in some schools abstract ends and concrete means are fused into one. This makes for a high effectiveness in realizing such ends, but, equally, it may make the task of changing goals so deeply embedded or altering structures so validated all the more difficult to accomplish.

III

So much for the strong but impalpable forces which condition the nature of boarding schools. More concrete are other organizations in the environment which impinge upon them. There are two kinds: those which mediate between the school and the wider world, such as governing bodies, local authorities, parental associations; and, secondly, organizations in the wider society such as the central government, examination boards, universities, and employers. The influence of such bodies varies markedly between the different types of schools.

Governing bodies or LEAs and their officers obviously influence the goals of schools. In most independent schools, particularly public or progressive ones, they are often as much concerned with expressive matters, with values and their manifestation in the school as with instrumental ones or matters of organization. The fact that a considerable proportion of governors of public and progressive schools were educated as boarders in the school or its group, and may have kin as pupils in them, adds to this stress on expressive ends and blurs the gap between the school and this outer body: in some religious schools the staff and the governing body are largely the same people exercising different roles as in an Oxbridge college. They can exercise a powerful pressure for continuity or change. By contrast, the governors or LEAs in maintained or socially integrated schools are less occupied with expressive matters, though inevitably active in their schools' instrumental

or organizational affairs. Most of them have not been educated
in their particular schools, do not have kindred in them and
have not been boarders themselves. Schools and governors thus
overlap less than in other schools. They tend to be less influential and more transient and effective power passes to permanent
officials or to chairmen. The inspectorate may be more prominent in state schools but in most other boarding ones,
beyond concern with material provision and minimum
efficiency, it scarcely affects the ends of schools, especially
expressive ones which are taken as given.[5]

In public and some other independent schools former pupils
are usually gathered into elaborate organizations, almost subcultures, with premises, officials, periodicals, insignia and rituals
of their own. They serve to maintain the stress on continuity
rather than change and provide the school with a continuous
perspective of its past. They seldom have direct influence over
policy as organizations but can in public or progressive schools
be powerful indirectly when individual alumni or groups of
them hold key positions or comprise substantial numbers on the
staff or governing body. They can provide invaluable support
for the school financially and in penetrating other bodies:
employers, colleges, local authorities and the like. By contrast,
in most state, progressive and coeducational boarding schools
old pupil organizations are less elaborate, tend to be purely
social and recreative, transient in membership and unconcerned
to influence the school's policy. They are unimportant.[6]

Parents of children in independent, public or progressive
schools are seldom as organized as former pupils: there are
fewer parents' associations in such schools than in state ones,
day or boarding. Though the traditional boarding schools work
closely with parents over individual children they tend to keep
the parental role out of the school and do not encourage the
parents collectively to share in the making or discussion of
policy. The latter, therefore, have little influence over
instrumental or expressive matters or the daily pattern of the
school, although somewhat more over organizational ones such
as uniforms.

However, the *negative* force of fee-paying parents can be
considerable: all independent schools are in fact dependent on
them in varying proportions according to the institution's

prestige and competition for entry to it. Parents in such schools exercise no direct influence, but, as headmasters frequently said in considering major changes of structure or methods, such as the adoption of CSE courses instead of O levels or the admission of girls, the school authorities felt constrained by the known expectations and values of present and potential parents. Some progressive, independent and most state schools possess parental associations which contribute materially to the school in daily affairs and discuss policy and practice. These schools often see their task as complementary to the family (not superseding it in term as do the others) and view parents collectively as having a supportive or innovatory function in the school. These parents are also more conscious of sharing responsibilities with the school rather than of having a clearly defined demarcation between school and home as do public school parents. But as state and integrated schools are not economically dependent on parents they can, if they so wish, ignore parents more than any independent school: the negative power of parents is less here than elsewhere.[7]

Secondary schools sometimes have other ones dependent on them, socializing pupils in preparation for them. As we have seen, public, progressive and independent schools sometimes possess their own junior or infants' departments so that integration with their ethos can start at three or six years of age and last until eighteen.[8] Most others have a general system of prep schools feeding them and interconnected with them in staffing, parentage as well as in the education provided. Some integrated and progressive and all state schools do not have a system of satellite or feeding schools of their own. Such schools need not influence the policies of the senior schools directly but their existence and dependence and the fact that they tend to be conservative educationally, can affect the capacity of the senior schools to change.

Professional bodies are the final kind of mediating organization. Among them the Headmasters' Conference is outstanding. Highly selective or traditional in membership, organized on a national and regional basis, with its own secretariat and journal and public relations advisors, it is a powerful means of emphasizing and maintaining a consensus on goals, standards and methods and on permissible changes among its exclusive

members and schools outside which follow its lead. For
example, along with the Governing Bodies' Association, it
issued statements of principle and negotiated on behalf of the
boys' public schools with the Public Schools Commission of
1965-8. It does not directly influence individual schools but it
continually helps to define what public schools are and stand
for to its own members and to the outside world and it
preserves their self-consciousness as a sector of education. To a
lesser degree the Incorporated Association of Preparatory
Schools (the IAPS), though much less exclusive, does the same.
The smaller Society of Headmasters of Independent Schools
which includes some twenty-seven independent schools is more
of a mutual information body than is the HMC. Special groups
have their own co-ordinating and strategic policy-making bodies,
like the Quaker Schools with their Friends Educational Council
or the Methodists who have recently formed a working party
which has issued a report on the future of their schools.[9] But it
is notable that the majority of independent, progressive and all
maintained boarding schools have no organization to represent
their sectional interests in boarding or to help support and
renew their goals.

Beyond these mediating bodies lie others more external to
the schools. Government educational policy has had little
effect on independent boarding schools in the past: they still
remain outside the pattern of national education despite two
government inquiries on the matter. State boarding schools are
very much influenced by decisions such as the move to comprehensive education and, indeed, they owe their existence largely
to a government policy report - that on support for children
with need for boarding (the Martin Report).[10] Other bodies like
the Schools' Council or the Nuffield Foundation are having a
major effect on the academic life of many boarding schools of
all kinds: such changes tend to affect methods rather than ends
however, and occur equally in day schools.

Universities and their examination boards condition the
curriculum of all schools which produce a large entry to them.
Between the public schools and the older universities of Oxford
and Cambridge there exists a special relationship which continues to influence their goals, methods, social prestige and
recruitment. Linked by a long intertwined history, by the fact

that over eighty-two per cent of the schools' staff and more of
their governors are alumni of Oxford or Cambridge, the public
schools and the two universities have profoundly influenced
each other's intellectual aims, curriculum, standards, teaching
methods, style of life, residential structure, daily routine and
expressive values, pastoral care, and the ideal of the
'gentleman'.[11] Though the proportion of public school boarders
entering Oxbridge is declining and the older universities regard
their traditional link with the public schools with some unease
nowadays, the proportion of public school boarders entering
Oxford and Cambridge is still greater than their share of the
total numbers entering all universities would normally warrant:
fifty-five per cent of public school boarders going to university
enter Oxbridge, compared with thirteen per cent leaving all state
grammar schools.[12] The Oxbridge open scholarship still remains
the highest academic aim of the school teacher and often of
schoolboys, [13] the headmasters and staff are still overwhelmingly
alumni, parents still expect the schools to gain their sons
favoured access and the schools' approach and culture are still
unconsciously focused on these two universities. Indeed the
increasing competition for entry to these universities (and
others) has affected the informal system of status within the
schools: academic attainment probably carries higher prestige
than ever before whereas athletic prowess, once greatly admired
and established in an elite of 'bloods', carries much less weight.
Other schools show much less influence of Oxford and
Cambridge, with important consequences for their academic
and expressive aims.

Potential employers have affected the aims of boarding
schools. Not only the churches but until recently also the
services have seen in independent boarding a source of recruits
to their way of life. In the past, service (particularly army)
officers were mainly recruited from public schools, and the
schools' own military organizations, OTC or CCF, helped to
prepare for this. Various professions, the diplomatic corps, the
higher ranks of the civil service, judges and barristers, the
episcopate, city business companies and financiers still come
largely from the public schools.[14] The connection between
them is, however, not specific: the schools prepare for this high
level or *grade* of employment by providing the necessary

general culture, the requisite cognitive or emotional patterns,
whereas other schools tend to train with more specific skills for
actual types of employment. Apart from a few vocational
schools linked to particular industries (farming or building), the
most signal instance of employers influencing schools is that of
the Industrial Fund of three million pounds set up by industry
in the 1950s which has since systematically financed the provision of science and engineering facilities in many independent
and most public schools. It has substantially affected the
balance of the academic goals and life of these schools towards
scientific, practical and even commercial pursuits. By 1970
nearly a quarter of public school boys left for careers in science,
industry or engineering.[15] Of all boarding schools the least
affected by vocational or employment consideration are some
progressive ones which do not see themselves as training for a
career or fitting for a job or even as preparing for conventional
society: they may indeed render their pupils - particularly
boys - anomic when they first move into the commercially
minded world and face the issue of earning a living.[16]

IV

The backgrounds of those who people the school: staff, pupils
and their families, form an important part of the culture in
which it operates and with which it interpenetrates.

Most teachers in public, independent and some progressive
schools come from social groups which correspond to those of
their pupils: the higher socio-economic groupings and the
majority of staff tend to come from families already established
in such groups. By contrast most of the staff in state and
integrated schools are of a socio-economic standing higher than
that of the parents of most of their pupils, but they themselves
are recent recruits into their present social class. They are
upwardly mobile, whereas the staff in the other schools are
already established in their social strata.[17]

The education of staff reflects this position and contributes
to the particular kind of ethos in their schools. Over seventy
per cent of staff in public schools were themselves educated at
public schools and about ten per cent of them were educated in
their own school. About sixty per cent of those in independent

schools were also educated in the independent sector. Teachers in progressive schools come from a wider variety of educational backgrounds, half of them from state schools. In integrated schools the staff are equally varied but with a third of them having been at state schools, another third at public schools and the remaining third at independent or integrated schools. Thus only a minority of teachers in integrated schools come from the same sort of educational background as most of their pupils, that is, the state sector. In the case of maintained boarding schools, over ninety-five per cent of the staff had themselves been to maintained schools as pupils.[18] The majority of the public school teachers had been boarders at school, the majority of state school teachers had been day pupils and at the other schools an average of forty-five per cent had been boarders as children.[19]

In public schools and boarding schools based on similar lines there tends to be a distinction between a hierarchy of residential staff on the one hand (housemasters, assistant housemasters) and teaching staff on the other who play no significant part in the boarding side and have a parallel and separate hierarchy of their own. In state or progressive schools and others like them residential duties are diffused more evenly over all the teaching staff. About eighty-five per cent of the residential staff in public and independent schools have been boarders themselves but in progressive and independent schools the percentage was forty-five and at state schools only five. The following tables show the trends of the education of both headmasters in schools and of housemasters or their equivalents:

TABLE 3:1

Schools attended by headmasters

	Own school	Public	Independent	Integrated	Progressive	Maintained	Day	Boarding
Public	4	17	1			1	3	19
Independent		6						6
Integrated	1	3		2		3	4	5
Progressive		3			2	2	4	3
Maintained		1				12	12	1

Source: intensive and extensive samples (called when combined the general sample).

TABLE 3:2

Schools attended by housemasters

	Own school Public	Indepen- dent	Inte- grated	Pro- gressive	Main- tained
Public	33	5			9
Independent	2	3	1		3
Integrated	6	8			10
Progressive	2	3		1	7
Maintained	1	2			16

Source: intensive and extensive samples (the general sample).

These differences are fundamental. The public, and to a lesser degree, the independent schools, tend to be cyclical and self-perpetuating in their intake, drawing staff from themselves or their own sector and staff mainly with boarding experience. The progressive and integrated boarding schools are eclectic, drawing staff more widely but with barely half of them having had experience in their own lives as boarders. State schools draw almost entirely from within the state system itself but almost exclusively from staff with day school experience alone in their background. Such differences in the background of boarding teachers profoundly affect their approach to residence and the flexibility of the schools in which they work.

They are intensified by other factors about the staff. Teachers in progressive, state and independent schools tend to be more mobile than those of the public schools. The contrast is most marked among staff with residential responsibilities. In progressive and state schools nearly all the boarding staff have had teaching experience in one and the large majority in two other schools, often day ones. The staff in integrated and independent schools have a somewhat less pronounced tendency of the same kind.

But in public schools seventy per cent of the housestaff at the time of our enquiries had never taught in any other school but the one they were then at. This pattern derives from the system of promotion in such schools. To climb up on the residential side in a public school means, after preliminary selection, waiting from the early days of teaching for succession to a house in one school. To ascend on the academic side to the headship of a department, however, in the same school a teacher is expected to have had a far broader experience. Thus in public schools teachers are often brought in from outside to become heads of departments on the teaching side but appointments are *never* made from outside direct to the residential post of housemaster. In progressive and state schools recruitment to a similar position on the residential side is often made direct from outside and breadth of residential experience in other schools is often deliberately sought.

TABLE 3:3

Teaching experience of housemasters

	Only in present school	In one other	In two others	In three or more others	Total
Public	28	13	0	0	41
Independent	3	6	0	0	9
Integrated	7	6	3	0	16
Progressive	1	2	3	4	10
Maintained	3	6	9	1	19

Source: general sample - depth interviews with housemasters.
The sample in public schools: 1:4; in others it varies from 1:1 to 1:2·5. Owing to differences in structure, there are proportionately fewer housemasters in the latter four categories of school.

Such contrasts of recruitment reflect themselves in the attitudes of staff to school, boarding and their roles. Teachers in public and independent schools go to them because they are familiar, because they are offered higher material rewards and status than elsewhere and distinct academic advantages such as smaller classes and better facilities. Public school teachers have a clear conception of and a high commitment to the public school ideal, tradition and a belief in the value of boarding education. Roles in these schools are not necessarily defined in terms of hours and duties or rewarded by cash in specific contracts; instead, they are defined more by the norms of the community and rewarded by public approval and by slow promotion up the system. But all this enhances the already pronounced commitment of staff to play wide and diverse roles and to sacrifice private or family life for that of the residential community. Similar widespread and intense commitment is found among the staff of progressive schools. They too have a clear conception of the goals of their schools. Indeed, it may be the philosophy or ideals, or such features as the hope of experiment, a more intimate scale and better facilities that draw individuals to these schools in the first place. The schools from which they come are often the very opposite of progressive ones. Roles and duties in these schools are not defined in contractual terms and commitment to them is produced again by community norms and dedication to ideals. There may, however, be a less general belief in the value *per se* of boarding and the schools may not be seen as conferring status. Staff who are drawn to integrated and state schools have a less clear and a less agreed conception of the ends of their schools, indeed, their own educational philosophies may in some cases be sharply opposing. They tend to be drawn not so much by ideals or by tradition or familiarity but by greater educational opportunity offered by these schools, (smaller classes, better staff/pupil ratios), by increased status over the less selective state system and by increased material rewards over day school teachers. In these schools roles and duties *are* defined by contract and specifically rewarded by cash; community norms play less part in motivation and performance of them. There is no familiarity with boarding, and belief in the value of boarding on the part of staff is less deep and general than in other schools. Many teachers or house staff in such schools move later to similar or parallel positions in day schools.[20]

Thus certain patterns emerge in this aspect of the presenting culture. Public and many independent schools tend to be self-perpetuating in the recruitment of staff, to have less lateral mobility and to generate high and wide commitment to one mode of boarding from those who often have experience of only this one kind. Progressive and integrated schools draw more openly and have more mobility and contain people with experience of diverse kinds of boarding or day education. In state schools where almost all the staff come from the state day system this is even more the case. In progressive schools, however, the pioneering ideal or experimental aims unify the widely drawn staff and generate considerable consensus. Such consensus and normative commitment is less prominent in integrated and state schools where contractual obligations are more pronounced. In all schools outside the public school system there may be less belief in boarding and less uniformity of conception as to what it should be and how it should relate to the family.

V

The family and parental background of boarders also helps to define the limits within which schools work. A fuller report on our research into the family and boarding is found in Chapter 10; here we are only concerned with it as a context for the schools' aims and operation.

In public and most progressive and independent schools parents tend to come from higher socio-economic groups than those with children at integrated or state schools. The latter are, however, not 'working class' by any definition: the majority of them might be termed 'lower middle class' (clerical or skilled workers) or just 'middle class' (teachers or self-employed businessmen and the like). Children of working-class parents, that is skilled or unskilled manual workers, in state boarding schools make up only ten per cent of the total population. Most public schools and some of the better known progressive ones draw more from families which have been securely established for more than one generation in their social class than is the case with a few minor progressive, independent and integrated schools. These contain proportionately more parents who are upwardly mobile, first generation entrants into their social class, or who are downwardly mobile, particularly on the mother's side. By contrast the majority of state boarding schools serve groups as settled in their class over a generation or more as are public school families: upward aspirations on the part of state boarding parents refer to their children, not to themselves.[21] Parents of children in the main public, progressive and independent schools tend to pay fees out of capital, insurance policies or trust funds not out of current income, but in the other fee-paying schools parents do not have this background of capital and tend to pay more out of their income, supplemented by insurance arrangements.[22]

The parents too have educational backgrounds which differ fundamentally. In most public and the leading progressive and independent schools a majority of parents were themselves educated at independent schools and a substantial majority of the fathers (eighty per cent) had been boarders themselves, mainly at public schools. Indeed, about twenty per cent of the fathers of boys now at public schools were boarders at the same schools as their sons, and, in the well-known schools, half the boys have some family tradition of boarding at their present school. In other independent and integrated schools the position is more diverse: nevertheless, in integrated schools for example nearly half the parents (forty-three per cent) possess some tradition of boarding. In sharp contrast are the parents of most state boarders. They were almost exclusively educated at state day schools themselves, contained far fewer who experienced secondary or further education, and less than five per cent who had any experience of boarding education.[23]

These differences persist when we consider why the parents chose a boarding education for their child. For a majority of public school parents we found, in our family study, that the decision was not taken according to educational principles or the needs of the individual boy, but according to class convention or family tradition: the decision was taken for many (eighty-six per cent) at birth and for the rest before the child was six. Of course, public school parents support their decision with educational arguments and may have grounds of 'need' for wanting their child to board, but these seem secondary to the primary one of convention. Maintenance or acquisition of status, educational grounds, need or denominational reasons are more to the forefront of the decision of parents in other independent and integrated schools: significantly, their decision about boarding is not automatic at birth or infancy and is taken later than is the case with most parents in the more important public school. This is the case with progressive school parents, too, who - somewhat more than the others - tend to relate their choice of boarding and of actual schools more to the character and needs of individual children aged ten or eleven: the entry system to these schools enables the decision to be

postponed more easily than does that of most other independent schools, where parents put their children's names down on
a waiting list at early ages. Reasons of 'need' for boarding
become much more decisive in these kinds of schools too.
About a third of pupils in progressive schools and over half of
those in integrated or state schools are there primarily because
of some social need for them to live away from their family and
most of them (indeed virtually all of them at state schools)
might otherwise, according to their parents, never have been
sent away to board at all. In this they differ from 'need'
children in public schools: the majority of these boys would
have boarded even if they had not this reason. Progressive
school parents without 'need' reasons seem to decide according
to their desire for an educational ethos not found in other
schools. Among other such parents - in integrated and state
schools - motives of attaining some form of selective schooling,
denominational or academic, and high status are prominent.
There is a real belief in the intrinsic value to children of
boarding experience and of residence as a method among most
parents of public and independent school boys and of substantial segments of parents of children in integrated and progressive schools. But among most state boarding parents and
those with need reasons in integrated and even progressive
schools there is significantly much less belief in the superiority
of boarding as a method over day education. [24]

These patterns are reflected in the way the parents go about
choosing actual schools. Public school parents often decide very
early on in the boy's life on the main secondary school. Fee-
paying parents in other schools tend to delay the choice of
secondary school until later when they consider alternatives.
But parents in integrated or state schools often have little
effective choice between schools: they have to take what is
available. Indeed, a substantial number may not even see the
school before the child is accepted. The future public school-
boy is seldom a party to the decision about boarding, may be
consulted about his likely secondary school but has no effective
say in the decision of his parents. In other independent schools,
among most progressive or state schools, the decision whether
or not to board is taken in close consultation with the child and
the child's own preference among schools carries considerable

weight. In state schools it may be through the child (reporting
from the primary school teachers) that the parents hear of the
possibility of boarding in the first place. This is one of several
areas of education and social life where we find parents of
public schoolboys taking decisions which, in progressive and
state school families, are either more shared with or even
delegated to the child. In public schools fathers seem to have
the greatest part in the decision, in progressive and state schools
mothers seem more crucial, factors which influence, as we shall
see, the kind of ethos chosen for children.

This variation of role implies and our research shows that
boarding has different functions for the families who use it.
Most fee-paying parents lead busy professional and social lives
outside the context of family or home. Though more mothers
of state boarders have full-time jobs the rest of their lives was
almost entirely contained within the bounds of family and home
as was also the case with their husbands. The wider activities of
public school and some other kinds of fee-paying parents and
inherited traditions of child rearing among families of such
status in our society lead to certain definitions of the child role
and parent-child relations in such families. The role of the
young child - unpredictable, all-demanding, tiring and sometimes physically unpleasant - may conflict with the demands of
the parents' social and professional roles. Many aspects of child
care are thus, from birth, delegated in such families to special
employees and confined to special places such as nurseries.
Though such parents now have much more to do with the care
of their infants than in the Victorian or Edwardian past the large
majority with sons in a major public school (eighty-three per
cent) on our family sample had employed another woman to
share in the care of their children (forty-two per cent had
employed nannies, twenty-six per cent au pair girls). No
mother of a state boarder in our family sample had had paid
help for her children in infancy.[25] Boarding then for the child
of public school and similar families, starting at the age of eight,
is but the continuation of the family's already established
pattern of sharing the physical care and some other aspects of
upbringing of the child with agencies outside the immediate
parents.

Parents at some progressive schools show the same pattern of

activity outside the home as public school ones: indeed mothers
in these groups may be more professionally employed. Though
they frequently have help with child rearing the parents themselves are more actively involved in the process, they are less
inclined to delegate or remove the child role from themselves
than are the traditional public school parents, though more
public school families are now tending to follow this pattern.
Indeed, though oriented outwards in some ways, this progressive
group of parents is child-centred to a degree that no others are.
Their children may have to board to suit the parental activity or
educational aims, but in so doing the mother - who is the
decisive figure in the matter - seeks a style of boarding which
itself is child-centred and family-like in its atmosphere, allowing
brothers and sisters to live together and with a recognition of
the affective and emotional needs of the child. Progressive
boarders thus move - usually at the age of eleven - to schools
which are also projections of the family's style and needs.[26]

State and integrated boarding is different. Unlike the other
kinds it has fewer positive functions for the ongoing family;
on the contrary it can be inimical to it. It functions primarily
for families which are defective units of care for the child. State
and many integrated boarders are reared directly by their
parents or kin, and the move to boarding is experienced much
more as a drastic interruption of the established pattern of child
care or family life, often justified only by the drastic abnor-
mality in the family anyway.

From these child-rearing patterns arise qualities which transfer
to the schools with children and staff and help to fashion their
ethos. When child rearing is delegated outside the network of
kin to paid employees, affective relationships between parents
and child may be rendered difficult or superficial, and
emotional expression on the part of the child more inhibited.
Children may be expected to display more grown-up attributes
of restraint, rationality and predictability. Early movement
away from home to an all-male society such as a boarding
school may enhance such tendencies and expectations: it may
enable boys to cope with figures of authority more easily than
with those of affection.[27] Public school mothers, we found,
said that they had to maintain a posture of affective neutrality
about their children. More of them than of state school

mothers found it difficult to talk about personal, sexual or emotional matters with their sons. Progressive school parents tend more to the pattern of the state or integrated families in their style of relationships. Boarding schools both reflect or reinforce these differing patterns of affective behaviour and in this respect the presenting culture profoundly shapes the style of residential life.

What then of other attitudes in the home?

Most fee-paying parents (outside progressive schools) tend to be politically right wing but - especially public school parents - more diverse or 'liberal' in their opinions on social, moral and cultural issues. Parents of state and integrated school boarders are less likely to be uniformly right wing in politics but tend to be more conservative on social, moral and cultural matters. On educational matters there is widespread agreement, although public school parents stress religion and leadership, whereas state school parents stress coeducation, physical development and the need for a 'homely' atmosphere. Few public school parents accept the need for this. Progressive school parents are less concerned with the transmitting of conventional expressive values and more with fostering the 'natural growth' of personality, creative expression, emotional development and democratic methods. They too value homely qualities in the school and want the usual instrumental skills to be transmitted.[28]

Parents tend to see the division of responsibility between themselves and the school in different ways. Most fee-paying parents (outside progressive schools) believe that the school and home have clearly separate responsibilities for more areas of the child's upbringing than is the case with state or progressive school parents. They also believe that the school or the home should be decisive on matters concerning their adolescent sons' cultural, social or sexual life. Parents of state or progressive schools, in contrast, want less of a demarcation between home and school: they believe school and home should share responsibility together to a greater degree and over more areas of their children's life than do public school parents. Likewise they are prepared to delegate more responsibility to their adolescent children in social and moral affairs - a tendency borne out in the way they involve their children in the choice of school in the first place.[29]

So much then, in brief, for the powerful, distinctive and subtle cultures of different kinds of families with which boarding schools interact and from which their own staff as well as pupils are recruited.

Apart from their family life the pupils who enter boarding schools bring with them the fruits of other experiences which may affect what their schools attempt to do and what they finally achieve.

Most boys entering public and many independent schools not only come from homes whch have delegated parts of the child role to special employees but have boarded away from home since eight in single-sex schools which prepare specifically for the public schools. Children at progressive schools enter at around eleven from a wider diversity of schools, including coeducational day schools. Though most of these schools have not prepared specifically for the progressive schools the child's own family by its particular ethos and style will already have acclimatized the child for the secondary school. State and integrated boarders are recruited again at eleven, mainly from a wide array of maintained primary schools, all coeducational and which are in no way preparatory for boarding schools. Unlike entrants to the other kinds of schools, a substantial minority of boarders at these (those who board because of ascertained 'need') may not basically wish to be there at all. Thus children at public, many independent and progressive schools are socialized into their school's ethos from an early age and frequently into boarding experience. State and integrated boarders have no preliminary socialization into boarding - and some may find that their secondary schools attempt a public school kind of ethos for which they have not been prepared either by their coeducational primary schools. This helps to account for some of the distinctive adaptations we shall find among pupils in integrated schools.

These primary school experiences and the relation between secondary school and outer society crystallize the social groups who act as the points of reference by which pupils judge themselves and their school. Public and some independent school boys have as their outside reference group mainly others of their own kind; present or former public school

boarders, though this is changing. At the other extreme, state
boarders have as their reference groups day pupils at state
schools or young wage earners. Progressive (and some other
independent) school children have more varied reference
points: fee-paying and state pupils, boarders and day pupils or
university students, but few workers. These groups external
to the school who act as models or provide social outlets for the
pupils can profoundly influence the attitude of boarders to
their school's aims and methods, helping to produce commitment at one extreme or alienation at the other.[30]

The social life of boarders in the holidays examined in later
chapters confirms further what we have already found about
the connection of schools with their particular societies. Two
basic patterns were found: one among public, independent and
progressive school pupils where the boarding society projects
itself into the outside holiday world as an anomic, artificial,
homogeneous, temporary but intense social network; the other
where, among integrated and state school pupils, the boarder is
himself left anomic and isolated in a day school world or reverts
into it, but is always caught up in the ordinary routine of
home.[31]

VII

From this survey of the presenting cultures, we conclude that
two very distinct kinds of relationship exist between English
boarding schools and the wider society.

The first kind exists where schools are an integral part of a
coherent sub-system of the wider society. Such schools have
been moulded by distinct traditions and educational
philosophies relating to boarding education; serve a traditional
and distinct clientele or subculture; recruit members at staff
and pupil levels who are socialized for them by other agencies
well before entry; are partly self-perpetuating and cyclical in
such recruitment; serve positive functions for the families from
which they draw and are closely attuned to them in values, style
and child-rearing practices so that there is little discontinuity
between family and school experience; penetrate the social and
family background of their members and are themselves
embedded in a network of other organizations with membership

and functions which overlap and which support them and knit them closely into the social sub-systems for which they prepare their children. Schools with this kind of relationship include the public schools, about a third of the independent schools and most progressive schools.

The second kind of relationship occurs when boarding schools are less integrally connected with a sub-system of society for which they prepare their children. These schools stand in no established tradition of boarding and serve no defined subculture; their membership is not self-perpetuating in recruitment, is heterogeneous in origins and seldom socialized into boarding by earlier experiences; they serve negative functions for at least half the families that feed them and there may be little continuity between the values and style of the family and those of the school; in some cases (in integrated schools) there is marked dissimilarity. Such boarding schools do not penetrate the background society and culture of staff, parents and pupils which all relate, congruously or otherwise, to the day school society; they are not supported by a network of other organizations with overlapping functions and membership. Schools with this kind of relationship are all state and most integrated schools, some score of small and less well-known independent and a few progressive schools.

4 The sociology of the boarding school

The external context has been set. The chief empirical factors which differentiate the schools have also been introduced. But, by themselves, these empirical variables are not enough: they neither adequately describe nor explain the nature and variation of the boarding-school society. To understand how and why these societies operate and differ we must look at more subtle aspects of their make-up: we must examine their sociological differences. In so doing we develop a general approach to the sociology of the school which has already been discussed in a previous publication and ask: apart from empirical and external approaches, how does one begin to analyse the community of a school?[1] By what other criteria can sixty-six schools and groups of them be compared? What factors explain the differences between them? Before answering these questions we must discuss the theoretical approach, the programme and concepts and the dimensions by which the schools have been explored.

The sociology of the school is a comparatively recent development within the sociology of education. For many years the school was studied sometimes in terms of a few of its constituent parts - the class, the peer group, the teacher's role - but chiefly in terms of its functions for society as a whole. Those functions, as we know, are administrative, allocative and integrative. After the Second World War most attention focused on the allocative functions of the school - its role in distributing society's human resources, in facilitating or obstructing social mobility or maintaining patterns of social stratification.[2] Research concentrated on the inefficiency and wastefulness of our educational system rather than on the school and classroom as a social organisation.

The other functions of the school have until recent years been comparatively neglected. Valuable studies were made of individual parts of the school, but its *integrative* function as a whole, in training for juvenile, adolescent and adult roles, in socializing into the values, norms and wider culture of society was not prominent in research. Lately however, in such studies as those of the communication of linguistic skills and the development of new learning programmes, the school and classroom have been examined as a society in their own right, as a whole complicated organism operating towards specific purposes of its own and having integrative functions for society in general.[3] In fulfilling such purposes of training the young in roles and socializing them into approved values and attributes, a boarding school is potentially one of the most powerful mechanisms available in education.

It is this view of the society of the school as a whole interlocking process, directed towards certain ends of its own, interacting with other societies in its environment and serving the three broad functions for society, that this book presents. Our approach derives initially from two areas of sociological study: that of complex organizations, and that of closed or 'total' social systems, for the boarding school has the attributes of both, but one should never forget that all schools are teaching institutions and consist predominantly of interaction between adults and children.

A complex organization is a social system constructed to attain certain specific goals.[4] Starting over forty years ago and developing through a series of classic studies, the sociology of organizations has now developed a substantial theory and methodology of its own. At first it was largely concerned with industrial or bureaucratic units engaged in producing inanimate objects and with the official structure and operation of such units, 'the formal system'. Later, emphasis switched to the informal network of human relations which pervaded the organization and their effect on the attainment of goals. These theoretical perspectives have been applied to all organizations, hospitals and prisons as well as schools, and there have been attempts to construct a general theory valid for all organizations. Interaction within the school has, until recently, not been systematically studied but much present research is examining the informal networks that exist among staff and pupils and the ways the social structure, curriculum and classroom organization affect these.

Though all schools belong to the species of organizations, boarding schools differ from day schools in that they are also closed or 'total' societies.[5] Such societies are marked by the exercise of complete control over their members' behaviour and value-orientations by the provision of all their basic necessities within their boundaries.* There have been many individual studies of such total societies as prisons or mental hospitals, and there is a famous study of the operation and effects of certain kinds of total institutions.[6] But this kind of society as a whole lacks a systematic analysis and this is illustrated when boarding schools are discussed. Total institutions tend to be confused together as though their nature, purposes and structure were all similar. Boarding schools are dealt with as though they were similar to concentration camps, prisons, mental hospitals, monasteries, armies, ships, isolated building sites or remote Welsh villages. Though we must not digress into a general discussion of total institutions, it is important here to examine the place of the boarding school in this sociological genre.

First some general propositions. We have to distinguish societies where the encompassing and controlling system is consciously articulated in pursuit of goals (e.g. a prison, a convent) from those where such controls are accidental or incidental to other main purposes (e.g. a lightship, a remote village). Total institutions of the former kind always serve goals related to the values of the general society. These goals can be *positive* goals, which involve preparation for and renewal of society's values or culture, as in a monastery, boarding school, army or kibbutz, or they can be *negative* goals which preserve society's values and culture from challenge, dilution or taint as in concentration camps, prisons, mental hospitals. Finally, while the internal structure of these societies can be highly differentiated, with considerable functional autonomy of their various parts, they are all characterized by an integration of areas of life or sub-systems which are normally kept distinct in the outside society: that is, by work, living and leisure being performed in one place, according to one routine and supervised by a unitary system of authority.

However, the nature of this all-encompassing control which

---

* This is our definition. Though closed societies are usually segregated from the wider one, their members may have regular access to it - e.g. certain orders of nuns. Totality, as the text explains, can be as much normative or expressive in kind as physical.

makes all such institutions 'total' can itself vary and these differences are critical. Total control can be physical, normative or both. Physical controls can cover activity, movement, time, dress, social relationships, and we shall call this *instrumental totality*. Normative controls aim to create high moral involvement and cover subtle areas of values, attitudes, modes of self-expression, norms of behaviour and belief: we shall call this kind *expressive totality*. Some total societies exhibit both kinds: a monastery, for example. Others exhibit only instrumental totality: a merchant ship for example, or a mental hospital or certain kinds of prison where reforming aims are low. Yet other societies can be total in the expressive sense but not in the instrumental one: a 'progressive' boarding school is an example of this, where there are plenty of physical freedoms but considerable and subtle normative control.

We end up therefore with three kinds of total societies. Some are *utilitarian*, a category which includes lightships and isolated building sites, where the totality is incidental to the goals, and where the society is close in its values to those of the general society. Its structure is marked neither by extreme expressive stress nor by the extreme physical controls which can lead to the mortification process of extreme institutionalization found in some institutions. Others serve *negative culture goals*. These exist to protect societal values from the inmates, are marked by high instrumental totality, rigid and distant relationships between staff and inmates, low selectivity and involuntariness of entry, little internal mobility, negative methods of social control and high alienation of the inmates. Prisons and some mental hospitals are good examples. A third group serve *positive culture goals* which exist to instil, protect or replenish society's values, such as monasteries, training colleges or combat units of the army. These institutions are marked by high expressive and perhaps by high instrumental totality, by selectivity and voluntariness of entry, by an interweaving of the relationships between staff and inmates, internal mobility and opportunity to achieve status, positive methods of control and high involvement by the members.

It is to this latter category of total institutions that boarding schools belong. They are usually much concerned with values. Indeed, sometimes they function as citadels to protect or preserve values, as in the way some public schools cherish 'traditional', social and moral values or the Christian faith, or sometimes they function as launching pads for the renewal of values, as for example in the assault on traditional values of child rearing mounted by the progressive boarding schools in the 1920s. Boarding schools, however, vary greatly and we shall discover that some have the attributes of the negative type. There are also variations in their use of instrumental or expressive totality and these variations, as we shall find, reflect differences in the nature and effects of the societies. Boarding schools are thus far from uniformly 'total'.

In any case, boarding schools are in some senses only partly total: their members leave at the end of every term and are then exposed to the freedoms and the values of the wider society. To fulfil educational ends the schools also have to admit aspects of the outside world within themselves. Total as their control may attempt to be for some time, the boarding school lacks the more complete and more permanent control found in some other institutions. This semi-total nature creates possibilities and problems of its own for the structure and operation of the society, for its individual members and for the outside units and organizations which share their lives and loyalties.

The boarding school is thus an organization of the total variety serving specific goals of its own and having broader functions for the wider society which we have already discussed. So much by way of generality. We can now introduce some of the chief features of the framework by which the schools in our sample will be compared and evaluated in the following chapters.

We begin by assuming that schools set out to achieve certain goals, the state of affairs which the school exists to attain or promote. These goals differ in content and we have found it useful to distinguish three types of goal. First there are goals concerned with the transmission of mental, physical or social skills or the acquisition of useful attributes, for example, examination qualifications, a disciplined intellect, good physique, social poise. We shall call these *instrumental goals*. The second kind concern not the transmission of skills but qualities or attributes which are ends in themselves, values of behaviour, belief, morals, taste and expression: things such as religious and moral awareness, cultural and intellectual interests, sportsmanship and the development of personality. These we shall call *expressive goals*. Finally, as all schools have to ensure their staff and pupil recruitment, maintenance and financial viability to survive over time, they pursue *organizational goals* which are concerned with such matters as administration, order, reputation, finance and efficiency.

All schools, day and boarding, pursue these three kinds of goals, though different schools or groups of them give prominence to different kinds, and the emphasis may change over time. Some boarding schools for many reasons put greater stress on expressive goals than do day schools, but we shall see in the chapters on styles of boarding that the emphasis varies widely. The balance between these types of goals contains many incompatibilities and generates tensions. Expressive and organizational goals have a tendency to conflict, and the demands of instrumental and expressive ones may not always harmonize. Different patterns of the predominance or subordination of certain goals therefore appear between schools or over a period of time within one school. These differing patterns and conflicts are crucial determinants of the varying structures, operation and effects of schools.

Goals, however, are not finite, concrete entities. They are moulded by the forces of historical tradition and the school's functions for society and consist of people's *perceptions* and evaluations. As schools are not homogeneous units, the governors, head, administration, groups on the teaching staff, the pupils and parents, may all have differing perceptions of the goals which the school is pursuing or those which it is attaining and those which they think the school should be pursuing. As we have just seen, these perceptions will be influenced by the presenting culture of the individuals in the organization. Likewise the goals *stated* to the outside world by the school may not coincide with the *implemented* goals pursued in day-to-day practice. Between the differing perceptions of goals, between stated and implemented goals, there are generated other tensions which provide the school society with conflicts and pressures for change.

There can be no understanding or comparative analysis of school societies without an examination of the goals to which they are directed but it is important to be aware that these goals are not static entities but consist of individuals' differing perceptions, which we shall discuss in the next chapter.

This approach enables us to examine individuals' support for the particular goals or sets of goals rather than assuming overall alienation or commitment. To attain its goals the school society is articulated into a formal social system. For example, various functions are allocated to sub-systems: the academic, social, athletic, religious/pastoral, bursarial and domestic, and these sub-systems can have elements of miniature societies in their own right - possessing separate roles, separate hierarchies of status, authority and privilege systems, occupying separate territories or buildings and sometimes generating norms, values, modes of expression and symbols of their own. We shall see that some boarding schools are remarkable for the profusion and the degree of autonomy of such sub-systems, while other schools are more centralized, as are most day schools. Like the goals which they serve these sub-units interact and produce conflicts which may promote, deflect or obstruct the attainment of ends. Knitting together all these parts of the school is a process of communication and of decision-making, a distribution of official statuses, of authority positions, and a complementary pattern of privileges and sanctions. These features differ between schools. The variations in the span and nature of authority delegated to pupils is, for instance, one of the chief variants between different boarding styles in this country.

To attain a degree of consensus on its goals and values and on the institutional means to attain them the society employs mechanisms of social control. This control is a complex process and can take many forms.[7] For example, there may be processes of assimilation by which newcomers are initiated and instructed in the norms of behaviour and values which he or she is expected to follow, a common and often elaborate procedure in closed communities. There may also be attempts to keep the society oriented towards the desired goals and values by developing a whole culture which symbolizes and expresses such values to those inside or outside the community. Rituals, traditions, cultural manifestations, approved patterns of taste or manners are among many aspects of such orienting devices found in boarding schools. To check deviation from such desired goals

and values is the function of the system of social control.
Usually, the control process also incorporates rewards and
sanctions which can be coercive, utilitarian, involving material
rewards or deprivations, or normative, involving the use of
symbolic rewards and penalties or the manipulation of status
or group feeling. Different sub-systems can use different
kinds of control, and the disparities between the kind of control
used in one and the other and between the nature of the
control and that of the goals it serves produce conflict and
repercussions which powerfully condition the pupils' adaptation
to the school. Control within a boarding school can also be
more pervasive and more subtle than in the more open society
of the day school. The two varieties of instrumental and
expressive totality which we introduced earlier are major
manifestations of controls available in a residential setting and
the degrees to which they are used are important distinguishing
factors between schools. The patterns of orientation and
control are vital to any society's effectiveness. The closed
nature of boarding schools gives greater resources for orientation
and greater scope and this is one reason why such communities
can have such a powerful and deep impress, positively or otherwise, on their members.

Within the formally laid down structure and pattern there
exists a whole network of values, norms of behaviour and value,
of relationships which are not formally prescribed by the goals
of the society. We call this world the informal social system.
Though analytically distinct from each other, the formal and
informal worlds interweave in practice in the roles individuals
play and the social groups and relationships into which they
enter. Indeed this very interlocking of the formal and informal
societies is crucial for the effectiveness of the society in attaining
its goals. Nevertheless the informal order can be analysed in its
own right and has been considered separately by us and by
many other writers.[8] There may be many informal networks in
a school. The governors, staff, domestics and the pupils all have
their own private worlds. The apparatus of the formal order is
often duplicated in these informal networks. For example,
there may be informal subdivisions, patterns of status and
privilege and power, informal modes of communication and
control, informal values and norms which are expressed in

traditions and rituals. Though the informal system among the staff and pupils can vary in the degree of its elaboration the closed nature of the boarding school gives it a special potency: indeed, the informal power and controls wielded by the pupils and staff to enforce their own code of norms over one another can be less escapable than the formal system of control and authority.

Thus the nature of these informal worlds and the degree of their influence is of vital concern to the formal system. In some schools the informal network of the pupils is penetrated and cut across by the formal one so that it is difficult to disentangle the two, but in others, as we shall see, they remain separate worlds, remote from each other. The informal world can be strong in that a large proportion of individuals acknowledge norms which control a wide range of areas from beliefs and interests to modes of dress and self-expression and which are enforced by strong informal controls. In contrast the informal systems can be weak in that they cover few areas and are not strongly enforced.

It is necessary here to comment on two assumptions that are frequently made about informal systems in institutions. First, strong informal systems do not necessarily reject the goals of the institution. This may be true in a few prisons or concentration camps but it scarcely applies in boarding schools. In fact, we shall see that the progressive schools have high commitment in all goal areas among the pupils despite having a strong pupil society. When the formal system is weak there will always be a strong informal society but where the formal system is strong, the informal societies can be varied, weak or strong. The other assumption frequently made is that one function of the informal system is to meet needs which are not met by the formal society. This is an important perspective derived from the work of Sykes and Becker,[9] but in many cases the situation is more complex than this. In some boarding schools we visited, for example, a harsh, repressive formal regime was supplemented by a violent and exploitative world that existed among the children. The pains of imprisonment were intensified rather than moderated. Generalizations about informal societies, therefore, should always be treated with caution, for the functions of institutions and perceptions of individuals differ so widely.

The formal system can vary in its approach to the informal one. In a boarding school many opportunities are available to the formal system to manipulate the informal system which are not possible in a day school. Most day schools have to operate through the classroom situation and the curriculum to influence the pupil world but boarding schools have the extra range of residential opportunities to achieve this effect.

Thus the *nature* of the informal order, the degree of its integration with the formal one, and its *orientation* to the school's goals are without doubt the most vital factors of all in determining the society's attainment of its ends. We shall see that boarding schools exhibit great differences along these critical dimensions of analysis.

This brief resumé of our approach to the sociology of the residential school is, of course, only one of many possible starting points, and though any conceptual system can be an intellectual straitjacket we believe that this framework is a useful beginning to our understanding of how boarding schools differ and why they operate in the ways that they do.

There are, of course, many weaknesses in this framework. In it, the conflict between a structural/functionalist approach and a phenomenological perspective tends to be blurred and the difference in pressures arising from the social structure and from the individual's perception of his social situation are not always clear.[10] Much that is elaborate description may masquerade as explanation and important non-sociological factors may have been ignored. There is also a danger that our categories may impose upon the situation perspectives that do not reflect the evaluations of the individuals concerned so that, for example, what we call 'organizational' may be viewed in an expressive way by the actors concerned.

Nevertheless despite these objections we believe that the conceptual framework we have outlined does offer a starting point to compare the great variety of schools that are included under the heading of English boarding schools. In the next chapters we shall develop these ideas and ask what do the schools set out to achieve, how do they do it and what effects do they have?

5   The goals of boarding schools

All schools work towards certain ends. Many of these they share as common aims. But residence enlarges the scope of the goals which a school can pursue. Though most day schools in this country have a broader set of aims than their continental counterparts, boarding schools can and do pursue an even wider range. Many of these goals found in residential schools reflect an expressive stress concerned with character and physical development and largely derive from the influence of the nineteenth-century public school. Some aims are common to all but we shall see that different schools emphasize different goals and give them embodiment in contrasting structures and residential styles. Boarding schools, therefore, exhibit a greater diversity of aims and a more extreme realization of educational philosophies than do day schools.

'My aim is to prepare my boys for death', claimed one headmaster. 'We exist to produce good farm workers', said another. 'The Christian gentleman sums up my aim', declared a third. 'Our chief object', said another, 'is to give them what they lack: a stable home'. 'Healthy, alert and responsible leaders are what we wish to produce', replied another head. 'Above all', stated another, 'we seek to·foster the growth of personality in the greatest possible freedom'.

Such brief snatches illustrate some of the diversity. These goals may at first seem nebulous. In fact, they radically differentiate schools from one another and ultimately determine the varying patterns of structure, operation and effect which we will explore in the following chapters.

II

Our research enables us to explore in several ways the *stated* goals of schools, those which the people primarily responsible for directing policy present publicly as their ultimate aims.[1] These *stated* goals may or may not coincide with the *implemented* goals which the school is seen to pursue in daily practice. We studied a large amount of literature prepared for presentation to the inside and outside worlds in all the schools on our sample: prospectuses, magazines, reports and handouts. We also observed and recorded similar presentations of a verbal kind: sermons, speeches, discussions, morning and evening addresses and so on. In addition we gathered material in the course of systematic interviews. As this latter material can be analysed in quantitative form we present only statistical material in this chapter but it is necessary to stress that, when collated with the other evidence, the patterns of goal emphasis and the subsequent styles of boarding that develop to implement them are remarkably consistent.

We interviewed all the heads in our schools and a sample of housemasters and mistresses for as long as three hours. During the discussions we asked them an open-ended question: what were their schools setting out to achieve as far as the pupils were concerned? This question produced careful and often lengthy replies reflecting contrasting educational philosophies

TABLE 5:1

Stated goals of public schools

The ten most frequently stated goals (numbers
mentioning them in brackets)

22 Headmasters		33 Housemasters	
Sense of service	(17)	Community spirit	(29)
Christian faith	(17)	Sense of tolerance	(26)
Community spirit	(16)	Sense of service	(24)
Sense of tolerance	(13)	Good O and A level performance	(22)
Cultural awareness	(13)	Moral sense	(22)
Intellectual training	(13)	Personal independence	(19)
Responsibility	(12)	Intellectual training	(19)
Moral awareness	(12)	Responsibility	(16)
Personal independence	(12)	Christian faith	(16)
Sportsmanship	(10)	Leadership	(12)
Sense of 'standards'	(10)	Good manners	(12)
Good manners	(10)		

Source: general sample, depth interviews.

from the sixty-two heads and sixty-nine housemasters or mistresses who answered this question. We shall discuss first the educational content of their replies and then analyse some sociological perspectives which underlie their statements.

Although all schools pursue some ends in common the forces which bear upon them lead to differences in emphasis between them and the goal patterns so produced follow closely the constitutional variations in English boarding education.

Public schools have a pattern of stated goals very much of their own, with a high degree of similarity among the individual schools. In Table 5:1 we see the stated goals which were most frequently mentioned by the staff in them.

Paramount to heads and housemasters of these schools is the development of certain moral attributes: service to others, Christian faith and practice, community spirit, the ability to control self in constructive concern for the welfare of others; tolerance and moral awareness. These socio-moral aims eclipse others in both priority and their repetition (they comprise six out of the ten most prominent goals). Indeed, many heads regard their schools as 'pattern societies', as model communities through the life and example of which pupils may imbibe these moral attributes. Some even regard them as isolated citadels practising and equipping their pupils with values to which society outside is either indifferent or hostile. As one head said of religion:

'this school is the nearest approach to a Christian community that these boys will ever have'. Or another, more extreme, passionately declaimed on moral values: 'this is a place where boys who have the right interests and the right standards are strengthened to spread their influence against the evil which is in the world'. A third expresses the importance given to the ideal of service: 'we try to get a boy to believe in what is bigger than himself - the school, the house and so on, and to make him *serve* these, not to live for himself, so that he realizes that service to the community is the most important thing when he leaves'.

Around this cluster of moral ideals others are related: responsible behaviour and loyalty, good manners and a sense of proper standards. Some housemasters still mention 'leadership', though in the goals of headmasters and housemasters themselves this Victorian conception has largely been replaced by the modern ideal of service. Three other goals not related to the moral cluster are stressed. Academically, the heads see their schools as training intelligence for its own sake, 'learning for its own sake' as one said, unrelated to applied matters or to paper qualifications. Though the housestaff, perhaps more concerned with down-to-earth matters, elevate exam performance to a stated goal, they too give high priority to abstract intellectual training. The second is equally important to headmasters: cultural awareness,

'a love of the best that has been thought, written and created', 'of the right things'.

The third goal is individuality or personal independence: defined by both heads and housemasters as a boy's ability to retain legitimate identity and self-reliance despite his concern for and absorption in the community.

These then are the elements which appear to the forefront of the modified Arnoldian tradition: a compound of strong moral and religious values, abstract intellectual training, cultural awareness and personal independence. The public schools set out to influence their pupils towards a certain ideal type of values, character and behaviour, a model which is clearly and uniformly defined by most schools.

Some possible aims are noticeable by their absence from this cluster. For intrinsic and comparative purposes we should consider some kinds of goal which do *not* appear prominently or even at all among the stated goals of the authorities in public schools. Vocational training, for example, was never mentioned, and examination performance had a low priority. The development of creative potential was mentioned only twice. The meeting of social or personal 'need' for boarding did not appear as a separate or prominent primary aim of these schools. Likewise only two headmasters and two housemasters included happiness among their stated objectives. This is not to say that public school staff are not concerned with the happiness of their pupils - of course they are - but, as much other evidence confirms, they see it as secondary, as the byproduct of the other paramount attributes which they set out to transmit -

'the happiness compatible with a good and useful life'

as one headmaster put it. Physical development figures little, far less than the ideal of 'sportsmanship' with its moral and character-training overtones. None of the heads or house-masters included the creation of a homely atmosphere among their aims; on the contrary, some explicitly mentioned that their schools should be 'bracing', have 'a touch of hardness' deliberately to contrast with the home. Finally, no head stressed the development of personality (apart from the imbibing of approved moral and cultural attitudes) as an end in itself, and none mentioned emotional development or emotional expression in their collection of stated ends. Once more, the absence of these specific goals does not mean that they are not, in some way or another, sought by public schools: but they have neither currency nor priority in the aims to which the schools are publicly directed. In this they differ significantly from some other kinds of boarding school.

Those independent schools, which are neither on the HMC nor 'integrated' with the maintained sector, pursue fewer stated aims and possess less consensus on such aims than do the public schools.

TABLE 5:2
Most frequently stated goals of independent schools
7 Headmasters

Moral awareness	(4)
O/A level results	(4)
Leadership	(4)
Tolerance	(4)
Responsibility	(4)
Service	(3)
Christian faith	(3)
Preparation for life	(3)
Meeting 'need'	(3)
Absence of pressure	(3)
Education for ability	(3)

Source: general sample, depth interviews. Only four housestaff answered this question, so their replies are not included.

One group of these schools models itself on the public school and prominent among their stated ends are moral or community values: religious and moral awareness, tolerance, responsibility and a sense of service. Leadership, now a passé ideal in the public school itself, still lingers on among some of this group. But to many of them qualifications and examination performance are openly stressed as aims, while abstract intellectual development is less prominent. Similarly vocational training or 'preparation for life' is emphasized more than in the public schools. Among a sub-group of these independent schools the stated academic aim is to adjust the education given to the level of ability of the child and among some, smaller and denominational schools, there is stress on the provision of freedom, or the removal of pressures as a setting for the development of the child and less concentration on reproducing an ideal type of person or set of values. A few also see the creation of a special environment to meet the requirements of children with 'need' as a chief aim.

The stated goals of a majority of these schools thus echo those of the public schools, but as befits their less elitist clientele and their pupils' wider range of ability there is more stress on practical objectives. Among some, however, appear aims which suggest a different approach to boarding education altogether.

These appear more markedly among the third group of schools: independent schools which are substantially 'integrated' with the maintained sector by the social composition of their intake. Not only are the goals which are prominent enough to be stated different in kind from the preceding kinds of school, but the divergence within this particular kind of school is more extreme.

Though the public school's moral and spiritual aims appear in answers by some heads of these schools the ideals of independence and of examination performance are more prominent. Equally high and highest of all among housestaff in these schools is the creation of an environment to meet the requirements of children with background 'need' for boarding. A substantial group see the creation of a 'homely' atmosphere as an aim in that direction - a goal which did not appear in the two former kinds of school. But sharp divergencies appear among other

TABLE 5:3

Most frequently stated goals of independent integrated schools

11 Headmasters		14 Housestaff	
O/A Level results	(9)	Meeting need	(13)
Individuality	(8)	Discipline	(12)
Meeting need	(8)	Moral awareness	(10)
Moral awareness	(7)	Homeliness	(10)
Responsibility	(7)	Education for ability	(7)
Freedom	(7)	Tolerance	(7)
Preparation for jobs	(7)	O/A Level results	(6)
Emotional development	(4)	Preparation for life	(6)
Education for ability	(4)	Christian faith	(6)
Happiness	(4)	Independence	(6)
Tolerance	(4)	Emotional development	(6)
Community sense	(4)		
Manners	(4)		

Source: general sample, depth interviews.

goals: while some schools stress exam results, others say they give more priority to adapting the education given to ability; while one distinct group stresses firm discipline and ideal types of moral behaviour as ends in themselves, another, mainly of coeducational schools, emphasizes absence of pressure and provision of freedom, scope for emotional development and happiness. Cultural, creative aims, the service ideal and abstract intellectual training do not figure prominently among the ends of any of those schools concerned in some degree with moral aims or character-training ends. Most integrated schools seem to be much more obviously preoccupied than do the former kinds of boarding schools with the practical educational, social and organizational problems presented by their kind of pupil. In setting goals to meet these two radically differing approaches to boarding two polar extremes of order and freedom appear among them.

With maintained boarding schools we find more consensus on aims, though by no means as much as among public schools and with a content significantly different from theirs.
Highest among the stated priorities of both heads and house-

TABLE 5:4

Most frequently stated goals of maintained schools

15 Headmasters		14 Housestaff	
Individuality	(12)	Meeting need	(11)
Happiness	(9)	Independence	(10)
Meeting need	(9)	Homely atmosphere	(9)
Cultural aims	(9)	Education to ability	(8)
Homely atmosphere	(7)	Preparation for jobs	(8)
Education to ability	(7)	Emotional development	(7)
Preparation for jobs	(7)	O/A level results	(6)
Emotional development	(7)	Happiness	(6)
Preparation for life	(6)	Self-confidence	(6)
Vitality	(6)		

Source: general sample, depth interviews.

staff are the fostering of independence, the creating of an environment to meet 'need', the pursuit of happiness, the creation of a 'homely' atmosphere and the development of emotions. Though examination performance is fairly prominent, the matching of education with ability is given greater stress as might follow from a group of schools which contain so many schools catering for less academic children. Career training is also prominent as is the development of self-confidence in the child (something which seems less called for in schools serving other social groups). Moral ends which are stressed are tolerance, responsibility, moral awareness, but the public school kind of pattern - service, loyalty, community and Christianity - figure in only a few of these schools. Cultural ends are emphasized by heads, good manners by housestaff. Among one group of schools freedom and absence of pressure appear again as ends but, in another group, discipline and a firm framework of life are stressed. Evidently, with a marked consensus on some ends, there are differing extremes in interpretation. Unlike the public schools this group is less concerned with abstract intellectual and moral ideals and more concerned with counteracting social dislocation and providing basic help to their pupils in social, academic or vocational ways.

Our final group of schools, the progressive ones, reveal

another distinctive pattern of stated goals and more consensus on them than even the public schools show. All the heads stress as their aim the development of intrinsic personality rather than the training of character according to certain approved values or an ideal pattern of them.

TABLE 5:5

Most frequently stated goals of progressive schools

7 Headmasters		10 Housestaff	
Development of personality	(7)	Development of personality	(8)
Emotional development	(7)	Emotional development	(8)
Absence of pressures	(6)	Independence	(7)
Creative development	(6)	Happiness	(7)
Cultural interests	(6)	Critical awareness	(7)
Vitality	(5)	Tolerance	(6)
Critical awareness	(5)	Creative expression	(6)
Happiness	(5)	Free style of life	(6)
Education for ability	(5)	Preparation for life	(5)
		Responsibility	(5)

Source: general sample, depth interviews.

Uniformly high among their expressed priorities are the generation of an atmosphere of freedom, the minimization of pressures, scope for emotional growth, for self-expression and cultural interests and the pursuit of happiness as an end in itself. Moral emphasis is on tolerance and responsibility, and, though some schools give prominence to the Christian faith and ethic, an equal number is concerned with 'spiritual' rather than specifically religious or denominational experience. Academic goals are related to individual ability and less concerned, in public expression at least, with abstract mental training or exam performance. Neither an elaborate and idealized pattern of character, nor severely practical aims of catering for need, preparing for jobs, gaining exam results or training in manners seem to have much prominence in the stated goals of the progressive school.

These then are the stated goals of boarding schools as expressed in interviews and confirmed by much other evidence.

Distinct educational approaches are found in three kinds of schools. Public schools stress character training towards an ideal pattern of moral, religious and cultural ends and abstract academic ends; state schools are more concerned with meeting the consequences of 'need' for boarding, with vocational training and basic academic education; progressive schools pursue the development of personality by reducing pressures, stressing freedom, creative expression and emotional development. The two other kinds of boarding schools tend to reflect these philosophies rather than possess their own. Most independent schools follow the public school style, but integrated schools exhibit features of all three different approaches; both kinds of school, however, stress practical training and concrete results. Consensus among staff on these ends is most marked in progressive schools and, to almost the same degree, in public schools. Our questionnaires showed that staff believe that their schools are implementing the goals they believe to be important. Less consensus is found among staff in independent and state boarding schools, although we shall see that there are important differences in style and approach among state schools which make generalizations difficult. Consensus scarcely exists among integrated schools which, as we saw, pursue strongly contrasting ends and there are large differences between what staff say the school should be doing and what it seems to achieve. All these differences derive in part from the varying historical or organizational pressures upon schools and from the coherence, or otherwise, of their functions for society which we have already examined.

Two further sociological interpretations of these stated goals are important for the rest of this study.

It is possible, first, to see whether these stated ends are primarily concerned with the individual pupil and his fulfilment or, instead or in addition, whether they are 'other-directed', primarily concerned with the individual's response to and interaction with other people. Of course, all schools pursue ends which are both individual and collective in their emphasis but, if we attempt to classify the stated goals of the heads and housestaff of boarding schools on this dimension, a clear demarcation appears between them.

TABLE 5:6

Collective or individual orientation of stated goals

Average frequency with which collectively or individually oriented goals were expressed by headmasters (HMs) and housestaff (Hse) in each kind of school.

Orientation	Public		Independent		Ind/Integrated		Maintained		Progressive	
	HMs	Hse	HMs	Hse	HMs	Hse	HMs	Hse	HMs	Hse
Collective	6·0	6·9	5·1	3·2	2·7	4·1	2·2	2·0	1·9	2·9
Individual	3·3	3·1	2·6	2·7	3·5	4·0	6·1	6·5	9·1	7·7

Source: general sample, depth interviews, calculated from the detailed content analysis and classification given in Table 1 in Appendix IV.

At one extreme are the public schools. Despite their stress on personal independence, the cultivation of intelligence and of cultural and some other values which are individual in orientation, the most frequently emphasized goals are those with a collective outlook. Independent schools show a similar tendency but integrated ones veer between the two kinds. With state schools the orientation of goals becomes predominantly individual and with the progressive schools we reach the opposite end of the dimension from the public schools: individually oriented goals emphatically outnumber the collectively oriented ones.

Such variations are not haphazard or abstract. The pronounced stress on goals with a collective tendency in the public schools and their followers derive from their function of training a governing and administrative elite, of sensitizing pupils socially and morally so that they can exercise responsibility over others. To this end, as one head put it on speech day,

'self-sacrifice is what matters, not self-fulfilment.'

At the other extreme the progressive school stresses goals which are individual in outlook in its effort to develop 'personality' and in fulfilling its function of rearing a deviant, nonconformist or creative subculture of the governing elite in society. The individual stress of state schools derives from their preoccupation with meeting the 'need for boarding' of many of their pupils. How far these abstract emphases concretely affect children we shall see later. Here it can only be said that they do profoundly condition - even in minute details - the daily working and structure of schools.

Our second interpretation is to classify these stated goals into three sociological categories: instrumental, expressive and organizational.[2] *Instrumental goals* concern the transmission of useful skills or the acquisition of qualifications. *Expressive goals* concern not means but ultimates: norms or values are transmitted, aspects of personality are developed or a particular desired state of affairs such as homeliness or care is fostered. *Organizational goals* concern not ends but the machinery by which the society operates. As stated goals represent long-term ideals we would not expect organizational ends to be much in evidence among them. Few headmasters would put prime among the publicly expressed aims of his school its own self-maintenance, internal reputation or economy; indeed, of the sixty-two who answered the question, only four did so. House-staff in contrast, were somewhat more inclined to mention such ends. Likewise, given the high stress on transmitting values of one kind or another in English boarding education, we would not expect instrumental goals, the transmitting of skills or equipping with qualifications to figure largely in stated ends of headmasters. Housestaff are inclined to stress them more. Accordingly, when we look at the frequency with which each

TABLE 5:7
Instrumental, expressive and organizational content
of stated goals

Average frequency with which instrumental, expressive or organizational goals were given by headmasters (HMs) or housestaff (Hse) in each kind of school.

Content	Public		Independent		Ind/Integrated		Maintained		Progressive	
	HMs	Hse	HMs	Hse	HMs	Hse	HMs	Hse	HMs	Hse
Instrumental	1·5	2·0	2·1	1·2	2·3	2·2	2·9	3·0	2·4	2·9
Expressive	8·1	7·8	4·7	3·8	4·1	5·3	5·3	5·3	9·1	7·6
Organizational	0	0·3	0·1	0·5	0·1	0·7	0	0·2	0	0

Source: general sample, depth interviews, calculated from the detailed content analysis and classification given in Table 1 in Appendix IV.

kind of goal was mentioned in our interviews, we find that the picture which emerges from Table 5:7.

In public and progressive schools expressive goals, those concerned with values, are stressed three or four times more frequently than are instrumental goals, those concerned with skills. In the other three kinds of school, however, this disparity is less marked: expressive goals figure only twice as frequently, and not even that in maintained schools where the disparity is least. In so far as organizational goals were stated at all it was mainly among one group of independent integrated schools. These patterns roughly correspond with the others traced between schools so far in this chapter and which are summarized in the diagram on page 91.

These, then, are the stated goals, the publicly expressed aims of the authorities in boarding schools. But it is only when we have seen how these aims differ from those pursued in day-to-day practice that we shall have established the full pattern of goals which determine the nature and practice of boarding education. To conclude this chapter, therefore, we turn next to the *implemented* goals of our sample of schools.

III

Goals are not finite, objective entities.[3] They exist largely in people's perceptions of them. Different individuals or groups connected with the school will perceive its goals differently. For example, we asked parents and senior pupils to rate the degree to which their schools actually pursue twenty of the aims more commonly professed by the authorities.

Our sample of parents who were interviewed in depth came from three schools: an archetypal public school, a state boarding bilateral school, and an equally typical state secondary modern boarding school. Obviously these parents may not be representative of those of other boarders, but their perception of the schools' goals are indicative.

The public school parents consistently rate higher their school's striving towards goals with a collective orientation, whereas the parents of state boarders rate higher their school's striving towards goals with an individual orientation. In this

DIAGRAM 5:8

Stated goals of boarding schools
Summary

Schools	Relation to wider society or subculture	Educational content of goals	Degree of consensus on ends	Collective or individual orientation of goals	Instrumental, expressive, organizational emphasis
1 Public	Clearly defined	Character training to ideal type of socio-moral values. Abstract intellectual training	High	Collective dominant	Expressive dominant
2 Independent	Moderately defined	Character training as above, more concrete academic aims	Moderate	Collective dominant	Expressive and instrumental
3 Ind/Integrated	Not defined	Elements of all approaches	Low	Individual and collective	Expressive and instrumental
4 Maintained	Not defined	Creating environment to meet needs of child basic social, vocational and academic training	Moderate low	Individual dominant	Expressive and instrumental
5 Progressive	Clearly defined	Developing intrinsic personality, freedom, creative expression, emotional development	High	Individual dominant	Expressive dominant

respect the perceived goals coincide with the stated ones of the school authorities.

TABLE 5:9

Parents' ratings of degree to which school authorities pursue implemented goals

Number of scores 80 per cent and over on collective/individual dimension

	A state bilateral school	A state secondary modern school	A well-known public school	Total possible score
Collective	2	5	9	9
Individual	3	5	2	7
Total ratings 80 per cent and over	5	10	11	16

Source: depth interviews with parents, goals questionnaire, the full data from which this table derives is in Table 2 in Appendix IV.

TABLE 5:10

Parents' ratings of degree to which school authorities pursue implemented goals

Number of scores 80 per cent and over on instrumental/expressive/organizational dimension

	A state bilateral school	A state secondary modern school	A well-known public school	Total possible scores
Collective	3	4	4	6
Expressive	2	6	8	10
Organizational	2	4	2	4
Total ratings 80 per cent and over	7	14	14	20

Source: depth interviews with parents, goals questionnaire; the full data from which this table derives in on Table 2 in Appendix IV.

The support given by public school parents for the goals stressed by the school authorities is confirmed by the way that they see their schools as giving in practice far more weight to a broader range of expressive ends than do the other parents. However, each group of parents see instrumental and organizational ends as more prominent in reality than might appear from the professed aims of the authorities. It is in these two areas that the major differences may occur between stated and implemented goals.

Our sample of sixteen to eighteen-year-old pupils in the sixth forms of schools was fully representative of all kinds of boarding. Their ratings of the degree to which their schools pursued the twenty goals most commonly mentioned by the heads and staff are thus more important. They show, more markedly, that in some boarding schools there is a high consistency between the authorities' professed aims and their most responsible pupils' perception of actual ones, but in other schools a marked divergence is apparent: what is said and what is done seem not to coincide.

First, how do pupils perceive the collective or individual tendency of their schools' implemented goals?

TABLE 5:11
Ratings by pupils aged 16 to 18 of implemented goals of school authorities

Number of scores of 60 per cent and over on collective/individual dimension

	Public	Independent	Independent integrated	Maintained	Progressive	Total possible scores
Collective	8	6	6	3	6	9
Individual	5	4	3	4	4	7
Total ratings of 60 per cent and over	13	10	9	7	10	16

Source: general sample, goals questionnaire; full data from which this table derives is given in Table 4 in Appendix IV.

Like their parents and their schoolmasters, the boys at public schools see their schools as striving harder towards a wider range of collectively oriented goals than is the case in all other kinds of schools. But they also see a broad stress on individually oriented goals as well: their perception of implemented goals is more balanced than the stated goals of the authorities. Sixth formers at other independent schools also see greater emphasis on collective than on individual goals, though the degree of stress is less than in the public schools. In integrated schools the pattern is more lopsided. Their pupils rate their aims as collective in tendency, though trying towards fewer collective goals and less intensely than public schools. Towards individually oriented goals these schools are seen as making least effort of all boarding schools: for example, they receive the lowest ratings for creativity or stress on the individual, though the highest for physical development. Equally distinctive are the perceptions of pupils in maintained schools. They rate their schools' efforts towards collective goals lower than do the pupils of any other kinds of boarding school. They see their schools as giving more stress to goals with an individual tendency, though the degree of stress on individual goals is less than that perceived by public school pupils in their schools. (See Table 4, Appendix IV). It is with progressive school pupils that the greatest discrepancy occurs between what they see as actual aims and what the school authorities state as aims. The latter, as we recollect, were heavily individual in tendency. The pupils' view confirms this: they rate their schools' efforts on five out of the seven individual goals more highly than do all the other kinds of boarders. (See Table 4, Appendix IV). It is on the collective side that the surprise occurs: unlike the authorities, the pupils see the schools as working more towards a broad range of collective ends. But these ends are very different from the collective ones of the public or independent schools: cultural, moral, social and democratic aims are given higher stress by them than by other pupils; whilst sportsmanship, exam results, and Christian values receive lower stress.

The pupils' perceptions thus provide a salutary check on the headmasters' and housemasters' professions of aim. They indicate that the public schools, though more heavily collective than others, also have a marked individual stress, while progressive schools, though more heavily individual than the rest, also have a distinctive brand of collective objectives. Table 5:12 sums up the discrepancies and congruencies.

TABLE 5:12

	Perception of goals	Collective stress	Individual stress
Public	Stated goals of authorities	High	Low
	Implemented goals perceived by pupils	High	High
Independent	Stated goals of authorities	High	Moderate
	Implemented goals perceived by pupils	High	Moderate to high
Independent integrated	Stated goals of authorities	High	Low
	Implemented goals perceived by pupils	High	Moderate
Maintained	Stated goals of authorities	Low	High
	Implemented goals perceived by pupils	Moderate	Moderate to low
Progressive	Stated goals of authorities	Low	Very high
	Implemented goals perceived by pupils	High	Moderate

TABLE 5:13

Ratings by pupils aged 16 to 18 of implemented goals of school authorities

Number of scores of 60 per cent and over on
instrumental/expressive/organizational dimension

	Public	Independent	Independent integrated	Maintained	Progressive	Total possible score
Instrumental	5	6	5	4	4	6
Expressive	8	4	4	3	6	10
Organizational (over 65 per cent)	4	3	4	3	2	4
Total high ratings	17	13	13	10	12	20

Source: general sample, goals questionnaire; full data from which this table derives is given in Table 4 in Appendix IV.

What happens when we turn to goals considered in their instrumental, expressive and organizational aspects? (Table 5:13) As with the parents there is among pupils in all schools a greater stress on instrumental and organizational aims than appeared in the aims of heads and housestaff. But major differences appear between schools of different kinds. Like their headmasters and parents, the boys at public schools rate their schools as working hardest to the broadest range of expressive ends. But they also see a wide and strong stress on both other kinds of goals, instrumental and organizational. In fact, in the pupil ratings public schools emerge as putting more intense and broad emphasis on each of the three kinds of goals than do other schools. The other independents show a similar distribution of emphasis, though scored less highly. Integrated schools produce a less constant pattern but, on the whole, instrumental aims are seen as more prominent than expressive aims. In these schools, however, the pupils think that three of the four organizational goals are pursued more intensely than in any other kind of school; a confirmation of a hint that appeared in the stated goals of the authorities (see Table 1 Appendix IV). Maintained school pupils see their schools as pursuing fewer expressive goals less intensely than any others, giving more priority to instrumental ones and relatively less to organizational ones. Finally progressive pupils rate their schools highly on a few distinctive expressive ends, variably on instrumental ends and lowest of all schools on organizational ends. Table 5:14 sums up the pupils' ratings.

TABLE 5:14

Senior pupils' perceptions of school's implemented goals

	Instrumental	Expressive	Organizational
Public	High	High	High
Independent	High	Moderate	Moderate
Independent integrated	High	Moderate	High
Maintained	Moderate	Low	Low
Progressive	Moderate	High	Low

Thus the pupils' perceptions endorse the stated ends of their heads and housemasters in so far as expressive ends are concerned but provide valuable indications of the nature and balance of the other two kinds of goals which inevitably do not figure much in stated ends. We begin to glimpse fundamental patterns of difference between the schools, which will be reflected in our later discussions of the styles of boarding by which they are implemented.

IV

It is not enough merely to compare people's perceptions of goals. As power is differentially distributed in institutions and as pressures arising from the school's functions for society limit the range of goals which are possible, some people's perspectives are more influential than others. The goals which schools pursue at any time, therefore, will be an outcome of all these conflicting pressures. These pressures will vary in intensity and direction so that at one time instrumental or expressive aims will seem to be prominent in the institution while at another time organizational emphasis will dominate. Over a long period, however, there will be a characteristic pattern of goals stressed. These are the implemented goals, the ends to which the resources are directed. Measuring these implemented goals raises methodological problems that we cannot consider in this book but, using a variety of material, the research worker has to assess these goals and evaluate the degree to which they are achieved. Thus, when we ask ourselves whether the actual, day-to-day ends which the school authorities pursue differ from the professed aims we have already outlined, we have to examine the perceptions of the groups we have discussed and on the basis of similar ratings, interviews, questionnaires, documents and observation try to distinguish patterns of implemented goals.

In so doing we shall break down the general categories of schools we have been dealing with, as not all the schools of one kind exhibit the same implemented goals. We shall also render the sociological categories of goals into patterns. Given the three kinds of goal, there are seven possible combinations of implemented goals which different schools might pursue. Five of the seven patterns were found existing in practice, the other two seem empirically difficult to realize.

Pattern one is that where the emphasis on all three kinds of goal is equally great, where the transmission of intellectual or social or physical skills, the concern with expressive values and attributes and the stress on organization, the running, routine, order, reputation and level of control in the school are all consistent and marked.

A substantial block of boarding schools falls into this category, representative of all kinds. Public schools preponderate and, indeed, a majority of them pursue this pattern of implemented goals, as their senior pupils perceived. Likewise, a significant proportion of independent schools follow this pattern of goals, but only small proportions of the other kinds of schools do so. Two progressive schools belong to this group because their particular styles of coeducation involve considerable stress on organizational aims.

Pattern two occurs when schools place an equal stress on their instrumental or expressive ends but relatively less on organizational ones, when the stress on routine, discipline, control, recruitment or disposal of pupils and reputation is less pronounced. This goal structure is close to that perceived by the pupils in progressive schools. Once more, a substantial proportion of boarding schools work towards these ends - most of the progressive and independent schools, a fifth of the public schools (those which are closest in style and effects to the progressive school) and smaller proportions of integrated and maintained schools.

Pattern three is found when school authorities put a high day-to-day stress on instrumental and organizational goals but a relatively lower one on expressive ones. Though the numbers of schools with these goals are still considerable their distribution is narrow. Three public schools belong to this group, each containing substantial numbers of state-assisted pupils. Half the integrated schools and a majority of the maintained schools on the sample follow this pattern of goals. It is thus a pattern which occurs in schools with a large entry of pupils from maintained day schools, though by no means all schools with such an entry exhibit it.

Pattern four appears when the school authorities pursue expressive goals to a degree not matched by their efforts towards instrumental or organizational goals. This is the situation which we found appearing so often in the *stated* ends of the heads and housestaff. In practice, however, it emerges much more rarely. Only two schools were found with this pattern, one a progressive school, the other the boarding side of a comprehensive school. Instances of the dominance of expressive over all other goals might be found somewhat more commonly in the day system, in some 'progressive' primary schools or in some independent progressive schools formed around a charismatic founder head.

The next *pattern*, *five*, is equally unusual. It occurs when the stress on organizational goals exceeds that on instrumental and, more emphatically, that on expressive goals. Though the latter two kinds may figure prominently in the stated ends of the school authorities they tend in practice to be subordinated to organizational goals: a preoccupation with order, routine, discipline, bureaucratic structure, efficiency or contractual performance of roles. We found such a pattern in three schools.

Two of the schools were maintained and one independent integrated. In one of the state schools, a secondary modern, and in the integrated school the resolution of large problems of order and control almost entirely frustrated the pursuit of the expressive goals so eloquently expressed as the stated aims of heads and staff, while it also diminished - though to a lesser degree - the implementation of orthodox instrumental goals. The third school, a state grammar, was so preoccupied with the maintenance of routines, of a bureaucratically structured pattern of life, and of order, that these organizational goals eclipsed instrumental ones, and expressive features could scarcely be discerned in the texture of everyday life and attitudes.

Two other patterns exist in theory but have not yet been found in practice. *Pattern six* would occur when instrumental goals dominated the other two. Such a case has not been encountered because a high stress on transmission of skills (unlike a high stress on communication of values) usually entails some organizational structure for effectiveness: instrumental and organizational goals in schools thus tend to go together. The other case, *pattern seven*, could arise when expressive and organizational goals together tended to dominate the instrumental ones. It does not seem to arise in practice, however, partly because there is an inherent imbalance, or competition for dominance between expressive and organizational goals in schools, but also because when organizational goals are emphasized in a school setting which in practice is expressively oriented, they develop both expressive and instrumental aspects; that is, they transmit values and skills. For example, some schools stress authority systems or house units (which are organizational features). However, staff in these schools not only connect these features with expressive aims such as the fostering of responsibility or loyalty, but also link organizational with instrumental aims such as training in adult roles, experience in organization, acquisition of tolerance and the development of social skills. To achieve acceptability in a school with expressive ends organizational features are thus translated and perceived in terms of the other two.

What do we learn about the different kinds of boarding school when we bring together the different patterns of goals which they actually follow?

TABLE 5:15

Implemented goals of school authorities by patterns

Schools	1 I=E=O	2 I=E(O)	3 I=O(E)	4 E(I=O)	5 O(I=E)	Total
Public	18	5	3	0	0	26
Independent	3	4	0	0	0	7
Independent integrated	1	3	6	0	1	11
Maintained	3	3	6	1	2	15
Progressive	2	4	0	1	0	7

Source: interviews with staff, documents, notes of observation.

From this table we see that three different groups of boarding schools follow distinctive patterns of implemented goals. Public schools emphatically tend to the first pattern of balance, while a minority tend to that followed by progressive schools and all stress instrumental and expressive ends. (Three public schools, however, all integrated, approximate more to the cluster of goals favoured by most state schools.) Independent schools, like public schools, follow patterns one or two. All the progressive schools also stress expressive ends. Most also stress instrumental goals but not organizational ones. Within each of these three kinds of school the variations may make for differences in practice and effect, but these differences are of degree rather than of kind. In each group there is a consensus on the importance of certain instrumental and expressive ends.

The two remaining kinds of schools exhibit among themselves not consensus but divergence. Thus while some integrated schools stress expressive ends others replace them by a stress on organizational elements. Maintained schools show still more diversity. Most give low priority to expressive ends and follow the day school pattern but others pursue patterns more favoured by public schools or by progressive schools, and two seem dominated by organizational ends. In both integrated and state schools these differences are not just ones of degree; they affect sizeable proportions of schools and they entail radical differences of practical objectives, methods, style and atmosphere in schools. Unlike the other three kinds of schools these categories contain schools heading in diverse or even opposite directions.

TABLE 5:16

*Factors affecting the real goals of school
authorities by patterns*

Schools	1 I=E=O	2 I=E(O)	3 I=O(E)	4 E(I=O)	5 O(I=E)	Total
Majority boarding before entry	17	8	0	1	0	26
Majority day pupils before entry	10	8	15	1	3	37
40-50 per cent have 'need'	7	5	7	1	3	23
Marked denomina- tional stress	18	6	0	0	0	24
Coeducational	6	4	3	2	0	15

Source: basic data in schools, interviews with staff, documents, notes of observation.

It remains briefly to consider some other of the empirical

factors which we discussed in Chapter 2, besides constitutional type, which might account for the differences in the goals which schools really pursue. Four important factors were: previous day school or boarding experience of pupils, the proportion of pupils with 'need', denominational character and sex composition.

The educational background of the pupils, whether the majority were day pupils or boarders before entering their present main secondary boarding school, partly correlates with the implemented goals of schools. When the majority have already been boarders *before* their secondary school their schools emphatically fall into patterns one or two. This is not surprising as the background of the pupils coincides with the constitutional type of school: those majorities with boarding backgrounds are chiefly at public, some independent and progressive schools. When most pupils have day school experience before becoming boarders at their present schools no clear correlation emerges, though the largest single block of boarding schools containing such pupils tends to the classic goal pattern of the day school. When the presence of substantial numbers of children with need for boarding is examined the picture is also inconclusive. It might have been hypothesized that the presence of large quantities of children with such need would have induced a pronounced expressive stress in the schools' aims to meet it. While thirteen schools do exhibit this expressive emphasis another ten do not, and three of them seem to be preoccupied with organizational matters. In fact need composition, as we shall see later, does not constantly influence the goals which schools actually pursue. Schools which are markedly denominational in their entry and practice do show a consistent pattern of goals: expressive ends are always stressed. Catholic and Anglican schools tend to follow pattern one, while nonconformist and other religions follow pattern two. The sex composition of schools also partly correlates with actual goals; not in the case of single-sex boys' schools, where real goals are diverse, but in the case of coeducational schools. Although numbers are too small to apply a statistical test, most of these have a marked expressive emphasis, sometimes accompanied by equal stress on organizational goals, sometimes not. This latter variation provides a vital clue to differences in coeducational styles of boarding which appear later.

Other variables were tested for significance but no correlation with the implemented goals of schools were found for the region of schools, their degree of selectivity, their proportion of day pupils. Apart from constitutional type and academic structure, the factors which do influence real goals are the boarding background of pupils, denomination and coeducation.

V

The goals of schools have been introduced. We have seen that historical forces, established and broad latent functions for society in general, as well as a defined role in an organizational or subcultural environment, give to each of three kinds of boarding schools - public, progressive and most independent schools - a consensus on ends. Though the content of the goals sought by public and independent schools on the one hand and by progressive schools on the other differed in educational content, in collective or individual stress, and in instrumental/ expressive/organizational balance, there was some degree of consistency between those goals which were stated by the authorities and those which were perceived to be pursued in day-to-day practice. The other two kinds of schools - integrated and maintained - were shaped by no strong boarding tradition, had special and limited functions for the general society, and played no clearly defined role in a subculture or an organizational environment. Though the stated ends of their authorities were distinctive and coherent they were not closely reflected in the implemented goals, which indeed show much less consensus than those of the three other kinds of school, a heterogeneity which spreads over all the basic patterns of goals and indicates extreme and fundamental differences between the schools in each of these two groups. Of other factors which might influence or correlate with patterns of implemented goals, only the boarding backgrounds of pupils, denominational and co-educational characters proved positive, while the presence of large numbers of need cases and other factors seemed to have no reflection in the goals pursued.

With all this and the five basic patterns in mind, we can now turn from abstract ends to the structure and working of our schools.

6 The different styles of boarding (1) Expressive styles

The preceding discussion of the very varied aims of the schools at least demolishes the supposition that boarding education in this country is a dated monolith. As the goals which are pursued in different schools vary widely, so the approaches to the residential situation and the consequent styles of boarding differ. Naturally such styles are, in part, moulded by tradition and by the functions which the schools have for society. The public schools, particularly some of the ancient foundations, have long trained a ruling elite in a semi-closed environment while, in contrast, other schools of more recent foundation have been designed to meet the needs of particular children. Consequently many of these schools are more homely and open to the outside world. Nevertheless the popular notion that the only two styles of boarding which exist are either for the very wealthy or for the very deprived obscures the range of other English boarding schools. Life in traditional public schools has been vividly and unsympathetically sketched in novels and films, but such hierarchical and monastic communities are distantly recognizable variants of but one style of boarding. Much of the emphasis of this book will be to show that other styles develop in different situations.

This stylistic variety makes it difficult to define the essential elements of boarding education. The goals emphasized, the roles played by pupil and staff and the controls stressed all differ so widely from school to school that it becomes impossible to distinguish boarding from day schools in these terms. As long as children have beds in the school and play roles within the residential unit the school takes on the features of a boarding school even though its residential style may vary from that of the monastery to that of a youth hostel.

Schools with the same functions for society, similar cultural or historical antecendents and identical goals will have broadly similar styles but within any one style there can be considerable variation between individual schools. Within some of the styles, the variation between individual schools is wider than in others.

Public schools, for example, all have similar styles of boarding even though other features such as academic standards and locality of intake may vary from school to school. Yet state boarding schools, while fewer in number, display considerable divergencies: contrasts in the levels of control, in the roles played by residential staff and in the proportions of children with specific need for boarding, and in approaches to them.

We have already suggested that one important aspect of the goal pattern of different schools is the degree to which expressive goals are stressed. It is quite clear from our previous discussions that certain boarding schools place a high premium on particular expressive goals such as character training, a particular life style, religion or even warm relationships between staff and pupils. In contrast other boarding schools emphasize the instrumental and organizational goals more than the expressive goals and, not surprisingly, produce different styles of boarding. This chapter examines the boarding styles of those forty-four schools in our sample which stressed expressive ends. These are the schools with goal patterns IEO, IE(O) and E(OI). In the next chapter we shall compare the styles of schools where instrumental and organizational goals are dominant and where the goal patterns are IO(E) and O(EI).

Public Schools

So much has been written about the merits and defects of the English public school system that it is difficult to furnish information on them which has not been already the subject of considerable argument.[1] Nevertheless much of this discussion has often concentrated on the more superficial aspects of public school life such as its ceremonies, sports, colours, prefects, fagging, school songs or discipline. There have been fewer attempts to relate these features of the schools' life style to the goals that they pursue.

Strictly, a public school is one whose headmaster is a member of the Headmasters' Conference but, while his eligibility for membership will depend upon his school satisfying a number of criteria, the proportion of boarders is not one of these. Thus some large city day schools may be public schools and apart from trivia, such as calling homework 'prep', may be indistinguishable from their maintained sisters the local grammar schools. Even within those eighty-eight public schools which are predominantly boarding there will be variations in size, in their history, in their selectivity and their allocative functions. For example, in our sample of twenty-six boys' public schools six of them had more than six hundred pupils while three had rolls of less than two hundred and fifty. Some public schools are ancient foundations while others date from the mid-Victorian period and are often associated with developments within the Anglican Church.[2] A few schools have also been founded in this century, yet whether large or small, rural or urban, Catholic or Protestant, the public schools have attributes which mark them off distinctively as a system from schools of other kinds.

There are fundamental similarities in structure, operation and values and even in the effects of their particular distinctive style. The schools are united by an ethos, that is a system of values embodied in the attitudes, expectations and behaviour of its members which differs markedly from those of other schools. If we explore the particular goals such schools stress, the roles played by staff and boys and the subtle, intensive, pervasive and unremitting control which these organizations employ, something of their distinctive life style should emerge.[3]

In the previous chapter we saw that the goal stress of most public schools placed an equal emphasis on instrumental, expressive and organizational goals. Moral and social goals such as the acceptance and practice of Christian faith, service to the community, the ability to manage others, the exercise of and submission to legitimate authority, physical and emotional self-reliance and loyalty to the group more than to oneself are all stressed as much as goals of academic excellence and scholarship. All these goals are pursued in an organizational framework which imposes high levels of discipline and control on the freedom, movement, privacy and activity of individual boys. Organizational goals are also stressed: public reputation, smooth administration, solvency and continuation over time. We shall see later that many of these achievements are demanded by parents and expected by employers. However, it is worth exploring a number of these goals further, particularly the way in which the schools link instrumental and expressive aims and achieve a high level of commitment among their boys.

Almost all the public schools have high academic standards. With well-qualified graduate staff, small classes, tutorial systems and impressive facilities, the schools stress academic skills. In this the public schools remain distinct from many other boarding schools and from recent trends in the state day schools. The curriculum remains that of a highly academic secondary school; it is designed to and usually does achieve good GCE results. The schools frequently stress the advantages that independence gives them in experimenting both in the ways in which subjects are taught and their relations with others in the curriculum, but increased concern with public examinations has worked against some forms of experiment in recent years. In the thirties the schools pioneered the teaching of engineering, farming and estate management, and in recent years Nuffield science, modern maths, business studies, economics, technology and creativity labs have been developed.[4] Several leading public schools have interesting variations in teaching techniques, such as varying group sizes, programmed learning projects and visual aids. Integrated studies have been developed in some. However, almost all these experiments have been relevant to academic children; there have been few serious attempts to provide courses catering for the less able or to revise the elaborate and relentless setting and streaming system. The table of careers of leavers from the public schools reflects quite clearly the academic emphasis of the schools' curriculum (see Table 6:1).

We shall see later that less able children in boarding education tend to cluster in the independent schools which adopt a different approach to the curriculum from that of the public schools and operate a very different style of boarding. Not only has there been less concern with the less able in the public schools but the tendency to allocate the less academic to 'modern' subjects has affected the status of many areas of knowledge. Particularly the practical subjects such as engineering and technical drawing, farming and estate management, horticulture and forestry are diminished in status. Modern languages, in spite of the pioneering of language laboratories in the schools, have suffered from similar associations with the less able, as have economics, geography and social

TABLE 6:1

Destination of school leavers from all boys' public schools in 1966

			Percentages
Continued Education	Oxford/Cambridge		13·5
	Other university		28·5
	Further education/art/music coll.		16·8
	College of education		0·9
	Other continued education		2·8
		Total	62·5
Employment	Industry/commerce		13·8
	Law		2·5
	Accountancy		4·8
	Engineering		1·3
	Other		2·0
	Merchant navy		0·4
	Armed forces		3·6
	Agriculture/forestry		3·4
	Civil service		0·3
	Local government		0·1
		Total	32·2
Transfer to other schools			4·2
Other			1·1
			N = 11,841

Source: Public Schools Commission, *First Report*, vol 2, p 107.

studies. Indeed, in spite of the greatly increased provision of subjects, the development of mixed A level courses and the discouragement of early specialization, the hierarchy of status of particular subjects has changed far less. As the schools' function is to fashion a particular grade or status of employment rather than a specific career, they have always prized and cultivated the abstract intelligence. Hence many schools still allocate a large proportion of their resources to abstract subjects, to classics, maths and the sciences and encourage their most able boys towards combinations of these subjects.[5]

In terms of curriculum development there were few boarding schools of any kind which could match the developments now occurring in the day schools. The only growth points in the curriculum among boarding schools for ordinary children were the courses in some of the vocational schools, such as in farming and building construction, and some specialist music schools. Indeed, it is mainly in special education, notably the approved schools, that there has been any radical redesigning of the curriculum to meet the needs of less able children. In nearly all the other boarding schools the children follow highly academic curricula. Even the progressive schools which are experimental in social and other expressive areas have curricula and teaching approaches which are suprisingly orthodox. Very few schools use their residential structure to enliven their curriculum. Nearly every school, we found, had an academic system which could have operated as easily in the day school and apart from occasional weekend projects, usually restricted to the physical and social sciences, the influence of residential life on the curriculum was negligible.[6]

The relationship between the curriculum in the public schools and their social structure illuminates recent educational discussion. The work of Bernstein and others has suggested that in day schools the design of the curriculum has affected all social relationships. Authoritarian fact-distributing teaching is facilitated in hierarchical, formal, controlled regimes while teaching in the open-class situation where children have choice, where teachers take up a more expressive, advisory role, radically changes the roles people play, both staff and pupils, and the relations between them.[7]

The evidence for our study of boarding schools would suggest that this can certainly be the case. Integrated studies, project work, activity-centred teaching break down the hierarchy of subjects and teachers. Open, flexible teaching leads to open, flexible relations between teachers and taught, for a system in which children move from an expressive teaching situation to an authoritarian school structure outside the classroom cannot operate successfully for long. The staff in those day schools where children are on Christian-name terms with staff in class

but are subject to an impersonal discipline within the school
find that such a system leads to insecurity and instability.
While an expressive teaching situation must be mirrored by a
complementary school structure the opposite is not necessarily
true. It is possible to combine a certain type of expressive
stress in the school (and to have close staff-pupil relationships,
high commitment to goals and multiple avenues to individual
achievement), with an authoritarian teaching situation and
structure. The public schools illustrate this, for they successfully combine expressive stress with a formal teaching system
and regime. By our indices, pupil commitment to goals is high
and staff-pupil relationships are at least as close as in most other
boarding schools.

The increasing academic stress of the public schools, which
reflects the increasing competition for the qualifications
necessary for university entry and other professional training,
has posed problems for them. The maintenance of an
equilibrium between goal areas has not been easy. All the
public schools have made changes of emphasis in the allocation
of resources in recent years. The failure of demand for
boarding to increase in the years 1961-71 and a perceptible
trend away from boarding altogether have deep implications for
the schools' expressive goal areas. Religious and moral ideas,
the abnegation of self, ideals of service, the propagation of
absolute values and a single cultural life style - such ends are
greatly facilitated by the isolation from the outside world that
boarding implies. Indeed, many of the traditional public school
values and the ways in which they were made explicit have been
eroded in recent years, in religious observance, in games, in
altruism and aspects of control. Competition with maintained
schools for university places has affected the goal equilibrium of
the schools both great and small. Between 1966 and 1970
thirty-six per cent of boys in the maintained grammar schools
gained two or more A level passes while forty-three per cent of
the boys in the public schools achieved similar results.[8] Indeed,
as many public schools exercise little selection on intake such
results, coupled with their virtual domination of the highly
competitive Oxbridge open award system, greatly enhance the
schools in parents' eyes. But such academic results have to be

bought at a price. Classics, which through its content and esoteric qualities did so much to weld the instrumental and expressive ends of school into one, has continued its decline but had long been in retreat before the changed Oxbridge entrance requirements recognized the inevitable. But its place in training the abstract intelligence of the schools' intellectual elite has slowly surrendered to maths and to science which with the help of the Industrial Fund has rapidly expanded in both public and preparatory schools. The stress on instrumental goals has increased, with wide implications for other aspects of the schools' structure, particularly in the strengthening of the power of the academic sub-units and change in the status and power distribution among the boys. This new intelligentsia in the schools, powerful and of high status, has vigorously questioned many sacrosanct expressive areas, particularly in religion. The idea of absolute values, the upper-class cultural style and the elitist function of the schools have been exposed to criticism from within; many fossilized expressive rituals have been swept away in religion, in games, and in the whole area of social relations between boy and boy and staff and boy. No doubt the greatest casualty in these changes of emphasis has been in the narrow loyalties to sub-units, particularly to that of the house and with it the power of the house captain and the housemaster.[9]

To prosecute these wide instrumental and expressive aims the public school adopts a federal structure which is in strong contrast to that of other schools. Indeed, many of its expressive goals can only be realized within a system of competing and largely autonomous sub-units. For example, the proper exercise of and graceful submission to authority, the swift and assured changing of roles, the sublimation of self or sectional interest for the corporate good, and the exercising of care without involvement, of service without identification all mean that responsibility and decision-making must be spread widely and are eagerly assumed by the boys. Many small units coexist alongside the main academic departments and each unit such as the chapel or library has its own leadership hierarchy, role systems, membership and particular rituals. Boys belong to houses, to sports teams, to societies, to clubs, to the CCF and

other groups as well as being in various academic sub-units.
Thus the role structure of the public school is a complicated
one as boys and staff are members of many diverse parallel
groups. As a result, the social structure of the school is a
federation of more or less autonomous units and power is
widely delegated. As the boarding house tends to be the most
important social unit, considerable power and autonomy rest in
the hands of the housemasters. There are many examples where
housemasters control admissions to the school, and reforming
heads sometimes find their zeal unappreciated and their
schemes blocked by the long-incumbent senior housemasters.
However, the strongest contrast between the public school and
other schools in the roles people play lies in the variety and
significance of the roles assumed by the boys. Senior boys are
particularly powerful. 'Remember', admonishes a house captain
to his successors 'you will never have quite the same power of
heaven or hell over others agains, so temper justice with
mercy'.[10]

The headmaster of the public school, in contrast, tends to be
an administrative manager rather than the authoritarian
director. One headmaster of a public school described his day
as follows:

'Every morning before chapel I come over to school at
8.40 am and quickly sort out papers, etc., before morning
prayers. One day a week instead of chapel I have my own
assembly. During the mornings I am usually at my desk
except for seven periods when I teach Latin. I take lunch in
school and in the afternoon I may have parents to meet,
staff to interview and some new entrants to see although the
housemasters keep in touch with prep schools and compile
their own lists. All admission forms finally end up in my
office. Often in the afternoon there are games to watch and
I usually have to work on plans, preparing lessons or seeing
staff or boys in the evening. I try never to take a day off
although as a justice of the peace I am often away for the
day. The deputy headmaster now deals with the timetable
and others with careers and university entry. I leave all
academic matters to the departmental heads although
occasionally I have to approve the allocation of finance. I

still try to be involved in all academic matters and to help any boy who wishes to see me. Not all boys get on with their housemasters, so I like to think that they can get advice from me or from the chaplain.'

It is not surprising, therefore, that of the public school headmasters who were interviewed only four had a role profile which reflected the expressive goal emphasis of the school. The majority play predominantly organizational roles, as the following table shows:

TABLE 6:2

The headmaster's role profile in different kinds of boarding schools

Role profile	Public	Independent	Independent integrated	Progressive	State
I = E = O	4	2	4	3	2
I = O(E)	6	1	2	1	7
E = O(I)	4	0	1	2	2
O(EI)	12	4	4	1	4
	26	7	11	7	15

Source: general sample.

It is interesting that in most other types of school the headmaster acts out roles which reflect the main goals stressed by the organization. For example, the expressive stress in progressive schools demands a paternalistic, trendy charisma which would be quite out of place in the instrumental and organizational pattern of state schools. However, in the public schools expressive roles are now delegated to others such as chaplains and housemasters. This represents a significant change from the nineteenth century when the great reforming heads carried all before them and it is a change not lost on the heads themselves.[11] 'I usually try to give the first chapel sermon of term', said one headmaster,
'but most of the boys gaze back at me unrecognizing or embarrassed at my spirituality. Some of my predecessors became bishops but my successors will probably be better

suited to the reorganization of ailing state industries'.

The housemasters in public schools scrutinize the academic, moral and physical development of the adolescent. When interviewed, most stressed as their important roles: pastoral care, vocational guidance, social training, the promoting of religious life, encouraging sportsmanship, the inculcation of cultural standards and the maintaining of discipline and loyalty. One public school housemaster describes his role, and it is typical of most schools:

'The headmaster admits boys but I have a free hand to collect any boys I want, such as boys who may be below our common entrance standards, so we get a cross-section of intelligence. I see parents when they visit, I like them to come to socials, and when the boy has settled in (the school has no visits during the first three weeks) although I get very few letters or phone calls from them. I am responsible for all discipline although prefects, who are chosen by nomination to the headmaster, deal with most offences. They have to get my permission to cane boys on the rare occasions this occurs. I tour the house at bedtime to hear appeals against any punishments given by prefects. I see it as my duty to place boys in a university, although the careers master provides the details. I see all boys every fortnight to discuss their worst grades and I watch and support all games but only coach boys if I am invited. I merely rubber-stamp the captain's choice of team and colours. I teach twenty-one periods a week - Latin, English and Divinity. I have house prayers once a week and five minutes' silence every night. I try to talk to any boy who is worried or anxious though I often persuade older boys to keep an eye on him and help him along. I also write to parents if anything is worrying. My matron deals with food, clothing and cleaning the house and my house tutors help with overseeing mark sheets, pocket money, leave lists and giving me information on any boys they know well.'

Indeed much of the school's social structure is suggested by this illustration. The housemaster clearly has entire responsibility for the running of his house and may in the grander schools even have his own secretary. Much real power is delegated to senior boys who have as much power as adults and usually more responsibility than junior staff members, who undertake administrative duties such as looking after pocket money or taking sports. In this way candidates for future housemaster posts can be scrutinized and promising material fashioned.

Inevitably it is a masculine world and ever since moving from the babies' class in their preparatory schools both boys and staff have learned to relegate women to marginal organizational and largely decorative roles. There are relatively few opportunities for women to make much relationship with the boys. Naturally the housemaster's wife has high status but as it is ascribed rather than achieved her real influence is minimal. She is restricted to entertaining visitors, particularly parents, gracing social occasions and arranging flowers. The matron is in a similar marginal position but without the status, and her roles are limited to domestic and health matters. Such ladies find that hovering on the fringes of an intense inward looking male world is peculiarly frustrating, particularly when their expressive roles are restricted to tweedy, shivering support for the Junior Colts.[12] There is no formal provision in the public school structure for the maternal role and until recently the impact of women on the community has been negligible. Pastoral responsibilities are closely guarded by housemasters and there is often considerable conflict with school chaplains who understandably attempt to extend their influence in this direction.[13] Also, twenty-two public schools in our sample had rules forbidding contact between boys and domestic staff, although this may spring less from a close guardianship of pastoral roles or cultural mores than from a keen awareness on the part of housemasters of the recreational possibilities of young Spanish kitchen maids. However, women have recently initiated welcome changes in the schools towards a more sensitive and individual approach to boys, particularly the need cases or the deviant intellectuals.[14] The shortage of able domestic staff, the virtual disappearance of bachelor housemasters and early marriage of most staff have thrust wives into a more influential role and they have been quick to exploit their advantages in modifying spartan regimes and extending pastoral support.

When the role profiles of housemasters in differing kinds of boarding schools are compared the relationship between their roles and the goals of the school is much closer than it was for headmasters. The following table gives details of housemasters' roles in different types of boarding school.

TABLE 6:3

Housemasters' role profile in different types of boarding schools

Housemasters' roles	Public	Independent	Independent integrated	State	Progressive
I = E = O	17	3	3	2	3
I(EO)	1	0	3	3	0
IE(O)	2	0	1	2	1
IO(E)	5	4	2	5	0
EO(I)	0	0	0	0	1
O(EI)	0	0	1	0	0
E(OI)	0	0	0	1	0
No comparable house-master system	1	0	1	2	2
	26	7	11	15	7

Source: general sample.

When in Table 6:4 housemasters' roles are compared with the differing goal patterns of the schools, therefore, a high correlation is found.* Eight schools had no comparable house system.

Within the public schools a hierarchy of prestige and power is accorded to the pupils. A small boy entering a public school is placed at the bottom of a formidable hierarchy; as he grows older his privileges increase until, as house captain, he has greater power than some members of staff. In the past new boys entering their house had to fag for older boys, although this has now disappeared in many schools and has been replaced by communal domestic work. At the other end of the hierarchy,

* $X^2 = 13 \cdot 0$ df = 4 on a 2 x 5 collapsed table $p < 0 \cdot 02$.

TABLE 6:4

*Roles of housemasters in schools with different
goal stresses*

Roles of housemaster	IEO	IE(O)	IO(E)	E(IO)	O(IE)	Total
IEO	16	10	2	1	0	29
I(EO)	0	1	2	0	2	5
IE(O)	3	1	2	0	0	6
IO(E)	4	4	7	0	1	16
E(IO)	0	0	0	0	0	0
EO(I)	0	0	0	1	0	1
O(IE)	0	0	1	0	0	1
	23	16	14	2	3	58

Source: general sample.

as house or school captain in a large public school, he may have
his own office, writing paper and even a telephone. He leads the
prefects who, as a group, are largely responsible for running the
house. Discipline, sport, routine and even pastoral care are
largely their responsibility. Although certain superficial features,
such as prefect beatings, are fast disappearing, there has been
little change in the expressive roles prefects play. For example,
although one house prefect in a more liberal public school
could neither beat other boys nor be waited on by fags, he still
organized all house routine, trained boys in sport, took
periods for absent teachers, supervised homework, coached boys
with academic difficulties, took prayers, kept minutes of
weekly prefect meetings and maintained discipline. The punishments he could inflict on other boys included making boys work
in the housemaster's garden, making them learn poems, write
essays or do fatigues, gate them, remove their privileges and
report them to the housemaster. With all this power went a
long list of privileges: freedom to go to bed at any time, the use
of certain paths and roads, certain clothes (e.g. white tie, suede
shoes, umbrella), missing Sunday breakfast, visits into town,
going to the front of the tuck shop queue and storing beer in
his study.

Senior boys in public schools, therefore, have as much power
as younger members of staff and many roles, including

expressive and pastoral ones, which are exclusively reserved to staff in other types of schools are delegated to them. Relationships between the senior staff and prefects are, therefore, close and equal. Public school character-training in management and leadership relies on such relationships and on the ability of such a hierarchy to restrict any emotional over-identification between senior boys and those whom they command.

This elaborate provision to promote good relations between pupils and staff ensures that the oversight received by each boy is impressive and as extensive as in any other type of boarding school. However, pastoral care in terms of pupils confiding their problems to staff or to senior boys is lower than might be expected. When the evidence for the levels of pastoral care in different types of school is examined in Chapter 8, it will be seen that while public school boys are willing to take academic, career and athletic problems to adults they are more reticent on family or emotional matters. Pastoral care on academic matters is high in public schools but in comparison with other boarding schools their pastoral effectiveness is reduced for family and personal problems. Norms operate in the society to repress displays of emotional feeling or expression and thereby limit the pastoral effectiveness in the schools.

Partly because of their federal structure public schools find it difficult to make radical structural changes, especially in those expressive areas which are given so much support by parents, governors, old boys and employers. There have been many changes in public schools in recent years, as is explained in Chapter 10, but we shall find that these changes affect neither the implemented goals nor the structure of roles and power in the schools. The changes that have occurred tend to be in instrumental areas and have been concerned with buildings, teaching and the curriculum rather than with other expressive features. The federal structure of the public schools makes it easy for housemasters and others to obstruct plans and presents the headmaster with serious problems in winning the consensus necessary to achieve effective change. Many minor changes, therefore, such as a reduction in the status of sport or in the power of prefects, may take many years to achieve.

A further consequence of this structure is that the most significant pressures on boys' behaviour come from the official hierarchy and from the roles inherent in it. Pressures from the pupils' own society and from the norms of behaviour which boys impose on their peers are reduced to a minimum by the endless manipulation of boys' attitudes, loyalties, aspirations and energies by the many formal sub-units which make up a public school and to many of which all belong. The pupil society is fragmented and oriented to official ends by this sub-division and by the incorporation of so many pupils in the official hierarchies of power or status. Our questions, designed to measure the strength of the informal pressures which pupils exercised on each other, show that, with the exception of two schools, the private aspirations and attitudes of public school boys tend more to coincide with those officially encouraged than in all other boarding schools except the progressive schools. Thus one question was designed to measure the status positions to which boys could aspire. Boys in the sixth forms of the schools in the intensive sample were asked to choose one such status position. In the public schools the position of academic status was chosen equally with the others, reflecting the breadth of goals of the individual in schools, whereas in the day schools three-quarters of the pupils selected the academic position, reflecting not only the more narrowly instrumental aims of the schools but also the instrumental orientation of the pupils.

TABLE 6:5

Aspirations of sixth-form boys (in percentages)

	Public	Progressive	Maintained boarding	Day
Outstanding scholar	31	20	49	74
Outstanding sportsman	25	16	29	13
Outstanding artist, musician	26	50	11	5
Head boy/committee man	18	14	12	6
Number of schools	17	3	11	4
Number of pupils	1486	103	572	261

Source: Extensive sample, day school comparisons.

When these boys were asked further questions about the

kinds of behaviour that would make them popular or unpopular with their peers, replies from boys in public schools were again different from those given by pupils in many other types of schools. While norms of social behaviour towards others, such as being generous or clean, were widely supported, very few public school boys suggested norms which were critical or antagonistic to school goals. In many other boarding schools the boys' informal social systems are more antagonistic to schools' goals, especially expressive ones.

TABLE 6:6

Some informal norms of sixth-form boys

		Public schools (N=23)	Schools where I/O goals stressed (N=16)
Social norms:	Be generous	72 per cent	63
	Don't be a big-head	83	94
Norms antagonistic	Be independent of staff	11	46
to school goals:	Smoke, drink, etc.	14	31
Norms supporting	Work hard	73	43
school goals:	Obey rules	86	38
		N = 2704	1406

Source: general sample.

Controls which public school boys face, therefore, come more from the multiple and subtle hierarchies of authority and from the structure of the school than from the boy's own world. A boy may be bullied or teased by his contemporaries in a public school, but offensive behaviour is usually such social behaviour as being conceited or selfish: official and informal values thus coincide. Boys who are unresponsive to the schools' goals are dealt with by the official control systems rather than by weak pupil society. Table 6:7 on the following page shows details of some of the offences which bring disfavour from peers.

The pupil society of public school boys, therefore, tends to be weak in that norms which reject the school's goals are neither widely supported nor rigorously enforced. Most controls are imposed by those in authority or by the rigorous system of restrictions which are built into school rules, and not by the demands of peers. The formal structure fragments the boys' world into small competing or parallel units and so ensures that hostile attitudes are confined to minority groups who are tolerated and manipulated.

TABLE 6:7

Offences considered most serious by the informal social system among sixth-form boys in public schools (in percentages)

Creeping round staff	41
Being over-friendly to staff	7
Being conceited	62
Being selfish	73
Being untidy or dirty	64
Slacking, lazy	32
Not doing things for house	38
N =	1726

Number of schools 15

Source: general sample.

Public schools exert a high level of control over their pupils. Indeed, much sociological literature has concentrated on the kinds of organizations which have been called 'total' institutions. An artificial routine bearing little resemblance to life outside the walls is imposed on people in the institution, and values and standards of behaviour which are accepted in the institution have little relevance to anything outside. Such a model, as we explained in Chapter 4, is hardly applicable to schools, where boys go home for holidays, where pupils are given positions of formal power, and where parents have willingly chosen this form of education; nevertheless, several studies have attempted to assess the degree to which the English public school matches this model.[15] The public school is certainly total in the sense that it sets out to influence its pupils' values by providing for all their needs within one social organization, but it has few of the adaptation patterns of the more negative total institutions.[16] We have tried to measure these features by devising scales. One is a scale of institutional control which assesses the amount of control over activity, movement, possessions and social relationships; the other is a scale of expressive control. While the numerical totals in each category must be somewhat arbitrary, as some categories have more items than others, a comparison of scores from different types of school is revealing. The following tables compare the levels of institutional control in schools of different categories:

TABLE 6:8

Means of scores in each area of control

Style of boarding	Compulsory activity	Restrictions	Movement and activity	Social relations	Time	Privacy
Public	17	8	14	24	9	30
Progressive	6	11	10	13	5	25
Independent integrated	11	14	16	20	16	33
Independent non-integrated	14	11	14	15	10	28
State	6	12	9	9	10	28

(For scales of controls see Appendix II.)

TABLE 6:9

Total scores for schools in each category

Score	Public	Independent	Independent integrated	Progressive	Maintained
0 - 50	1	0	0	1	2
51 - 75	3	3	0	1	7
76 - 100	6	3	4	5	2
101 - 125	7	0	2	0	2
126 - 150	6	1	3		1
151 - 175	3		2		0
176 - 200	0				1
201 +					
Mean of totals:	112	82	118	68	84
Standard Deviation	33	26	27	21	38

It can be seen that public schools exercise higher levels of control than other types of school in the areas of compulsory activity and social relationships, and in general are more controlling than the other kinds of school, except integrated ones. Many public schools still have strict controls over boys' relationships with people outside school such as the family, and inside school often restrict boys' social contacts with domestic staff and with boys of differing age groups or in other houses. In many schools even the day boys have to keep rules and regulations during the hours that they spend at home. For example, areas of town are often out of bounds, while day boys are expected to conform to rules of dress, chapel attendance and homework. Public schools, therefore, do impose high levels of institutional control, and are in this respect similar to total institutions, although in certain other schools these controls are even higher.

There is another important dimension of totality which the concept of institutional control fails to explore because physical restrictions are only one kind of control. Many other organizations have features of total institutions in that they cater for all individual needs in one social system, but they do not impose high physical controls. For example, groups of missionary priests have all their needs met and are controlled expressively by one social organization although they are free from physical restrictions. Among boarding schools the progressive schools, as Tables 6:8 and 6:9 show, have low levels of institutional control, yet in their wider, expressive sense they are as total as public schools. Public schools combine both institutional controls with high levels of expressive control in that they lay out clear expressive standards which have to be achieved.

This expressive control covers many personal areas of values, beliefs, intimate relationships, social relations, taste, access to the outside world and cultural expression. The class and cultural background of the staff and pupils leads to a belief in the absolute value of certain expressive values of manners, speech, morals, politics and modes of evaluation of other people. Adult behaviour, rationality and loyalty are all accepted while adolescent roles expressed in social life and distinctive dress tend to be discouraged.

The following table gives the scores for expressive control which have been derived from a scale similar to that used to measure institutional controls. As can be seen, the public schools impose much greater control of this type than any other type of boarding school.

TABLE 6:10

Means of scores in each area of expressive control

Style of boarding	Religion	Games	Leader-ship	Style of life	Means of totals	SD	N
Public	26	44	28	98	196	18	26
Independent non-integrated	21	32	15	96	172	26	7
Independent integrated	10	23	10	47	89	24	11
Progressive	12	12	3	60	76	13	7
State	5	15	8	40	68	25	15

(For scales of control see Appendix II.)

This high level of expressive control shows how the public school takes responsibility for many of the functions which are normally fulfilled by other social institutions such as the family and peer group. Pastoral care, for example, and oversight of emotional development are entrusted to staff and prefects. The family's direct influence on the boy's education and development is limited. This has important consequences for the types of control which are predominant in public schools which again contrast with those found in the classic model of total institutions. From the age of eight the public school boy has been away from home in boarding schools and has become very dependent on his school for emotional and social support. This dependency is an emotional state of attachment and is not the same as institutionalization which is a state of mental disintegration. In an earlier report, we saw that it is because boys in public schools are so dependent that they are so loyal to their schools.[17] More important, though, are the controls which can be used because of this high dependency, for boys can be effectively sanctioned by engendering shame and guilt arising from damaged relationships or trust. Although punishments such as beating or fatigues are still commonly used in public schools, the shame and dishonour associated with the administration of the punishment are probably greater than any physical discomforts they produce.

This approach is effective because boys who go to public schools have generally been to preparatory schools as the following table shows, and this pre-socializes them into accepting such a pattern of expressive control and high organization. Over eighty per cent of boys in public schools have been to a preparatory school.

TABLE 6:11

The previous schools attended by entrants in 1964
(in percentages)

	Public Schools	
	Boarding	Day
(a) Maintained primary	3	44
(b) Independent primary	80	45
Both (a) and (b)	8	6
(c) Maintained secondary	3	2
(d) Independent secondary	1	1
(e) School abroad	6	2
	N = 3420	923

Source: Kalton, *The Public Schools,* p 28.

Our own intensive survey shows that eighty-five per cent of the boys in our sample boarded at their preparatory school.

Although they are small, preparatory schools reflect much of the life style and goal stress of the public schools and are important socializing agencies. Preparatory schools also represent the only style of boarding which is commonly employed for children under the age of eleven. There is little other boarding provision for younger children in state or independent schools. As a style, therefore, preparatory schools are worthy of further discussion, for they not only lead to a deeper understanding of the public school ethos but form a distinct style of boarding in themselves.

Preparatory Schools

The preparatory schools educate about 60,000 boys between the ages of seven and thirteen. Of this number approximately 31,000 at any given time are boarders and of the five hundred schools in the IAPS (Incorporated Association of Preparatory Schools), which is the junior equivalent of the HMC, about a quarter admit only boarders while more than half of the schools admit day boys as well. Very few prep schools are entirely day in composition; when they are, they tend to be the junior departments of large independent city grammar schools. Prior to their arrival at the prep schools about a quarter of the boys have attended state primary schools, the rest small private schools, particularly those boys who come from abroad.

It is difficult to provide for comparative purposes any significant number of other boarding schools that educate children of this age. The state is reluctant to make boarding provision at junior levels and even the junior departments of progressive schools discourage parents from boarding their children before the age of eleven. However, a number of these schools were studied in our survey of prep schools (see Appendix II), and something of their distinctive style will be illustrated.[18]

The IAPS, which met first in 1892 to standardize the size of cricket balls for junior players, has developed into an association which seeks to exert an influence over the curricula in the preparatory schools, to co-ordinate member schools' relations with the public schools, and in recent years it has been increasingly concerned with the presentation of an attractive public image for the prep schools and has even acted as a political pressure group. Membership of the IAPS confers on any particular school some external seal of approval, as a number of requirements must be met concerning staffing, standards of accommodation and the success of their pupils in the common entrance examination for the public schools. All prep schools are independent and, as few are endowed, most charge fees which cover the full cost of tuition and accommodation, though concessions may be made for old boys, the sons of clergy, the forces, etc. A proportion are still owned by their headmasters (137 out of 498 in 1966) but

the financial advantages of forming limited companies or
charitable trusts, particularly during the period of selective
employment tax, and the need to ensure some sort of continuity for individual schools has led to a continuing decline in
the number of owner-headmasters.

The preparatory schools claim to do more than prepare their
boys for the public schools and suggest that subsequent
successful adults' careers owe much to their schools' early
influence.[19] While this may be true, the fact that only fifteen per
cent of their boys fail to go on to the public schools (and these
hardly represent the schools' most vaunted successes) suggests
that the major task of the preparatory schools is to familiarize
boys with the goal stress of their forthcoming senior school, the
roles they will play there, both formal and informal, and teach
them to accept as legitimate many aspects of the senior school's
process of control. This pre-socialization function of the
preparatory school begins early; a third of the boys start
boarding before the age of eight and about seventy per cent of
all boys in the preparatory schools are boarding before the age
of nine. However, rapidly increased costs and changes in the
upper-middle-class patterns of child rearing have tended to raise
the age of first boarding in recent years.

TABLE 6:12

Age of first boarding

Average age of first boarding in a sub-sample of 9 schools
(in percentages)

Up to 7 years	6
7- 8	24
8- 9	31
9-10	19
10-11	12
11+ (to 13)	8
	100 N = 948

Source: prep school sample. (See Appendix II.)

The three schools which have the highest number of boys in

need of boarding are the only ones which have over eight per cent of their pupils boarding before they are seven years old (the highest percentage is 18·7). The usual age of starting boarding in many prep schools is the seven and eight age group. Only those schools with a large day element have many boys coming as boarders into the day school after the ages of nine and ten.

The allocative functions of the school for society are clear from the schools' close relations with the public schools. Many of the prep schools furnish the first rungs of the ladder of upward social mobility for the sons of parents who did not themselves attend public schools (sixty per cent). In these cases the mother exercises far greater influence on the choice of school than does the father, and a far greater influence than she is likely to exercise at senior level. In recent years mothers have exerted a powerful influence on the prep schools to be more open or flexible in their boarding arrangements or local in their composition and even, in some cases, more homely in their regimes. However, a small number of more exclusive preparatory schools which send their boys to several leading public schools have a different clientele. Such schools are status-maintaining, for almost all the boys have fathers educated at leading public schools, sometimes even at the same prep schools as their sons. Here the fathers exert much more of an influence on the selection of the prep school than the mother; there is much less shopping around. However, not all parents board their children because of a belief in the merits of

TABLE 6:13

Children in preparatory schools with need for boarding (in percentages)

Boys with parents abroad	29
Boys with broken homes	9·3
Boys in need through parental illness, or boy's maladjustment	3·8
	42·1 = 408:1117

Source: prep school sample, sub-sample of 1117 children in 12 schools.

residential education, because of family tradition or the desire to achieve a higher social status for their children. A large proportion of boys in many of the preparatory schools have a need for boarding and the administrative functions of the schools should not be ignored. Table 6:13 above provides a very conservative estimate of the numbers of need cases sheltered in the schools.

This table uses a very circumscribed definition of 'need' since it takes no account of personal discord in the home, boys with special gifts needing extra-ordinary teaching, with special medical requirements such as asthma, geographical isolation of homes, etc. We found also considerable variation in the proportion of children with boarding need in individual schools. The highest level of need in a school visited was sixty-four per cent, and in the twelve schools the breakdown (in percentages) was:

60	3 schools
50-60	1 school
40-50	1 school
30-40	2 schools
20-30	3 schools
15-20	2 schools

Not only is it clear that the greater the number of need cases the higher is the proportion who start boarding early, but it was noticeable that schools containing the most children with need made greater efforts to make the school homelike.

While individual schools may be influenced by such specific considerations, the style of most prep schools is determined by their integrative functions, that is, the reinforcing of upper-middle-class values, norms of behaviour and cultural patterns and the inculcating of certain instrumental skills.

'Our true purpose is to go between the home and the harder life of the public school. To provide the first stepping-stones on the road to the senior school and university'.

Such a statement from a headmaster leaves us in little doubt that the goals of the preparatory schools are closely linked with those of the public schools. We in fact find that the same balance between instrumental, organizational and expressive goals that characterizes the public schools is reflected in the smaller world of the preparatory schools. Headmasters, both at senior and at preparatory level, maintain that many of the boy's values are fixed in his earliest schools and that this inculcation should begin early by boarding in enclosed communities. Many heads maintain that the separation from home is less disturbing when the boy is young: 'When he is old enough to tie up his shoes', maintained one head, 'he is ready to grow up and to make his way in the school community'.

In the prep schools the skills that the boys are encouraged to acquire are academic, athletic and social, and the values that they are expected to display are those of religious belief and life, dependability, industry, a belief in the corporate good, and control of self. All these reflect the similar emphases already noted in the public schools. The headmaster of a prep school stated that:

> 'The aim of this school is to produce on a foundation of individual health and happiness and by a judicious combination of hard work, vigorous exercise and leisure time, a sound training for body, mind and spirit so that the boy may be in all respects fit to pass on with high ideals to the larger life of the public school and later the world outside. The exceptionally large number of old boys who have in recent years won places at Cambridge and Oxford would seem to indicate that these school aims are being achieved'.

The criterion of success is illuminating as it suggests how far the schools are wedded to an ideal of academic excellence and to the conviction of the academic and social pre-eminence of Oxbridge. It is also clear that the schools do not hesitate to take some credit for pupils' subsequent success; as many prep school headmasters emphasize: 'a tree is only as good as its roots'. Such academic concerns in the prep schools and their pre-occupation with inculcating adult behaviour in their pupils mean that the prep schools reject much of the child-centred stance of state primary schools and the few preparatory departments of the progressive schools with their stress on

creative play, on happiness and individuality where, in the words
of Plowden,

> 'Children need to be themselves, to live with other children
> and with grown ups, to learn from their environment, to
> enjoy the present, to get ready for the future, to create and
> to love, to learn to face adversity, to behave responsibly, in a
> word, to be human beings'.[20]

The preparatory schools' stress on academic values, their
concern with a number of organizational goals, particularly
with efficient running and their public reputation, and their
stress on certain expressive areas: values of community life,
physical and moral development and particularly religion, all of
these clearly emerge in the goal perspectives of heads and staff.

There is high consensus among the staff and little conflict
with the goal priorities of their headmasters, whose attempts to
balance institutional, organizational and expressive concerns
are evident from their replies. The staff express some unease
at the schools' organizational goal stress, deprecating the
emphasis on good public reputation and on keeping the
children busy. Staff also feel that the demands of public school
preparation inhibit a more child-centred approach in the
preparatory schools. However, such doubts clearly do not
haunt headmasters who firmly reject those goals, stressed by
progressive and state primary schools, of personal development,
of education suited to ability and of developing critical
faculties in the child. The low estimates given to the importance
of homeliness in a school setting are clear in the replies to us of
both heads and staff in the preparatory schools.

Not only do the goals stressed in the preparatory schools
differ from those emphasized in most junior day schools, but
also the means used to achieve instrumental goals, to ensure
high academic success, also contrast strongly with the
approaches of other schools. Learning is achieved less through
self-directed activity and experience and more through an
authoritarian, formal teacher-pupil relationship. There is a stress
on factual knowledge, on precise and orderly presentation.[21] If
life is formal and regulated for prep school boys outside the
classroom, so it is within. Indeed the schools, in rejecting the

considerable external criticism of their limited curricula and dull approach, stress their boys' considerable successes at O and A levels and the fact that many of them may be in a position to pass examinations, particularly in Latin, maths and English, several years in advance of contemporaries in the state system.[22] In fact, the prep schools have little freedom of manoeuvre because their curricula are largely determined by the requirements of the public schools' common entrance examination which has defied repeated attempts at radical change. Because the schools are particularly vulnerable to parental pressure, especially as most are small and have few capital resources, scholarships won by their boys to the senior schools greatly enhance prep schools' prestige. During the period of our research, when many schools were in an insecure position and faced with a temporary decline in numbers, it was the highly academic schools which were full and enjoyed long waiting lists of potential pupils. As the head of one such school commented:

> 'While I feel the attention we give to the arts is somewhat perfunctory, we have a long tradition that attracts boys from homes where such values are held high. Professional people send us good material to work on and we maintain the best of the old tradition: academic excellence based on the classics'.

The prep school master has to teach facts because this is largely what is still being tested by common entrance. He is compelled by the situation to spend at least three-quarters of his periods in formal teaching. Project work and discovery methods of learning, which are regarded with considerable suspicion by most teachers, are relegated to Saturday morning school or to a weekly optional activities period. This is less true of the junior departments of large public schools where common entrance is less of a hurdle and transfer is more automatic. When it is realized that nearly three-quarters of the boys in the prep schools have begun Latin before the age of ten and may spend as much as a fifth of their lesson time on it, the contrast between the preparatory and state primary school approach becomes clearly evident.[23]

The reasons for the retention of Latin are also particularly revealing. Headmasters frequently justify the stress on classics in the prep schools because, as one head said,

> 'its whole emphasis is unashamedly on accuracy and self-discipline'

and they value its supposed ability to train the abstract intelligence and to further the schools' aim of inculcating the pursuit of knowledge as, 'a habit of mind instead of a duty'. These preoccupations are noticeable even in creative activities such as music and art, so that it is possible for a school prospectus to state:

> 'An attempt is made to teach boys how to work and train them in industry and concentration. They have a full opportunity for doing creative work in art, craft and music and special emphasis is laid here and throughout the school on neatness and accuracy'.

In fact, many schools give little time to creative areas and a sum total of about five per cent of classroom time is spent during the boys' later years in the schools on art, handicrafts and music. Were these schools not largely boarding schools with considerable time at evenings and weekends which can be and often is devoted to such creative areas, the stated and real goals of the institutions would be very far apart. The contrasts between different sectors of education at junior levels emerges clearly from the following tables.

TABLE 6:14

Ages at which boys in prep schools begin Latin

	No.	Percentage
Under 9 years	84	17
9- 9.11	283	57
10-10.11	113	23
11+	5	1
No Latin taught	1	0
Question unanswered	9	2
(74 per cent before the age of 10)	494	100

Source: P.L. Masters, *The Preparatory Schools Today* (Black 1966), P 120.

Progressive schools do not teach the classics as form subjects at any level and they have declined in importance in the state sector, where they do not exist before the secondary level. A comparison of the time spent by boys on various subjects across different types of school shows the diverging pre-occupations of the preparatory schools.

TABLE 6:15

Percentage of total time spent by junior boys on lessons: subject analysis

Subjects	Preparatory			Primary	Progressive
	Lower: age 7½-9	Middle: age 9-11	Upper: age 11+		
Art	4	3	2	14	11
English	25	16	13	15	11
French	9	15	15	0	14
Geography	7	6	6*	16*	16
Greek	0	0	5	0	0
Handicrafts	3	1	1	10	5
History	7	7	6*	16*	16
Latin	5	16	17	0	0
Mathematics	20	19	18	14	14
Nature study	3	1	0	0	0
Physical education	5	4	4	8	11
Science (physical or biology)	1	2	4	10	14
Scripture	6	5	5	2	0
Singing/other class music	1	1	1	5	5
Any other subjects	1	1	1	0	0

* Taught as integrated studies.

Source: Full sample of preparatory and comparison schools. (See Appendix II.)

The dominance of Latin is clear in comparison with other schools: even after the age of eleven when boys in the state system of education may have started Latin they are unlikely to spend seventeen per cent of their time on it. Comparison with boys in the progressive schools reveals that science, physical education, integrated studies and arts and crafts are given greater stress in the latter.

Not only are there significant differences in the allocation of resources to various academic areas by schools but also in the perspectives that boys have of the status of different subjects. In answer to the question:

'To have a worthwhile successful career, in which subjects do you think it is necessary to excel?',

the following table gives the rank order of boys' preferences.

TABLE 6:16

Rank order of boys' subject preferences

Subject	Boarding schools				Day
			State		Secondary
	Prep	Progressive	Primary	Grammar	Modern
	(21)	(2)	(1)	(juniors)	(juniors)
Mathematics	2	4	1	1	1
English	3	1	2	3	5
Science	5	3	3	2	2
Humanities/geography/ history	6	7	7	6	6
Art, music, drama	7	5	8	7	8
Craft, metalwork, woodwork, printing	9	6	5	9	3
Engineering	8	8	4	5	4
Latin, greek, ancient history	1	9	9	8	9
Modern languages	4	2	6	4	7
N =	1124	159	151	368	210

Source: preparatory and comparison schools.

This pattern raises interesting questions concerning the extent to which the schools' wider functions for society, particularly the allocative and integrative functions, determine the allocation of resources in the schools and the status of subjects in the eyes of staff and pupils: theoretical questions which have been explored elsewhere.

The small size of the prep school means that many of the

functions delegated to other teachers in senior boarding schools can be adequately met by the headmaster alone. Hence the schools are autocratically run in that the head exercises far greater power in almost all areas of school life than do assistant staff. Inevitably from a public school background himself and usually from an Oxbridge college, a headmaster has usually spent all his teaching life in preparatory schools. Unlike the public school headmaster, he is frequently appointed from the senior staff of his prep school and is much longer as a head in any one school. His expressive roles are emphasized more than we have seen to be common in public school headmasters and are brought into balance with organizational concerns. In many prep schools the head also has an important instrumental role in that he teaches the top forms, coaches scholarship candidates and devises the timetable. He interviews parents and candidates for admission, he frequently acts as bursar and estate manager and he fulfils many public relations functions such as juvenile magistrate. He also maintains his links with housemasters in those public schools that take the majority of his boys. He acts as the chief disciplinary agent within the school and publicly awards the weekly accolades for academic and sporting pre-eminence among the boys. The headmaster and his wife are often the principal pastoral agents for boys and he may take some major sport. He is in fact ever-present and he familiarizes the boys with much of the housemaster's role in the public schools. He eats breakfast, lunch and tea with his prefects at the top table, withdraws *en famille* in the evenings to leave organizational matters to house tutors and prefects. He preaches in Sunday chapel, entertains public school house-masters and chosen boys to Sunday lunch. He attempts to make palpable the ideals of hard work, selflessness and controlled, conditional love for his charges; he is unremittingly correct.

As in the public schools, his assistant staff come from within the system, for example, about eighty per cent have never taught in anything other than prep schools and over ninety per cent come from public schools.[24] Indeed, the emphasis on their background is much greater than it is in the senior schools. For not only are university, usually Oxbridge, qualifications given in school prospectuses but school awards are also prominent and, for the unqualified staff, public school education and armed service experience are considered quite sufficient experience to teach younger boys. The temporary staff usually consist of old boys waiting for Oxbridge entrance and, in some, visiting staff may come from local public schools.

Preparatory schools have considerable difficulties in recruitment of staff. Colleges of education are hesitant to co-operate with them even for students' teaching practice and before qualifying as a recognized teacher a year must be spent in state schools. Thus a source of teachers with different ideas rarely penetrates the system. Neither is prep school teaching a job that attracts the able graduate or excites the recommendations of university appointment boards. Staff are found from within the system by a network of personal contacts. A contribution particularly significant to the schools' ethos comes from the retired service officers who are found in every common room.

The head's key position in so many areas and the relative inexperience of many of the assistant staff mean that little autonomy is accorded to them, in contrast to staff in the public schools. They may have integrated role structures but exercise in fact little authority within the schools' many sub-units. And frequently these sub-units and offices within them exist in little more than name only, such as the chapel or the library. An elaborate hierarchy is devised to familiarize boys with the more meaningful structures of public schools. Even the house units within the prep schools are more devices for academic and sporting competition than they are the expressive focus for community life as in the public schools. However, even if they enjoy little power in reality, the elaborate hierarchies of the public schools are mirrored among masters and boys in the prep schools. There are second masters and house masters, heads of departments, house tutors, staff in charge of major sports and minor sports. Among the boys there are heads of schools, deputy heads of schools, heads of houses, school and house prefects, monitors in charge of forms or of sub-units such as the library. The separate chapel hierarchy is already in embryo with its choir, its servers, its readers, etc. Indeed, in schools numbering rarely more than a hundred boys and ten staff, the weight of office for some would be overwhelming if it implied anything more than adding another list to the already crowded noticeboards. Because much of the federal nature of the

school's structure is a fiction and power is centralized in the
headmaster, changes can be more swiftly made in the prep
schools than in the senior schools. However, as their real goals
are set by the public schools and not by themselves, little
experiment and few radical changes in structure have in fact
occurred in them.

In the process of control, the preparatory school foreshadows
much that will reorient and direct the boy in his public school.
He learns to exercise and submit to authority gracefully and be
increasingly aware of its legitimate scope and boundaries.
There are an extensive number of organizational constraints
upon boys: elaborate and inescapable uniforms, strict control
of possessions and a tightly scheduled day followed with groups
of others. There is no privacy. Similarly, control by orientation
and pressure in expressive areas is elaborate and relentless. There
is great competition in academic, social and sporting areas; the
virtues of hard work, loyalty, obedience and success are
rewarded by various insignia, dignified by ritualistic presentations and public callovers. Much of this is reinforced by a
strong religious stress that teaches self-abnegation, honesty and
morality, and usefully gilds much that is organizational: respect
for those in authority and loyalty. Senior boys control the
junior ones and contact between all is distanced by the use of
surnames and by the emphasis on adult acceptable behaviour.

Rewards are frequently utilitarian for the younger children:
the Saturday sweet, the coveted television programme are
permutated with an elaborate mark system which puts a premium
on effort as well as attainment. But for the older boys the
rewards are increasingly normative: the approval of adults, the
esteem of others and symbolic tea with the headmaster, trips
out and showing visitors round. Particularly clear are the
rewards that come to the orthodox over time: each age group
has its own particular privileges and obligations in dress, in bed-
times, in meal places, in access to forbidden territory and to the
outside world. Finally, a most effective form of control is
exercised by the parents, for while the school excludes them
from any direct participation in the regime, parents are used to
dignify expressive events considered important by the school.
They attend chapel, support games, house plays and concerts,
open days and prize givings, and informing parents of a boy's

success is considered the highest form of reward possible by prep school boys and, in the case of failure, their most feared sanction.

TABLE 6:17

Rank order of most favoured rewards
(in percentages)

		1st-3rd choices
1	Tell parents	87
2	Good marks for the house	74
3	Private approval	70
4	Public approval	35
5	Mars bars - or other favoured confection	20
6	Sit by staff at mealtime	16

N = 1124

Rank order of most feared punishments
(in percentages)

(i.e. those ranked 1 are *least* disliked)

		5th-8th choices
1	Private censure	6
2	No sweets	15
3	Early bed	25
4	Bad marks	29
5	The stick	62
6	Public censure	64
7	Tell parents	65
		N = 1124

Source: full sample of prep school boys.

Sanctions again move from the utilitarian to the normative with age. Sending to bed is replaced by ostracism and public disapproval and frequently the staff manipulate the supportive informal world of the boys to achieve maximum impact on the deviant. As a diminutive head of house aged twelve volunteered:

'If a boy has a big minus total at the end of the term he is excluded from his house until they choose to vote him back in, he has to give up his house tie and wear a black one, and cannot take part in any house games'.

Boys are seldom beaten or expelled and here again it is the 'awful' ritual that accompanies such events in which control is vested, rather than the pain of the sanction itself.

We have seen in our consideration of the public schools that they exercise not only institutional control over privacy, compulsory activities, times, movement and activity, but also considerable expressive control through religion, games, concentration on the creative arts and encouraging a particular style of life. In the same way it is possible to identify these items in the preparatory schools and assign to them arbitrary scores which for comparative purposes between schools suggest different levels of control.

TABLE 6:18

Scale of institutional control

	Possible		Prep schools (20)			Girls' prep schools (3)	Co-educational progressive (2)
	Min.	Max.	Min.	Max.	Average	Average	Average
1 Compulsory activities	0	11	6	11	8	7	3
2 Restrictions	2	37	8	31	19	20	12
3 Movement and activity	0	26	12	20	14	12	6
4 Times	0	16	5	11	7	9	5
5 Privacy	0	16	4	14	8	4	3
6 Total	2	106	41	70	55	54	29

The boys' prep schools have a high score on privacy, which suggests that the schools offer boys very little. This contrasts with the two other types of school, particularly the progressive schools, one of which provided each child with its own room. The progressive schools exercise much less control in all spheres, but their highest scores for items in the scale of expressive orientation which follows in art, music, drama, suggests that in their own way they too exercise over their pupils considerable non-physical direction.

TABLE 6:19

Scale of expressive orientation

	Possible Min.	Possible Max.	Prep schools (20) Min.	Prep schools (20) Max.	Prep schools (20) Average	Girls' preps (3) Average	Co-educational Progressive (2)	State (1)
1 Religion	0	26	5	21	13	11	0	15
2 Games	2	34	14	26	20·5	19	3	2
3 Leadership	0	42	0	32	25	26	2	2
4 Creative arts	0	70	25	50	37	34	50	26
5 Style of life	0	29	12	24	17·5	11	4	9
6 The staff world	0	34	11	26	20·5	17	13	8
Total:	2	235	67	179	133·5	118	72	62

This table is much more suggestive of the totality of schools because it examines areas of life that are significant in determining the whole ethos of a school. In the boys' and girls' prep schools the high emphasis on games and leadership and the low emphasis on the creative arts is apparent. The state schools' relatively low expressive orientation in games, in leadership and the arts among the pupils is clear and there are weaker attempts to influence the life style of the school through the staff. The progressive schools' concern with the arts has already been mentioned. They have a low formal emphasis on many aspects of their pupils' life style. However, in these schools the pupils' informal norms exert considerable control on their peers' life style.

It will be noted that these two scales of control are linked in so far as the highest scores in the areas of one scale are often the highest scores in at least one area of the other. Where there is a high scale of institutional control and a low scale of expressive control it is very likely that it is a small school which usually scored low on areas such as the arts. Schools high on compulsory activities tended to be low in privacy and high on restrictions over movement and activity.

However, the preparatory schools' most significant contribution in primary socialization lies in the style of relationship that exists between the formal world of the staff and the informal world of the boys. By fragmenting the informal world of the boys through aspects of the control process, the emphasis on adult values by the school can be turned into reality. Boys find themselves living in a fragmented social world of their own which is penetrated and manipulated by adults and divided in itself by aspects of the control process, such as competition and the elaborate hierarchies just described. The boys are accustomed to having all aspects of their lives, even their most intimate behaviour and attitudes scrutinized by others and, if found wanting, reported on. This common acceptance of penetration and manipulation of their world legitimates early much of the kind of control that staff and senior boys will exercise over them later in the public schools, and it is all the more effective because long stay in single-sex, isolated communities leads to an emotional dependence on the school.

When laid out in this sociological way, the structures of the prep schools can be clearly seen to be intelligibly designed by adults to stress absolute values. Aspects of the control process such as competition exert pressures which are reinforced by the supportive informal norms of the boys' peer group. Unlike the situation in the junior schools in the outside world or in the senior schools to which the pupils are destined to go, escape is impossible. Neither on the staff nor among the boys exists an explicitly deviant group questioning ends and means and substituting alternatives. Rebellion is rare among the boys; indeed, the problems are those of over-conformity, particularly to academic ends and the collective good. However, overt signs of distress in the boys are very rare. Few suffer from prolonged homesickness or symptoms such as bedwetting and stealing, but a more significant proportion mask their distress and failure in all-round development by over-compensating in those areas that the schools stress: in academic and sporting achievements, and this is suggested by the fact that a number of boys in the prep schools may be quite capable of passing several O levels by the age of twelve. In contrast to approaches in state primary schools, much that the preparatory school attempts to do may seem to be calculating, even antipathetic to the child's fullest development. However, the progress from the ritualistic casting aside of teddy bears at the end of the first term to the dizzy heights of dormitory captain seems to pose few problems for most boys. They seem happy, highly committed and fulfilled in the gregarious world of pre-adolescence, although the long-term impact of early boarding may be less beneficial. Using a wide variety of indices it is clear that the commitment to their schools' formal goals is widespread and deep. In a number of ways the prep school boy shows patterns of adaptation which characterize those noted in the public schools, and in their aspirations they do not differ markedly from boys in the senior schools, except for a greater emphasis on position in the hierarchy.

TABLE 6:20

Aspirations 'What would you like to be best at?'

(percentages)

	Scholar	Prefect	Games	Art/music/ drama	Total
Boys' prep schools (21)	54·0	9·4	25·3	11·3	100 = 1672
Coeducational progressive schools (2)	40·3	0	22·2	37·5	100 = 88
Girls' prep schools (2)	32·0	1·5	35·5	31·0	100 = 150
State junior boarding (1)	50·0	9·0*	25·0	16·0	100 = 63

* The coeducational progressive school and state junior boarding schools had no prefect system so this response is artificial in that it is not based on a system of status or rewards.

Source: prep schools sample.

It is also clear that academic pressures already pose considerable concern. The following table illustrates the anxiety that preparatory school boys feel over failure in a number of areas.

TABLE 6:21

Items causing any worry, in rank order

Rank		Average percentage
1	Getting bad marks for bad work	80·0
2	Losing things at school	66·7
3	Getting bad marks for bad behaviour	66·2
4	Being sent for to go to the headmaster's study	65·0
5	My parents might die	63·4
6	I might fail my exams	61·7
7	The feeling I must get a scholarship so my parents won't have to pay so many fees	61·2
8	My future	60·3
9	Having to obey the bell at once, whatever you are doing and even if you haven't finished it	60·1
10	Coming back to school at the beginning of term	59·7
11	I sometimes feel a fool	58·3
12	My work	57·0
13	Having to report to staff if you break anything	55·2
14	Having to be on time for classes	54·5
15	What it will be like at my next school	53·6
16	I am not good at work	53·3

Source: full sample of prep schools.

TABLE 6:22

Replies per cent of first choices presented in a rank order of ten items

Rank		Percentage
1	My parents might die	40·5
2	My future	28·8
3	The feeling I must get a scholarship	10·3
4	The feeling I must pass my exams	9·1
5	Getting bad marks for bad work/behaviour	5·4
6	The thought of leaving this school	3·3
7	Coming back to school at the beginning of term	1·6
8	I miss my pet	0·8
9	Having to obey the bell at once	0
10	Losing things at school	0

Source: full sample of prep schools.

Such a pattern of anxiety might be expected from boys under the considerable pressures of preparatory school life, but the repression of these tensions beneath an imperturbable front also appears early. In areas of pastoral care the public school pattern seems to be well established by the ninth or tenth year. There is rather low communication of personal problems to staff in the prep schools, although it is not markedly lower than in children of a similar social class in progressive and other schools. However, it is quite clear that the development of the public self, the correct image, militates against communication with peers, for only twenty per cent of them will communicate problems with a friend. In their competitive world to be known by others is to be vulnerable, and this is in marked contrast to the replies from children in other boarding situations. It is significant how much less pastorally isolated are boarders of the same age in progressive schools, chiefly by their recourse to friends.

TABLE 6:23

Pastoral Care

School	Staff	Friend	Outside	No one	Number
Family problem taken to (in percentages)					
Preparatory	30	23	15	32	1043
Junior depts. (state)	34	27	18	31	318
Progressive	33	41	11	15	196
Girls' preparatory	33	34	10	23	350
Personal problem taken to (in percentages)					
Preparatory	26	20	12	42	1043
Junior depts. (state)	32	29	17	32	318
Progressive	27	44	14	15	196
Girls' preparatory	29	34	17	20	350

Source: prep schools sample. For pastoral care questions see Chapter 8, Table 8:19 and Appendix II.

In retrospect boys in the public schools look back on their prep schools with great satisfaction. As one boy wistfully writes:

'It was a make-believe world of games and innocent enthusiasm. Each day our world seemed to get better, with more to do, you knew more, you mattered more and you were safe'.

If the prep schools were limiting in their perspectives or causing problems by the practice of early boarding, at least the boys in the senior schools do not reproach them for it.

TABLE 6:24

Looking back, how would you say you got on at your prep school(s)?
(sixth-form boarders)

	percentages			
	A	B	C	D
I thoroughly enjoyed it	21·7	32·9	24·3	12·7
I was happy most of the time	42·0	36·5	35·6	48·2
I found it tolerable	16·3	11·3	13·0	14·5
I was unhappy at first but happy enough later on	8·0	7·9	9·6	10·0
I was unhappy for much of the time	2·9	2·7	2·9	3·6
I hated it for most of the time	1·1	1·8	2·9	2·7
Grew to dislike it, more unhappy in last years	7·3	6·3	10·5	4·5
Generally happy, certain aspects unpleasant	0·7	–	–	–
Other	–	0·7	0·4	1·8
N =	440	239	189	67

Source: intensive sample, general survey.

However, while the majority of boys state and recollect satisfaction with their life in the preparatory schools, the minority that do not is particularly significant. Those boys who disliked their prep schools suffer more frequently from homesickness and there are positive correlations between low enjoyment of boarding at an early age and low attainment in the senior schools,* in feelings of rejection† and high anxiety in social situations.‡

In conclusion it would be wrong to think of boarding at junior age levels as a monolith dominated by the style of the

* $r = 0.32$ $p < 0.01$.
† $r = 0.16$ $p < 0.01$.
‡ $r = 0.21$ $p < 0.01$ (product moment correlations)
        $N = 1,027$.

IAPS schools. We have hinted that even these have considerable stylistic variety, depending on a number of factors of which the proportion of day boys, the relationship with particular senior schools and specific clientele are particularly important.

However, one state primary school is predominantly boarding and a number of primary schools have boarding hostels. In these a different residential style has developed where none of the expressive stress of the preparatory schools is evident. Homeliness and support, particularly stress on pastoral care and relationships, give much to an ethos that is influenced by child care institutions. The style has the affectivity and casualness of the small children's home with none of the pre-socialization devices that are so significant in the preparatory schools. The child-centred curriculum of primary education is linked with similar approaches in the residential situation. Staff have greater autonomy than in the preparatory schools, many more women hold key expressive roles. The heads are paternalistic and decisions can be influenced through frequent staff meetings and consultation. In these communities boarding is not regarded as an essential tool to further ends but more as providing shelter for children deficient in or forcibly absent from family life.

The junior departments of the independent progressive schools, though differing radically in style, share with the preparatory schools the task of socializing young children to accept the goal stress, pupil roles and control process of senior schools. The more expressive the goals of institutions, as in the public and progressive schools, the more essential is some preliminary socialization of prospective members. In the junior schools that prepare for progressive schools the accent is on allowing the child to develop at his or her own pace, free from external pressure. Academic excellence is less prized, and the mechanisms of competition and conditional approval are little employed. Also we have noted that the curriculum is very different, the arts and crafts have much greater stress than in the preparatory schools, particularly painting and pottery, weaving and handicraft and, almost unthinkable for the potential public school boy, dance and free expression in drama and music.

In such child-centred regimes, many aspects of family life are imitated, housemothers and fathers act as parent substitutes, offering unconditional love and acceptance of the child for what he is. More activity takes place in small groups, the schools are coeducational, there is more noise, more tears, more childlike behaviour. In contrast to the preparatory schools, adult values of sobriety, perseverance and responsibility are at a discount and there is less stress on the corporate good. Individuality and self-realization are prized and emotional display encouraged, rather than the suppression of the self. Control is exerted by the expectations of the peer group, the values of which can be easily manipulated by adults. Already in embryo are the community meetings where all seem to have a say in decision-making. Adults exert an influence through the easy, relaxed style of relationship where they and the children are all called by Christian names, and they seek constant pastoral involvement with the children.

However, such communities share in some ways the isolation and inward-looking qualities of the more traditional preparatory schools. While these schools are open in the sense that institutional controls are kept to a minimum, control in expressive areas can be high, and because of their life style and values the schools seem to suffer an expressive isolation from the local community. While the staff may come from a wider variety of backgrounds, they are deeply committed to the pro-gressive ideal and they may espouse it as a secular religion. Cut off in campuses of great size and amenity, the children flower unpruned, enriched by health foods. Over-protected from adult realities, bare-footed, bejeaned and precocious, the children are as clearly marked and as effectively prepared for the experiences of their senior schools as are any of the grey-suited, scrubbed products of traditional prep schools. While the style of preparation is very different, the long-term allocative and integrative roles of the preparatory and progressive junior schools seem very similar.

Progressive senior schools

There are many pressures in education which are inducing schools, both day and boarding, to give more emphasis to expressive goals. Schools of all kinds are attempting to widen their impact and to do more than impart discipline and transmit fundamental academic skills. Many day schools, for example, are accepting greater responsibility for the social welfare of their children; many primary schools have radically redefined the teaching programme and learning situation. 'Approved schools' are now part of the wider provision of residential care for deprived and disturbed children: some teacher training courses offer a perspective which is wider than the technical skills required for imparting knowledge.

The kind of expressive stress which is generated in all of these cases is far removed from the expressive goals of the public school where young children are trained into adults who are thought capable of taking elite, administrative positions in our society. The expressive qualities sought are of a different kind; there is a move towards a more child-centred approach, scope for greater self-expression and development of the individual in an atmosphere of warm supportive relationships with adults, and a participation of everyone in decision-making. As we have seen, such an approach has been practised by certain boarding schools for many years. Some of the seven senior schools which fall into our category of 'progressive' schools enshrine such an educational philosophy.

Within our category of progressive schools, however, there are still wide variations in the real goals pursued and in the consequent styles of boarding. One group of schools of great importance is that associated with the Quakers. Apart from the one boys' public school run by the Society of Friends, three other Quaker coeducational schools are included in our sample. Another group of schools identify themselves as 'progressive schools' but even among them there is much variation of style. Some of these schools, such as Abbotsholme, Bedales, Clayesmore, Bembridge, were founded at the end of the last century and developed a style incorporating certain features of the progressive ethos, such as absence of corporal punishment, more democratic procedures on decision-making, more freedom for children to go out or to visit homes, while maintaining an orthodox approach to teaching and curriculum. They have now tended to drift into the orbit of the public schools. Another group of schools founded in the 1920s, such as Summerhill, Dartington and the Malting House, set out to do more than this and to offer the children an environment which put little pressure on the individual and allowed the personality to flower at its own rate. The styles of boarding in such 'radical' progressive schools contrast sharply with those of the public schools already discussed. These 'radical' schools are coeducational, there is no official pupil or staff hierarchy, democratic meetings make rules and regulations, few controls over movement or dress are imposed and barriers between pupils and staff are reduced.[25.]

To understand this wide variety of approaches to the residential situation found in the progressive sector, we shall discuss two particular styles: that found in the Quaker schools and that found among the 'radical' schools. Naturally the Quaker schools differ among themselves, but they do offer an approach to boarding which is worthy of separate discussion, as most of the progressive schools tend to adopt this style. We shall call this the 'paternalistic' style or progressive boarding.

The paternalistic progressive schools. Boarding schools which are coeducational in our sample fall into three distinct kinds.[26] In one, which we shall call the divided community, boys and girls are kept apart for all activities except for teaching and, in reality, the boarding arrangements consist of two separate schools, one for boys and one for girls. A second group of schools are more freely integrated, in that boys and girls are mixed for all activities and that there is no clear distinction between the living quarters of either sex: these schools we shall call 'egalitarian' or 'radical' communities. Yet others in our sample have developed a style of boarding which falls between these two extremes, and we call this the 'mixed' kind of coeducation. While certain areas of the school, such as dormitories, playing fields and changing rooms, are restricted to one sex, many opportunities exist for boys and girls to mix for teaching, activities and leisure. Common rooms, classrooms and arts centres are all used freely by boys and girls so that frequent and relaxed social contacts can be maintained. Staff are encouraged to interact with pupils rather than merely supervise them, although house systems are rarely distinct as in public schools and are often controlled solely by the unmarried teachers who live in school rather than by married housemasters appointed for this specific purpose.

The Quaker progressive schools adopt this paternalistic style.[27] While consultation exists both with staff and pupils the headmaster sacrifices little real power, he is omnipresent and his influence is all-pervading. The expressive goals of relationships, of close pastoral care, of warmth and acceptance are clearly demonstrated by the insistence on coeducation, on the large proportion of women staff, the schools' close links with the pupils' families and with the local communities.

Unlike the public schools few of these schools are federal and the most significant sub-units are the academic departments and, in one or two schools, the residential units. Consequently there is little hierarchy developed amongst staff or pupils and all members of staff are expected to play similar roles. Pastoral care, for example, is not the responsibility of particular adults even though some schools have developed a tutorial system. Staff roles tend to be defined by the expectations of the community and each member of staff is expected to contribute to the relationships which prevail in it.

Unlike the more authoritarian structures of the public and preparatory boarding schools just considered, these paternalistic progressive schools are more democratic at both staff and pupil level. Far from exercising a mainly organizational role the headmasters of these schools have a major expressive role, supporting pupils and staff by frequent discussion and personal contact, engendering and maintaining a consensus. This is not always easy, for these schools have a highly involved staff and there are clashes over freedom and control and over the style of education.

Committees which enable staff and pupils to debate important school matters are important features of these schools, though there is less attempt to use whole-school assemblies, senates or moots as is frequent in the more radical progressive schools. However, unlike those in radical progressive schools, few pupils in these paternalistic communities actually believe that they have any real power to influence decisions. The pupil world is in fact manipulated by staff to accept and support the school's goals and the authoritarian powers of decision are reserved to the adults in most areas of importance.

These schools also give children more freedom than the

public schools to go home and to visit local towns, and offer them wide scope for self-expression in clothes, decoration and possessions. In this respect they are more homely than the public schools and more tolerant of the expression of adolescent roles. They also rely more for control on a consensus of accepted behaviour among staff and children, so that other sanctions are few. For example, in these schools there is no corporal punishment and little control is used other than per-suasion, the arousing of guilt or of feelings of responsibility and other emotional pressures. This reliance on consensus can lead to tension in those areas in which pupils, particularly older ones, and staff disagree. Nowhere is this clearer than in the nature of boy-girl relationships permitted by the staff. Young children benefit from the paternalistic oversight but are not sufficiently mature to be frustrated by their school's attempts at democracy, though older pupils often feel that while staff are benevolent they are insufficiently progressive to trust them as young adults who are free to control their own relationships and make decisions.

Admission to the Quaker schools is different from that to the others, for boarding education is available for children of Quaker parents who pay fees according to income. Quaker children are admitted irrespective of wealth or, in most cases, ability. Most of these children, however, tend to be pre-dominantly middle class, although the remaining places are not automatically made available to the wealthiest or most intelligent children of other fee-paying parents. The education and boarding provision in Quaker schools is often used by local authorities to place children who, for some reason, need boarding education. Many officials argue that the style of boarding found in this kind of progressive school, with its mixture of freedom, support and respect for the individual, is more suited to meeting the needs of such children than many other styles and, of course, coeducation enables brothers and sisters to be at the same school.

In all the nine Quaker schools, about three hundred Quaker parents receive financial assistance with fees under the Joint Bursarial Scheme for Friends. This is just over twelve per cent of the total intake. The amount of assistance given is large, being on average nearly half the school's fees, and in some cases the parental contribution is reduced to one pound a week. The table below gives the intake into one such school.

TABLE 6:25

The fee structure of one Quaker boarding school in 1968

	Boys	Girls	Total	Friends		Not Friends	Total
Boarding	201	196	397	–		–	–
Day	4	10	14	–		–	–
			411	162		249	411
				39 per cent		61	100

	Friends (N=162)		Not Friends (N=249)		Total (N=411)	
Supported by LEA wholly	4	(2 per cent)	39	(16 per cent)	43	(10 per cent)
Supported by LEA partly	11	(7 per cent)	7	(3 per cent)	18	(4 per cent)
Supported by other funds	1	(1 per cent)	6	(3 per cent)	8	(2 per cent)
(Quaker bursary scholarship)	79	(49 per cent)	0	(0)	79	(19 per cent)
Supported by scholarship funds	0	–	12	(5 per cent)	12	(3 per cent)

It is not only among the pupils in this school that there is a minority of Quakers. Only half of men and one-quarter of women staff were Quakers and this was the result of a deliberate policy to make the school wider in its intake and ability range. The headmaster himself said:

'It's important not to bring in all your own sort of people. We deliberately bring in people whose beliefs are counter to the establishment, as long as they are positive people. The more individuals I have, the better and healthier the climate'.

This style of progressive boarding, therefore, emphasizes certain expressive aims of individuality, relationships and social responsibility, and contains staff and pupils from a wider variety of social classes and cultural backgrounds than do public schools. Although the schools are selective in intake the range of ability within them is wide. They have to construct a curriculum which is more relevant to the less able child than that of the public school. Streaming, for example, has been abolished in many schools and many children leave at sixteen, an age when in a public school they would scarcely qualify for a private study. Nearly forty per cent of leavers left the Quaker school above at the age of sixteen, as the following table shows. Most children obtained some O levels, which shows that the intake is wider in comparison only with public schools and not with day, comprehensive schools.

TABLE 6:26

Leavers from a Quaker School in 1968

Total leavers:	80	(100 per cent)
Aged eighteen	30	(37)
Aged seventeen	20	(25)
Aged sixteen or below	30	(37)
To university	20	(25)
To college education	6	(7)
To technical colleges	5	(6)
Further education at lower level (business course)	14	(17)
A levels elsewhere	6	(7)
Family business	16	(20)
Jobs requiring O levels	10	(12)
Jobs not requiring O levels	3	(4)

The curriculum in many of these schools is very similar to that of comprehensive schools and is more deliberately geared to less able children than that of public schools. Creative work, art, drama, music and technical pursuits, project work and needlework are given greater emphasis in these schools; sculpture, social work, pottery and jewellery making accompany the usual sports and outdoor activities. There is far less sexual segregation in activities than is found in other co-educational schools: for example, boys happily do cookery and make jewellery and the girls enjoy woodwork and play cricket.

Although expressive aims are much stressed, these differ from those found in public schools and are implemented differently. The Quaker schools are democratic and paternalistic as well as being less total than the public schools. The institutional control scores for the four paternalistic progressive schools in our sample were 98, 76, 76 and 77 respectively, whereas the mean score for public schools was 112. Expressive controls also tend to be lower than in the public schools: on our score the mean for these paternalistic schools was 101 whereas that for the public schools was 196. The communities tend to be self-questioning, tinged with idealism, and statements such as the following are frequently heard:

> 'Our aim must be to produce a state which takes away the occasion for sanctions. This depends on a relationship between staff and pupils which, while preserving authority, attempts to break down the traditions of "us" and "them". To achieve this the effect of personal example is the biggest single contributory factor.'

Such a style is beginning in fact to develop a goal structure in which, unlike the public schools, warm relationships, caring for individuals, homeliness and choice are achieving parity with instrumental aims. However, many such schools are trapped in an uneasy balance between the divided and integrated policies of coeducation. For younger children the schools strike an acceptable balance between care, individuality and organization. For the older pupils, however, they are too paternalistic to win high commitment.[28]

The radical progressive schools. It is not the paternalistic schools, just described, whose cosy coeducational style rouses the ire and controversy associated with progressive education. This is reserved for the seven egalitarian or radical progressive schools which in this country educate about 1,500 pupils.[29] They are small and coeducational, but their goal stress is different from that of other boarding schools in that certain expressive goals dominate instrumental and organizational ones. However, the expressive aims pursued are not those of the public schools. In radical communities the main expressive aim is the development of the individual child's personality at its own rate, free from external pressures and restraints. This self-realization is to take place in a tolerant community where adolescent tastes, spontaneity and pleasures are held in high esteem, where the children will receive the maximum support for adult and peer relationships and will be liberated from the pressures of competition, parental expectations and orthodox aspirations. The personal, intellectual, athletic and manual aspects of an individual's development also receive great stress. Controls are few, and those sanctions which are thought to hinder relationships are minimized. Some of these schools have formerly been associated with certain esoteric practices such as vegetarianism, theosophy or naturism, though these are manifestations of a wider philosphy such as bringing up the child in an environment which is in tune with natural development.

In most of these schools the social provision tends to be superior to academic facilities. This is the opposite emphasis to that in many other boarding schools, such as the independent integrated schools. Also certain activities such as art, drama and music are sometimes cultivated at the expense of others such as sport or outdoor ventures. Staffing is generous, particularly in social areas, and many schools divide their pupils into small family-style groups with houseparents or housemothers in charge. The use of 'housefathers' and 'housemothers' signifies a world of difference from the public school style of 'housemaster'. The prominent role of women in these schools is not matched in any other styles of boarding except those found in schools for special populations like the handicapped or subnormal.

The egalitarian schools operate by reducing the controls imposed on the pupils so that, officially, there are few restrictions on movement, possessions, clothing and self-expression. In some schools even classes are voluntary, though most schools have abandoned this policy in recognition of the children's needs for defined boundaries and in order to improve their academic standards. In most of the schools there is no compulsion to attend religious meetings, to practice sports or to partake in social activities. Generous facilities are provided but pupils are expected to organize their own leisure and to do things voluntarily as the individual's personality and sense of purpose dictate. The children are given as much privacy as possible. In one school each child has its own room even at junior levels. Boys and girls mix freely and, in the most radical schools, corridors, lavatories and bathrooms are all mixed as in a family setting. Institutional control is therefore low, as Table 6:8 shows, though this table includes progressive schools of the paternalistic style. The mean scores for other schools are: public schools 112, independent 82, maintained 84 and all progressive 68. But the mean score for the four egalitarian communities which we studied is 51 (SD = 21) and one of these schools had a score of only 26, the lowest score of all the sixty-six boarding schools in our sample.

Nevertheless, despite this diminution of institutional control, pupils are subject to considerable pressures on behaviour, dress and values from their own pupil society. The informal society of the children sets the normative standards on which control rests so that informal norms define the limitations of dress, permitted relationships, political attitudes and modes of self-expression. The staff, too, find that they have to manipulate many of the pupils' attitudes in order to make relationships with them and in extreme cases find that their own values are greatly influenced by the pupils. Thus while control is essentially normative in that it is based on staff and community expectations, there is considerable manipulation by staff of the informal society of the pupils through their strong informal relations with them.

Despite such communities' apparent liberalism, therefore, and their radical stance, the power of the pupil society, the tendency to recruit from certain limited social groups, and for the children to be introduced to progressive values from an early age invest these egalitarian communities with elements of expressive totality. For example, on our score of expressive control, these schools scored significantly higher than in areas of institutional control, 70 as opposed to 51. Indeed, as Table 6:10 shows, the expressive control in these free schools is close to that of integrated and state schools which we will find to be so much more controlling in other respects.* This expressive totality leads to isolation and self-preoccupation. Relationships with the local community can be poor and the pupils' society can exert pressures and controls which are as encompassing as anything that might be imposed from above in a public school.

* Mean scores of expressive control: public schools 196, independent 172, integrated 89, progressive 76, state 68.

Nevertheless, the schools still win high commitment from the pupils, particularly as instrumental stress is slight, participation in decision-making is expected and pupil power is considerable.

Despite the generous social provision and the high ratio of staff to pupils, however, the informal system of the pupils puts less stress on academic skills than in other schools. Examination results can be poor, in spite of the small size of teaching groups and the fact that the children are often those of the radical intelligentsia. Such academic under-achievement may of course spring from a variety of causes. For example, many boys who attend such progressive schools are those who have presented problems of adjustment in different settings. It has long been one of the contradictions of the egalitarian progressive philosophy, ostensibly free in its educational and social approach and radical in ethos, that it seeks justification for such means by success in orthodox academic areas. Much recent research would suggest that there is a correspondence between what is defined as elitist knowledge and the mechanisms by which it is attained.

In terms of teaching methods and curriculum, the radical progressive schools vary. Some are very poorly equipped and less up-to-date than many other schools although classes generally are small. In some, the curriculum tends to be flexible and much free time is filled with activities such as spontaneous art, craft and music, while other schools are more orthodox. Competition and streaming are absent although for the older children the curriculum has to acknowledge the demands of O and A level examinations. Such schools have developed a curriculum which has much to offer the less able middle-class child, and the absence of academic pressure has helped many inadequate or insecure children who have under-achieved elsewhere. The developments in craft and engineering that these schools have pioneered will probably have helped in widening the social intake of the schools. Only recently, however, has any radical progressive school applied this approach to a number of working-class children.

Control in such schools is strictly normative in that it relies on the relationships between staff and pupils. Other than individual persuasion there are no major sanctions, apart from expulsion, which can be used in the schools. Members of staff have to gain control by force of their personality, which can cause considerable strain. Although all pupils are given a very considerable share in defining the school's role, routine and reputation, and often discuss in community meetings the suitability of sanctions, staff often manipulate such meetings to ensure that the children's power does not venture into unacceptable areas. Hence in reality much power rests in the hands of the headmaster whose role is almost quasi-religious, that of a charismatic leader of an expressive community. Far more than the paternalistic Quaker headmaster, the headmaster of a radical school has to act as an ultimate manipulator and unifier, ensuring that consensus is maintained and that democracy does not become disruptive. The secret is in seeing that the democratic processes work in accordance with his wishes. We saw earlier that roles of public school headmasters were not related to the goals of the schools. However, when schools of different sizes are compared it is clear that in small independent and progressive boarding schools, which usually have expressive aims, the headmaster has to take over expressive roles of pastoral care and leadership. The following table gives details of the headmasters' roles in schools of different sizes and confirms this:

TABLE 6:27

Size of school

Headmasters' role-sets	0-150 pupils	151+ pupils	Progressive School
Expressive roles dominant	7	18	5
Expressive roles subordinate	2	38	2

$\chi = 5\cdot1$, applying Yates' correction, $p < 0.05$.

Naturally the parents and governing bodies of progressive schools are from groups of the upper middle class whose attitudes to education and child rearing are more liberal than those of parents and staff in the public schools. Many such parents work in the communications industries, in the arts or in academic circles but, apart from including fewer clergy and commissioned officers, the intake in terms of occupation scarcely differs from that of a public school. Obviously all such parents are highly committed to this form of education and, unlike the public schools, opposition to change, if it occurs, tends to come from these groups rather than from pupils or staff in the school.

The structures of progressive schools make it easy for headmasters to introduce changes of a radical nature as there are few status positions among the staff to be threatened, little federalism of structure, and consensus is more easily obtained than in the public schools. However, while the stress on expressive goals and the expressive commitment of parents and old pupils can block the speed with which radical change is introduced, two radical-style progressive schools in our sample had been able to change their real goals in a short space of time.

In their social structure the radical schools fell into two kinds. One group caters for the same social class as public schools and has few children outside that economic level. They have no relationships with local authorities or state schools. They may have some children on reduced fees but most of their pupils are both upper middle class and educable to GCE standards. These schools therefore function like the public schools to fashion an elite, albeit a creative, nonconforming one. The other group of schools, usually smaller, less well equipped and economically precarious, is sought after by fee-paying parents with children who have experienced educational difficulties and by local authorities anxious to place pupils who are psychologically maladjusted or educationally in need of special help. These schools are therefore socially broader than the former: as many as thirty to forty per cent of the pupils may be sponsored by LEAs. They are in fact closer to special schools in their composition, objectives and problems than are the other radical schools or maintained boarding ones for less problematic youngsters.

It would be wrong to assume that progressive schools are disordered, promiscuous and unacademic. The style of co-education is free, sexual liaisons do occur between boys and girls and are often deep, but the informal society of the pupils does much to ensure disapproval of promiscuity and the staff are sensitive in the handling of these situations. Sexual problems are not particualry prominent. Much more serious is the tendency for the strong pupil society to introduce a conformist culture and limit the impact of staff. Also, intense social life and the joys of adolescence can result in an under-use of facilities and under-achievement academically. The absence of of external structure and direction is not always matched by the young person's own firmness of aim or self-discipline.

The radical progressive schools succeed in winning a higher commitment from children in a residential setting than in any other school.[30] Such commitment comes from all pupils, even those educated in different styles beforehand. More boys come from other schools than girls because parents are more reluctant to consign their sons to the unpredictable progressive style than their daughters unless the boy has some serious need or has failed elsewhere. Not a few of the girls in radical progressive schools have brothers in the top public schools. This pattern leads to a tendency for the radical schools to be dominated by the girls, with the apparent emasculation of boys and isolation for those who cannot or do not wish to partake in their rich social life. It is not surprising, therefore, that the influence of the radical progressive schools has been greatest in special and in primary education, for here, away from the academically competitive world, are their nearest parallels.

Though other schools have become more child centred and flexible, the radical schools are still unique at secondary levels in their approach to the child, in their freedom, their co-educational living, their participation in decision-making, and in the closeness and informality of staff-pupil relations. The freedom of the coeducational structure varies, as we have seen, but boys and girls are generally free to mix socially and grow emotionally in a way that they are not in other schools, and there is a genuine attempt to allow children to use staff of the opposite sex for pastoral purposes. Indeed our tests reported in Chapter 8 show these schools to be pastorally the most effective of all those on our sample. We have seen elsewhere that the commitment in the more egalitarian schools is the highest of all boarding schools. One problem of such communities is, however, that the pupil society can become uncritical in its commitment to the school and because of its cohesion can induce a rigid conformity in its members and so reduce the benefits of the school's liberal regime.

Smaller independent schools. Yet another constitutional category of independent schools produces a distinctive style of boarding with a pronounced expressive emphasis. These are those government-recognized independent schools which, from the point of view of academic standards, social structure and educational classification are not public schools but still admit a majority of fee payers. Many are small in size and some are even owned privately by the headmaster although most, like prep schools, are now administered by private trusts.[31]

We visited six smaller independent schools which as a group filled some of the inadequacies presented by the selective nature of the public schools. The common entrance to the public schools may not be a steep hurdle to most boys but it defeats some; in addition a few boys in their preparatory schools can clearly be seen to need more support than would probably be forthcoming in public school structures. Parents who believe in boarding, with less able or with sensitive children, but who do not subscribe to the progressive ethos, support these smaller independent schools which rarely have more than a hundred and fifty boys and are more flexible in their organization. They attract not only middle-class parents but also the interest of the local education authorities for placing maladjusted or difficult children.

Some schools in their structures reflect small public schools. There is a stress on group loyalty, service and independence and also a strong Christian emphasis. Their official goals are largely expressive with an official emphasis on cultural, managerial and moral qualities. However, the resources at the schools' disposal are meagre compared with those of HMC schools. Staff-pupil ratios are lower, facilities and buildings are poorer, the curriculum is narrower and less imaginative, and academic standards are lower. It is these schools which consistently show the largest discrepancy in our questionnaire on goals between what pupils think that the school should do and what it is actually trying to achieve, between its clients' aspirations and their realization. The attempt to apply the public school model to children who are less academically gifted, when facilities are poor and limited by the small size, leads to a situation where pupils' alienation, as measured by such tests, is higher than in any other group of the schools we studied (see Appendix II, Table 4).

Not all the remaining independent schools, however, are of this type, for there is another group which pursues some of the expressive qualities of the public school, such as pastoral care and moral training, but which have developed structures and a curriculum for the less able or emotionally immature children who have failed to enter the more prestigious establishments.

In these schools a hundred or fewer boys spend their time isolated in the depths of the English countryside, in buildings which cluster round crumbling mansions once owned by prosperous businessmen or landed gentry. No wonder then that this group of schools is often identified with the least attractive image of boarding education. Small, isolated, single-sex, and sometimes poorly equipped and unaccountable to public authorities, these can be variations on a 'Dotheboys Hall' from which occasional scandals of excessive punishments, starvation diet or perverted staff emerge to titillate the readers of the Sunday papers.

Such an image, we found, is largely unmerited. The ministry-recognized schools of this type among our random sample had none of these dubious qualities. Indeed these small schools which support the inadequate middle-class child represented an important contribution to boarding education, a unique style with certain features which distinguish them from all other styles.

The instrumental emphases in these schools is very strong and, as we shall see, tends to relate to the low academic ability of the intake by concentrating on the narrow areas of gaining good results in public examinations. For example, one such school had a thirty-eight-period weekly timetable and home-work every day, including Sunday. The expressive emphasis, however, differs from that of both public and progressive schools. While there is an emphasis on care for the individual and his needs, this is less pronounced than in progressive or Quaker schools and is combined with some, but not all, the expressive goals stressed by public schools. Though leadership and elite preparation are rejected as goals because of the intellectual limitations of the children and the small proportion of older boys, which prevent the establishment of a public school house or prefect system, goals of social responsibility, sportsmanship and ethical Christian standards are all stressed.

Cultural standards, too, are less high pitched, one school, for example, proudly presented *Seagulls over Sorrento* for its annual play. Nevertheless the structure is still authoritarian in that there are no democratic committees or participation and boys are expected to obey orders from staff and to undergo considerable academic pressure. Expressive control is high on our scale at a mean of 172 compared with 196 in public schools and scores of below 89 for the other kinds of boarding schools. The organizational stress, however, is much less pronounced than in public schools, although restrictions and control are high in some special areas such as compulsory activity. The schools' mean score on our scale of institutional control was only 82, as against 112 in public schools, 118 in integrated and 84 in maintained schools. Other features of the boarding style are more like the radical and Quaker styles, which we have indentified; thus uniforms scarcely exist, and the more homely atmosphere and flexibility of routine which intimate size and centralized power make possible reduce the need for rigid, impersonal organization. Hence the goal pattern in these schools has features found in both Quaker and radical schools.

Some of these small schools are also among the most 'integrated' of all independent boarding schools, for as many as one-third to a half of the pupils are paid for by local authorities. Most of these are lower-middle or working-class children who are in the care of the authority or whose family circumstances necessitate placement in a boarding school. The style of boarding found in these schools, a straightforward academic education set in a regime which offers more individual care and support and is less competitive than that of a public school, is attractive to authorities who seek boarding schools which are for the individual child but which do not have the facilities and, some would say, carry the stigma of a special school.

Most of the children, however, are from middle-class fee-paying homes. Very few of these have been sent to such schools as a matter of family tradition and many are those who hold the unenviable position of being the less able child in an upper-class family. Some of these children present great problems to the school in that they have feelings of failure and rejection, especially when their brothers and sisters are doing well at famous public schools. Some cases are even more tragic, those of children who have been virtually abandoned by parents who choose to solve their marital problems by shedding their children into the care of a minor and relatively cheap boarding school.

These features of the intake into these small schools are shown in the following table, which examines the intake into one small independent school.

TABLE 6:28

Features of intake into a small independent school

Total boys in school	84	
Paid for by LEA	25	30 per cent
Parents abroad	10	12
Fee-paying but from very bad homes	6	7

Nearly half the children had needs other than those shown by poor academic performance.

Although in the better schools there are original projects taking place, there tends to be considerable cramming for O level and other examinations such as those of the Royal Society of Arts. Parents want the school to give their children elementary qualifications to allow their boys to enter professions. From one small school, in 1966, the fourteen leavers joined banks, the forces and the police, but few went on to colleges, as the following table shows:

TABLE 6:29

Jobs taken by leavers from one small school in 1966

Farming	4	
Services	2	
Accountancy/surveying/bank	3	
Police	4	
Apprenticeships		
Building		
Mechanic	1	
Technical college		Total: 14

The style of teaching, therefore, tends to be based on

individual tuition and teaching groups of less than ten, but the range of subjects and content of lessons are extremely orthodox, as examination passes are so important. While the organization of the teaching is geared to less able children, the methods used tend to be pressured. This tendency is reinforced by the backgrounds of staff, who are usually fully trained but limited in their experience of teaching less able boys. In one school, for example, three of the nine staff had gone to public schools and only one had taught in a non-selective state school. Few staff have had experience of modern remedial teaching methods and, in any case, often have to teach three or more subjects. The shortage of money for facilities also limits what the staff can achieve, and in times of economies teachers may be sacked, which leads to a feeling of insecurity and a ritualistic approach to their work. Again, it is only fair to point out that individual schools are different and that there are extremes. For example, in one school there was good equipment and imaginative, experimental teaching while in another, boys were regularly caned for failing exams.

Despite the advantages of the informal, relaxed atmosphere and the individual care given to boys, the small size and correspondingly small number of staff pose problems of lack of facilities and activities. Shortage of money also limits the scope of what can be offered. This is particularly true at weekends, when geographical isolation often forces boys to remain in a school which offers little variety in activities other than games. In one school the research worker's diary noted that it was hard to believe that the boys who were happily sitting in a comfortable house room round the television and eating their tea from a kitchen trolley were the same group who had spent the afternoon idling away at table-tennis, the only indoor activity provided on a wet day.

These small schools, more than any other type, are greatly influenced by the calibre of the headmaster and two or three of his senior staff. They carry the brunt of the teaching, discipline and expressive example and in a way the schools are very similar to the preparatory schools in this respect. One headmaster, for example, described his predecessor's educational theories as:

'When they couldn't think of anything else to do, they

played hunt-the-thimble,'

and he described how difficult it was to reinvigorate the community on his arrival. By contrast, even in small progressive schools the quality of the school depends less on the policies of the headmaster, for the expressive goal stress of the school, its emphatic and distinct philosophy and the cultural expectations of parents define clearly the roles that staff have to play. In the smaller independent schools the goals are less clearly defined and consequently headmasters are more free to work out the school's policy.

These schools, therefore, are an appendage to the public school system in that they admit fee-paying children who have failed to win places in more prestigious schools. In goals and curriculum they show many features of the public schools but many schools are more personal and homely and offer greater individual attention.

Conclusion

Those schools which give stress to expressive goals, either giving them parity with instrumental and organizational goals as in the public and smaller independent schools or allowing expressive goals to predominate as in the radical progressive schools, all share certain structural features. They recognize the importance of the informal world of pupils in a way that schools with an instrumental goal stress do not. This world is either fragmented or penetrated by various structural devices which allow official values great influence, as in public, preparatory and independent schools, or a strong coherent pupil world survives which can be subtly manipulated by staff, as in the progressive schools.

All these schools take children who board early, are isolated from home and local contacts either deliberately, in the case of the public, preparatory and independent schools, or involuntarily, as in the case of progressive schools. Long stays in residential communities build up a dependence on them to meet a whole variety of physical and emotional needs. While this dependence should not be confused with institutionalization, which is a form of personality disintegration, it does make all children who have boarded for a long period susceptible to the normative control processes and value manipulations of their schools. This is in strong contrast to children in those schools dominated by instrumental ends. They have boarded for a much shorter time, are therefore less dependent on their institution, are controlled by more utilitarian means and respond in a much more calculative way.

Naturally schools which pursue expressive goals differ. We have noted that the distribution of power is more explicit in public schools and their expressive goals of loyalty, obedience and selflessness are compatible with a high organizational level. It may be that much of the high control levels in public, preparatory and independent schools are survivals from a period when they were avenues of upward social mobility and were inculcating new values in the young rather than reinforcing class mores as they do today. All schools with expressive goals share another common feature: they are part of a wider allocative system in a way that the schools which pursue instrumental ends are not. The destinations of their pupils are the executive and administrative positions in society. They may either view them, like the public schools, as an inevitable duty, covet such positions like the independent schools, deny their relevance as do the progressive schools. However, they cannot escape their functions for society and in this respect, as a group, they differ from the more instrumentally oriented schools to which we now turn.

7 The different styles of boarding (2) Instrumental and organizational styles

Not all the sixty-six schools in our sample display the strong expressive stress which characterizes public, preparatory, progressive and smaller independent schools. The fact that these schools form a majority of our sample should not divert our attention from other important schools where the emphasis of goals is more instrumental and organizational. In two of our constitutional categories, the integrated independent and state boarding schools, the goal stress of most schools shows this pattern. The variations among the individual schools which compose these categories, however, are wider and more extreme than for public and progressive schools. State boarding schools vary even more widely than integrated ones as they do not belong to any clear tradition of boarding and have developed independently of one another. Nevertheless, these state schools in general share a distinct ethos and will be discussed as a separate group.

We shall treat first those boarding schools which, although constitutionally independent of the state system, admit a large proportion of children, half or more, whose fees are paid by local authorities.

The independent integrated schools

These schools link themselves to the maintained sector of education in a variety of ways. Some schools were founded long ago as charitable institutions for the deprived and continue at the present time to offer shelter for children with needs for boarding. Other schools are used by local authorities because of the vocational stress or specialist training they offer, such as in agriculture or forestry.[1]

We have already seen that some small independent schools are integrated in that the local authority pays fees for individual children with boarding need, but these schools offer a regime

which is suitable for such children and are not formally
'integrated' as a matter of deliberate policy or because of their
vocational teaching.

A number of independent integrated schools were originally
founded as charitable institutions. They once had clear welfare
functions but with the growth of the social services and higher
standards of living their present role is less clear. Many of these
schools are now classified as independent schools, although such
a constitutional character masks the unique nature of their
intake.

They form a clear group among boarding schools both in the
functions they serve for wider society and the styles of boarding
that they operate. They set out to provide care for orphaned
or under-privileged children and some were specifically
endowed for this purpose alone. Before the growth of the child
care services and special education these schools, some of which
are called hospitals or blue-coat schools, were an important
agent in residential child care. A number of famous public
schools, for example, were originally founded to provide
education for the poor and neglected; few continue to serve
such aims and most have become fee-charging schools for the
well-to-do. However, many charitable trust schools still have
funds or foundation awards available to enable needy children
to receive a free education.

Owing to the rising cost of education the foundation funds
of these schools have been insufficient to maintain educational
and residential standards and most of these schools have had to
find other sources of revenue. This has posed considerable
ethical and organizational problems for them and several
solutions have been devised. Some schools have now become
voluntary aided or direct grant schools with a minority of
boarding places which can be paid from the foundation's funds.
Others have remained completely boarding and have sought to
admit children whose fees are paid by local authority social
service departments. A number of others have opted for
compromise and have kept a minority of foundation awards
for their needy children while offering the remaining places to
fee payers from wealthy backgrounds.

Integrated schools differ from the public schools in their
stress on instrumental and organizational areas. They do not

have the features of residential schools which have been specifically structured to meet the special needs of children such as maladjusted schools and community homes. In fact these charity schools provide shelter in a very spartan environment and offer an academic education rather than a caring regime. Schools that have become part of the state system operate predominantly as if they were day schools to which small boarding sections are attached; while the provision and standards in the academic departments are high, boarding provision is usually limited, poorly equipped and haphazardly staffed.

In some of them the contrast between the academic and the social provision is very striking. Large dormitories are often unheated, recreation rooms are ill equipped and over crowded and dining halls are institutionally furnished, with long antique tables and benches worn thin by years of use. Privacy and comfort are minimal. In one school, for example, on our last visit in 1972 sixty boys slept in one large bare dormitory lit by curtainless windows and two bare bulbs and store their clothes in baskets under the serried ranks of beds. There were no recreational facilities for junior boys or individual studies for senior boys. Yet the poor facilities of the boarding side often stand in sharp contrast to the well-equipped libraries, modern laboratories and open classrooms of the academic sub-units, a clear reflection of the predominantly instrumental stress of these institutions. The boarding accommodation is usually separate from the main school, housed in one gaunt institutional block rather than distributed as houses across a wide campus as in most public schools. Social subdivisions are by dormitories or landings.

Many ancient rituals of dress, showers, church walks, feet and hands inspections and ceremonies of admission still persist in these schools, reminding us of the negative stripping of identity and compulsory routines described by Goffman in his studies of custodial institutions.[2] The boarders, who are accorded little privacy, are often supervised by resident teachers. Such men have none of the status, rewards or power of their public school housemaster counterparts and receive relatively less help from the prefects, whose roles are confined to mere matters of discipline and organization. For example, a housemaster in such a school described his role as follows:

'I have nothing to do with admissions. I never deal with mail and only see parents at parents' evenings or plays. Most I never see. I am, of course, a teacher but my main job in the boarding house is keeping discipline when I am on duty two nights a week and one weekend in four. The prefects see that the boys go to bed but I am responsible on my duty nights for keeping discipline and might have to cane a boy or give a detention. There are four of us, all single, and we get free living in the block for doing these duties. Naturally I get to know some boys very well, especially those in my sixth form, but I have no official responsibility for this. The careers master, for example, does university entrance and fitting up boys' jobs.'

Housemasters' duties in this school are predominantly organizational and, unlike the case of the public school house-master, little official emphasis is placed on pastoral care or on exercising a moral influence on the boys. Residential duties are the price of free living for young single teachers, many of whom are saving up to get married and who are not, as are public school housemasters, in a position of influence. The few women employed in such schools are confined to organizational, domestic and health duties and they have little contact with the boys, less than in public schools. Naturally, this should not imply that in practice staff neglect the boys, indeed many of them are highly involved simply because they view their boarders as being deprived of home comforts and having less status than the day boys. Hence they take boys out at weekends, entertain them and offer considerable support and pastoral care. But the important contrast lies in the narrow definition and haphazard organization of staff roles in such schools when compared with the complex and precise arrangements of the public schools.

Such schools are frequently autocratic and all important decisions are made by the headmaster. He delegates little of his authority and frequently runs the school as if it were a day school, showing little interest or concern for the boarding side. Few members of staff, including senior ones in these schools, have anything to do with the boarding houses, and the main sub-units and positions of responsibility are in the academic departments much as in the ordinary day schools. Boarding staff have little influence on policy decisions, and the boys none at all. Prefects in these schools have little of the authority and independence and none of the expressive role of public school prefects and even in the boarding houses their duties are confined to organizational matters such as supervising prep and controlling dormitories.

Many of these integrated schools exert high levels of institutional control, especially by according the boys little privacy. The mean score for schools of this type in our sample is 105 (SD=22), very similar to that of public schools. Naturally in schools with such an instrumental and organizational stress, expressive control is low; rewards and sanctions therefore tend to be utilitarian, showing little of the control and the manipulation of relationships, feelings and expectations which are found in public and progressive schools.

The absence of hierarchies and of small sub-units means that the informal system of both boys and staff tends to be stronger and to cohere in a way that is different from that of the public schools. However, as the goal stress is instrumental and many boys are selected on academic criteria, there is little alienation from the predominantly academic goals. But the spartan living conditions are less easily tolerated. In such communities the needs of the less able and emotionally deprived are not met and it is in this group that withdrawal and rebellion are most evident. Unlike the public schools, where rebellion is highly functional as it highlights moral and political issues, in integrated schools such a response on the part of the pupils questions the orientation of implemented goals. Hence rebellion or criticism by the pupils is ruthlessly suppressed. However as expressive goals in these schools are few and little emphasized there is little of the extreme alienation from such ends found in other integrated schools.

Far more staff appear to be alienated in these schools than in public schools even though their roles are largely confined to teaching and administration. There is often a cleavage of interests between the majority of the day staff, who know little of the boarding situation, and the resident staff, who resent the disparity between academic and social provision in the school. The informal social system of the staff, as in many day schools, puts a high premium on academic achievement and on discipline and is very conservative with regard to change, and suspicious of the informal relationships between staff and pupils that the residential situation fosters. Hence the staff in such schools lack consensus and some have disintegrated into hostile camps.

A second group of charity schools has faced the problem of increasing costs and inadequate resources in another way. Some have developed close liaisons with local authority social service and education departments which buy places for children who have specific boarding need. For example, one such school we visited had only fourteen per cent of its children financed from the original endowment and it filled the remaining places (322 children) with nominees from the local education authority. The background of these children clearly shows considerable family dislocation and a proportion of children whose parents are overseas are also admitted (see Table 7:1).

Although pressures caused by their pupils' background force these schools to be more aware of, and to make provision for, the needs of their clientele, such as the tolerance of enuresis, absconding or tantrums, many elements of the charity foundations still prevail both in the instrumental goal stress and in aspects of school structure. The boarding provision is, however, normally better equipped than in the previous type of charity school but institutional features in dress, routine and aspects of staff-pupil relationships remain. However, the residential provision is strengthened: houses are small and often purpose built, housemasters are status appointments, having more independence and well-defined pastoral responsibilities. While power still resides in the hands of the headmaster, he is more open to influence at staff meetings.

Some of these schools are coeducational but their style is usually cautious, that of a divided community with virtually separate schools for boys and girls rather than the mixed style common in Quaker and the integrated one found in radical progressive schools. Rules such as:

'The opposite sex must be treated with respect and consideration, as shown in a good family atmosphere.
Clandestine meetings are not to be arranged.'

are common. Sometimes the schools for senior boys and girls

are separated by many miles and there is little mutual contact. Other schools are single-sex at secondary level but mixed for juniors. Nevertheless these schools have made some approach towards designing a boarding experience which offers the children more support than the academically oriented charity schools.

TABLE 7:1

Social categories under which children were admitted to one integrated school (see p. 175)

(January 1966)

Social categories	Boys	Girls	Total
Parents divorced	42	26	68
Parents separated	24	28	52
Parent widowed	58	70	128
Illness in family	21	15	36
Bad home conditions	8	2	10
Travel difficulties due to living in isolated area	–	5	5
Mother not married	8	4	12
Adopted	2	1	3
In care of local authority	4	4	8
Orphans (both parents dead)	9	2	11
Staff children	3	3	6
Total	179	160	339
Social categories			
Overseas: missionary	8	14	22
Overseas: diplomatic service	6	2	8
Overseas: services	23	28	51
Overseas: others	11	7	18
Total	48	51	99
Total number of children	227	211	438

NB Each child has been put in one category only, though many come under more than one. However, the primary reason for the child's admission has been chosen. In some cases circumstances have changed since entering the school, e.g. remarriage of the parent, death of parents, etc.

In contrast to the first kind of charity schools, the informal social system of staff in these is usually more committed than that of the boys to the aims of the school. More staff are involved in residential duties and many are motivated by religious or social beliefs. Residential duty also carries more status and reward than in other charity schools. Nevertheless the high controls and the unwillingness to give any responsibility or power to pupils, especially in mixed schools, leads to alienation among older pupils who find such a regime overpowering and fraudulent in its concern. Many expressive features of warm relationships and pastoral care are therefore rejected by the pupils, and their alienation can spread to influence their attitudes to academic matters. In several coeducational schools of this type a rich compensatory under-life had developed which afforded the pupils the chance to meet the opposite sex. It was notable that the opportunities given by a coeducational system and an involved staff were lost because the regime was unable to relax control and grant the pupils some individuality and influence.

The third group of independent integrated schools have kept a core of their foundation places and made other places available to fee payers. These schools face more serious difficulties than other integrated schools, for it is difficult to meet adequately the goal expectations of the different groups in the school. For example, the foundation boys from lower-middle and working-class homes resist much of the expressive stress, the public school tone, which is required to attract fee-paying parents. Minor issues which symbolize such conflict, such as rugger versus soccer as a major sport, or the wearing of a distinctive uniform, engender conflict between boys and staff and among the boys themselves. Other pressures multiply; for example, one headmaster in a desperate effort to achieve sufficient GCE results to ease his election to the HMC, increased the number of teaching periods to forty-three a week and then wondered at his boys' resentment.[3]

In such situations divisions between the staff intensify. Young teachers become swiftly disillusioned.

'I didn't come here to teach the sons of local snobs but to help unfortunate lads', said one teacher. 'I don't get much of a chance'.

The pupils also become divided, as their ratings on goals show.[4]

The working-class group show instrumental commitment and expressive alienation, a position which is reversed amongst the less able fee payers. External bodies, such as old boys' organizations and governors, debate whether the school has sold its soul to independent education, while aspirant fee-paying parents demand more of public school style, endlessly requesting more distinctive uniform or the introduction of cadet corps. These informal attitudes and the narrow concept of residence which these integrated schools display mean that apart from instrumental skills little is offered to either foundationer or fee payer. Indeed everyone in the community becomes a casualty of the lack of consensus on goals. To weld these disparate groups together these schools frequently become highly custodial. An evil potential is seen in almost every activity. For example, a rule from a mixed charity school ran as follows:

> Contraband articles are: matches, cigarettes, lighters, lighter fuel, explosive and inflammable mixtures, air rifles, air pistols, ammunition of any kind, keys, sheath knives, stilettos, or any other form of dangerous weapon, playing cards, undesirable literature, electric razors, cosmetics, certain articles of jewellery, comics unless approved, and then only to members of Form One.

Indeed this administrative solution to problems which face several charity schools seems to be the least satisfactory of all, for the inability to reconcile conflicting goals leads to serious hostility among staff and to alienation among all senior pupils.[5]

Vocational schools

Some integrated schools are vocational: they bring together pupils who require a specialized training such as musical education, ballet tuition or preparation for life in the armed services. Although instrumental in the sense that they are training children for specific careers, this does not mean that these schools lack an expressive component. For example, ballet dancers or Royal Naval officers require expressive involvements which are fostered in the ethos of vocational schools. Loyalty, reliability, service and perfection are all qualities that such training aims to foster in addition to furnishing technical skills. But others, such as the farming and building schools which we studied, had little expressive stress and the real goals remained predominantly instrumental.

Naturally, these schools belonged to others of our constitutional categories and therefore reflect features of these styles. We visited six boarding schools which were vocational: three were state boarding schools, one a technical grammar school and two were independent integrated schools in that local authorities paid for boys to attend. Two schools prepared boys for the navy: one for the royal navy and one for the merchant navy. One school trained future farmers, another building workers, another engineers, and the sixth was an independent school run by a Catholic group of missionary priests, which granted free admission to boys who were contemplating the priesthood. As would be expected, these vocational schools which are very instrumental in their goals are less total than those which stress expressive aims. This is generally the case, as the following table shows.

TABLE 7:2

Scores of institutional control in the six
vocational schools visited

Implemented goal stress instrumental only:	50	72	101
Implemented goal stress instrumental and expressive:	157	155	97

Thus the level of institutional control is low in the schools which offered a training in technical and practical subjects. The curriculum and activities were all centred round these subjects and few other controls were imposed. As the pupils were self-selecting, they could legitimately be asked to leave courses if they showed no interest or were troublesome. But vocational schools where the stress was more expressive tended to exercise far greater institutional control.

There was, however, one exception. This was the school which admitted working-class boys who were considering joining a group of missionary priests. Although this was a religious community, the curriculum was that of a good grammar school and the atmosphere was designed to create an environment in which boys could carefully consider their vocation. Far from being a closed community, this school was one of the most sensitive of all to the needs of its working-class intake and most of the institutional control score of 97 was made up by the lack of privacy due to old buildings. In other respects this school was open, flexible, democratic and allowed considerable scope for self-expression.

Sometimes these vocational schools were rich in interest for the sociologist. For example, the naval schools were characterized by strong pupil informal systems rich in informal rituals and traditions. The boys used slang that had survived unchanged from Trafalgar. In hierarchies both formal and informal and in the nexus of relationships between inmates these schools resembled ships of the line. Indeed boys who ran away were posted up on the noticeboard as having abandoned ship. This style, its bugles, pipings, log-keepings, which seemed so strange to the participant observer, created an expressive ethos geared to the officer roles that boys would soon be playing at sea. Many of the rituals and traditions fostered a sense of security for, interestingly, one such school had more boys from disrupted and disintegrated homes than any other school in our sample.

These vocational schools therefore fall very clearly into those that stress instrumental goals and those that add expressive features to their primary training role. The former schools are practical and non-total and residence is secondary to the acquisition of skills. However, in the second group expressive goals are as important as instrumental ones and residence is significant in maximizing expressive stress. These schools are among the most highly controlled of all that we visited. Such control, however, does not alienate the majority of the boys, because they are committed to such training and they are in their schools voluntarily. Similarly, the concern of staff for boys is greater than would be expected in other total institutions. Yet such regimes do cause great suffering to those boys who have lost interest in the specified vocation. In these schools, therefore, there is usually a number of rebellious boys who, unlike their counterparts in a public school, have no legitimate or semi-legitimate outlets through which they can express their hostility.

The experience of these vocational schools should be more

widely known, as should the contribution in this vocational area of the erstwhile approved schools, now community schools. The ability of these residential communities to re-motivate boys who have failed in other schools and to use the working situation as a base from which many other skills may be practised or mastered could be of relevance to all those in their last years at secondary schools.

State boarding schools

Most of the boarding provision which we have been discussing is in the independent sector of education. It would be wrong to assume, however, that local education authorities make no provision of their own for residential education. Some authorities choose to buy places in independent schools for children in need of boarding and we have seen that the Quaker, charity and many small independent schools admit children whose fees are paid from public funds. Nevertheless there are nineteen boarding schools which are under the full control of the local authority and these provide places for nearly four thousand children. In addition to these schools there are a further hundred and twenty hostels which are attached to maintained day schools. These provide accommodation for children from remote areas, whose parents are abroad or mobile, or for children who have other needs. In all, these hostels provide nearly seven thousand boarding places.

Table 7:3 gives further details of the numbers of schools operated by local authorities and the places they provide. It is clear that in any consideration of boarding education the State's contribution should not be ignored.

The nineteen state boarding schools which have a majority of boarders have a very varied history. Some have grown out of past residential provision such as camp or open-air schools, some from ailing private schools taken over by local authorities, while others have been purpose built to provide facilities for local children such as those from remote rural areas or whose parents serve in the armed forces. The resulting provision is therefore haphazard and lacks common purpose.[6] Some schools are academically selective and others are not, some are coeducational and others are single-sex. Some can show off exciting gleaming

TABLE 7:3

Incidence of state boarding provision for ordinary children
in England and Wales

	No. of schools	Grammar	Secondary Modern	Comprehensive	Technical	Bilateral	Primary	Boys	Girls	Mixed	Places	No. of LEAs having provision
Fully boarding	13	2	10	0	0	0	1	4	1	8	3000	9
50-100 per cent boarding	6	4	0	0	2	0	0	5	0	1	900	5
Less than 50 per cent boarding	123	97	5	11	2	4	4	57	27	39	6500	52

buildings while others are forced to exist in squalid encampments of nissen huts. Indeed, while the physical provision varies greatly, generally state boarding schools are smaller in size and less generously provisioned than most public schools. In playing fields and capital equipment such as swimming baths, libraries and residential accommodation they are deficient. For example, fourteen per cent of public school boys sleep in single or double rooms compared with two per cent of boys in state boarding schools. At the other extreme twenty-seven per cent of state boarders sleep in dormitories of more than twenty boys, compared with only fifteen per cent in the public schools. Nevertheless these figures are averages and they mask the considerable variation that exists within the system. In some ways, however, state boarding schools are of considerable relevance, for some have developed styles of boarding which are particularly suited to working-class children.

We have already seen that the goal pattern of the state schools is much more instrumental than that of others. Indeed many staff and pupils believe that the real benefit of boarding is the increased opportunities which it offers for study. Only a few schools stress the expressive goals of close relationships between staff and pupils or pastoral care. Many state boarding schools were highly organized, controlled and inflexible.

As the philosophy of state boarding schools and the functions they serve for society are ill-defined, their structure and style depend largely on tradition and the imagination of heads and senior staff. They varied extremely. Hence some state boarding schools, sensitive to the needs of their children, were co-educational of the mixed kind and had many features of the radical progressive schools in their reduction of pressure on the child and democratic decision-making processes. Other schools were custodial and repressive. The state boarding schools seemed open to change, for their functions and their goals are less rigidly defined by parents, governors or old pupils. Some of these schools were innovating local, weekly or flexible boarding patterns by which children can easily transfer from boarding to day education as their age and needs vary. In some cases the level of institutional control in these schools was even lower than that of the self-styled progressive schools. Their atmosphere was warm and homely. A number of other schools developed close contact with parents by having regular parents' meetings or by encouraging parents to come into the school to take activities or to help in moments of crisis.

In contrast to these original, forward-looking structures, some other state boarding schools enshrined all that can be negative in boarding education. They were more restrictive than any of the public schools and imposed high levels of institutional control; in fact the highest score of 192 was greater than that of any other school in our sample. Such schools were closed to the outside world, saw little of their parents and offered children very little stimulation in the residential situation.

Despite these contrasts between individual schools, there are many features of state boarding schools which are common. They stress instrumental aims and have a high organizational goal stress. They are bureaucratic in structure and staff are accorded little autonomy. There is no clearly organized house system in them and correspondingly nothing which resembles the powerful position of a public school housemaster. The schools are more centralized in structure and most of the financial allowances to staff are for academic responsibility. In some state schools, housemasters are appointed specifically to run a boarding unit and may be given a small payment and free living, although they are expected to teach a full timetable. In other schools the staff in charge of residential units are merely those single ones who wish to live in and get cheap accommodation in exchange for undertaking residential duties. However, in all state boarding schools residential responsibility is paid at a much lower rate than academic position and, unlike their counterparts in the public school, the house staff only have responsibility for day-to-day decisions, as the headmaster retains overall power. Although the headmaster is rarely involved in the boarding side the housemasters are not the powerful, highly paid or prestigious group that can be found in any public school. In state boarding schools housemasters can also be heads of academic departments and this provides them with more status and rewards than their residential office. From the point of view of the staff, state boarding schools tend to operate as if they were predominantly day schools where the residential side forms one department. Although facilities differ the staffing is usually less generous than in most independent schools.

There are fewer sub-units than in a public school and little responsibility is delegated to house staff. In general, however, some schools have separate house units like public schools, some attempt family-style 'home' units, others use the form or dormitory as the basic unit of organization and pastoral care. There is little need for the endless procedures for communication among heads of sub-units which occur in public schools. Among the pupils, also, there are fewer hierarchies or positions of status than in a public school. Prefects, for example, play only organizational roles of getting children up and keeping order and accept none of the expressive involvements of their public school counterparts. Pastoral care, fostering spirit, loyalty and sportsmanship are not the roles sought by prefects in state boarding schools.

In their curricula state boarding schools reflect their equivalents in the day system. Six of the schools we studied offered a rather unimaginative grammar school curriculum with all their children working towards A or O level examinations. Ten schools were equivalent to secondary modern schools with CSE dominating the curriculum and no advanced work. In these schools team teaching, integrated studies and project work were more widely in evidence. However, unlike some public and progressive schools, few state schools of whatever academic orientation seemed to use the residential situation for academic purposes. Usually the teaching and the residential aspects were distinct and little attempt was made to benefit from the boarding situation by re-timing lessons, projects or extended local visits. This is in strong contrast to the public and progressive schools, where academic activity is stimulated by evening sessions, visiting lecturers, external visits and projects.

In other areas there are also considerable differences. The levels of control, for example, vary considerably in different state boarding schools. While expressive control is normally low, institutional control varies very widely, the scores ranging from 19 to 192. The mean score for institutional control was 84 but the true standard deviation for this was 38. A small number of state schools have adopted a flexible system of boarding which allows the pupils access to their homes and to the outside world, a recognition that seventy per cent of state boarders come from homes in the immediate vicinity. The informality, openness and homeliness of such regimes are a significant growth point for residential education and are reminiscent of many of the features of special residential education. Other state boarding schools impose high restrictions on dress, access to the outside world and a whole range of academic and social activities yet they make little effort to influence the moral and spiritual stance of their pupils.

Consequently the state boarding schools are not homogeneous when it comes to making comparisons with our earlier group of schools. Some are rigid and highly controlled, others are flexible and open to the outside world. In about half of the co-educational schools boys and girls were segregated: one school even had an invisible dividing line down the playground. In the others mixed styles of coeducation prevailed. One state boarding school allowed its pupils no personal contact with home or parents during the term, and even forbade the use of the telephone, whereas two other schools allowed contact every weekend. In comparison the public schools tend to be much more consistent and almost all allow visits from parents every few weeks and outside excursions for their boys.

There may be many explanations for this variation. Commitment to instrumental goals is less influenced by high levels of control than is commitment to expressive goals, and widespread ritualism on the part of pupils in instrumental areas still

achieves a level of success in academic and work skills. In some
cherished goal areas the schools can see themselves as achieving
considerable success. Other cogent reasons for state boarding
schools adopting a cautious approach to the opportunities
offered by the residential setting is their staff's unfamiliarity
with anything other than day school situations. Less than two
per cent of staff in state boarding schools had been educated in
residential schools themselves and many seemed quite unaware
that boarding can mean more than a bed, undisturbed homework time and the occasional game of ping-pong.[7] As these
schools have developed few of the mechanisms for penetrating,
fragmenting and manipulating the informal world of their
pupils, the problematic nature of much of the pupils' informal
activity thrusts some schools into a highly custodial stance.
The informal world of the pupils is more turbulent in state
boarding schools because the pupils have received little prior
socialization into boarding and all schools have a high need
component.

Nearly all these state boarding schools have considerable
welfare functions in that at least a third of the pupils are admitted
on grounds of needing education for some reason. Hence a core
of children have parents who live abroad (twelve per cent of all
pupils in the schools), parents who are in the forces, who live in
remote rural areas or who cannot provide adequate care or a
suitable environment for their children. Places not filled by
applicants with boarding need are made available to parents
prepared to pay the boarding costs. This is attractive to many
parents who want a boarding education but cannot afford a
private school.[8] In state boarding schools all tuition costs are
borne by the local authority responsible and this greatly cuts the
cost of residential education in comparison with fully independent schools. In some schools this situation causes those
problems that we noted in the independent integrated schools.
The demands of fee payers seeking a public school life style
conflict with the requirements of those with boarding need.[9]

This lack of well-defined functions in society, unlike those of
the public schools or the day grammar schools, can have some
advantages. For example, it reduces the difficulties of introducing change. In state boarding schools a new headmaster can
often make rapid innovations. In one school visiting arrange-

ments for parents were altered overnight and in his first term a headmaster introduced flexible boarding whereby pupils were only required to spend four weekends a term in the school. In later chapters we shall see that of all schools it was the state boarding schools that have made the most structural changes.[10] In some cases schools have altered their implemented goals on important elements of their structure such as the pastoral or tutorial systems. Their centralized structures and the absence of powerful parasystems make such changes possible even in those expressive areas such as the pastoral, religious or sporting, where the public and progressive schools find innovation more difficult.

With such polarization of styles among the state boarding schools it is not surprising that commitment of pupils varies in different schools. The replies to children's ratings on goals show clearly that the commitment of pupils can be very high in schools which combine a meaningful instrumental stress with a liberal regime. One state school which prepared boys for the building trade showed this most clearly, for here boys who had found little satisfaction in, and withdrawn from, ordinary schools found an education system which met their needs. Many of the secondary modern boarding schools also seem able to win a commitment from pupils that is as high as in any other schools. Lowest pupil commitment, however, was found in those state boarding schools where institutional control was high and where staff were reluctant to enter into any relationships with the pupils except those of a scrutinizing/disciplinary sort. Here pupils' support was restricted to instrumental goals alone, staff-pupil relations were poor and the children's own values avoided enthusiasm for school activities or co-operation with staff. Some state boarding schools faced difficulties in that few staff had any contact with the boarders outside the classroom. The informal social system of staff tends to reflect that of the day school and avoids the close relationships and the interdependence fostered by the boarding situation. Staff are unwilling to participate in extra-curricular activity but are more concerned with status, bureaucracy and order. In this situation boarders can receive little attention or support from the teaching staff, who are frequently insensitive to the boarders' problems. In these schools, therefore, where the staff's attitudes are those of the day school, pupil commitment can be low.

As a result state boarding schools show varied abilities to influence the pupils' informal systems. Some schools do have the styles of boarding which win the commitment of children who do not come from the social classes where boarding is a convention. In such schools, while the informal social system of pupils remains cohesive, it can be manipulated towards official goals by staff, who learn to tolerate many of its manifestations. Other schools are less tolerant of the pupil world; their efforts to control rather than to influence or manipulate pupil values lead to widespread hostility on the part of the children.

In addition to these boarding schools there are many other types of residential provision offered by the local education authorities. There are about a hundred and twenty small hostels attached to day schools in England and Wales. In spite of their number and considerable possibilities in meeting the needs of deprived children they show few original developments. Such provision could be widely used to help deprived or delinquent children, for they can receive boarding when they need it without changing their day school and being removed from the locality. In theory such units could complement the provision of the day school and in some cases this has been developing. However, most of the hostels we visited were custodial and offered little to the school or meaningful residential experience to the children they sheltered.[11] No attempts were made to use these hostels in a wider sense for residential courses or for weekend activity and the minority of boarders in them tend to be isolated and look jealously at the freedom of their day contemporaries as they themselves trudge back to a forbidding boarding house at four o'clock in the afternoon. The experiments in the educational priority areas quite clearly show the advantages of such hostels to all age groups when they are intelligently used.[12] They clearly suggest that more imaginative use of centres which have some residential provision attached to the large day schools can be a great advantage. These could have a wider use as youth centres, evening and weekend activity places, extra classrooms and sites for play groups. They could also act as centres for children with short-term residential needs which are insufficient to warrant a full care order.

As they exist at present, however, the majority of hostels attached to the day schools will have to change radically to widen their educational impact.

It is clear then that schools which stress instrumental and diminish expressive goals have a number of common features. They have a high organizational level and are bureaucratic in structure. Little power is delegated, particularly because in the state sector these schools are part of a wider bureaucracy. Sub-units in these schools rarely achieve anything of the autonomy of those in public and even in some progressive schools. Indeed the academic sub-system clearly both in resources and status outstrips all the others. Staff roles are simple, defined and even in residential areas contractual.

Because of their predominantly day background and because of the instrumental goal priorities of their school staff tend not to view the residential situation as an enriching experience in itself. Boarding is usually viewed as little more than a device to ensure undisturbed pursuit of academic and work skills. As expressive aims, that is, the moral and spiritual states of the children are of less concern, there is little attempt to penetrate, fragment and manipulate the children's informal world. Unless the informal world overtly challenges official goals (when it is largely suppressed) the formal order usually ignores or tolerates aspects of the pupil culture.

There are many indications that the children are committed to their schools' instrumental goals and most are not alienated by the organizational stress in the schools or the high levels of control they exert. However, in social and sporting areas some withdrawal and rebellion is noticeable.

A number of schools have defied this pattern. Because education in a state boarding school is not part of a wider allocative process, as it is in public or progressive schools, and because the state boarding schools have a very varied genesis, a number of approaches have diverged from a strictly instrumental goal stress. A number of schools, particularly those of the secondary modern style, have begun to recognize their administrative and sheltering role and made attempts to meet the needs of a large proportion of their children who are social casualties.

Such styles are beginning to share features of special education, particularly the maladjusted schools and community homes. Such state boarding schools can be seen as resurrecting expressive aims and bringing them into parity with their instrumental and organizational concern.

Styles of boarding schools where organizational goals are predominant over instrumental and expressive goals

As we have discussed styles where instrumental and expressive goals are dominant, it is only logical to consider those boarding schools which show the fifth goal pattern, where organizational goals dominate all others. Only three schools in our sample show such a pattern. One of these is an independent school which takes children whose fathers are in the navy and offers an orthodox education in a school run on naval lines, although few staff have naval backgrounds. The other two are state boarding schools.

Although these three schools do not fall into one constitutional category there can be no doubt that this goal emphasis is self-perpetuating and gives rise to a distinct style of boarding. All three schools had an intake of boys from social classes which do not normally send their children to boarding schools and many boys had various need reasons for being there. The behaviour problems that this caused only accentuated the organizational preoccupation.

In all three schools the style of boarding was total in that very high levels of control were imposed over possessions, activities, relationships, privacy and individuality. The scores for institutional control were 155 for the independent school and 192 and 101 for the state school. The school with the 101 result allowed boys out each day before tea and gave older boys single rooms, which reduces its overall score, but even then this score is much higher than the average for state boarding schools, 84.

In each of the schools privacy was negligible, self-expression in taste and dress was not permitted and activities provided other than sport were few. All three schools had little expressive stress of any kind and stood in sharp contrast to other instrumental and organizational schools which were far less total.

In these schools staff-pupil relationships, as measured by our criteria, were the worst of all the schools in our sample, and for use of corporal punishment they came easily at the top of a frequency table. In one school there was a complete turnover of staff every three years but in another, where posts were well paid, there was a tendency for staff to stay longer. In one school half the six hundred boys were caned in any one year, and in another boys in the first three forms received an average of three canings each per term. Nearly all the offences involved breaking minor rules. One boy received six strokes for smoking, another the same for talking after lights out, and three boys aged fourteen who went to a fish and chip shop received eight, ten and twelve strokes respectively from the master on duty. None of these punishments was recorded or officially witnessed.

There appeared to be little effective pastoral care. Staff merely kept discipline and in reply to our questions less than ten per cent of the pupils recorded any comments implying that they had close contacts with staff. The norms of the pupil informal society were strongly enforced and were opposed to the schools' limited goals, particularly the academic ones.

The private world of the pupils exerted great pressures over the behaviour of pupils although, in contrast to the cold brutality of the formal system, in one school the pupil world was non-violent and centred round an elaborate system of homosexual liaisons, which offered younger boys much of the care, protection and attention that they wanted and failed to get from the staff, and gave the senior boys expressive outlets which did not exist in legitimate forms.

The most serious problem in all three schools, however, was that the informal system of the pupils rejected the wider aims of the school, such as academic achievement, while the staff informal system centred round the maintenance of order and discipline at the expense of relationships, so that the more aware teachers soon became frustrated and moved elsewhere. A vicious circle had been reached. The more these schools increased their attempts to influence the pupil world, the more the informal system of the pupils rejected the goals of the school. For example, friendly adults who sought to help boys were dismissed as homosexual, while disapproval of such gestures expressed by colleagues reinforced these self-perpetuating attitudes. The more often indiscipline and manifestations of many of the boys' problems, such as smoking, non-co-operation and absconding, occurred the more discipline was applied, so that public canings and mass punishments were common, all of which served to reinforce the boys' antagonism. All three schools had almost reached a deadlock situation where the pupil society completely rejected the formal goals, and any attempts to bridge the gap merely accentuated the differences.

This unfortunate state of affairs gave these three schools a distinctive style of organizational domination. The boys realized that they received few benefits from residence and tended to under-achieve in a wide variety of areas. Needless to say the academic results in the schools were very poor. In only one school did the warmth of peer relationships compensate for the deficiencies of the formal system. In the other two schools it added only more misery to the situation, as bullying and extortion flourished.[13]

The intake of a large proportion of children who had need for boarding was a feature common to all three of these schools. It is significant that schools which do admit a large quota of children with need seem to polarize in their goal stress and in the types of control that they exert. This was discussed fully in the report *New Wine in Old Bottles?*.[14] These three schools where the goal emphasis was predominantly organizational represent the one extreme of such polarization. Other boarding schools, including many charity and state boarding schools, have adjusted more successfully tothe problems posed by their intake. Other factors such as tradition, the background of the staff, and the personalities of the staff with key positions all accentuated the dominance of organizational ends in these particular schools.

As these schools so clearly show the great danger of increased organizational stress is that beyond a certain point the relationships inherent in such a style become self-perpetuating and only very drastic action can remedy the situation. Only three schools in our sample had reached this state of affairs permanently, but other schools had cycles of control which occasionally approached this pattern.

Conclusions

Our broad review has defined at least seven major styles of
boarding coexisting under the umbrella of residential education:
that associated with the public and prep school, with the two
kinds of progressive school, with independent, integrated and
state schools. Within each category, however, there exist
variants of the main style and, going deeper still, there are hosts
of smaller differences between smaller groups of schools. These
differences are created by the differing functions for society,
the contexts, cultures and classes in which schools operate and
the goals they pursue. They resolve themselves into internal
features such as systems of control, the roles played by staff
and pupils, the structure of subdivision, the relations between
formal and informal systems, and it is consistencies between the
patterns so formed which produce an identifiable style. Table
7:4 summarizes the styles found according to the features
which define them.

Theoretically some other factors might have been likely to
affect boarding styles. Thus coeducation might have been
expected to produce a boarding style in its own right. In fact,
however, we saw that schools adopted three basic modes of
coeducation and that these three appeared in different degrees
as part of three distinct residential styles: progressive,
integrated and state. Likewise it might have been expected that
schools with a large proportion of day boys or with a heavily
regional or even local composition would have produced styles
marked by greater flexibility between day and boarding,
between school and home and the local community. The only
uniformity that could be discovered between most such schools,
however, was their failure to use their day boy or local composition in any such way. So too with location. One might have
expected the thirteen schools on the sample sited in large urban
populations to have produced a distinctive urban style of
boarding (as have the Soviet schools), but with very few
exceptions their urban situation produces no perceptible effects
except in enlarging some approved cultural opportunities and
other disapproved subcultural problems.

One other curious feature of the English boarding styles is
their insularity. Though all English schools have been affected

TABLE 7:4

	Public	Preparatory	Progressive
Functions for society	Allocative Integrative	Allocative Integrative	Allocative Integrative
Goals	IEO	IEO	E(OI)
Sub-units	Many	None	None
Communication:			
Horizontal	Complex and frequent	Regular	Regular
Vertical	Complex and frequent	Regular	Regular
Curriculum	Academic Orthodox	Academic Orthodox	Wide, but for middle-class children
Institutional control	High	High	Low
Expressive control	High	High	High
Roles: headmaster	O	IEO	E(IO)
housemaster	IEO		E(IO)
Authority among pupils	Complex hierarchy	Prefect system only	None
Pupil informal society			
Nature	Weak	Weak	Strong
Commitment	High	High	High
Staff informal society			
Nature	Strong	Strong	Strong
Commitment	High	High	High
Ability to change	Change slow and complex	Easy but limited by functions	Easy

Quaker	Independent non-integrated	Independent integrated	State
Allocative Integrative	Allocative Integrative Administrative	Administrative Integrative	Administrative Integrative
IE(O)	IEO	IEO	IO(E)
Academic and boarding only	Many	Academic and boarding only	Academic and boarding only
Regular	Regular	Staff meetings only	Varied
Regular	Regular	Infrequent	Varied
Wide, but for middle-class children	Academic Pressurized	Academic Pressurized	Orthodox Day school
Low High	High High	High Low	Varied Low
OE(I) IE(O)	IO IEO	IO IO	IO IO
None	Complex hierarchy	Prefect system only	Prefect system only
Strong High	Weak Low in senior pupils	Strong To I goals only	Strong Varied
Strong High	Strong High	Strong in limited areas To I goals only	Strong in limited areas To I goals only
Easy	Slow and complex	Varied	Easy

by the style of the public school, even if only by reaction, as with the 1920s progressive style, all have developed independent and separate traditions. Each has significantly failed to learn from the experience of the other. Indeed until recently some kinds of boarding were generally unknown and there was no common platform by which workers from them all could come together to pool experience.[15] In this too boarding for ordinary children lags behind that for children with special needs.

Given the recognition of the substantial differences within residential education, the debate about boarding can never be the same. It is no longer a question of the merit of boarding versus day education as of the value (if any) of different styles of residence for different children or situations, be they the training of a managerial elite or the meeting of kinds of deprivation. Also it is only when all the possibilities and varieties of residential education are considered that future policies can be constructed and growing points discerned.[16] Boarding, we may fairly conclude, may be one educational method, but in this country it has developed several styles, some of which may be useful for some children at certain times.

8 Some effects of boarding (1) General

Many claims have been made about the effects for good or ill of boarding upon those who experience it. But there has been no conclusive evidence on the matter.[1] It is doubtful if there ever will be such evidence because of the difficulties of isolating and then controlling the effects of the variable of residence from hosts of others. As *The Times* has said, in commenting on this research project, the best way to measure the effects of boarding would be to take pairs of identical twins who had lived together in the same environment and make one twin a day pupil and the other a boarder at the same school and then follow through their progress. Even this would not give an absolutely controlled situation, however, and is of course an experiment which is impossible to realize in practice.

What we have been able to do in real life during our research in schools to measure the variable of boarding is inevitably far more crude. As it was impossible for us to match individuals on all or many factors except that of being a boarder or day pupil we have had to match groups. In order to hold constant as much as possible the similarities between the groups we compared day pupils with boarders *attending the same schools*, schools which are predominantly boarding but in which at least a third are day pupils who, as far as we could ascertain, comprised the same spread of intelligence and social background as the boarders themselves. We did this in twelve schools, two public schools on our intensive sample and ten from our extensive sample, comprising two public, one integrated, two progressive and five state boarding schools. In addition, to make even broader comparisons, we chose four day schools and compared their boy pupils on certain criteria with boy pupils from boarding schools similar in social, economic composition, size, constitution, style and aims. These day schools were one large independent school, two neighbourhood or sub-regional comprehensive or bilateral schools (both with girls) and one secondary modern school for boys.

When these comparisons showed up significant differences,

which was not always the case, we could point to boarding as a potential cause, though it may not be the only or even the determining one. All that the evidence presented in this chapter can do is to indicate more clearly and with more support than hitherto some observed effects (or lack of alleged effects) which the boarding as distinct from the day situation *may* produce on comparable groups of pupils.

Generalizations on the matter, of which there have in the past been too many,[2] are bedevilled as well by other factors. Not only does the life history and personality of the individual profoundly affect his response to boarding but the age at which boarding starts and the length of time in residential education are also crucial variables, as we know. Thus the effect of spending long periods in single-sex communities concerns mainly those boarders who, since the age of eight, have attended schools of the public or preparatory school kind. Such effects may be less extreme for boarders in state or other schools where boarding starts later at eleven or thirteen, where stays are shorter and the control of the school also less total.

This introduces yet another variable equally ignored by many contributors to the debate about boarding education. As the last chapters have shown in detail, styles of boarding vary extremely, more extremely than styles of day education. Before proclaiming an 'effect of boarding', one has to consider which kind of boarding is producing such an effect and whether the other kinds also produce similar or different effects. Even in making comparisons with day education, we must bear in mind the differences in approach, structure and opportunities within day schools in this country. Day schools apparently similar can themselves produce different effects: M.J.Power, for example, contends that within one working-class area different day schools produce different influences on delinquent behaviour by pupils.[3] In any comparison therefore we must bear in mind the style of boarding and the kind of day education from which our evidence comes and be wary of extending the results to all other schools in these sectors.

We shall start by looking at the opportunities created by the residential situation and assess the degree to which they are realized by different kinds of school. These opportunities are wide, ranging from academic and cultural stimulation to the creation of intimate staff-pupil relations. Later in the next chapter we shall explore as far as we can the effects of boarding on individual children.

(i) Effects of boarding on academic achievement

It has been often said that residential schools offer an environment more conducive to academic fulfilment than day education: the organized life, controlled periods of private study or prep at evenings and weekends, the good staff-pupil relations, the constant presence of teachers to help, the use of facilities at evenings and weekends, it has been claimed, give the boarder many advantages over the boy who departs for home at four and leaves all these things behind.[4] On the other hand it is counter-claimed, the fragmentation of life, the parcelling of time into many separate sections, the endless and varied demands of boarding life prevent the single-minded and protracted concentration, and the greater self-control of study which the day pupil can often achieve at home.

Little of this discussion has been supported by evidence and some of the evidence has been vitiated by invalid comparisons. Thus Graham Kalton compared the academic performance of public school boys with that of day grammar school boys, to the obvious benefit of the former.[5] Such comparisons do not measure so much the effects of boarding and day education as demonstrate the very different systems and approaches to education and, above all, the enormous cultural differences in background between pupils. In his comparison neither the aims, structure, selectivity and facilities of the two sets of schools, nor the social class and cultural backgrounds of the two groups of pupils, could be held constant.

It is, however, possible, using Kalton's research and that of the Public Schools Commission as well as our own, to draw some evidence on the matter from day pupils and boarders of roughly the same intelligence range and the same social class, attending the same school as each other, or day and boarding schools which are comparable. The data is entirely from public schools: that from direct-grant schools is less useful because of the well-known fact, which our research has substantiated, that the intellectual level of the day boy entry in such schools is higher than that of the boarders, while the social spread on the day side is wider.[6] Day boys constantly do significantly better in academic terms than boarders in direct-grant boarding schools, but this clearly has little to do with being a boarder or a day pupil.

If we compare boarders and day boys in the same or comparable public schools we find that the sixth-form day pupils spend more time in private study than the boarders.

TABLE 8:1

Average hours per year on study by sixth-form pupils

	Boarders	Day
Preparation, private study at school, or homework	561·7	594·1

Source: Public Schools Commission, *First Report*, vol II, appendix 6, p 53.

Also more day boys in a sub-sample of the day-boarding schools we investigated in depth tended to see their schools as promoting attributes of hard work than did their contemporaries who were boarders.

TABLE 8:2

Sixth form pupils seeing the school as promoting the habit of working hard (in percentages)

School	Boarders	Day	Number
State	19	42	82
Public (1)	25	40	150
Public (2)	28	42	86
Public (3)	25	41	274

Source: general sample; subsample of day/boarding schools.

The hard worker tends to be less badly thought of among day boys than among boarders anyway.

TABLE 8:3

*Sixth-form respondents ticking 'working too hard' as an
element of unpopularity (in percentages)*

(list of features of unpopularity in a closed question)

School	Boarders	Day	Numbers
State	38	16	82
Public (1)	32	19	150
Public (2)	35	17	86
Public (3)	33	12	274

Source: as Table 8:2.

In other words, as much other evidence showed, day pupils tend
to be oriented towards academic achievement while boarders
are more expressively motivated towards the wider range of
ends which their schools serve, of which academic work is only
one.

We can examine the public school pupils' performance by
the results of public examinations, the only fairly objective
criterion we have. At the first public examination taken at
sixteen (O level) the evidence collected by the Public Schools
Commission, by Kalton and by ourselves corresponds and shows
that the performance of day pupils tended to polarize somewhat
compared with that of boarders: fractionally more of the day
pupils tended to fail or to get fewer passes and more tended to
get a larger number of passes than boarders.

TABLE 8:4

O level achievement of public schoolboys (in percentages)

	Boarders	Day
No subject sat	3	4
All subjects failed	2	2
1-3 passes	8	10
4-7 passes	49	42
8 or more passes	38	42

Source: Public Schools Commission, *First Report*, vol II, appendix 6, p 104.
See also Kalton G., *The Public Schools*, Table 6:7, for similar findings.

The differences are in fact small and suggest that the structure of boarding may help pupils to work at this age compared with similar day pupils, though determined day pupils can collect larger quantities of passes than boarding life (or school policies) permit. In general, however, at this level being a boarder seems to have no marked effect compared with being a day pupil in the same school or between similar ones.

At the more intellectually and organizationally exacting level of the public examinations taken at seventeen or eighteen years of age (A levels) more pronounced differences do emerge. Once again there is very little difference in terms of those who fail, although more boarders tend to fail all subjects than day pupils. In terms of those who do best, however, as measured by the acquisition of three or more passes at this level, then day pupils do significantly better than boarders.

TABLE 8:5

A level achievement of public school boys (in percentages)

	Boarders	Day
No subject sat	32	31
All subjects failed	9	6
1 pass	11	9
2 passes	19	14
3 passes	24	34
4 or more passes	4	6
	N = 7770	N = 2813

Source: Public Schools Commission, *First Report*, p 106. See also Kalton G., *The Public Schools*, Tables 6:10/11 for similar findings.

In gaining public and open scholarships for the older universities day pupils agains do perceptibly better than boarders (see Table 8:6). It seems that public school boarding at this age level and among abler pupils to some degree obstructs the kind of academic performance which the abler day boys can obtain. This finding paralleled in our own evidence, did not surprise us as in our interviews and questionnaires sixth formers frequently stressed the disadvantages of boarding to those at the top of the school. Frequently, they claimed, their time for study was broken up

TABLE 8:6

Open awards to public school boys at Oxford and Cambridge

	Percentage	Number
Day pupils: mainly day schools	42	113
Day pupils: day/boarding schools	37	295
Boarders: day/boarding schools	27	571
Boarders: mainly boarding schools	26	619

Source: Kalton, G., *The Public Schools*, Table 6:16.

into fragments by rituals such as house prayers and their energy
and attention diverted by their important organizational roles
such as policing the house, running games and other activities
and the many areas of life in which seniors were expected to
participate and lead. The able and committed day boy from the
same background could usually devote himself to study more
continuously and with fewer distractions.[7]

This finding from public schools is confirmed by evidence
from most other kinds of boarding schools and by the comments
of many members of staff in them. The academically abler day
pupil, provided he has a supportive home and the same background advantages as the boarder, tends to do somewhat better
academically than his counterpart when he reaches the top age
level in the school.

Paradoxically, and most importantly, the reverse is true if we
divide up our school population and look at pupils who are *less*
able to cope with academic work. In both independent and
state boarding schools teachers and staff claimed that boarding
helped the less able, while scarcely affecting the more able child.
Indeed in one state boarding school where this hypothesis was
put forward fifty-five per cent of the pupils had failed the
standard selection test for entry to a grammar school, the exam
at eleven plus, yet fifty-two per cent of these got at least four
O level passes. Though in this case the facts that the pupils
were in a selective secondary modern school and had aspirant
parents to get them there make comparisons with day secondary modern results valueless, there is more convincing evidence
from comparisons within the public schools again which
supports the general hypothesis. Thus when less able pupils

within the same public schools or from comparable public
schools (those who failed the eleven plus exam), are examined
by their day and boarding composition, the boarders are seen to
perform better at subsequent public examinations than comparable day boys.

TABLE 8:7

Subsequent examination achievements of public schoolboys who
had failed 11 plus exam (in percentages)

		Boarders	Day
O level passes			
	None	2	7
	4 or more	82	68
	8 or more	28	19
A level passes			
	1 or more	43	35
	2 or more	34	28
		N = 294	N = 231

Source: Public Schools Commission, *First Report*, p 103.

This evidence tends to confirm what staff and pupils say: that
the intensive life and the supportive structure, the organized
pattern, the constant presence of teachers and help, though it
may in some ways hold back the brightest from the highest or
most extensive flights of performance, can on the other hand
positively boost the less academically inclined in a way which
even positive and aspirant homes cannot.

Indeed this very success of boarding raises in some schools
attendant problems. In five of the state and three of the
independent schools we investigated the heads and staff com-
plained that the children were *over*-stimulated academically
to levels of performance which could not be maintained when
they left for work or further education where the framework
was inevitably less supportive or controlling. Equally it was
found that the vigorous life of school, its cultural provision, the
opportunity to exercise skills of management and responsibility,
led pupils to construct career aspirations which even their somewhat inflated academic performance could not hope to sustain.

Our figures show more demand for teaching and professional, skilled and white-collar careers among boarders from secondary modern boarding schools compared with day schools of the same social class background and these differences cannot be accounted for by differences in background. As one cynical teacher said to us:

> 'Once they're here they decide not to be dustbin men, so they get ideas of acting even if they've never been to a theatre.'

Though our research experience leads us to maintain that these general conclusions apply widely over boarding schools it must be borne in mind that individual schools or groups of schools may differ in motivating their pupils to academic work. Thus in the progressive kind of school the informal norms of the pupils may place little stress on hard work or academic achievement for its own sake and therefore academic performance, at least as measured by examination results, can be less valued in both the formal aims and the pupils' own aims in such schools. This situation is less true of other kinds of schools. We saw this in the responses by senior pupils given in Table 6:5 above to the question: if you could be only one of these things at this school, which would you choose to be?

Pupils in progressive schools seem, as much other evidence shows, less oriented to work and more to other areas of school life. Their academic performance as measured by public examinations tends to reflect their attitudes.

We can conclude then about the academic effects of boarding, first, that more specific research needs to be done than could be attempted in our extensive survey. Nevertheless, from the evidence we have discussed from public and that which we gathered from other schools, it does seem that in general there are few dramatic differences in academic performance between boarders and day pupils when the school, social class and cultural backgrounds are held as constant as possible. However, able day pupils tend to do better than able boarders particularly at sixth-form level, whereas less able boarders seem to do better than less able day boys at all ages. To the one group boarding as it now is may be a hindrance, to the other it is a positive support. The latter factor suggests, as does other evidence, that boarding experience of some appropriate kind may positively help those children, whether able or not, whose backgrounds circumstances seriously handicap the achievement of their potential.

(ii) Enlargement of cultural horizons

One of the most common arguments in favour of boarding is that residence enables schools to offer wider cultural, physical and social opportunities and more purposeful activities than those of day schools. The use of evenings and weekends as well as actual amenities and environment give boarding schools, it is said, the chance to develop more thorough, more continuous and more ambitious programmes of educational activity outside the classroom in order to enlarge and develop the talents of children. Thus John Wilson, a former public schoolmaster, writes that:

> 'No home, even combined with outside services, can offer the same facilities for adolescent development as a community specifically designed for the purpose can offer: games, work, clubs and societies and all the other activities which we have noted in the public schools cannot flourish without great difficulty unless they are all contained in one community.[8]'

John Dancy, another proponent of boarding, adds that:

> 'Whereas in day grammar schools there are facilities for the *best*, in the public schools *all* boys are given a chance and the encouragement to enjoy physical exercise and acquire physical skills.'

And,

> 'it is in, perhaps, these three activities [music, art and drama] more than any other that the opportunities of the boarding school are so obviously superior. No home can possibly offer the same range of them; no day school can find it anything like as easy as a boarding school to provide the time and space for them.[9]'

These confident statements come from the more expensive and best equipped public schools. In fact, as we have seen, provision varies so widely between schools that it is difficult to make such generalizations about boarding education as a whole. As we saw in earlier chapters some schools have extensive provision and set out to offer a wide range of stimulating activities while many others give their children little more than teaching and no more of other amenities than many day schools. One of the public schools on our sample offered a choice of six team sports on games days and other individual sports, twenty-two societies which met regularly, eight holiday trips or expeditions, and creative opportunities including the use of a large theatre, three Bechstein grand pianos, a full-size indoor swimming pool, a weekly film on the current national circuit and a library of fifty thousand and more volumes. At the other extreme were not a few schools dominated either by poverty or by organizational goals. At one of the latter, a relatively wealthy school aided by charitable funds and with six hundred boys, only one sport was available and was compulsory for all, there were no active clubs or societies at all, the nearby river and sea were not used for activity, there were few visitors or expeditions, an ancient film was shown on Saturday evenings, the small and ill-equipped library was locked outside teaching hours along with the gym and craft rooms, and the art room was smaller than the cricket store. Needless to say the pupils' own elaborate under-life and escapades richly compensated for the deprivations of the school's formal provision and outlets.

Not only what the school offers but also what the home environment offers is important in deciding whether cultural opportunities for children are increased. A child from a supportive and well-off home in London may have little to gain by removal to a rural boarding school. But children from less well-off, less supportive backgrounds or those in rural areas may, on the other hand, find that boarding compensates richly for some deficiencies at home. That boarding in a well-equipped and lively community can open up possibilities and talents not explored even in good day schools was shown when twenty-one boys from grammar and secondary modern schools in Swindon entered the sixth form as boarders at the large Marlborough public school nearby. We followed their progress in a separate research enterprise and found that over the two years of their stay the boys' interests broadened enormously. When they arrived, their aims were heavily academic but when they left a transformation had taken place.

TABLE 8:8

Aspirations of Swindon-Wiltshire boys at Marlborough

	At end of first term	On leaving	Other Marlborough sixth formers
Outstanding scholar	12	5	21·8 per cent
Outstanding sportsman	2	4	25·5
Outstanding in creative arts	5	8	27·4
Outstanding prefect	2	4	22·3
	N = 21	N = 21	N = 453

Source: Swindon-Marlborough research project data.

Many of the boys felt stimulated by the interest and encouragement of others (staff and boys) as well as by the school's many facilities. Most participated in existing activities. Others brought new impetus to them as with folk-singing in one house or the creation of a wine-making society by two of the boys. Some did indeed 'make their mark' in the school: one boy edited the school magazine, another played in the First and Second Fifteen, a third became captain of athletics, and another became one of the school's most well-known painters; eight were house prefects and three later became heads of house. In this whole area, the energies of the newcomers and the expressive life and ethic of the public school combined fruitfully for both: the possibilities of integration were realised.[10]

When we compared sixth-form boarders and day pupils in different schools on our sample (Table 6:5 in Chapter 6) we saw that boarders in all kinds of schools have interests and aspirations distributed fairly evenly over academic work, the arts, school power and politics, and sport, whereas the interests of day school boys tended to concentrate almost exclusively around academic matters and, to a lesser degree, sport. It does seem then in general that boarding widens the interests and energies of its recipients.

But, such is the variety of provision, it would be unwise to rely entirely on generalizations of this kind. The widest range of facilities and stimulation in our survey was provided by schools with strong expressive aims, even if the style of provision often reflects upper-middle-class cultural interests and attitudes. In schools with a strong instrumental bias we found fewer such cultural activities and outlets and they were pursued with less intensity but, in these schools, there was less control over children and more opportunity for them to sample the more diverse culture of the neighbourhood. Such local provision varied enormously but it often meant that the pupils had elements of several cultural styles available rather than the officially approved kind found so often in the expressive type of school. Schools with organizational ends dominant, however, offered least of all: the pupils endured a combination of poor facilities and an all-encompassing repressive regime more impoverishing than almost any day or home environment, though the resulting deviant pupil under-life offered scope for talents and creative enterprise of all kinds.

When boarding pupils on our intensive sample were asked to rank which of eight aspects of residential life they had personally found most rewarding, in all schools but one creative opportunities (in music, art and drama) ranked after teaching, sports opportunities and close relations with friends. It is, however, clear that purposeful activity of an athletic and cultural kind is highly valued by them (see Table 8:9).

We can now explore more deeply the differences between day pupils and boarders in this area. From our extensive sample of boarding and comparison day schools we present the answers by sixth formers to a question in which the boys were given lists of qualities which boarding and day education might promote. Three items on the list were relevant to our present concern: interest in cultural things, breadth of mind, lack of knowledge of the outside world. The table and correlation between rankings are given below (Tables 8:10-12). In schools with differing patterns of goal stress there are corresponding differences in the boys' opinions on what their style of education produces.

From all this data it does appear that boarders in general do think more than day children that their schools promote among themselves cultural interests and breadth of mind, though they obviously feel that the price of this is a lack of knowledge of

TABLE 8:9

Aspects of life found most rewarding: rankings by sixth formers

| | Public schools | | | | State boarding schools | |
	A	B	C	D	E	F*
Teaching	2	1	2	1	2	1
Sport/games	3	2	1	2	1	2
Organizing and running things	7	5	5	5	3	4
Living with other boys	4	7	6	9	9	3
Contact with individual masters	10	6	7	6	8	6
Opportunities for art, drama, music	5	4	4	4	4	8
Living to a regular pattern	8	8	9	8	7	7
Relations with a few boys	1	3	3	3	5	5
Being able to get round rules	9	8	8	6	6	9
N =	239	440	189	67	97	83

* In school F, a mixed secondary modern school, the answers are from fifth-form boys and girls.

Source: intensive sample.

the outside world, which day pupils obviously experience less in their education.[11] More valid are the differences which emerge among the boarding schools themselves. The greatest cultural impact is claimed by pupils in those schools which have expressive aims prominent, though when the school also has organizational aims to the fore (goal type I = E = O) the pupils are significantly *less* conscious of being out of touch with the world outside. We have seen earlier that this phenomenon is accounted for because the boys in these schools, mainly public schools, have been socialized from an early age into accepting a high degree of control and do not feel as strongly as other boarders that such control isolates them from the outside world, thus illustrating the dangers of generalizing about adaptation in total institutions.[12] Hence there are only weak correlations between levels of institutional control over pupils and low cultural effectiveness. Among all schools, however, there is an

TABLE 8:10

School promoting cultural attributes (in percentages)

		Goal stress	Interest in culture	Breadth of mind	Lack of knowledge of the out-side world	N
Public schools						
	A	IEO	67	48	58	90
	B	IEO	81	71	52	110
	C	IE(O)	97	92	44	75
	D	IEO	93	71	46	161
	E	IEO	35	31	52	189
	F	IEO	33	29	52	239
	G	IE(O)	63	78	35	106
	H	IEO	32	34	55	440
	I	IO(E)	28	20	24	80
	J	IO(E)	15	12	68	65
Independent (non-integrated)						
	K	IEO	29	80	29	45
	L	IEO	90	70	48	33
	M	IE(O)	77	77	46	31
	N	IO(E)	60	40	57	60
	O	IO(E)		23	75	51
Independent integrated						
	P	IE(O)	18	29	72	65
	Q	IE(O)	31	58	47	26
Progressive						
	R	IE(O)	78	70	51	80
State						
	S	IO(E)	33	100	15	27
	T	IO(E)	13	38	58	97
(Sixth-form boys and girls)	U	IEO	27	42	28	84
Day schools						
Comprehensive	A		25	20	23	52
Independent	B		43	36	25	80
Mixed bilateral	C		18	24	24	90
Secondary modern (Fifth forms)	D		10	21	6	88

Source: Extensive sample and day school comparisons.

TABLE 8:11

Spearman rank correlation coefficients among the schools

		P
Between order for promoting interest and culture and breadth of mind	+0·60	·01
Between order for promoting interest and culture and lack of knowledge of outside units	−0·15	not signif.
Between order for promoting interest and culture and institutional control	−0·32	·05
Between order for promoting breadth of mind and lack of knowledge of outside world	−0·88	·01
Between order for promoting breadth of mind and institutional control	−0·48	·05
Between order for promoting lack of knowledge of outside world and institutional control	+0·46	·05

TABLE 8:12

Means for percentages for schools of differing goal stress

Goal stress	Interest in culture	Breadth of mind	Lack of knowledge of outside world	Standard Deviation		
IEO	54·1	60·6	26·5	26·6	19·6	10·3
IE(O)	52·9	67·3	38·8	27·7	19·9	11·3
IO(E)	46·7	49·2	37·5	19·0	29·1	24·1
Day schools	24·0	25·5	19·5	12·2	6·4	7·8

inverse correlation between cultural effectiveness as perceived by the boys and their sense of lack of knowledge of the outside world. It is not surprising, therefore, that schools which do not stress expressive goals have less cultural impact than others. The high standard deviation from the mean for the item 'lack of knowledge of the outside world' confirms what we saw earlier, that schools with low expressive stress tend to polarize into those that are open and flexible, allowing plenty of interchange with the world outside, and those which are repressive and poorly equipped with the highest levels of institutional control in the sample.

The ability of schools to enlarge cultural horizons thus varies widely. One feature which works against effectiveness in this area is the inherent tendency for residential communities to be inward-looking. Though facilities may be many and activities varied, as in some public and progressive schools, they may still be inward in focus and are often accompanied by consensus of values and life style on the part of school, staff and pupils which makes the community as a whole far from an enlarging experience. As we know, the frequent uniformity of com-position in staffing and recruitment, and the concentration on certain kinds of approved expressive aims, and the controls imposed to prohibit others, all make it unlikely that many boarding schools will contain, as many day schools have to do, sharply diverging styles of life and values. Issues that divide or challenge the ethos of these schools are frequently excluded from the start or repressed rather than assessed.

The lack of competing values which is so marked a feature in many boarding schools is reflected by the boys' opinions on controversial moral and social issues. The sixth formers' response to our attitude questionnaire based on acceptance or otherwise of 'traditional' viewpoints produced the following responses.

TABLE 8:13

Scale of acceptance of 'traditional' values in percentages

	Low acceptance—High acceptance			Schools	N=
Sixth formers	*1–6*	*7–12*	*13–18*		
Public schools	12·2	57·9	29·9	16	1542
Independent	11·6	60·4	28·0	6	245
State and integrated	33·0	46·0	21·0	17	818
Progressive	81·0	19·0	0·0	3	103

Source: general sample.

We see that in the public and especially other independent schools there is a strong tendency towards traditional viewpoints, a stronger diversion between unorthodox and traditional views in state and integrated schools and an overwhelming bias towards non-traditional views in progressive schools. The tendency to consensus found in the public schools and their satellites on the one hand and the very different kind of consensus found in progressive education can only be reinforced by the limited experience provided within the schools and by the high levels of institutional control found in the one and of expressive control found in the other.

Far from enlarging experience schools can therefore help to narrow the experience of competing values and life styles to which the day child in the outside world might be more exposed and this, as well as the deep commitment which many expressively oriented schools generate among pupils, may make it difficult for boarders to adjust to the wider pluralistic culture on leaving and may instead lead them to reproduce the sub-culture of school in their later lives. Indeed the totality of most schools, the limits on personal privacy and self-expression and on movement outside the school which are so common again may limit cultural development. Likewise the events of school life are cloistered in the sense that they are relevant only within a narrow framework. Routine, structure, the roles played, the age and sex composition of the age population are often quite unlike life outside the school. The texture of daily life is also less varied than that experienced by day pupils. There is often therefore no real point of reference outside for values, statuses and roles which are cherished within the schools. Pupils come to accept a system of values, rewards, status, privileges and ways of judging others which may bear little resemblance to what goes on outside. This makes many boarding schools custodial not in the usual sense of protecting society from the inmates but in the opposite sense of protecting inmates from the wider society.

To sum up: boarding schools can and, our evidence shows, actually do open up the cultural, social and physical horizons of their pupils in ways that day schools seldom can emulate. Their ability and desire to do so varies extremely. The cultural impact of some schools is limited by the narrow definition of permitted cultural activity, by narrowness of social composition and by the inward focus and the irrelevance to the wider culture outside of the style, structure and mores of the school itself.

The issue of widening children's horizons is only one area where schools can influence their pupils. One obvious feature of boarding schools is that the residential setting enables adults to have a deeper and more continuous influence on pupils and their own world than the more limited time and interchange afforded by day school life. How far was this opportunity met?

(iii) Influence on the pupils and their world

In any organization there are many unwritten expectations of behaviour that are enforced among those who belong to it but which have neither the organization's official support nor even acknowledgement. These codes of behaviour make up what we called in earlier chapters 'the informal social system'. In schools both the staff and pupils are subject to these codes which lay down accepted patterns of behaviour, attitudes and modes of expression. These expectations are not prescribed as part of a role but they are enforced by peers or colleagues. To take a small example, there may be no formal agreement about the dress of members of staff but in some schools those who wear denim jeans or who do not wear gowns may find themselves subject to criticism and teasing and even in some cases social rejection by colleagues attempting to enforce the formal/ informal norms.

As such norms affect both staff and pupils they are crucial to the effectiveness of the school in realizing its aims. If the norms current among the staff disapprove of involvement with school outside teaching or in making informal relations with the pupils, then the school is unlikely to be effective in realizing its aims (especially the expressive ones) and all the more so if the pupils' own norms are hostile to the school's goals or policies on such matters.

Many researchers have studied the informal systems which are generated among the staff and inmates in organizations such as prisons, mental hospitals, army units and even schools. Some have suggested that in custodial or total institutions there is usually a distinct split between the worlds of the staff and the inmates: an 'us' and 'them' cleavage so deep as to prevent the formation of relationships across the gulf and thus to displace any reformative or therapeutic goals.[13] Such a two-camps model is inadequate for all total institutions and particularly for residential schools in which there is far more variety in the nature and relations between informal networks than this model allows. Thus in some schools the informal society of the pupils may reject many of the school's goals but may also be cruel or benign to its members and conservative or radical in outlook. In other cases the pupils' norms support the school's goals and encourage conformity to official demands. In a separate paper on this topic,[14] we have suggested that all informal systems have three important dimensions: first, the degree of consensus which exists on specific norms, that is the proportion of members endorsing certain values and patterns of behaviour; second, the strength of informal control, that is the rigidity with which norms are enforced; and third, the pervasiveness of norms, that is the range of activities and beliefs controlled by them.

Those schools where all three - consensus, strength and pervasiveness - are high may be said to have strong informal systems, though the norms may themselves be directed towards or away from the school's official goals. Schools where the pupils' and staff's informal systems show low consensus, low levels of informal control and low pervasiveness have weak or diffuse informal systems.

As informal systems differ in their strength and orientation to goals it follows that the commitment and satisfaction of pupils and staff vary widely. This extreme variety is a remarkable feature of the schools on our sample. For example, when we asked the boys in the intensive sample to evaluate their satisfaction we found a wide range of experience between schools. We also noted that there was a greater tendency for boarders' responses to polarize at extremes compared with those of day pupils: just as there could be much more intense and widespread commitment at the one extreme, so there could be much deeper and more widespread alienation at the other. Most day pupils, however, tended to be in the moderate regions of response in between. We shall come back to this phenomenon soon.

TABLE 8:14

Enjoyment of school by sixth formers in percentages

| | Public schools | | | | State schools | | Independent day | State day | |
	A	B	C	D	E	F	A	B	C
Enjoyed it all time	35	34	37	4	66	27	19	21	18
Happy in last years	15	8	10	11	6	12	12	17	15
Tolerable all time	38	42	38	41	16	32	60	54	62
Happy at first, not now	3	8	3	12	12	17	8	4	2
Disliked it all time	9	8	12	32	0	12	1	4	3
N =	189	441	239	67	84	97	80	52	90

Source: intensive sample, day school comparisons.

Individual responses of this kind fall into more coherent patterns when we consider the collective adaptations of the pupils as a whole. To examine the degree of commitment of the pupils' world to the school's official ends, we compared discrepancies between the aims which the pupils wanted the schools to pursue with those which the school pursued in practice. We found (see the data given in Table 4, Appendix IV) what much other evidence confirmed, that commitment to official ends was highest and most widespread in progressive schools, followed next by public schools and then by maintained schools; there was least commitment in intensity and range in independent and integrated schools. When we examined the informal systems of these schools we found that in all the public schools except two the informal order of the pupils was weak and diffuse when measured by the three criteria above but that that of the staff was strong, for example, generating strong informal obligations to participate in extra-curricular activities or pastoral situations which in other schools had to be laid down by the official system in formal contracts. In progressive schools, on the contrary, we found that the pupil informal world was very strong on all our three dimensions with a rigid enforcement of norms stronger than that of the staff, though that too tended to be strong. In other words the informal systems which support the goals of school can be either weak as in the public schools or strong as in the progressive ones. Among state boarding schools there was less uniformity, both in the nature of the informal networks of staff and pupils and in the overall levels of commitment of both.

In general, however, we found it was the case that informal systems were strong whenever the formal structure of control was weak, though, in such cases, the orientation to the school's aims could be either supportive or rejecting. There are, however, exceptions to this finding, particularly in the sector of integrated schools or those where organizational goals were more prominent than expressive ones. Thus in the schools which we found dominated by organizational ends and where there was a high degree of external control, the informal society of the pupils was itself extremely powerful, rejecting all the aims of the school and imposing its own standards of behaviour. The nature of the controls used, however, varied in each case. In one school the brutality of the official regime was reinforced by a brutal pupil world with a prevalence of bullying, extortion and racketeering, close to the stereotyped prison model. In another school, by contrast, where the official system was strong but the staff informal system was diffused and uninvolved, the boy world was paternalistic and pastoral, centred round a network of supportive homosexual liaisons between older and younger boys.

These aspects of the pupils' world are reflected in questions which aimed to discover the pupils who possessed high status in the informal world, boys whom the sixth formers we questioned thought new boys would look up to and respect (Table 8:15).

In public schools we see how the informal system of the boys supports the official one by according high status in the pupils' world to positions which in the school's official system also carry high formal status. But in the two schools where organizational goals were dominant and the pupil society was alienated from official aims the positions which carried most status in the informal world were frequently deviant in terms of the official system.

TABLE 8:15

Replies of sixth-form boy boarders on positions which carry high informal status (in percentages)

Summary of replies	Public schools in intensive sample				Schools with goal stress O(IE) on extensive sample	
	A	B	C	D	A	B
Leading prefects	62	75	51	73	11	31
Leading sportsman	31	16	29	22	21	22
Leading academic	6	4	11	3	11	5
Leading artist/musician	2	1	4	2	0	5
Boys who hold anti-school attitudes or who have strong political ideals	0	2	1	0	31	15
Boys who are always in trouble	0	2	4	0	5	2
N =	440	239	186	67	105	60

Source: general sample.

If we now examine more closely the relationship between the informal world of staff and pupils and the formal ones we find complex patterns of interaction. In some cases the formal system of the school manipulates the informal one of the pupils. This is most systematic and thoroughly done in the public schools in which the society of the pupils is divided into numerous competing fragments and a wide diversity of official roles is distributed, all of which units and roles are in some ways directed towards the official ends. In progressive kinds of school a similar manipulation occurs through a deliberate blurring of the distinction between formal and informal systems, by the encouragement of participation in decisions and in the quality of relations, and by the cultivation of warm personal loyalties between adults and pupils. In the other kinds of schools, however, these techniques were used less and less effectively and more often the formal system tended to ignore, to suppress or even to be unaware of the pupil world. In some cases the residential setting permits the boy world to cohere and to resist formal influences, especially expressive ones. In our sample of schools we found that this had happened in four integrated independent and three state boarding schools. The nature and relations of the informal systems of schools varied too greatly to generalize and in Table 8:16 we give the kinds that we found most prevalent.

TABLE 8:16

The nature of staff and pupil informal societies in different types of boarding school

Style of boarding	Nature of informal system				Orientation to goals		Type of relationship between formal and informal systems	
	Boy		Staff					
	Strong	Weak	Strong	Weak	Boy	Staff	Boy	Staff
Expressive goals dominant								
Public		/		/	Support	Support	Manipulation	Manipulation
Small independent	varied			/	,,	,,	Passive	,,
Quaker	/			/	,,	,,	Manipulation	,,
Progressive	/			/	,,	,,	,,	,,
Instrumental/organizational goals dominant								
Charity	/			/	Support I	,, IO	Passive	Reject
State	/			/	,, I	,, IO	,,	,,

One salient characteristic of all the evidence we gathered on the adaptations of pupils individually and collectively to the aims and methods of their schools was the tendency to extremes in boarding as compared with day schools. The extremes were both in quantity and intensity. Thus we found that in general there tended to be more boarders who were committed to their schools on the one hand or alienated from them on the other, while in day schools a semi-committed ritualism (going along with the system but with little real commitment to its ends) was more common. In particular, schools with expressive ends such as public and progressive ones generated commitment of an intense kind seldom found among day pupils even in the same school. There was an emotional commitment, a deep internalization of the ends and means which led sometimes to a disorientation on leaving the school from which it took a long time to recover. At the other extreme these schools also provoked among a minority an intense alienation. Here there was a passionate rejection of ends and means as a reaction to the all-encompassing expressive controls which seemed to some individuals an assault on their very identity and which led them sometimes to self-destructive behaviour resulting in expulsion. We found equally extensive alienation in many instrumentally and organizationally oriented schools both day and boarding, but the reaction was seldom of this extremely intense kind. The same applies to the response of withdrawal from the school's aims, structure and life. It is difficult for us to say whether this is more or less common in day or boarding schools but it does seem from our evidence and interviews with medical and other staff and pupils that it takes more extreme forms in closed societies, where the response of withdrawal, such as a protective eccentricity, is almost institutionalized among staff and pupils. In short, though the adaptations of pupils varied as much between boarding as between day schools, there was a tendency for polarization in the former and among expressively oriented schools in particular for a more intense kind of adaptation altogether.[15]

Among staff the most general and intense commitment was again found in the expressive schools, with more ritualism in the others where the pattern corresponded with day education except that, in boarding schools, there seemed fewer alienated staff. Alienation in so all-embracing and inescapable a society is less tolerable than in the world of day school teachers; in boarding schools alienated teachers leave together. Withdrawal may not have been a more common response among boarding staff but it seemed more tolerated in the expressive schools as a means of keeping deviant staff and the children gathered round them away from downright alienation. Such withdrawal was often picturesque in its expression. When such personality problems arise among staff, the pupils cannot escape from their impact as can those in day education.

In conclusion then, while residential schools have greater opportunities of influencing and directing the informal worlds which arise amongst staff and pupils than do day counterparts, there is a wide diversity in their success in doing so. The limitations in what boarding can offer, the lack of relevance of some styles of it to pupils' needs, the dominance of organizational ends or expressive controls all limited the achievement of schools. At their most effective, however, residential schools can exercise a control over the adult and pupil informal worlds and generate patterns of adaptation, the extent and depth of which cannot be paralleled by comparable day education.

(iv) Staff-pupil relationships and pastoral care

When staff and pupils live together in a community it is obvious that there are greater opportunities for them to mix than is the case in a day school. This leads, claim the protagonists of boarding, to closer staff-pupil relations through which pupils and staff get to know each other well as individuals. George Snow, a former public school headmaster and recently a bishop, tells us that

> 'the housemaster is head of a family: his caring for boys is a family relationship and its exercise is normally the most important influence in a boy's life.'[16]

It is true that many children who first arrive at a boarding school are surprised at living in close contact with their teachers:

> 'I saw the housemaster's wife in her dressing-gown,'

noted one startled newcomer. But before we examine the assumption that this communal existence leads to better relations between staff and pupils, and better pastoral care of pupils by adults, we should remember that many boarding schools limit regular access by children to their families, peers and girl friends outside the school who do, as we shall see, perform pastoral functions for the day school child. If boarding provides special opportunities in the pastoral area, it therefore also brings some deprivations as well. Equally we should remember that boarding does create some of the very problems that its pastoral machinery sets out to solve. When housemasters told us that their boys felt free to discuss problems of worry about home, sexual frustration, homosexuality and the like with them, they often failed to realize that some of these problems were created or exacerbated by the regimes they were operating.

So much by way of caveat. When our extensive evidence on staff-pupil relationships is reviewed, we find again and again a great range between schools but some important patterns between particular kinds of schools, between boarding and day schools and, finally and most significantly, between the boarder's pastoral care and that of the day pupil in his school, his home and outside life.

First some particular aspects of staff-pupil relations. Coming back to Snow's contention, we actually asked sixth formers in the four schools on our intensive sample with house systems how close their contact with their housemasters had been.

TABLE 8:17

Sixth formers' contact with their housemasters (in percentages)

	Public schools			State boarding
	A	*B*	*C*	*E*
I have got to know well as a person	10	21	2	3
I have got to know fairly well as a person	47	51	40	44
Our contact chiefly confined to discipline or formal meetings	33	18	39	22
I scarcely know as a person	7	6	13	7
We have virtually nothing to do with each other	3	3	5	24
N =	440	239	80	97

Source: intensive sample.

Though these boys were all in the sixth form, at the top of the house structure, substantial numbers seemed not to know their housemasters well, except at school B, a Catholic one. This casts some doubt on the 'family relationship' claimed by Snow. Such doubts are reinforced if we recollect that when we asked the boys to rank aspects of school which they found most rewarding, contact with individual masters was rated surprisingly low, whereas teaching appeared usually at the top. Clearly the closeness between staff and pupils and its value to the recipients can be overstated by the advocates of boarding. In so far as satisfaction with teaching measures pupils' confidence in staff, we found that this was somewhat higher in our intensive sample boarding schools than in the four comparison day schools as the following table shows.

TABLE 8:18

Satisfaction with teaching of sixth-form boarders in the intensive day school sample (in percentages)

	Public schools				State boarding schools		Day schools			
							Independent	Comprehensive	Comprehensive	Secondary Modern
	A	B	C	D	E*	F	A	B	C	D
Yes, generally satisfied	58	66	52	36	89	51	61	32	41	27
No, generally dissatisfied	39	33	54	60	9	37	36	61	55	69
N =	440	239	189	67	83	97	80	52	90	88

* Mixed secondary modern schools, replies from sixth-form boys and girls.

Source: intensive sample and comparison schools.

It seems then that the satisfaction with teaching among pupils is more pronounced than their friendship with the staff and that the official pastoral role may not be as effective as some advocates make it out to be.

We measured the pastoral effectiveness of schools by the pupils' ability and willingness to turn to others with their problems, both adults in the community and their own contemporaries. We suggested three different kinds of problems, an objective 'work' kind, a problem concerning someone else in the family, and finally an intimate personal problem and asked who, if anyone, from a given list the pupil would turn to with each

TABLE 8:19

*Replies to questions as to with whom (if anyone)
you would discuss problems
Fifth and Sixth forms in percentage*

	Staff	Friend	Other	No one	Number of Schools	Replies
A *Work problems*						
Boarding						
Public	63	20	8	10	10	1413
Other independent	69	11	11	9	5	254
State	50	30	8	13	9	503
Progressive	70	16	8	6	3	106
Day						
Comprehensive	37	26	6	31	2	142
Independent	42	16	10	32	1	80
Secondary modern	31	12	9	48	1	84
B *Family problems*						
Public	42	24	10	25		
Other independent	47	19	11	23		
State	41	25	9	25		
Progressive	46	32	8	14		
Day						
Comprehensive	5	41	15	39		
Independent	14	10	6	70		
Secondary modern	11	12	7	70		
C *Personal problems*						
Public	27	29	10	34		
Other independent	33	28	14	25		
State	30	27	6	36		
Progressive	31	34	10	25		
Day						
Comprehensive	15	24	9	52		
Independent	21	7	12	60		
Secondary modern	9	11	4	76		

Source: general sample and day school comparisons.

kind of problem inside the school and for day pupils repeated the question for pastoral agents outside the school as well as inside. Obviously the results showed considerable variations between individual schools and different kinds of pastoral agents within them. But in general terms certain clear patterns emerged, as can be seen in the summary of the pupils' replies in Table 8:19.

The pastoral effectiveness of all schools is naturally greater for the objective 'work problem' but slumps notably for the more familial and personal problems as is shown by the rise in the percentage of pupils who can turn to no one. Only between a quarter and a third of all the pupils in our sample felt that they could discuss personal problems with staff at their school. In general, progressive schools are the most pastorally effective according to our criteria, with consistently fewest pupils without some human outlet for their problems and with a relatively high recourse to staff and to peers.[17] It is notable that in public schools, despite their elaborate official structures for pastoral care and the evident considerable success of this in dealing with problems of the work variety, there is a considerable reluctance to turn to adults or anyone else at all with problems of an intimate character. We shall see that this may derive not necessarily from defective school structures but from pre-socialization, from the boys' own deep inhibition in discussing deeply personal matters with anyone, which we shall describe later in their emotional relations with the other sex and with their parents. The staff agencies in state schools were also less used than others and the schools contained most boarders who could turn to no one. This reflects very much the state day school pattern, as we can see, but also we found in practice that state boarders more frequently referred their problems *outside* the school to parents who, as we know, live in the region and to others with whom they had less difficulty in discussing such matters anyway.

Instrumental pastoral care based on knowledge, in which the adult is continuously informed about the child's development and background and uses this information and the organization of the school in the interests of the child, is evidently effectively achieved in most boarding schools by official agencies such as housemasters, tutors and teachers and it is clear that day pupils have substantially less of this objective and informed guidance.

Pupils and staff in boarding situations know and trust each other enough to discuss this kind of matter. But the second, expressive, kind of pastoral care based on deeper communication and more affective relationships, in which the child has a sympathetic and warm support encouraging the discussion of deeper issues, is achieved far less, though again far more in day schools which may leave this kind of care of the adolescent to the families and friends and others outside their boundaries.

Great differences occur between the levels of pastoral care achieved by various schools; there is greatest variety in state schools and most uniformity of achievement among public and progressive schools. In state schools the proportion of pupils who would tell members of staff about personal problems ranged from fourteen to thirty-eight per cent and those who would tell no one about personal problems from nineteen to sixty per cent. Variations on the same intimate matters in public schools were more narrow, eighteen to forty and thirty to forty-four per cent respectively.

Why do all these variations occur? No one system - house, tutorial group or form - seemed to produce consistently better results pastorally than another. No patterns emerged when these factors were examined. Neither does pastoral care appear to be related to the level of control or totality of the school because rank correlations between pupils turning with deeper problems failed to correspond with the order according to institutional control ($p = -0.13$ and -0.05.) Effective pastoral care on the family problem also failed to correlate significantly with the personal one ($p = +0.29$, not significant) indicating that some schools are effective in some areas but not in others. This is particularly true in progressive schools where family problems are more discussed with staff than personal ones.

Very contrasting regimes can achieve high levels of pastoral care: structural features are therefore less important than attitudes and the informal systems involved. The informal norms of the staff are here very important because, although the prison, the 'us' and 'them' model of institutions, suggests that the inmates avoid relations with staff even in positive and therapeutic institutions, in boarding schools we found that the informal norms of the staff could disapprove of and control over-involvement with pupils however much the official policy of the school promoted staff-pupil relations. These informal norms were partly a defence against personal exhaustion, against manipulation by the pupil society, against severe conflicts of roles and a means of avoiding over-involvement with individuals. Pastoral effectiveness in the more intimate areas was greatest when pupils were allowed choice of formal agents, when pastoral groups were small and when women, domestics and ancillary staff were brought in to the pastoral system. Individual situations in which conflict occurred between the roles of discipline and administration on the one hand and pastoral care on the other made for low effectiveness. Most pastoral effectiveness, however, depended on the informal norms of the pupils and staff and on the standards that these laid down for acceptable interaction. Consensus among the staff in particular towards intimate pastoral relations promotes the most effective pastoral care, although the structural features we have mentioned help in this direction.

Nevertheless, despite the variety between various kinds of schools and their levels of effectiveness in dealing with different kinds of problems, the boarding schools in our sample were altogether more effective as centres of pastoral care than the four comparison day schools which we examined. Recourse to staff with work problems in these latter schools was significantly less and for the other problems was absolutely negligible, friendships being as much used or even more for them. The numbers of children in the day schools with no one to discuss such problems inside the school were large for academic work and enormous for the more intimate problems, over twice the proportion found on average in boarding schools. It is also noticeable that far fewer of the pupils in day schools were prepared to discuss the two more intimate problems with friends, some evidence in support of the hypothesis that boarding generates deeper relationships among peers than occurs outside. But, it will be at once and rightly objected, day pupils do not need expressive pastoral care inside their schools as they have families and friends and others outside them with whom to discuss intimate problems and who may abundantly make up for what the society of the school fails or does not wish to offer.

In fact there has been no systematic research in this country into the important subject of pastoral outlets for adolescents in day schools or at work. We therefore subjected our day school comparison pupils to an extra scrutiny, asking them not only to whom they would go with problems inside the school but then, a second time, to whom outside the school they might also or separately go. We analysed the results as shown in Table 8:20, differentiating between boys and girls.

TABLE 8:20

Pastoral care on intimate problems: day pupils (in percentages)

| | Family problems | | Personal problems | |
	Girls	Boys	Girls	Boys
Inside school				
Staff/adults	0	0	21	16
Friends	45	11	46	11
No one	55	88	33	73
Outside school				
Parents/other adults	35	31	15	10
Friends	45	18	45	10
No one	20	50	40	80
N =	147	310	147	310

Source: 4 day school comparisons, sixth-form sample.

We see that for girls and boys there is little recourse to school staff on family matters and more recourse to parents, but the pattern reverses for personal problems. Day girls rely heavily on friends and when school and outside agents are considered together, this leaves them with slightly fewer pastoral isolates on family issues than boarders and somewhat more with no outlets on personal matters. Our concern, however, is more with boys because, of the twenty-seven boarding schools for which we produced data in Table 8:19, twenty were exclusively for boys. When we look at the day boys in the table above we find that their pastoral position is worse than for the girls in their own schools and infinitely worse than for all boy boarders on our sample. On family matters eighty-eight per cent of the boys in our day schools could turn to no one at school and fifty per cent could still find no one to talk to about such problems out-

side it. On more personal problems seventy-three per cent had
no outlet, adult or pupil, in their schools and eighty per cent
still had no outlet outside it. Not only are parents much less
used by boy adolescents than by girls, but fewer boys than their
girl contemporaries or than boy boarders elsewhere had friends
with whom they could talk on such issues, at least in our four
schools. This evidence adds yet more weight to the probability
that one important effect of boarding among boys in both
single-sex and coeducational schools is to allow deeper relationships between contemporaries than seems to occur among boys
of like age in day schools, who paradoxically possess potential
scope for male and female contacts both inside and out of
school. It also shows, in so far as the evidence of our four day-
schools dare be generalized, that boarding schools in spite of
all their pastoral limitations and artificialities offer their boys
aged fifteen to eighteen more effective pastoral outlets, both
formal and informal, than day boys find in school, home life
and the outside world combined.

*(v) Ability of boarding schools to meet need for residence away
from home*

Another important function served by boarding schools is their
ability to act as a welfare service for families with problems that
affect their children's education. These may arise from
inadequacies in the family unit, from the emotional and health
needs of the child, from the location or environment of the
child's home or from the mobility of the parents. While there
are many ways besides full-time residential education by which
such problems can be overcome, boarding schools in fact do
shelter a large number of children and it was proposed by the
Public Schools Commission in 1968 that they should take in
still more. The proportion varies in different schools, as we saw
in previous chapters. In some charity and state boarding schools
nearly every child had some need for boarding, whereas in
public schools the proportions are less.

The anxieties and insecurities of children with need for
boarding impose great pressures on schools. Many schools
which admit large numbers of these children have designed
regimes and structures to meet their problems and to reduce

the inevitable strains which are imposed by life in a residential setting. Nevertheless despite these developments there is still a wide variety of schools which seem able to cope with an intake composed largely of need cases. For example, preparatory schools make little obvious provision to meet need, yet care for many orphaned, deprived or damaged middle-class children. These schools often cope more satisfactorily with these problems than do some of the secondary schools to which the children proceed. The secondary school with most boys from broken homes on our sample provided a naval training and managed to surmount these problems and to satisfy the children. Why is it then that schools so very different from each other seemed to operate successfully despite the nature of their intake while other schools we visited were unable to meet the problem presented by difficult children and resorted to the implementation of custodial regimes where organizational goals dominated everything else, ignoring fundamental problems and individual requirements? Why can so many different approaches, ranging from naval and preparatory school regimes to charity and special schools run on cosy family lines, cope successfully with such children?

Obviously no boarding school can provide the unconditionial love that a child expects to receive in his family and the successful schools do not seek by substitution to replace the affective unit and relationships of the home. Once this limitation is acknowledged many types of regime seem to be suitable for meeting other requirements which children with need may have. The essential success of these regimes depends not so much on whether schools recognize their pupils' needs as whether the pupils are able to adjust both to the deprivations of leaving home and the cultural pressures imposed by the school. The child with need for boarding from an upper-middle-class family is likely to go to a public school whatever his private circumstances, and his problems are therefore those of adjustment to a residential setting rather than those of cultural adaptation. If the school sets out to minimize any problems of cultural adaptation among pupils with need for boarding, then children from a variety of backgrounds can be helped in a residential setting which imposes minimum controls and is effective in winning pupils commitment.

There is no evidence, therefore, that any one style of boarding is generally more effective in meeting need for boarding than any other. Obviously the question of social background has to be considered in deciding what regimes suit particular children so as not to aggravate their existing problems. Because public schools may cope successfully with need occurring among their clientele it does not follow that they can repeat the success with children from other backgrounds and other cultures with need for residence. In *New Wine in Old Bottles* we suggested that public schools could not meet the needs of less able or working-class children without a drastic re-structuring which would alter their whole ethos and role, away from their elitist functions for our society.[18]

The emphasis on the ability of schools to cope with pupils for whom boarding is a necessity must not distract us from wider arguments about the types of care most suited for children in need. Boarding schools can be a useful solution to certain problems as they offer care in a predominantly educational setting and demand no new emotional relationships from children. Nevertheless alternative approaches which are beyond the scope of this book should not be ignored. Care in the community, for example, may often be preferable to residential schooling. The style of residence that could be developed in hostels or centres associated with day schools may have the advantage of keeping the child in his home area while providing residence in a setting where educational and social activities such as play groups and weekend courses take place. This is one way of removing any stigma or feelings of rejection that can arise when a child feels 'sent away'. Hardly any of the boarding hostels that are at present attached to day schools are used in this way and it is only by a radical redefinition of their functions that they could develop such a potential. Most of the small hostels attached to day schools display all that is worst about boarding in this country, but centres such as Northorpe Hall near Leeds or Red House, Denaby, both in Yorkshire, are seeking to exploit the benefits of residential education for children in need while eliminating the defects. Their experiences could well lead to an extension of residential provision of this intermediate kind and so provide an important point of growth.

9 Some effects of boarding (2) Personality

We can now turn from our survey of the general effects of boarding to the way in which it influences the personality and growth of individual children.

(i) Increasing self-reliance

Virtually all the advocates of boarding claim, as a favourable effect, that it produces 'independence', self-reliance, 'the ability to stand on your own two feet'. When these concepts are probed their precise meaning is often difficult to establish and unfortunately impossible to measure. It is often difficult to know the kind of children or situations with which this essentially relative quality (independence of whom or what?) is being compared. Sometimes at interviews those who suggested this effect contrasted the boarder with a mythical, over-indulged, affluent, spoon-fed day child completely tied to the sybaritic life of home and the apron-strings of mother. When the tables are turned and the contrast is made between the boarder on the one hand, protected and controlled by a semi-closed institution where food, hot water, clean sheets, entertainment and pocket money just appear and school is two minutes away from the house, and a fifteen-year-old day boy on the other, who rises early, does a paper round, gets his own breakfast before setting off in all weathers by bike for school, the picture can be reversed. Who then *is* independent?

It is clear that important class factors are at work here. The twenty-one lads aged sixteen years who moved from the upper-working-class homes and day schools in Swindon to become boarders at Marlborough sixth-form college found not independence but a drastic loss of it.[1] It is clear from their experience and from parallel contrasts between the entry of working-class sixth formers and the others at the progressive school at Dartington discussed in Chapter 12, and from the evidence presented in the next chapter on family backgrounds, that in working-class or lower-middle-class families adolescents still at school are far more used to taking fundamental decisions for themselves, earning money for themselves and choosing friends and styles of life for themselves than upper-middle-class children whose parents exercise a far more pervasive control and interference over their lives and even friendships throughout their sixth-form careers. Removal to boarding school for boys and girls from the former group may thus mean a sudden curtailment of independence. Removal from the home and parents for the second group, even to a closed and controlling institution, may nevertheless make for greater personal independence.

Whatever initial qualifications we may make eighty-three per cent of the staff whom we interviewed considered that self-reliance and independence were among the most unqualified effects of boarding. Not only the staff. For boarders of all kinds stressed this, state boarders more even than the public school boarders, with only a substantial minority of progressive school sixth formers doubtful about it. In a reply to the question: what does being at this school promote, the numbers who ticked the item 'self-reliance' in a long list of probable effects was as follows.

TABLE 9:1

Boarders claiming that school promotes 'self-reliance'
(mean percentages for schools of each type)

Boarders	Sixth	Fifth	Third to fourth	N		
Public	70	82	96	(1362	274	186)
Progressive	59	61	97	(164	192	140)
State	98	85	98	(124	416	520)
Independent integrated	82	81	93	(200	206	217)
Independent non-integrated	75	79	93	(64	127	136)
Day pupils						
Public	41	42	46	(211	146	306)
Comprehensive	31	32	35	(96	307	680)
Secondary modern	—	12	15	(—	83	88)

Source: general sample and comparison day-schools. This figure includes day pupils in the intensive sample as well as those in the comparison schools.

This impressive and unusually unanimous chorus from all kinds of school and all age ranges commands respect. What then do boarders in their interviews with us and glosses on our questions seem to understand by the 'self-reliance' which is promoted among them? First, it means to them taking responsibility for your own actions without having parents to back you up, to bail you out or to prod you along. Secondly, it means knowing how to express yourself and answer for your actions verbally in company and publicly and before authority. Thirdly, it means organizational competence, knowing how to organize your own affairs in a situation of little privacy and to promote them on your own in a complicated society. Finally, it means a form of self-control, the ability, necessitated by close living, to scale down reactions, to hold yourself back from overdependence on the goodwill of others, a sort of inner reserve. We discerned by observation and experience that all these qualities occurred in boarders of all kinds and former day pupils arriving at boarding schools found themselves rather painfully acquiring them, as their parents frequently noticed and mentioned to us.

But the independence of the boarder in this sense occurs within a narrow organizational context. How far it applies outside the school is much more difficult to determine. Boarders, it is true, may become independent of their families but for early boarders in particular this independence may go too far in that they may lose meaningful relations with their parents as well. Independent self-control can also become at its extreme an inability to express deeper feelings; so, too, boarders in expressively oriented schools, however independent in the senses above, can nevertheless often become deeply dependent on their school and unable easily to break out of its context on leaving. Finally, as is indicated by the levels of control we have described earlier, boarding schools, except for progressive ones, often remove from young people of sixteen to eighteen powers of decision on a wide variety of daily, even detailed and petty, matters which the majority of sixteen to eighteen-year-olds outside decide for themselves. In other words boarding may promote certain kinds of self-reliance but often within the limits of a deeper dependence on and even deference to an external and pervasive system of authority and control.

(ii) Gregariousness and social sensitization

Our scales of control have already amply demonstrated that
privacy, time spent alone, is not much found in the English
boarding school. Meals, recreation and study often take place
in large groups. Only two schools in England, Eton and
Dartington, provide a single study bedroom for every pupil of
whatever age in their society. Some other schools provide
studies, sometimes shared, for sixth formers but even in most of
these cases the boys sleep separately in dormitories. For
virtually all boarders under sixteen and for the majority over
that age, sleeping and living are in dormitories and common
room or shared group rooms.[2] Our intensive sample of schools
covered most of the prevalent kinds of accommodation and
fairly represents the privacy of the boarders. The sixth-form
boys estimated the time spent alone during waking hours on a
normal weekday as follows.

TABLE 9:2

Time alone in waking hours during weekdays in percentages

	Public schools				State schools		Day boys at B and D	
	A	B	C	D	E	F	B	D
5 minutes or less	4	6	14	8	20	15	0	0
5–15 minutes	11	11	11	12	18	29	12	10
16– 30	17	13	16	18	19	14	14	8
31– 60	28	19	20	10	22	20	8	12
61–120	24	15	23	23	12	13	32	35
121+	14	35	26	30	6	10	34	35
N =	440	239	189	67	97	84	85	36

Source: intensive sample.

Between a third and a half of the sixth form boys were alone
for less than half an hour and a half to two-thirds of the boys
for less than an hour, whereas day boys at two of the same
schools had sixty-four and seventy per cent of their members
who were alone for over one hour each day. The boarders,
however, are well conditioned to and even like such an absence
of solitude, for when we asked them if they would like to have
more time alone, two-thirds or more did not want it and those

at the school with the least privacy wanted it least.

TABLE 9:3

Sixth formers wanting more time alone in percentages

	Public schools				State schools	
	A	B	C	D	E	F
Yes	30	31	31	33	33	20
No	65	65	68	68	61	80

(N = as in previous table).

What then is the effect of this endless living with others? To what degree do such children become dependent on the group? Obviously again this factor is not easy to measure but, first, what do the boarders and the day pupils think of their own experience? When we asked in the questions on what the school promotes, whether the school promoted herd instinct or individuality, there were no significant differences between boarders and day children in answering. It was state school boarders who thought that their school least induced the herd instinct and most promoted individuality.

TABLE 9:4

Percentage who say that being at school promotes a herd instinct

(Figures are means of percentages for each type of school)

	Forms					
	Sixth	Fifth	Third to fourth	N		
Boarders						
Public	48	29	48	(1362	274	186)
Progressive	32	27	28	(164	192	140)
State	4	20	26	(124	416	520)
Independent integrated	44	23	18	(200	206	217)
Independent non-integrated	15	33	21	(64	127	136)
Day						
Public	42	39	51	(211	213	306)
Comprehensive	16	19	28	(96	307	680)
Secondary modern	—	17	19	(—	83	88)

Source: general sample and comparison day schools. These figures includes boarders in the intensive sample as well as those in the control school.

TABLE 9:5

Percentage who say that being at school promotes individuality

	Forms					
			Third to		N	
	Sixth	Fifth	fourth			
Boarders						
Public schools	58	77	78	(1362	274	136)
Progressive schools	54	68	72	(164	192	140)
State schools	98	81	84	(124	416	520)
Independent integrated	76	78	73	(200	206	21)
Independent non-integrated	83	59	79	(64	127	136)
Day						
Public schools	61	75	83	(211	213	306)
Comprehensive schools	68	82	71	(96	307	680)
Secondary modern schools	–	49	54	(–	83	88)

Source: as Table 9:4.

Our attitude tests and tests on responses to authority have also been elaborately analysed to see if day pupils and boarders at the same kinds of schools have more or less consensus, more or less heterogeneity of opinion. When social and cultural factors are thus held constant, no significant differences emerge. Boarders are neither more nor less conforming or prone to accept authority than day pupils of their own social group and at their own school. It is when we turn to the more subtle effects of gregarious living that distinctions begin to appear between the two experiences.

To examine any differences in relationships, we took children at the end of the second year of boarding, ten-year-olds in our preparatory school study. One group was from a boarding preparatory school, another from a day preparatory school and the third from a state primary school. All the children were matched for academic ability and for social class, for the primary school was in an upper-middle-class suburb. Each child was asked to select a classmate to help him do certain hypothetical tasks, such as helping him with arithmetic, at playing football in a game, going out for a cycle ride, doing a jigsaw puzzle, shovelling snow, going out to tea, helping fight enemies, and helping paint a picture. It was found that the boarders chose different people for different tasks, most choosing five or more friends, whereas the day boys from both other schools relied on fewer friends, no more than three, for every task.

TABLE 9:6

Number of different friends chosen for the eight tasks

No. of friends	Boarding preparatory	Day preparatory	Day primary
1	1	6	5
2	1	4	9
3	3	7	6
4	4	5	6
5	7	2	3
6	6	3	0
7	6	2	1
8	2	1	0

(N = 30 for all schools)

Source: preparatory schools study, sub-sample.

From an early age therefore boarders seem to interact more with a wider and looser group of friends than do day children. And we shall see in the next chapter how marked this tendency is in the holiday times. Not a few boys who were recent boarders at school commented to us that whereas formerly at their day schools they had one or two close friends they now found their friendship groups were much larger in size.

This social tendency is confirmed by yet other evidence. Sixth form boarders at schools in the intensive sample were asked to choose from a list of qualities which they most liked to see in other people. They were given a list of eight qualities, scattered among which were four primarily social or other regarding ones (leadership, tolerance, ability to mix easily and to co-operate with others) and four of which were primarily individual or self-regarding ones (independence of mind, imagination, originality, and sensitivity). Boys were asked to select the four qualities which they most liked to see in other people and their replies were scored thus: +1 for every social quality and −1 for every individual quality selected.

TABLE 9:7

Qualities preferred in others: social/individual (in percentages)

Score for choice of qualities		Boys who boarded before ninth birthday	after ninth birthday	at schools in the intensive sample Boarders	Day
Social	+4	12	2	8	2
	+3	31	9	21	3
	+2	42	11	29	10
	+1	6	14	9	13
	0	5	11	8	9
	−1	2	27	12	28
	−2	1	11	5	15
	−3	1	14	7	18
Individual	−4	0	1	1	2
		N = 443	674	1117	121

Source: intensive sample.

The results showed that boys who had been boarders from an early age preferred social attributes in people more than boys who had boarded later, who somewhat preferred individual ones, and that day pupils preferred individual attributes even more markedly than the later boarders.

Thus boarding does not seem to make its recipients slavish adherents of the group but it does seem to condition those who experience it, especially those who board from an early age, to prize social rather than individual qualities in others and to lead them to interact in larger groups of sympathetic peers.

(iii) Development of skills of management and authority

Though day pupils play many roles of which the boarder is dispossessed temporarily during term, boarders at school in turn have some roles given to them which few day pupils experience so fully. Virtually all the schools on our sample expected their pupils to play adult roles and nearly all passed over to their pupils roles of management of others and of exercising authority. In public, preparatory and schools of similar styles, the diffusion of roles of authority and management among pupils is wide over many areas of school life and the pupils move progressively up parallel hierarchies by which some control over or responsibility for others below them is matched by obedience to those above them. At the top of these hierarchies in house, school, games, CCF or social organizations are boys who exercise more real power over others than sometimes the junior teachers in their own schools and many other teachers in day schools outside. Day pupils have nothing like the scope and reality of this dual training in responsible authority on the one hand, and obedience on the other; nor have boarders in other kinds of schools such as state, progressive and integrated ones. Authority in the public school style of boarding is not only instrumental in the sense that prefects at day schools understand authority (checking boys in, supervising dinner queues, etc), but it is also *expressive* in that the system expects boys with authority to exercise pastoral care over those in their charge, care which is frequently taken seriously and exercised sensitively in practice.

In the other three main kinds of boarding school the roles of authority exercised by pupils are more varied. In progressive schools there is none of the hierarchy and structure of authority as found in public schools, but pupils are instead invested with a considerable adult role of decision-making, both for themselves in their daily life and for the whole community in democratic situations. The more radical kinds of progressive school pass over real individual and collective decision-making to their pupils. Virtually no other schools in this country, day or boarding, go so far. The rationality, deferment of gratification, and the self-control demanded are highly adult qualities which not all the children find it easy to display or sustain. State and integrated schools fall somewhat between models of the public school on the one hand and the more paternalistic progressive schools on the other, but nevertheless distribute adult roles and responsibilities. All three kinds of school exact managerial qualities in the sense of passing the running of communal undertakings over to the pupils.

Once more, differences on this score between boarding and day education were difficult to measure. Obviously the day pupil also exercises adult, responsible or managerial skills though of a different kind from those of the boarder. Our care-

fully devised tests exploring the differences in response to
managerial situations or authority figures produced no significant differences between the boarders and day pupils who took
them. Perhaps the tests were inadequate or the differences too
elusive. Boarders themselves, however, certainly think that
their schools offer training in management more than do day
pupils, as their ratings of the goal 'provides us with experience
in managing people' tend to show.

TABLE 9:8

*Ratings in percentages by sixth formers on the goal 'provides us
with experience in managing people'*

Boarders	Tries	Should try	Succeeds
Public	72	80	60
Independent	58	76	54
Independent integrated	62	77	56
State	55	70	52
Progressive	60	69	58
Day			
Public	64	79	51
State	41	48	27

Source: extensive sample, see Table 4, Appendix IV.

The same pattern applies when the question of promoting
qualities of leadership is answered, though progressive school
boarders, in accordance with their general attitudes, reject this
effect and public school boys endorse it more than others.

Nevertheless, despite claims and counter-claims that public
school training in authority either created or wrecked the British
empire, there is no evidence to prove at the moment that boy
boarders as they were in the late 1960s were more or less skilled
at wielding or responding to authority than comparable day
pupils. The exploration of such hypotheses would require very
rigid definition of authority and its exercise and a long follow-
up study of pupils and old boys. It is true, as we shall see in the
next chapter, that early boarders from public school styles of
boarding more often tend to have good relations with their
father, the authority figure, than with their mother. This may

give some slender support to the notion that protracted
boarding in public school styles makes for adjustment to
authority figures. But no more. This type of effect of boarding
needs either more research to analyse or does not prove
significant or obvious in practice.

(iv) Effects of boarding on emotional and sexual life

One area of life in which boarding education as it now is in this
country provides a sharply different experience for its
recipients from day education is that fundamental area of
adolescent growth and concern, the emotions.

Boarding schools permit much less scope in their official
life and policies for emotional development than does the day
school/home situation. In the first place, however sympathetic
and pastorally effective the staff in boarding schools may be,
they cannot by definition offer the unconditional love of a
parent for a child: a love not conditional on performance and
expectations as is that bestowed by trained and changing paid
professionals in a school situation. Secondly, the vast majority
of boarders live in single-sex schools. Very few single-sex
schools for boys or girls have anything more than superficial
contact with schools of the other sex, and few regularly allow
individuals of the other sex on to their premises. As a result the
vast majority of the sixth-form boy boarders on our intensive
sample (eighty-six per cent) had no girl friend locally compared
with thirty-five per cent of their day boy contemporaries. The
long isolation from the affective unit of the home and from
emotional outlets with the other sex seems to have some dis-
cernible impact on those boys who have boarded in such an
emotional vacuum from an early age. As we have already seen
and shall see again in the next chapter, it seems to induce or
support 'affective neutrality', an inhibition on expressing
feelings, and a tendency towards more strained relations with
affective figures such as the mother. Even coeducational
boarding need not remove all such problems; for in the majority
of coeducational schools, which are of the divided type, little
contact is permitted between boys and girls and emotional
relations can be severely discouraged, while unconditional love
from the family may be as remote as in the other kinds of

schools. This is perhaps the most signal area where the limitations of present-day boarding as an environment for balanced growth are most glaring.

Boys' schools. It was no part of our research brief to question children about their own emotional or sexual lives, though much material on the matter inevitably came our way, some of which we used in *The Hothouse Society*. Our statistical evidence is thus of a general nature.

Of course the boys on our sample overwhelmingly said that they saw too little of the other sex and wanted more contact with girls. When our questions asked them to express the effect that being educated apart from girls had had on their perceptions, their answers polarized into extremes which were found much less commonly among day pupils in single-sex schools. On the one hand a substantial group of the boarders on our intensive sample (thirty-five per cent) claimed that they had found girls difficult to comprehend, unreal and unapproachable, while a small minority of fifteen per cent at the other extreme claimed that they regarded girls principally as vehicles for sex, particularly in the holidays, which a much more substantial minority of thirty-six per cent said were times for gratifying desires unfulfilled during term, a compensatory attitude borne out by evidence in the next chapter. Early boarding once more seems to affect the adjustment of boys to emotional figures, this time not to mother but to those of their own age. Over sixty-one per cent of the sixth-form boys on our intensive sample who had boarded before the age of nine gave reactions to girls of these two extreme kinds, while only twenty-one per cent of later boarders did so and only eight per cent of day sixth formers. This surely indicates that an inability to accept girls as real and complete people, a tendency to polarize in perception of them towards the unreal goddess model on the one hand or machines for gratification on the other, may be induced by long isolation in boarding communities.

This is borne out by the answers to our questions on how the boys felt when they were actually in the company of a girl. A majority of boarders (fifty-six to sixty-seven per cent) were uneasy or lacking in assurance with girls compared with a majority of day boys in the same or similar single-sex schools

TABLE 9:9

Sixth-form boarders' reactions in company of a girl in percentages

| | Boarders | | | | | Day (single-sex) | |
| | Public schools | | | | State | Public | State |
	A	B	C	D	E		
I'm usually quite at ease	44	40	42	33	33	58	63	65
I look self-confident but don't feel it	20	18	24	23	23	18	14	15
I tend to put on a bit of a show	15	9	10	20	20	15	15	12
I feel a bit embarrassed	11	10	13	7	7	6	6	6
I feel uneasy	11	7	9	13	13	3	2	2
N =	239	189	440	67	97	196	96	52

Source: intensive sample, day school controls.

TABLE 9:10

Sixth-form boy boarders giving a tendency to increased homosexual feelings as a result of boarding in a single-sex school (in percentages)

| | Public | | | | State |
A	B	C	D	E
66·7	67·0	70·0	67·8	62·9
N = 239	441	189	67	97

Source: intensive sample.

(fifty-eight to sixty-three per cent) who claimed to be perfectly at ease in the company of the other sex. How deep or enduring these marked reactions to girls may be we cannot say. We do not know what, if any, effects they may have produced on the boarders as they are now or as they might be in later life. There is, however, evidence that more boy boarders have marital difficulties in later life than those from either single-sex day or coeducational schools.[3]

Just as single-sex boarding may affect attitudes to the other sex, so it may influence boys' reactions to their own sex. When we asked in an open question the sixth formers on our intensive sample to state what they had found were the least desirable effects of single-sex education, the most frequently mentioned one among several others was the tendency to increase homosexual feelings (Table 9:10).

When, among the possible effects that their own particular school might promote in practice, we also listed homosexuality, the following proportions of boys from the same schools and in two comparable coeducational schools ticked it as being the case. Over half the boys in the boarding sample thought that their schools produced homosexuality whereas less than two per cent of those in the coeducational schools thought that it did.

TABLE 9:11

School seen by senior boy boarders as promoting homosexuality (in percentages)

	Public			State	Two coed. state schools (including school F)
A	B	C	D	E	
50	55	60·8	54·8	53·8	1·5
N = 239	441	189	67	97	105

Source: intensive sample and one extensive sample.

In our open-ended questions, which allowed the boys to write about any worries caused personally for them by life as a boarder at school, the following proportions volunteered homosexuality as such a problem.

TABLE 9:12

Senior boarders giving homosexuality as a problem for them caused by school life (in percentages)

	Public			State	Two coed. state schools (including school F)
A	B	C	D	E	
9	21	26	18	15	0
N = 239	441	189	67	97	105

Source: intensive sample, one extensive sample school.

Again, substantial though fluctuating minorities seem to be deeply personally worried by this effect.

Whatever these figures may mean in reality, it does seem that most boy boarders on our sample believed that their schools' single-sex nature activated homosexual instincts in them and that substantial minorities of them volunteered that they were personally worried by the effects on themselves. By contrast this sexual response and worry seems entirely absent from the sample of boys in coeducational schools.

This sensitization to their own sex and to homosexual situations among boy boarders was indicated by two incidental pieces of other evidence from our research. In a question probing informal norms, on the elements of popularity among the boys at schools, we listed as one of the items which might make for popularity as 'good looks'.

TABLE 9:13

'Good looks' ticked as an element of popularity
(sixth-form boy boarders in percentages)

						Day boys	
	Public			State	Public	State
A	B	C	D	E		
41·9	42·0	40·0	41·0	38	17	15	15
N = 239	441	189	67	97	211*	90	52

* This figure includes day boys at schools C and D as well as in the comparison schools.

Source: intensive sample, day school comparisons.

More than twice as many boy boarders as day boys valued physical attractiveness on the part of their own sex as an element of popularity. Next, as part of a series of projective tests which we used to examine reactions to authority, we gave each pupil a picture showing in the foreground a boy dressed in a T-shirt with his back to us, looking at a man whose face was deliberately ambiguous, benign or awesome according to the beholder's reaction. When the test was applied in day schools, the pupils saw it and reacted always as to a test of authority. In boarding schools, however, a minority of boarders saw it, to our surprise, as a homosexual situation and some of them quite seriously saw the child as naked.

That single-sex boarding may make boys more aware of homosexual feelings in themselves, in others and in situations, does not mean that the schools they inhabit are hotbeds of homosexual activity and relations. Their feelings may be stimulated but before they are translated into action, into relationships and social patterns and norms, quite other and controlling factors intervene. But even in the schools on our intensive sample which have so far produced such uniform reactions the situation considerably alters and diversifies when we turn from the reactions of individuals to the attitudes of the community of the boys towards actual homosexual behaviour or towards homosexual individuals in their midst. Among a list of items which might make a boy unpopular with others we suggested someone 'too keen on his own sex' and among a list of slang epithets which were the worst someone might be called by another in the school we gave the item 'queer'.

TABLE 9:14

Sixth-form boy boarders ticking homosexuality as element of unpopularity (in percentages)

	Public				State
	A	B	C	D	E
Unpopularity					
'too keen on own sex'	59	69	30	31	65
Worst epithet					
'queer'	80	72	41	45	68
	N = 239	441	189	67	96

Source: intensive sample.

It will be seen that at schools C and D the odium of being a practising or alleged homosexual is significantly less than at the other schools, and it was very obvious to us on our stays at these two schools and from much other evidence that came our way that some forms of homosexuality were approved or tolerated and were fairly widespread in them whereas at the other schools they were disapproved of, restricted and concealed by the boys

from each other. We estimate that the former situation of
tolerance by the pupil society of homosexual behaviour and
relationships occurred in no more than ten of all the schools on
our extensive and intensive samples.

If all or most boy boarders are sensitized to homosexuality
by their experience, why does it only result in widespread
patterns of activity in some schools? The matter is complex.
First of all we should remember that homosexual activity falls
into certain kinds, some of which may coexist or any one of
which may exist by itself and be approved: physical experimentation among younger boys, which seems widespread; emotional
and physical relationships between boys of the same or different
ages; emotional relations between boys of the same or different
age not accompanied by physical ones; promiscuous physical
relations not accompanied by obvious emotional ones. (This
latter kind occurs in school A in the table above and accounts
for the discrepancies between the two figures given there.) In so
far as we can judge we found schools with all of these kinds of
activity. Evidently the attitudes of staff and the official
system were irrelevant to the existence of a widespread homosexual underlife: sometimes the official attitudes were
repressive, at other times they were manipulative and, in some
schools, uninformed altogether of what was going on. We
subjected the ten schools with an obvious homosexual underlife
to an analysis by such factors as isolation, denomination, level
of control, goal patterns, relations between the informal and
formal systems, but no consistent linking factors emerged
between them. Obviously all the schools are single sex and
obviously it is the informal system of the pupils which controls
the situation rather than the formal system and attitudes of the
staff and it must be either tolerant or supportive rather than
hostile. What then makes the informal norms of the pupils
positive among such a diverse group of schools and negative in
others which are equally diverse, when the basic situation and
other features are so similar between them? Why should
homosexual orientation be fashionable for some time in a
school and then swing to being taboo later, as we found in some
of the schools concerned? It seems that this is one of those
situations attributable to personality, to the sociological
accident of the rise to influence of an individual or group of

individuals who, aided sometimes by tradition, sometimes by the quality of staff-pupil relations and often by the degree of isolation from heterosexual outlets, can activate and legitimate a homosexual tendency which remains latent in many other similar schools. Beyond that we have no explanations.

All this is not to say that homosexual activity is widespread in boarding schools; on the contrary, except for the experimental kind, it seems remarkably restricted as a social as distinct from a private phenomenon. We have no means of knowing its long-term effects or that of the more widespread stimulation of homosexual feelings among boy boarders in their later lives.

Coeducational schools. Boarders at coeducational schools are a tiny fraction of those in residential education. We saw above how these relatively few schools subdivide into three groups: those which separate the sexes ('the divided communities'), those which mix them more frequently together ('the mixed communities') and those which encourage complete integration ('the integrated communities'). Each kind of coeducation produces different structures and problems. Obviously in several ways boys and girls in coeducational schools feel less frustrated than those in single-sex schools, though the level of frustration varies with the level of co-education. Thus when we compare the levels of commitment or alienation among sixth formers in such schools we find that far more pupils of both sexes in the integrated schools were committed to their schools than in those of both the other kinds, and more of those in mixed schools than in those of the divided kind (Table 9:15).

More frequently too the norms of the pupil society in the integrated kind of school coincided with those of the staff. The opposite was the case in schools of the divided kind, and the mixed kind fell once more between the two.

These results and similar ones for pastoral care and other areas of school life makes it clear that generalizations about co-education are perilous.[4]

There are, however, some effects of coeducational boarding which were not found in the single-sex boys' schools we visited and which seem to be less prominent in mixed day schools.

TABLE 9:15

Level of satisfaction with school by nature of coeducation in percentages
(sixth-form pupils only)

| | Divided | | Mixed | | Integrated | |
	Boys	Girls	Boys	Girls	Boys	Girls
Satisfied	23	31	55	62	93	89
Mixed	9	21	10	12	1	0
Alienated	63	45	25	20	2	8
No answer	5	3	10	6	4	3
N =	104	97	89	63	51	55
Schools	5	5	4	4	2	2

Source: general sample.

TABLE 9:16

Dominant norms in coeducational schools

| | Divided | | Mixed | | Integrated | |
Sixth form	Boys	Girls	Boys	Girls	Boys	Girls
No. of dominant norms pro goals stated by staff	3	4	6	8	9	11
No. of dominant norms anti-goals stated by staff	7	9	4	3	1	1
No. of replies	104	97	89	63	51	55

Note: dominant norms were derived from an open question on what makes a boy popular or unpopular with other boys. If a norm was listed by seventy per cent of the pupils it was accepted as a dominant norm. Its content was then compared with staff ratings of real and achieved goals.

When we examined boy-girl friendships within the schools and then compared them with those of day pupils we found that, among sixth formers, there were more girls than boys without a close emotional relationship with someone of the opposite sex. Also far fewer girls in coeducational boarding schools had boy friends than those in day schools. The trend was more marked in coeducational styles of the divided and mixed kind.

TABLE 9:17

Sixth formers with boy or girl friends (in percentages)

| | Boarders | | | | | | Day | |
| | Divided | | Mixed | | Integrated | | | |
	Boy	Girl	Boy	Girl	Boy	Girl	Boy	Girl
Boy or girl friend	55	28	62	30	69	57	75	77
No boy or girl friend	43	65	31	65	26	38	22	21
No answer	2	7	7	5	5	5	3	2
N =	104	97	89	63	51	55	310	147
Schools	5	5	4	4	2	2	4	4

Source: general sample.

Deprived of boy friends outside the school the girls were left with the boys inside, but these boys frequently had girl friends among the younger age groups. This left the older girls peculiarly frustrated, without emotional outlets but with the pressures of a cloistered community and academic work bearing upon them.

The effect among them was sometimes (and especially in the divided and mixed sort of school) an intense claustrophobic frustration, almost a hysteria, which is impossible to express statistically, but which was not paralleled among boys in the same schools or in single-sex ones, was not found in coeducational day schools and has not been suggested by research in single-sex girls' schools either.[5] No wonder that in some of the schools the girls turned their attentions on some younger male members of the staff and this caused further problems, especially when their interest was reciprocated. In day school society, where girls were freer to pursue their relations in and out of school, these problems seldom occurred.

Those schools which thoroughly integrate the sexes and where the norms of the pupils encourage or even enforce pairings-off between boys and girls produce a peculiar social situation of their own. The girls preserve a network of girl-girl friendships which seem compatible with their intimate friendship with a boy. The boys involved, however, seem much less able to sustain the close relationship with a group of other boys that we found in the less mixed or single-sex school and which seems to exist also in coeducational day settings.

TABLE 9:18

Boarders with close friends of own sex

	Divided		Mixed		Integrated		Day coed.	
	Boy	Girl	Boy	Girl	Boy	Girl	Boy	Girl
Yes	85	92	78	91	46	92	60	94
No	11	5	18	5	51	6	37	5
No answer	4	3	4	4	3	2	3	1
N =	104	97	89	63	51	55	310	147
Schools	5	5	4	4	2	2	4	4

Source: general sample.

In other words the society of the boys becomes fragmented and dissolved by the coupling process whereas that of the girls does not. In such schools the girls also often seem to be more dominant in controlling the informal norms. As a consequence certain norms or common attributes of boyhood such as physical aggression or interest in team games can be minimized in such schools, leading to the frequent comment that the boys seem to be emasculated or feminized by the society. Promoting this phenomenon, too, is the fact that in such progressive schools the parents also often seem to have a mother as the dominant figure, at least in the determination of the son's education. In day school settings boys seem, like the girls in integrated boarding schools, to be able to handle the coupling relationship without losing their part of a boy peer-group or the reference point of male behaviour and norms.

One final feature was found in all coeducational schools but much less commonly in single-sex or day schools, and seemed to result from the presence of girls or norms ordaining heterosexual liaisons combined with the lack of outlets for other relations outside the school. This is the concealment of sexual deviation of any kind. In single-sex schools, however puritan in mores or rigid in hostility to sexual deviations the pupils' informal system may have been, there seems to be always a large measure of tolerance of deviation from approved sexual norms: perhaps induced by a consciousness of common deprivation of normal life and the fact that in any case sexual and emotional activity was always underground. In coeducational schools deviation from heterosexual norms seldom seemed to be tolerated and pupils who were solitary or social isolates, particularly boarders who did not fit into the coupling patterns of some schools, were controlled by the epithet 'queer' and made to feel odd. Obviously this uniform enforcement of norms and styles is much less controlling over the day pupil, at least outside the school.

On deeper and long-lasting effects of coeducational boarding this research cannot offer fresh evidence. That boys living in coeducational schools feel themselves more adjusted to the other sex than those in single-sex schools is only to be expected.

TABLE 9:19

Sixth-form boy boarders' reactions in company of a girl

| | Single-sex schools | | | | | Coeducational | | | |
| | Public | | | | State | school | | | |
	A	B	C	D	E	F	G	H	I
I'm usually quite at ease	44	40	42	33	33	77	82	80	88
I look self-confident but don't feel it	20	18	24	23	23	4	9	9	6
I tend to put on a bit of a show	15	9	10	20	20	13	8	9	5
I feel a bit embarrassed	11	10	13	7	7	1	0	1	1
I feel uneasy	11	7	9	13	13	0	0	1	0
N =	239	189	440	67	97	53	110	52	61

Source: general sample.

Boys in coeducational schools differed too from substantial minorities of those in single-sex ones in that their perceptions of the opposite sex did not polarize on the idealistic-mechanistic dimension discussed above, and they tended too not to compensate for sexual deprivation in holiday periods. Indeed in all that was written for us by pupils, and in their general conversations and discussions which we recorded, there was much less sexual imagery, reference and preoccupation in the coeduca-

tional schools than in the others. The sexual temperature in
these schools seemed noticeably lower than that in boys'
schools.

Beyond this it would be unwise to go: there are simply no
facts available on the later lives of boarders from the two sorts
of school. Considerable evidence has been produced by
researchers on the differences produced in pupils by coeducational and single-sex day settings: the most recent even
attempting to show that adults educated in coeducational day
schools have more stable patterns of marriage than those from
single-sex ones.[6] If this were to be an effect of day education
one would expect the impact of boarding on such a pre-
disposition to be even greater. But there are many technical
obstacles to the acceptance of such research conclusions. Here
it needs only to be stressed that the adjustment of boy boarders
in single-sex schools to adult society may be easier than sus-
pected because the established culture, the roles, the familial
patterns taken up in the society to which they move reflect and
accommodate the responses we have found operating in the
single-sex school. Paradoxically there is some definite evidence
that boarders from the integrated kind of coeducational schools
of the progressive variety find adjustment to adult society,
which is not universally marked by the acceptance of egalitarian
relations or indefinite demarcations of role between the sexes,
presents them too with very considerable problems.[7]

Clearly here is yet another topic where further research could
most fruitfully be done.

General conclusions on the effects of boarding

Given the emphatic claims and counter-claims on the merits and
defects of boarding education by its sponsors and detractors,
the effects that our researches have been able to suggest or
determine are surprisingly sparse and tentative. Many of the
tests we devised to ferret out the differences between boarders
and day pupils at similar or the same schools and from similar
backgrounds produced no clear results at all. Perhaps the tests
were inadequate and certainly each of the alleged effects we
have explored and described in this chapter deserves an
elaborate and carefully mounted study involving the follow-up

of pupils after they have left school altogether. Nevertheless our researches, as elaborate and careful as the broad scope of our inquiry and the time we had available would allow, does indicate that the effects of this intensive, removed and expensive kind of education - for good or ill - are much less obvious, less crude, less uniform than the debate about residence has admitted. We can now bring together our own findings or indications, bearing in mind the diversity of styles of boarding and the difficulty of generalization.

It does seem that the effects of boarding on the academic performance of the majority of boarders are not substantially different from those of day education on pupils in controlled day situations, except that the more able day pupils seem to do better than boarders, whereas less able boarders seem to do better than their day counterparts. In terms of a general widening of horizons it was clear that the potential of residence was broader than that of day education and was sometimes realized, though in many cases the residential situation introduced severe limitations of its own which detracted from any such enlarging effect. Boarding schools were also found to have greater scope than day schools to direct the informal world of pupils and staff to their ends, though sometimes again this power was obstructed by the weaknesses of the system as it now is. Boarders seem to adapt more extremely to their schools than day pupils in terms of commitment or alienation and also of withdrawal. Undoubtedly boarding schools offered greater pastoral care by adults to pupils than was found among day pupils both at school and outside, and seemed to induce more pastoral care among pupils themselves, significantly among boys who seemed to have more and deeper relations with contemporaries then adolescent day boys, who seem appallingly bereft of pastoral agencies both among adults and among their peers. The ability of schools to cope with need to live away from home varied and depened on their ability to cope with the primary need and the secondary ones resulting from removal.

In terms of the effect on individuals, no clear evidence emerged on the alleged promotion of 'self-reliance' among boarders, though it is likely that certain kinds of 'independence' are fostered as other forms of dependence may also be increased. The same ambivalent effect was found when we

examined skills of management, though boarders clearly had
more training in some kinds of adult roles than day pupils.
More clear was the tendency to induce gregarious living and to
condition those who have experienced it from an early age to
value social rather than individual characteristics in people,
though there is little evidence of more conformity to the group
among boarders than among day boys. We found that early
boarding also may affect the emotional development of boys:
leading them to difficulties with affective situations or in
dealing with affective figures, but easing their relation with
authority figures. Single-sex boarding induces, besides widespread frustration, a sharp divergence in attitudes to the other
sex: making girls seem remote and unreal or engines for
gratification to substantial numbers of boarders. There was
plenty of evidence that single-sex boarding sensitizes boys to
their own homosexual instincts or to homosexual situations,
though no evidence that homosexual activity was widespread.
We have little comparable evidence about homosexuality for
day pupils and less about the later lives and adjustment of boy
boarders, but what there is shows more difficulties for them in
later life. Coeducation removes the frustration of single-sex
education but, compared with day experience, certain styles of
it induce some further severe frustration among girls, a fragmentation of boy society and an intolerant rigidity about
deviation from heterosexual norms.

One important finding is that the age at which boarders leave
home seems to induce important individual adaptations among
boys, in their approach to others, in their handling of emotions
and authority figures and in their sexual lives. It also reminds us
that one important and fascinating area involving boarding
schools and their effects has hitherto not been discussed by us:
the boarder and his family life. This is the subject of our next
chapter.

10 Boarding and the family

One of the most outstanding features of English boarding
education is its separateness from the family. To most people
outside this kind of education, boarding is seen as a threat to
family life, while to many people inside it the family, in turn, is
seen as a threat to residential life. Boarding and the family are
often conceived as irreconcilable opposites, both possessing
virtues which cannot be woven into an integrated educational
experience for a child.

The vast majority of parents in England, as our surveys of
9,953 parents living in seven local authority areas all over the
country showed, would not be interested in residential education of any kind for their children even if it was financially
possible for them to have it. For the child to live away from
home, even not very far, seems to them incompatible with a
proper family upbringing and with parental love, care and
responsibility. Boarding, they feel, is an unnatural state suitable
for the unnatural, that is, for the very rich on the one hand or
the delinquent and depraved on the other. It is true that the
survey showed that about twelve per cent of parents *were*
interested in having some form of boarding for their child if
funds were available to help and this projected at the national
level would mean a potential 327,000 extra boarders, more than
twice the present number. But significantly, the majority
(sixty-five per cent) of these parents wanted boarding *only* if it
was consistent with continuation of family life: that is if the
child was near enough for regular contact with home and if the
school was unconventional enough to permit this contact in
other ways too. In other words those who wanted boarding
showed the same hostility as those who did not to the present
system because it seemed inconsistent with family life.[1]

These widespread attitudes are reinforced by more
sophisticated critics of residential life who see removal from the
warmth, security, flexibility and varied age structure of the
family unit to an institution, monosexual in composition and
narrow in its age range, as a deprivation of basic nourishment
for healthy growth and likely to produce damage or distorted

development. It is significant that in the areas where such educational critics have had greatest practical effect, as in that of special education for children with disabilities, needs or delinquencies, schools are frequently subdivided into small units which deliberately try to reproduce the structure, relationships, style, atmosphere and even name of home and family.[2] None of the boarding schools and only a couple of the small boarding houses which we visited attempted this family kind of organization: it was not necessary, they claimed, as their pupils were not special cases and already had proper families of their own.

'School is school,'

said one housemaster,

'and family is family.'

Surprisingly therefore the conception of boarding and the family as being distinct or even hostile experiences is supported by the practitioners of the method themselves. It was after all one of the most enlightened public school headmasters we interviewed who defined a parent as

'a nuisance created by the motor-car.'

Of course boarding schools have much more regular contact with families than have comparable day schools and are frequently in touch with parents about individual children and their problems and therefore often know the parents and their problems too. But they seldom go beyond this kind of communication about individuals. Not only does the geographical remoteness of many schools from the parents' home areas genuinely make more meaningful types of contact difficult (sixty-four per cent of parents of public school boys live more than fifty miles from their sons' school) and not only does the scattered location of parents make solidarity among them more difficult than in the case of neighbourhood day schools, but deeper attitudes are at work which tend to the same outcome.[3] As we shall see later, that group of parents which we call the conventional boarding school kind regard it as the school's job to take over full responsibility for their child and do not want to or cannot be continuously involved in the child's life during term: they delegate many of the functions of the family to the school during term and some of the functions of parents to paid employees during the holidays. Even where, chiefly in progressive, state and some independent schools, parents do not share this attitude, the schools themselves are remarkably uniform in their approach to the family. Wide as are the differences of style between them in so many other ways, on this matter there is, with only a few exceptions, a general uniformity of approach.

For pupils to go home frequently and regularly and for parents and siblings to visit or stay at the school frequently and regularly, let alone be involved in its life, would be physically a problem and organizationally difficult for most schools. Secondly, most schools think that the mobility outwards and the invasion inwards would disrupt the closely knit sense of community which virtually all of them seek to foster. This community feeling, they contend, can best be sustained by deliberate isolation, apartness and immobility. Thirdly, many schools, especially those wedded to expressive goals of the collective kind, see the outside world, even the family environments of their children, as a threat to the moral and social values they seek to inculcate. The less the pupils are exposed to outside contamination by alien values, such as 'gin and jaguar' ideals, the better. Finally, many schools have never reconsidered conventional practices which derive from the long journeys and complex timetables of the railway age and even the smaller boarding hostels of day schools in which a different atmosphere and practice might have been attempted mainly tend to follow the tightly custodial pattern of larger schools, without being able to offer their internal facilities.

As a result we found that most schools allowed the pupil home to sleep only once or twice in a long term, and most rationed the number of parental visits to children during term to three or four, while restricting the school's own contact with parents to special events and meetings about individual children.[4] There are far fewer parents' associations attached to boarding schools than old boys' associations and, where they exist, they are mainly concerned with social or fund-raising matters rather than with educational debate. Some schools, chiefly small independent or state and progressive schools more concerned with home and less uniform in their style, go beyond these norms. Thus we found four schools on our sample which allowed boarders to go home at any weekend and another two which did the same except for three 'residential weekends' when special projects took place for the whole community. Smaller numbers remaining at weekends gave the chance for a deliberate change of atmosphere to something more intimate, more based on small group activity and individual attention. Two preparatory schools were deliberately trying weekly boarding on a large scale so as to minimize the trauma of separation from the family for young boarders in their care. In general, however, weekly boarding is regarded with suspicion by most schools. Only three schools on our sample encouraged parents to participate in their life. At one, a preparatory school, local parents took evening and weekend activities for which they received some nominal payment, releasing staff for more work with difficult children. One or two schools have tried to overcome the geographical problem by forming regional groups to which the headmaster and some staff go regularly for discussion on school and educational matters.

These attempts to open school and family more to each other are still exceptional in the 1970s. Most of the expressively oriented schools often do not wish to be open to outside and conflicting values and the non-expressive type of schools are often bound by organizational preoccupations which would be disrupted by such flexibility. In fact such openness and flexibility certainly seem to ease some of the discontents frequently found in the more closed schools and undoubtedly help individual children and families. They also present problems of organization especially those of imaginatively changing the atmosphere of school at weekends and of constantly facing the challenge to values and style brought by frequent contact with the outside world. When children were given a free choice we found that relatively few of them went home regularly and those who did seemed to need the emotional support which the home provided. Pressures for flexible boarding systems of this kind and for more parental involvement are on the increase both from frustrated adolescents and from some middle-class parents whose family relationships and educational reference groups are altering. They constitute, as the next chapters explain, an important and badly needed point of growth for the system.

II

Who then *are* the tiny minority of parents who at present have children in boarding schools and why have they opted for this kind of education? So very little is known about the motives, attitudes and life of the boarding family that we undertook a special survey in depth as part of our general research to find out more. For reasons of economy we had to restrict our study and therefore chose to compare public school families with state boarding families and both with another more mixed group in between the two. For reasons of access and to enable comparisons with the evidence we were separately collecting from their sons and schools, we chose parents from three of the schools we had studied on our intensive sample. We shall call them schools A, B and C.[5]

School A is one of the most famous boys' public schools in the country, emphatically within any 'top ten' of HMC schools, a large Victorian foundation dominating a small town in the south of England. School B is an old-fashioned local authority boarding school, a small grammar (or bilateral) school for boys over thirteen housed in a substantial mansion, founded and run at the time on the lines of a minor public school in a prosperous southern county. Its intake is local (except for five per cent overseas and seven per cent forces parents) and by no means confined to cases of need for boarding. Parents pay according to means. The third school, C, was also a small state boarding school but this time a secondary modern one for boys and girls from eleven onwards, in the home counties, a more recent creation housed largely in prefabricated buildings. Its intake is from a large county and it takes about twelve per cent of children from overseas. About half the entry have ascertained 'need' for boarding and all parents contribute to fees according to means.

At the public school A, where the intake was national and international, the survey had to be restricted to England and Wales on grounds of cost. To ensure a fair geographical distribution, the country was divided into eight regions from which a one in four random sample was taken from those parents with a boy who had been at the school for four years or more. This gave us a sample of fifty-seven families, all but one of which, a

family abroad for a year, was visited and interviewed at home.
There were a hundred and seven interviews, mothers and fathers
being interviewed separately. At school B a one in three random
sample of parents of sons of fifth- or sixth-form age was taken
and as most lived within the county we undertook no
geographical stratification. Twenty-two families were eligible,
one refused to participate, and thirty-seven interviews were
completed with parents seen separately at home. At school C
we took a random sample of one in two of parents of boys only
(not girls) in the fourth or fifth years almost all of whom lived
in a large and very varied county. This gave us a sample of
twenty families, all but one of which was visited, making thirty-
five separate interviews in all.

TABLE 10:1

Survey of parents

	Families eligible	Parents interviewed
School A	57	107
School B	22	37
School C	20	35
	Total: 99	179

The 179 parents (another thirty-five were interviewed on a
pilot survey but their replies are not included in this report)
were interviewed in depth for about three hours and the
questions covered not only factual data but attitudes to
boarding, reasons for selecting schools and satisfaction with
them, child-rearing practices and opinions on social, ethical and
political issues. Information was also gathered on the parents'
community life, their work, their income and interests, their
sons' life at home during the holidays and the parents' view of
them, and the ways in which boarding had affected themselves,
their children and their relationships. Details of the research
are given in Appendix II and this chapter summarizes some of
the main findings.

In some purely statistical respects the three groups of families
were similar. Thus mean family sizes were 2·9, 2·6, and 3·3
respectively for the schools and there were few large families, as

the low standard deviations from these means demonstrate (1·1, 1·0, and 1·7). There was no preference in any of the groups for boarding for boys in particular family positions. The mean family size indicates, what other evidence had amply proved, that there were very few purely working-class parents at the state schools B or C.*

The public school families were solidly established in their social positions (eighty per cent of the fathers and ninety per cent of the mothers had parents who had held high professional or executive positions) and according to comparative indices, they were typical members of the upper middle class. Parents in state school C by contrast were from families fairly well established in the region of what could be called the lower middle class or the upper working class, distinguished from others in these groups only by their high aspirations for their sons. The school B parents fell between the two camps, with much more social mobility upwards and downwards in their backgrounds than was found in the other two groups. There were more fathers at school B who were, in economic and occupational terms, more upwardly mobile than fathers in the other two groups and the mothers at the school contained significantly more who were downwardly socially mobile in comparison with their parents' occupation and status. School B, like many other charity-based public or independent schools, clearly served the aspirations of those climbing upwards from backgrounds like those of school C or seemed to help arrest the fall or preserve the culture of those moving downwards whose reference group was the parents in school A.

The public school fathers came mainly from the higher professions or ranks of business (twenty-one per cent were doctors, eleven per cent clergy, twenty-five per cent directors and ten per cent ex-officers of the forces), those in school B were more mixed and less highly placed in their professions, whereas fathers in school C contained clerical workers, commercial travellers, shopkeepers and a train driver. Half of the mothers at school C did full-time work whereas only a quarter of the public school mothers did a job and that tended

* This contrasts with an average of 5·6 children per family (SD = 2·7) found among the 1138 families of boys in the approved schools we have studied subsequently

to be part-time. The mean family incomes per annum reflect these social and occupational differences: that for the public school family in 1968 was £4,800 per annum and there was a background of inherited resources, many of the mothers frequently having private incomes. Eight of these families had annual incomes of over £10,000 per annum. The child's fees were paid principally out of capital or trust funds (in fifty-four per cent of the cases) though insurance policies (fourteen per cent) or money from relatives (seven per cent) sometimes helped as well. Only in five per cent of the cases were fees met mainly from parents' current income. The mean family income for school B in 1968 was £2,300 per annum and though thirty per cent of the parents had incomes of over £3,000 there was no background of inherited money, their prosperity was recent and contributions to fees were met almost entirely out of earned income. The same was true of families at school C where the mean income was considerably lower at £1,600 per annum.

TABLE 10:2

Joint income per annum of parents from all sources 1968
(in percentages)

£	A	B	C
501–1000		20	13
1001–1500	8	30	44
1501–2000	8	20	31
2001–3000	10	25	6
3001–5000	38	5	6
5001–10,000	23		
Over 10,000	13		

The life style of the parents contrasted sharply between schools A and C, with those of school B having some characteristics of both extremes. Public school parents, for example, entertained more often at home, went out more often and had friends scattered over a wider region than the others. Apart from informal networks of friends, the public school parents were much more involved in local organizational life than the others. The mothers tended to be particularly active, thirty-six per cent of them doing regular social work, twenty-nine per cent doing regular church work, twenty-one per cent attending the Conservative Club and twenty-seven per cent attending the Womens' Institute or similar bodies. The fathers tended to do less welfare work but were equally active on local church councils (thirty-two per cent), in professional associations (twenty-eight per cent) and in local golf, shooting, fishing or other sporting clubs. Though the mothers at school B were fairly active in local organizations, both sets of state school parents were much more homebound than the other group. Entertaining and visiting friends were rare, half claimed that they had little contact with the neighbourhood, but there was more visiting of the extended family which tended to be more local than was the case with families in school A. Mothers at school C were much more occupied during the day with home and children than were any of the others. None of them had domestic help and fifteen had children still attending local day schools. Most of their day, if they were not in full-time work, was occupied with housekeeping and their personal hobbies were such things as watching television, reading and knitting, whereas school A mothers did gardening ('they are so difficult to get now'), sewing (only two knitted), dressmaking or such artistic hobbies as painting or weaving. Fathers at school C, though spending more time out of the house at sports clubs or the like than their wives, were nevertheless more homebased than the professional men in the other schools, who claimed to have little time for watching television or for doing the odd jobs which so much occupied school C fathers. All the public school parents read *The Times* or the *Daily Telegraph* though often taking a lighter paper of a right-wing kind, particularly one with a good gossip column for the wife. The state parents took fewer papers and more of the middle-brow (*Daily Mail*, *Daily Express*) or popular ranges such as the *Daily Mirror* and so on. In short the public school parents are active outside the home, mothers as well as fathers, and they belong to a wide informal and formal social network, whereas state school parents are more confined to home, preoccupied with children and family.

These differences become even sharper when we consider the educational background of parents which in turn powerfully conditions their choice of schooling and attitude towards education in general. The length of education of the parents varied according to the school. At school A two-thirds of both mothers and fathers were university graduates and only two of the parents had left school before eighteen. At school B only one was a graduate but over eighty per cent of the fathers and ninety per cent of the mothers had stayed on at school beyond fourteen. At school C most of the fathers had left school at fourteen and a third of the mothers had done so. The public school parents, ninety per cent of them, had been to private schools; at school B over half of the mothers and one-third of the fathers had been to private schools. No fathers and only one mother had been privately educated at school C.

Boarding patterns show similar disparities. Over half the mothers of the public school boys and four-fifths of the fathers had themselves been boarders at school. Of the boys in the family sample from school A, over three-quarters were at least the third generation of boarders in the family. In ninety per cent of the families there was a boarding tradition and in a third of them it was associated with one particular school, school A. Nearly half of the public-school mothers had themselves been reared by nannies, which may also help account for their attitudes to their sons, but only two mothers at school B had this experience and none at all at school C. More than fifty per cent of the parents at school B had some boarding tradition in the family and a fifth of the fathers had been boarders at public schools though more mothers had had this experience. There was no boarding experience at all at school C, as only one parent had been a boarder. Clearly the approach to boarding is profoundly affected by the extremes of familiarity and unfamiliarity we have found. One other major difference between the parents was that boarding was used at some stage for all sons and most daughters of parents at school A, but only for individual children by parents in the other two schools.

This gives a clue as to why and how the public school parents chose boarding for their child. Many (eighty-three per cent) had already delegated the care of the child in their homes to nannies or *au pair* girls and continued the process by delegating it to the school. When we tried to classify the parents' reasons for wanting their child to board, ninety-one per cent gave reasons of convention such as 'this is the pattern in our family' or 'his father was there, so school A was an automatic choice'. Though twenty-one per cent of the boys and sixty-two per cent of the daughters of the public school families started at a local state primary school, the decision to board in the independent sector is taken very early, a practice encouraged by schools anxious to ensure stable recruitment by full waiting lists. In the case of ninety-one per cent of the boys at school A it had been decided that their main education should be boarding by the time they were seven and in the case of eighty-six per cent it had already been decided at birth. This contrasts extremely with the other schools where the boarding decision is taken when the boy is ten or eleven years of age or even later and then, something which seldom occurred in families at school A, in consultation with the boy himself. Only seven per cent of the parents at school A had seriously considered long-term day education for their sons at secondary level though more of them (twenty-three per cent) chose it for their daughters, but there were signs that this rational choice between boarding and day education is on the increase in this sort of family. Only two per cent of the parents at school A explicitly gave reasons of 'need' for boarding though there was evidently somewhat more need of the usual kind, such as family difficulties or movement, and in this kind of family the busy and far-flung public lives of both parents created a more prevalent need to delegate care of children to someone. Decision to board among the established upper-class parents seems a mixture of ingrained family and social tradition and a disguised need to delegate care deriving from style of life. Very little attention is paid to the suitability of the individual child for boarding in general or for a particular public school, whereas much more attention is paid to both these factors by the state-school parents.

Convention too plays a large part in the selection of the actual secondary boarding school. For fifty-four per cent of the boys in our sample at school A it was chosen because it was 'the family school'. The other half of the parents made a more rational choice between this school and others and chose it because of its general reputation, because of the quality of old boys and academic standards, because of its scholarship successes and because of the locality and environment in which it was placed. The vast majority of them, ninety-three per cent, visited the school before deciding on a firm entry for their sons, but looking at buildings and facilities and meeting the staff were less important for the undecided ones than the preceding factors: they said the visit had made little difference to their choice which was virtually already made. At this late stage less than a third even passingly contemplated the possibility of day schooling for their sons now aged twelve years.

Far more rational choice is exercised by such parents over their child's *preparatory* boarding school. Three-quarters of the boys in our sample at school A began boarding at eight. In these cases only three of them went to the same preparatory school as their father. Our parents tended to choose schools within a certain radius which enabled easy visiting from home and then carefully selected a particular school by visiting and deciding on grounds of locality, academic standards, reputation, the staff, and especially the quality of the head and his wife. There is an increasing tendency to use primary schools and delay the age of starting boarding for boys among such parents.

Choice of boarding and choice of school is utterly different for the parents and children in the other two kinds of school. True enough, in school B, the state boarding school with a public school ethos, the boarding backgrounds of some parents led to a positive belief on their part in this mode of education, a belief which was entirely absent in school C. A considerable section of parents, over thirty-three per cent, in B had already used private day prep schools for their sons and one significant motive was to gain the benefits of a public school education without the cost, boarding being largely incidental to the securing of increased life chances or, on the part of those down-wardly mobile, the securing of the status and affirmation of the upper-middle-class culture to which they still aspired. Several parents referred to B as 'the poor man's public school'. Even at school C this motive was also present, for not a few parents admitted that a boarding secondary modern school which was inevitably selective in its entry gave their children greater chances and status than the local day secondary modern school which was completely unselective.[6] In both groups boarding as such was a subordinate adjunct to social advancement by education, 'giving our son the best chance possible', 'doing our best for the boy'. Unlike the public school parents these ones explicitly acknowledged 'need' for boarding. No less than twenty-one per cent of the boys at B and thirty-one per cent of those at C came from homes in which one parent was dead or both were separated, compared with only eight per cent at the public school. Of the parents, fourteen per cent at school B and thirty-seven per cent at school C gave need reasons as their main grounds for sending their son away from home to board. These basically negative reasons for wanting boarding and the parents' evident reliance on the school for help creates, as we shall see, a special attitude by the parents to the school.

The state school parents heard of the particular schools either from friends in the locality, from their children who had heard about them from day school, or were recommended to apply by the heads of their sons' day schools, particularly when need for boarding was obvious. Local reputation and recommendation by other families were important factors to those without an obvious need for their children to live away from home. One father in school C said, for example:

> 'We heard quite by chance about applying. I didn't like the idea of Johnny going to Newlands (the local day secondary modern) and I was talking to someone in the village in the holidays and he said that applications had to be in by the second day of term. I saw the head at once but he knew even less about the boarding school than I did.'

Sometimes, a situation which never occurred in the public school sample, the boy himself proposed going to the school about which his parents knew nothing and in over half the cases the boy was consulted carefully before the initial application was made. Some of the wealthier parents at school B had a choice between it and the cheaper independent boarding schools whereas those at school C had no choice but the school concerned or the local day one. Perhaps this situation as well as ingrained day school habits accounted for the fact that more than sixty-three per cent of the parents at school C and over a third of those at school B, though without knowledge of the school in question or of boarding education in general, did not even go to see the school before their sons were accepted at it. For them there was not even the conventional visit of confirmation made by public school parents whose minds were already almost made up. Virtually none of the sons of the two state schools had boarded elsewhere, though about nineteen per cent of children in the two schools, mainly forces children who did not appear in our sample, had been boarders earlier. Ignorance of the system, aspiration and financial dependence made the parents unaware of alternatives, blindly grateful and uncritically accepting of all that the two schools provided for their children.

III

How then do the parents react to the schools to which they send their sons?

Perceptions of goals vary with each group.[7] The public school parents had clear ideas of what a public school should be and do. When they were asked to rate what goals the schools did pursue, should pursue and then actually achieved, their answers very much reflected the day-to-day aims that we found the schools and staff pursued in practice. Thus they placed a high emphasis on expressive goals (except the one of homeliness) and the only areas where their answers indicated that the school was failing to correspond with their aspirations were for the instrumental goals of preparing the boy for a vocation and adapting education to ability. In these areas the parents seemed to want more change than the school was producing. They also wanted more success in some of the expressive areas, notably religion, morality and creative development, but nevertheless still rated the school's efforts in these directions very highly indeed.

In the other two schools the parents, as follows from their dependence, also show little discrepancy between the goals they believe that the schools should pursue and those which they felt the school was successfully attaining. Differences between what the parents wanted and what the school succeeded in doing were even smaller than for the public school parents. At school B among some parents there was clearly pressure for more stress on expressive areas, coming mainly from that group of parents who wanted a more conventional 'public school' style. At school C the cultural, creative and individual outlets were the only ones seriously criticized.

Some significant differences of emphasis emerged between the parents. Though state school C parents placed more weight on successful organization and such things as discipline they also stressed the pursuit of individual attributes, whereas public school parents, like the schools themselves, tended to stress as desirable far more collective attributes. Public school parents stressed managerial training, leadership and collective values, whereas state school parents, especially those at C, emphasized more the need for homeliness, for physical development, discipline and order and, paradoxically, more democratic involvement of the pupils in the running of the school. Actual dissatisfaction was rare in public school parents: in all, only six out of fifty-six families said that they would not send their son to the school again if they had the chance and only two couples at the state boarding schools felt the same way. The largest group with minor reservations was at school B, that aspirant group who were pressing for more stress on academic and expressive values.

In general social attitudes as tested by standard scales the parents of school A tended to take a conservative viewpoint reflecting values which we found, using the same tests, were prominent among the boys and staff of the school. Only in a few areas was this general consensus between parents, sons and staff disrupted: on issues such as freedom and independence for young people and on a few religious and political issues such as the welfare state. On these the parents' attitude was more conservative than that of their sons but in other areas, such as cultural ones, there was very close agreement between the two. In both the state schools, however, there was much less consensus between home and school and pupils. On social, cultural, religious and moral and political issues the boys and parents tended to differ more markedly. There was less of a continuum between outside and inside culture than is the case in the public school and within the school there was more heterogeneity and extremes of opinion. Between groups of parents differences are equally marked. Apart from being less religious than the others, the parents in school B shared many attitudes with those of the public school. At school C parents were more conservative on sexual and cultural matters but tended to be more liberal on social and political issues and on matters of family life than those in the other two schools.

In general then we see a close continuum in attitudes and

convention between the public school and its parents. This continuity in social, political and expressive values and academic standards makes for smooth recruitment and socialization but embeds the school in a web of rigid expectations which undoubtedly limits its capacity for change. By contrast the diversity, lack of pre-socialization and sharply differing motivations of state school parents make it difficult for the schools, even if they were so inclined, to develop a thorough, high and uniform stress on collective goals of the expressive kind. As long as the school has produced the instrumental goals which the parents approve, and does not challenge the parents' emphatic family values and attitudes to child rearing the parents are content and the schools are free to change and experiment radically in other ways. We see how the stress on homeliness and access to the home in the style created by some of these schools reflects the background culture of the children, just as totality, spartan living and delegation of family roles and more limited contact with the home reflects the attitudes and practices of public school families.

IV

How then does the experience of boarding seem to affect the family and relationships within it?

Preoccupation with the family and home was paramount among the boys in our survey schools. When asked about the advantages and disadvantages of being a boarder, lack of contact with family and home was given as one of the major disadvantages by the majority of boys under sixteen in all the schools surveyed except two. Significantly these two schools had both made experiments to establish closer and more frequent contact between pupils and their homes. When we asked again, in all schools on the intensive sample, what aspects of school life caused most worry, lack of contact with the family was again one of the four most prominent concerns of all pupils including those of sixth-form age. Though it is often claimed, frequently by the schools themselves, that boarding education fosters 'independence' by removal from home and few of the boys actually wanted to go back home and live, it is significant that the pupils so uniformly wanted more contact with it. Few schools gratified this wish and few staff seemed aware of the pupils' needs. The general policy of rigidly limiting access to the home may thus actually increase the level of anxiety and frustration in the school, causing deeper problems than those which might result from a more open and flexible policy.

Almost all the boarders in our extensive and intensive samples had suffered from homesickness on first leaving the family and in general schools usually had a deliberate policy of meeting it. A vast majority of them deliberately limited visits to the school by parents for a period and tried to settle the boys by an organized round of activity and rituals of initiation. At a few progressive and state schools, more flexible in their contact with home, policies were diametrically opposite, parents were encouraged to come and help their boys to settle down, even staying in the school for a week or more while doing so, and the school stressed that boarding did not mean loss of or basic separation from the affective centre of the child's life. Homesickness seems more widespread and is experienced more acutely and over a longer period among children in state boarding schools who come into the school at eleven. Public school boys seem to experience it less acutely or protractedly, though in this case the fact that our respondents are recalling memories of

TABLE 10:3

Sixth-form boys' assessment of duration of their homesickness (in percentages)

	Intensive sample schools					
	Public				State	
	A	B	C	D	E	F
Homesick						
More than one year	9	5	6	4	15	12
For first year only	31	31	29	16	47	42
Occasionally	35	36	36	40	24	26
Rarely or never	24	27	28	34	14	20
N =	289	441	189	67	97	84

Source: intensive sample, sixth-form questionnaire.

eight years ago may minimize the trauma implied in our statistics. It is more likely that for public school boys the trauma was reduced by the affectively neutral pattern of their upbringing in which they were looked after by paid employees from an early age and not expected to display undue emotion anyway. This latter inhibition may help account for the fact that, when we compared the mothers' and their sons' recollections of homesickness, we found that the public school mothers grossly underestimated the suffering experienced by their sons compared with the state school mothers who tended to exaggerate their sons' homesickness. Perhaps the public school mothers were not even told. And even if they were their own tendency to affective neutrality may have led them to dismiss the problem.

TABLE 10:4

Estimates of homesickness by mothers and boys (in percentages)

Son or self (boy)	A Public school		B State school		C State school	
	Mothers	Boys	Mothers	Boys	Mothers	Boys
Severely homesick	15	5	38	9	5	6
At first/part	40	68	52	55	63	50
Never homesick	42	27	5	36	26	44
Don't know/other	3		5		6	
	N = 56		N 20		N 17	

Source: family survey.

Not that public school mothers were unemotional on their sons' departure to board at eight years: on the contrary fifty-nine per cent of those at school A were very distressed, although patterns of convention made them accept it.

'It is as much a part of family life as having children', said one, 'but I felt awful all the same'.

Forty-two per cent of the mothers said they were not distressed at all when their child left home. Naturally more state school mothers were extremely distressed, despite the fact that their sons were eleven on leaving home for school C or thirteen for school B and the school was nearby. Parents recalled terrible times of weeping and despairing phone calls and being plunged into a void.

'We seemed more upset than him', said one mother, 'the house suddenly became quiet and empty, just us left by ourselves. We were lonely and sick with anxiety about him and guilty about letting him go.'

Very few of them were resigned and only some ex-boarding mothers at school B were cheerful at the time. Perhaps these different reactions led the mothers to project their feelings on to their sons, for only thirty-eight per cent of the state school mothers said that their sons' first reactions to boarding were cheerful, compared with sixty per cent of the public school group.

TABLE 10:5

Response of mothers to son leaving home (in percentages)

	A	B	C
Distressed	59	75	95
Resigned	22	5	5
Unaffected	19	20	0
N =	56	21	19

State school parents, too, tended to be more in contact with their sons and the school once their boys were there, though this may reflect the more welcoming policies of both the state schools (parents are encouraged to drop in at one and to participate at the other) compared with the public schools' more orthodox approach.

TABLE 10:6

Number of visits or other contact with school last term by one or both parents

	A	B	C
None	15	33	0
1–2	69	24	41
3 or more	16	43	59
N =	56	21	19

The long-term effects of this separation, seen by one group of parents as necessary and usual, and by the others as more unnatural, though by both as beneficial to their boys, are much more difficult to ascertain than the short-term ones. All the public school parents thought that for their own lives the boy's absence was either a positive gain, releasing them for professional or social life or other freedoms, or at least no loss. Fewer state school parents saw any gains to themselves in their child's absence and substantial minorities experienced it continuously as a strain or deprivation.

TABLE 10:7

Absence of child as seen by parents (in percentages)

	A	B	C
Positive for parents' own lives	47	38	14
Negative or a strain	0	31	29
Making no difference	53	31	57
	N = 107	37	35

So too with the differences between the couples which result from the boy's absence. Though the largest groups of parents saw their relations as being unchanged or even improved by having their child board, more state parents thought that the relationship between father and mother had got worse as a consequence.

TABLE 10:8

Parents' views of effects of child's absence on their relationship (in percentages)

	A	B	C
Got better	31	42	21
Unchanged	40	32	53
Mixed	20	5	5
Got worse	7	21	16
	N = 107	37	35

Their sons are somewhat more emphatic that their relationships with their parents have been improved by removal from home, though again more state boarders than public school ones think things have got worse.

TABLE 10:9

Sons' views of effects of boarding on relationships with their parents (in percentages)

	A	B	C
Got better	73	53	53
Unchanged	7	11	16
Mixed	12	12	17
Got worse	8	24	14
	N = 441	97	84

Source: intensive sample.

Indeed, despite all their anxieties about home and desire for more contact with it, a majority of the boys in our general sample liked living away for most of the time and seventy per cent of all boarders claimed that they had learned to appreciate parents and home more as a result of absence. Removal from the intense emotional stresses between parents and siblings which occur in adolescence, and the objective perspective gained on the affective unit of the family from the distance of the unaffective institution of the school may indeed, as the majority of boarders claim, lead to a deeper appreciation of home, parents and love, and to a greater ability to handle relationships without conflict, at least in holiday time spells. But whether the secondary problems which result from removal from home, or from life in single-sex schools as they now are outweigh these gains is another question. Indeed, though some children might well be damaged by the pressures of living at home continuously during adolescence, removal from its stresses and conflicts, its emotional texture, the give-and-take of family life, may damage others by depriving them of deep, maturing experiences which may be beneficial and which they, in later life, may never learn to cope with. Perhaps - although there is no evidence - most adolescents could benefit by a mixture of both experiences. But certainly the boarders' own strong witness should remind us that some form of residential experience, not necessarily that of the conventional English boarding school, may be a positive help to all concerned in the process of adolescence.

It was impossible for us to measure or compare what the depth and quality of relationships were like between the boarders and their parents. Parents fondly thought that the boys turned to them with their problems more often than the boys said that they in fact did and day boys turned more often in practice to parents with problems than did boarders. Nevertheless most parents felt that their sons would not bring personal problems to them, though most of them had no difficulty in discussing such matters with their sons if they arose. Significantly public school parents felt that their sons were less likely to turn to them than state school ones and far more of them (thirty-four per cent at school A compared with ten per cent at school C) said that they could not discuss personal matters with their boys. Thus though public school boys are so emphatically more confident that their relationships with parents are good it seems that more of them find it difficult to communicate deeply than state school boarders whose relationships are more varied: perhaps the relationships between public school boys and parents may be excellent but at the price of being superficial. Perhaps again it is the affectively neutral style of life or earlier removal from home which inhibits this deeper communication among a significant minority. We shall see in a moment how more loose and superficial the public school boy's relations are with other people at home.

When we asked parents about their own relations with their sons, we noticed, among a minority of fathers and mothers who did not get on well with their sons, that when strain occurred in public school families it was more often between the mothers and their sons while in state school families it was more often between fathers and sons. In examining our data from the intensive sample we saw the same phenomenon emerging, but more clearly in relation to the age at which the child boarded than according to the type of school attended. Whereas late boarders and day pupils have roughly equal relations with their mothers and fathers (though day boys get on slightly better with their mothers), early boarders have significantly worse relations with their mothers than their fathers, a majority experiencing some strain. All but a fraction of these early boarders were at public schools.

TABLE 10:10

Replies of sixth-form boys on relations with their parents (in percentages)

	Boys boarding before nine		Boys boarding after nine		Day boys	
	Mother	Father	Mother	Father	Mother	Father
Good relations	48	67	65	66	67	61
Mixed or strained relations	52	33	35	34	33	39
N =	443		674		121	

Source: intensive sample, sixth-form questionnaire.

We can only speculate on the causes of this finding. We know that the mothers of such boys often felt guilty at their sons going away so early and perhaps the boys themselves felt deeply rejected at being removed from the centre of affection so young and these feelings obstructed relationships thereafter. Perhaps too, having lived so long in all-male and affectively neutral surroundings, the boys found it difficult to deal with the expressive and affective mother figure and found it easier to handle the authoritarian male figure with whom they were familiar. Certainly this is borne out by the difficulties which similar boys had with other younger members of the opposite sex. Or perhaps early boarders have families which are more affectively neutral, more difficult homes or more difficult mothers than others, though the latter reasons are unlikely. Whatever the causes and whatever the consequences for these boys' intimate and public lives (hence possibly a reinforcement of the tendency to authoritarian situations and all-male fraternities by former boarders), it is clear that early boarding does correlate with peculiar effects on family relationships which exist seven or eight years after the boy started to board, effects which distinguish a significant minority of public school boys from other boarders in this country.

V

When term ends and the pupils return home they face questions of relationships and perpetuation of school values. Most boarders regret the loss of friends at home and contact with the neighbourhood. State boarders coming from local day schools at eleven experience this most acutely when they return. Over a half of those on our sample had no friends at all locally in the holidays, for the friends whom they had made earlier at the local primary school had drifted away, forming new interests and new friendships, so that the boarder coming back at intervals found no place for him. Sometimes the situation was aggravated by suspicions about him being sent away - 'they all think I'm a snob round here'.

The independent or public school boarder is not faced by so drastic a problem. He has the same basic difficulty of adjusting to a situation in which school norms and relationships do not prevail, but on the whole his peers at home also tend to be boarding school children. He does not have to break into a circle which has been continuing happily without him while away, but rather comes home to rejoin one which has been in suspension during its members' absence. Only four of the public school parents said that their sons had no friends and twenty-seven per cent of them said that their sons had over twenty friends or more. Replies by the children themselves indicate how public school children drew their holiday friends from other public school boarders, whereas state school children drew theirs from

TABLE 10:11

Friends at home of boy boarders (fifth-form age)

	Percentage of all the friends in schools		
	State (2)	Public (7)	Progressive (2)
Friends			
State day pupils	78	21	51
Public, prep school boarders	8	61	31
At work	6	7	2
University, etc.	8	11	16
No. of respondents:	192	651	96
No. of friends listed:	674	5,140	738

day children and progressive school children from a mixture of the two.

When the depth of friendship is considered these figures and the detailed evidence gathered from the parents' survey showed that though state boarders had fewer friends in the holidays than public school boarders they saw them more frequently and were more intimate with them. Public school boys had far more friends, but proportionately fewer of them compared with the state school boarders had, according to their parents, close relations with any of them. In other words the public school boarders' friendship network is large and loose, taken up at the beginning and dropped at the end of the holidays without much trouble, whereas the state boarders' group is tighter, more intimate and consequently all too easily irrevocably broken.

Most of the boarders enjoy the holidays, though a third are glad when they end and can get back to school. One reason they are so much enjoyed is that children resume roles of which the schools disposess them during term. We have earlier noted how many schools expect their children to behave with adult attributes of rationality, sobriety, restraint and responsibility. On returning home for the holidays these are shed. Children resume diverse roles in the family, become the recipients or the givers in affective situations. Above all, the adult role is shed in favour of that of the adolescent. Most boarding schools by their system of values and control severely limit the adolescent role, only a few state and most progressive schools incorporate the role of adolescent fully into their regimes. Most schools prohibit many aspects of adolescent culture, limit emotional expression, ignore temperamental difficulties, suppress demands for independence and aspects of the adolescent quest for identity by experiment. What school does not permit, holidays and parents do. The dichotomy between school and home throughout boarding school education is seen at its most extreme and sometimes grotesque in the holidays.

For many boarders the absence of school norms leads to an almost frantic assertion of the adolescent role and a wholesale abandonment of the school mores if not school values. Regular church going, which so many schools enforce, is reduced (except for school B below, a Catholic school), smoking, drinking, associations with girls, which most schools prohibit,

TABLE 10:12

Percentage of sixth formers reporting activities during last holidays

	Boarding						Day		
	A	B	C	D	E	F	Public	State	
Go to church once/twice	48	14	51	42	32	34	48	24	20
Go to church regularly	21	81	24	25	10	6	17	4	3
Smoke	41	57	44	33	50	65	25	21	25
Drink intoxicants	89	88	80	83	91	88	70	62	64
Go out with girl friend	67	59	63	67	71	62	57	48	51
Go to club, society near home	44	36	35	42	55	43	44	59	60
Go to or give a teenage party	66	73	71	33	59	57	36	30	29
Take a paid job	—	16	—	—	34	25	27	36	33
N =	239	189	440	67	97	84	211*	80	52

* This includes day pupils at schools B and D as well as the day school comparisons.

Source: intensive sample and day school comparisons.

become all the rage and party going is common. These compensatory activities described by boarders are confirmed, with the exception of going out with girls about which parents may be ignorant or the boys exercising their fantasies, by our interviews with the parents and by other research.[8] In the three schools on our parents' survey holiday activities went thus:

TABLE 10:13

Parents' reports on sons' activity last holidays (in percentages)

	A	B	C
Went to a party	87	55	5
Went regularly to social club/group	64	52	42
Went out with girl friend	26	21	33
N =	56	21	19

It was also clear that only a few parents exercised the same rules over their children during the holidays as the schools did during term. Both boys and parents were asked about rules or understandings on behaviour and especially about adolescent modes of expression. In general the parents' replies suggested an even lower amount of parental control than did those of the boys, as the following table illustrates.

TABLE 10:14

Rules or understandings by parents with boys in holidays, described by parents and their sons (in percentages)

	Public				State		Day (3 schools)
	A		B		C		
	Parents	Boys	Parents	Boys	Parents	Boys	Boys
Time for being in at night	18	19	35	32	37	44	44
Against smoking	11	42	9	36	21	55	16
Against drinking	22	24	5	17	11	31	13
Going to church	4	17	5	14	5	16	1
Doing school work	4	18	5	22	11	36	51
Tidiness, housework	2	–	29	–	16	–	–
Seeing too much of girls	2	4	0	3	0	4	1
	N = 56	440	21	97	19	84	311

It is clear that very few parents from any of the schools exercised anything like the controls over adolescent behaviour that are imposed by the schools themselves. The replies from day boys also show that the only times when their parents laid down clear expectations were in the two most obvious areas of being home at a reasonable hour and doing school work. Boarding parents were more protective than day ones in most other respects also.

This gap in values between school and home, which our evidence suggests occurs generally except for some state and most progressive schools, is obviously serious. It focuses round the adolescent role. The schools' efforts to limit it lead to over-compensation during holiday time and to a preoccupation during term with trivial manifestations of adolescence (dress, hair, etc,) which often deflect schools from their ends and lower pupil commitment.

The normlessness, the lack of roots and sense of belonging to anywhere but the school obviously helps this extravagant pattern of behaviour during the holidays. Social class differences enter in here, too, as we can see if we look in the tables above at the somewhat different patterns of public and state school behaviour. But both state and public school boys seem to have distorted patterns of behaviour if we take the day pupils of the same social background as the norm. Perhaps the infrequency and unfamiliarity of close contact with sons leads some parents to over-indulge, to compensate at their end by being more permissive. Public school parents tend more often to help organize the contrived social round which many of their sons enjoy. Indeed public school boys spent more restless holidays than the others, thirty per cent of them spending five to ten weeks of their twelve-week period of holiday away from the home itself. They also went to far more parties.

TABLE 10:15

Attending party in last holidays (in percentages)

	A	B	C
None	13	45	95
Only 1	11	15	5
2–4	32	35	0
5 or more	45	5	0
	N = 56	21	19

Of course most families enjoyed quieter moments together and virtually all the parents on our sample did something with their sons. Those from school A went on cultural outings to the theatre, church, sports events or on expeditions while the state boarders tended more often to visit other members of the family with their parents and to go to the cinema or just to go shopping with them.

VI

The family thus constitutes one of the unresolved problems for the boarding system of this country as it now stands. School and its values and style of life stands somewhat apart from the family and the values and style it adopts. Though in the case of the public schools there is a close continuity in style and expectations between the two, in the anomic holiday periods many school practices are abandoned by the home. Only in two or three state schools and some progressive and many special schools is there a real continuity of values and practice between school and home based on a close working partnership between them. The isolation of the ordinary boarding school from the background of its pupils, its failure to inter-penetrate with that background obviously impairs any long-term impact it may have. This is realized by many day schools, which see a close relationship with the home as crucial, though this is attempted by remarkably few boarding schools at present.

In one way boarding may strengthen the family by making pupils more aware of its virtues and removing them from its strains but in other ways it may undermine it by reducing depth of interchange, distorting some patterns of relationships and rendering the family's holiday-time existence unnatural, by spreading anxiety, and by preventing regular contact with the affective centre of a child's life which school can seldom be. It is significant that both pupils and parents on our surveys overwhelmingly believe in the values and strength of boarding, nevertheless want more contact with each other than is provided. As the style of life of the public school parents, who produce the majority of boarders, moves more and more away from affective neutrality and delegation of the child role, these pressures for contact will mount.

The challenge for boarding schools, if they are to survive, if they are successfully to transmit their values, if they are to maximize the help they provide for the child and to minimize the damage they do and if they are ever to accommodate children from social groups with intensive family lives, is how to work with, through and alongside the family, recognizing what those in day and special education long ago accepted, that the home offers what no school can and that the school and home linked in a continuum offer the most supportive environment for the growth of a child.

11   Decay and growth

So far we have been dissecting the styles and context of
boarding in somewhat static terms. But individual schools and a
whole sector of education are not like corpses. They, and
residential education in general, are in a continual process of
change, of perpetual growth and decay. It is time to turn from
anatomy to dynamics.

What tendencies are affecting the area of boarding as a whole?
How is the pattern of provision changing and according to what
pressures? Within the schools themselves or within the
groupings of them with which we are familiar, what changes are
taking place and what forces are promoting or resisting change?
Finally, reviewing the general picture again in the light of the
last ten years, what growing points have emerged, significant for
the future? These are the questions with which this chapter is
concerned.

II

Educational provision since the Second World War has continued
to expand at pre-school levels, at sixth-form levels and in the
hugely developing area of higher and further education.
Boarding provision has shown no such boom. There was
significant growth in the 1950s but not on anything like the
scale comparable in day education in either the maintained or
independent sectors, and since the mid-sixties there has been a
slow, variable but perceptible tendency for boarding provision
of the long-term kind to decrease. Signs of this are to be found
even in the more established and academically selective public
schools catering for boys of secondary age where no growth in
boarders has occurred for over ten years. Thus between 1946
and 1961 the number of boarders in public schools rose by
28·6 per cent and that of day boys by almost twice as much,
46·1 per cent. In the decade 1961-71 however the proportion
of boarders in such schools remained static (35,346 in 1961 and
35,347 in 1971) while the day boy population in the schools
continued to rise by another 16·3 per cent.

TABLE 11:1

Boarding and day boys in public schools

	1946	1961	1971
Boarders	27,922	35,346	35,347
Day	11,038	16,129	18,812
Total	38,960	51,475	54,159

As these figures include the principal thirty-nine public schools where some growth of around 1·76 did occur in the last decade, they mean that the other forty-nine schools experienced an actual decline in boarders and have had to struggle to keep their places filled.[1]

In public schools the recent move towards coeducation discussed below is due as much to the presence of empty beds as to changes of educational outlook and there are indications that the levels of academic selection have fallen in some schools. The established boys' public schools are, however, too conspicuously placed in the allocative system and are thought by their clientele to offer such obviously enhanced life chances to their pupils to be seriously threatened by a declining demand at present. If demand were to slacken in such schools there are substantial numbers of academically less able boys anxious to come in. It is minor public, independent and integrated schools which are most affected by a declining demand. The ever-rising costs of boarding are apparently not compensated for in such schools by the good facilities, the high level of instrumental success, and the secured status and route into the elite found in the major public schools. The boys in such minor schools are, as our evidence proves, the most disaffected of any boarders, conscious of their school's inability to realize their own high educational aims, and the parents share the trend among upper-class parents to doubt the value of boarding.[2] As a result of these internal and external pressures, increasing numbers of such schools are closing as parents prefer to put their sons and financial investment into the major public schools or to transfer out of boarding altogether to state day schools or to day independent ones which are on the increase.[3] Boarding schools of this kind which remain tend more and more to become repositories of children with definite 'need' for living away

from home and often of lesser academic capacities.[4] Even at
the primary age boarding among boys has fluctuated in the last
ten years. Partly because of the long, heavy and sustained
financial outlay required if boarding starts at the age of seven
and continues to eighteen, partly because of changing parental
views of sending boys away before puberty, the age at which
boys go to preparatory schools is now tending to become nine
or ten rather than seven or eight. This redistribution of age
does not mean that boarding prep schools are fast disappearing:
in the 1960s there was a decrease but in the early 1970s
boarders of prep school age actually increased, as did the proportion with clear 'need' to live away from home. This increase
has always been less than that of day pupils of the same age,
and new day schools to cater for them are on the increase.[5]

The pattern in this area of boys boarding is one of somewhat
fluctuating stability as far as the majority of public schools are
concerned and slow decline in other kinds of school. It is not
just a matter of sharply rising fees (boarding fees rose 130 per
cent in independent schools between 1952 and 1968)[6] which
make parents prefer the secure academic and status rewards of
public schools to the much less obvious returns of independent
and integrated schools, nor is it principally the marked restlessness of boys in such schools. The trend to state or independent
day education is caused as much by changes in roles and
attitudes within the families of those who, in the past, might
have chosen boarding for their sons. As servants and nannies
and paid help with infants become more scarce more mothers
from the upper socio-economic groups experience the role of
sustained motherhood, of caring directly for their children from
babyhood to infancy. This, as well as changing assumptions
about the role of parents in child care and the role of the child
as a unifying factor in the family, seems to make parents,
particularly mothers, resistant to the idea of boarding for their
sons at an early age or, indeed, at any age. The prevalent convention about boarding in such social groups, though still
tenacious and accompanied as we have seen by the dis-
possession of the role of the mother and by the care of infants
by others, is slowly disintegrating.[7] Boarding tends to be more
of a conscious choice for an individual child accompanied by
guilt feelings on the part of the mother or is more related to

actual reasons of need for living away from the family. These
basic changes in the family's approach to boarding constitute
another challenge, possibly even a growing point for the
residential system as we shall see later. All these factors then
account for shifts in the demand for and provision of boys'
boarding.

Much more dramatic changes are occurring with regard to
girls or boarders in state schools. Girls' boarding schools are
withering away: there are now about seventy and they have
been closing at the rate of up to five a year. Boarding has never
been favoured in any society as much for girls as for boys and
in England it never conferred anything like the same life
chances or status or academic success as boarding for boys.
Given the increased costs, the small and scattered nature of the
schools, problems of staffing, the narrow range of curriculum
offered, especially at sixth-form level, no wonder there has been
a pronounced flight from such schools by parents and their
offspring.[8] Exacerbating the problem is the reaction of
adolescent girls to the extremely closed, controlled and 'total'
way of life in such schools. Dr Wober's researches confirmed
what others had predicted: that adolescent girls deprived of the
company of the other sex and of normal outlets for self-
expression, of youth culture and of various domestic, family
and maternal roles, undergo a crisis of identity, the intensity of
which is seldom paralleled among boys experiencing similar
deprivations or controls.[9] Throughout our researches it was
girls rather than the boys who responded most acutely by mild
hysteria, depression or claustrophobia to being 'cooped up' by
boarding, whatever the actual amount of restriction to which
they were subject. As their parents have no incentive for them
to stay on unless there are 'need' reasons, the girls are tending
not to go to board or to leave before the sixth form for the
apparent freedom, heterosexuality and cultural plurality of the
technical college or to more progressive, coeducational boarding
schools. Apart from the very few which are academically
reputable and confer social cachet, the girls' boarding schools
are tending to become places principally for those who need
boarding and the declining number of places may not be
enough to meet the considerable number of girls with such
needs.

The same is true of another area of marked contraction in the system: the boarding hostel attached to state day, usually grammar, schools. This, one of the most ancient forms of boarding, no longer seems viable, despite the substantial numbers of children with 'need' for boarding seeking places and a large-scale development of short-stay boarding centres attached to single or groups of day schools within maintained education. Again, it is not only finance, though small boarding units, of which there were 122 in 1964 and are now less than a hundred, are uneconomic to run. They are often small and fail to provide the boarders within them with an adequate peer group or a varied social existence and this is reflected in the alienation of boys and more severely of girls inside them. Moreover they frequently lack any coherent residential policy and aim, fail to relate to the needs of day children at the school and operate somewhat negative and unimaginative hostels, marked by isolation and high levels of control.[10] Even the sixteen public day schools with boarding sides experienced a ten per cent reduction in boarders between 1961 and 1971.[11] Where bolder policies are pursued, where the boarding provision is regarded not as beds for a disadvantaged minority, left to fend for themselves at four oclock, but as providing opportunity of residential experience for the whole school and a focus of twenty-four-hour community, then such boarding hostels are full, lively and constitute one of the most important growing points within the system, as we shall see. Such residential centres with positive policies relating to day education are usually found attached to comprehensive, not grammar, schools. Amid the general decay in this sector of boarding there is to be found at a few points some very significant new life.

The involvement of the local educational authorities in long-term boarding also seems to be tapering off. After the Second World War there was a burst of creativity, of local authorities establishing their own boarding schools, largely but not exclusively to meet cases of 'need'. Nineteen such schools were established, ranging from well-known grammar schools, such as Wolverstone, run by the former London County Council, and Ottershaw, run by Surrey County Council, to less well-known but equally interesting secondary modern schools such as

Fyfield, run by Essex County Council, the City of Coventry
School or the largest coeducational boarding school in western
Europe set up at Wymondham by the Norfolk County Council.
Some of these schools, as we have seen, pioneered new
approaches to boarding largely out of necessity, evolving from
the social background and assumptions of staff and pupils
trained in the day system or based on patterns of child care.
Unconscious of their originality and unpublicized until our
research enquiry, the schools and the LEAs are somewhat
embarrassed by their existence as anomalies within the state
system. Some three of these schools, including Adcroft School,
Trowbridge, Wiltshire, one of the most fascinating and realistic
attempts to attune boarding and comprehensive education to
working-class boys and their style of life, were swept out of
existence between 1968 and 1970 by plans for comprehensive
reorganization of day education. Several other schools await a
fate on similar grounds or on that of finance.[12] Children with
need for boarding are increasing in numbers[13] and the LEAs are
meeting the situation, not by developing boarding schools or
centres of their own, but by scattering such children around the
cheaper, independent or integrated schools. It is ironic that just
when the state should have been developing its own highly
important, sometimes fresh and, according to our indices,
sometimes successful style of boarding, financial and planning
pressures should lead to a withdrawal and to the removal of
children from a boarding context based around their culture
and needs to an independent school education which, as the
evidence shows, is sometimes alien and unsympathetic to
both.[14] Even so, according to the limited criteria of need which
LEAs variably operate there are children, less able ones and
girls in particular, for whom it is still difficult to find places and
for many of whom nothing is done.[15] There has been no
expenditure on residential provision for such children remotely
comparable to the lavish outlay on the delinquent on the one
hand or those who reach higher education on the other.[16] In the
few cases where constructive policies have prevailed, as described below, it has been found possible to combine the interest
of day comprehensive reorganization with those of boarding
provision and to minimize the undoubted financial difficulties
of direct provision of boarding places by local authorities. But

these cases are very exceptional. The general arrest in the growth of the state sector, against the advice of the Public Schools' Commission 1968,[17] has checked one of the most vital sources of renewal of this kind of education in this country. The burgeoning of short-term boarding supported by LEAs, important as it is, is no substitute.

One sector of the boarding scene is healthy, if not flourishing: the progressive schools. True, there has been no growth here, for no boarding schools claiming to be of the progressive creed have been established in England since the foundation of Wennington in 1940.[18] But there is no contraction either. Indeed, some schools have never been so successful. As parental preferences change towards coeducation, towards a more 'family' style of boarding and towards less restricted approaches to the adolescent, progressive schools which are established and well equipped find their style in demand and, possibly for the first time in their history, are more than able to fill their places with children from normal, rather than abnormal, backgrounds.[19] The smaller, less well-equipped progressive schools still cater mainly for cases of 'need' for boarding of one kind or another. It is not that parents are attracted by the experimental nature of such schools, for there are no more significant experiments going on in this sector than in the public school one. It is simply that parental values and adolescents' demands have at last caught up with what were the advanced progressive school values of the 1920s. Even more traditional schools are beginning to adopt some of the fashionable externals, if not the thorough reality, of the progressive style of boarding.

The general picture of boarding provision in the late 1960s was one of stagnation overall, with particular areas of gradual or rapid decline. In the early 1970s, however, there seems to be a slight increase in boarding at junior levels associated with proportionately increased entry of those with 'need' for residence. Rising costs, the improvement of state day educa-tion and availability of independent day education have been accompanied by subtle shifts in familial roles and relations and therefore in attitudes and by vocal reactions on the part of boarders themselves to which many parents pay heed. All these factors account for the general contraction and changes of emphasis going on within the system. There are few signs of

steady growth of provision and, given the factors just
mentioned, little can be expected in the future. What development there is consists mainly of changes of style and approach
within the system. These may be of vital importance if
residential education is to survive. But before turning to them,
we must switch from the general to the particular, to the
schools themselves to see how they are responding to the
forces of change now bearing upon them.

III

Schools can change in three different ways; in the goals
they actually pursue, in their institutional structures, and in
other ways which do not redefine formal structures or the roles
played within them. [20] In our work in schools we sought to
chart as minutely as possible all changes in recent years, in our
interviews with the heads, housestaff, teachers and pupils, in our
examination of records and school literature. From all this we
derived a fairly accurate picture of changes, from small ones like
the alteration of privileges or timetables to large ones like the
creation or abolition of junior houses. Using all this evidence

TABLE 11:2

Index of change 1960-8 (i) in implemented goals

	Instrumental		Expressive		Organizational	
	Towards high academic emphasis	Away from high academic emphasis	Towards expressive emphasis	Away from expressive emphasis		Total
Public	0·0	0·0	0·0	0·0	0·0	0·0
Independent	0·0	0·0	2·0	0·0	0·0	2·0
Independent integrated	1·0	1·0	0·0	1·0	0·0	3·0
State	0·0	3·6	0·7	2·1	0·0	6·4
Progressive	1·4	0·0	0·0	0·0	0·0	1·4

Source: general sample, the index is composed by analysing and classifying each
change according to given indices, and then dividing the total number of schools into
the total of changes: the index thus represents the average change per school of each
kind, but has been scaled up by a uniform multiplier of 10.

we went on to construct an index of each kind of change in the schools between 1960 and 1968 so as to quantify the general trends.[21]

As would be expected there were few changes in the implemented goals, those long-term, permanent ends which schools actually pursue. They were least in those schools with very clear goals and with a strong stress on expressive values and with a defined, interdependent relation with outside bodies or a section of society, those para-systems we discussed in Chapter 3. There were no changes during the years concerned in the implemented goals of public, most independent schools and only slight change in those of progressive schools: just as there were no changes in their functions for society and their particular clients. Integrated and especially state schools show markedly more changes in real goals. In some schools this was in instrumental areas, caused by the move away from grammar school aims and training towards the altogether broader objectives, different styles and structures implicit in radical and thorough implementation of the idea of comprehensive education. In expressive areas too there was some change in some of these schools: in most cases a deliberate abandonment of attempts to impose uniform expressive values and the controls by which they were enforced, conscious adherence to ideals of more thorough freedom, and self-direction for pupils and

TABLE 11:3

Index of change 1960-8 (ii) in institutional structure

	Instrumental		Expressive		Organizational	
	Towards high academic emphasis	Away from high academic emphasis	Towards expressive emphasis	Away from expressive emphasis	Total	Total
Public	0·0	0·0	3·2	2·6	5·8	11·6
Independent	0·0	0·0	12·0	4·0	2·0	18·0
Independent integrated	1·0	1·0	5·0	0·0	6·0	13·0
State	0·0	4·3	12·0	4·3	5·7	26·3
Progressive	0·0	0·0	10·0	2·8	4·3	17·1

Source: general sample, see Table 11:1.

heterogeneity of values and expression within the school. These state boarding schools changed direction more easily than others because their position was less well defined, they were less embedded in a network of expectations and of well-recognized functions for coherent sub-groups in society. As a result their purposes and composition could alter more than those of other schools and they could more readily alter course according to the winds of educational philosophy.

Of course all schools made more of the next kind of change: that in institutional structure (Table 11:3).

Once again, however, it was state boarding schools which made most. There were numerous changes on the instrumental front associated with the change from systems imposing a common academic level to others in which children pursue aims more individually or from the base of multi-ability groups. Even in these schools there were far more changes on the expressive side. Pastoral systems have been improved, houses modified, various kinds of horizontal and vertical groupings attempted. The ease with which state schools created or altered such structures is notable and is perhaps related to the relative lack of expressive meaning which we found that such things have in these schools (thus, it is far easier to abolish a house which has so much less meaning for its members in a state school than in a public one). Other changes were to lower expressive control: prefectorial systems were abolished, participatory systems of decision-making were established, units were set up by which seniors live free of restrictions and the like. Some independent and progressive schools shared the same trend, making as many changes in their expressive structures towards improved pastoral care and decreased control and hierarchy, but they tended to be less root-and-branch changes than those in state schools. Integrated schools faced with the problem of a social and cultural mix tended to polarize, some moving towards greater rigidity of expressive control in order to surmount the problems and the others moving towards the model of expressive freedom and individual adjustment found in the progressive type of school. All schools made regular changes in their organizational structures, bursarial, domestic and administrative.

In public schools such organizational changes were nearly as great as in all the other ones put together. Again the public schools made far fewer changes in their structures during our research period than did any other kind. None of note were made in the academic spheres and those that were made in the expressive areas concerned the creation or abolition of junior house units, the setting up occasionally of sixth-form centres with greater freedom (of which there were twenty by 1973), the experimentation with tutorial systems to supplement the standard house unit, the abolition of fagging in some schools and of certain types of authority and hierarchy systems among the boys in others. Significant as this trend was, such deliberate changes in structure were few. It seems that the constraints against structural change were greater in the public boarding schools than in others.

These schools obviously felt the same pressures for change as the others, particularly for greater expressive freedom from pupils and even from some parents, but could not or perhaps did not want to alter their structures to meet them. Once again their part in a closed social network prevents change; the fact that governors, old boys and parents have such defined expectations of the school and relatively greater power than in other schools acted as a brake on several changes wanted by some headmasters. The federal structures of decision-making in public schools by which housemasters can together have considerable negative power can also obstruct change. In all the other kinds of schools power is more centralized in the hands of a head or diffused more widely over staff, and this can make for greater flexibility. The complex subdivided structures of public schools also makes the process of change more complicated and more slow than in others. Such complex structures mean that individual members of staff play more diverse and subtle roles than in schools which have simpler patterns. Thus apparently specialized changes, such as enlarging the choice of games or rendering chapel voluntary, affect the roles of more staff than would be the case in other schools. Likewise, as we have seen, public schools create separate cultures out of their subdivisions as a means of generating commitment by the pupils to them: cultures based on the house, the team and the academic group and the hierarchy. State and progressive ones significantly either fail or do not set out to give such expressive emphasis to their parts. They thus find them much easier to change than the public school. Finally, as we know, the public schools contain far more staff, particularly on the residential side, who have no experience outside their own system. All other schools, again particularly state and progressive schools, have staff with wider experience and deliberately make appointments to residential positions from outside. This breadth undoubtedly makes for flexibility in the way structures are approached, for greater receptivity to change and for a knowledge of other relevant areas of experience such as the special boarding schools in this country.

TABLE 11:4

Index of change 1960-8 (iii) non-structural change

	Instrumental		Expressive		Organizational	
	Towards high academic emphasis	Away from academic emphasis	Towards expressive emphasis	Away from expressive emphasis		Total
Public	23·7	6·3	10·5	17·4	21·6	79·5
Independent	14·0	12·0	8·0	20·0	30·0	84·0
Independent integrated	16·0	6·0	11·0	15·0	27·0	75·0
State	5·7	5·7	6·4	12·2	12·8	42·8
Progressive	12·7	14·2	11·4	8·6	17·0	64·1

Source: general sample, see Table 11.1.

When we turn to the third kind of change which does not demand those fundamental redefinitions of staff and pupil roles which the complex society of a public school makes so difficult, to changes which are non-structural, then the situation is very different. Naturally enough, more changes of this kind occurred in all schools, though least in state boarding ones because their changes were concentrated elsewhere. Public schools figure highly on this particular kind of index but with some very distinctive differences of their own. All schools made many academic changes, some towards lessening academic pressures, others towards increasing them. This divergent emphasis is equally distributed over the independent, state and progressive schools: some schools responding to mounting demands for

examination results by universities and parents, by
strengthening their academic system and expectations, others
responding to the comprehensive principle in the secondary
system of education in England by lowering pressures and
readjusting expectations. Quite exceptionally uniform,
however, was the amount of change stressing the academic side
in the public schools. In the last fifteen years there has been
accumulating emphasis on public examinations, signal improve-
ments in science, teaching and facilities, extensions of the
curriculum to cover subjects outside the old grammar school
canon (from business studies to archaeology or political
thought), increased lesson and prep periods, re-equipping of
libraries, experiments in teaching techniques and syllabus and in
areas of the curriculum such as SMP maths, Nuffield sciences
and so on. These kinds of academic emphases have been far
more uniformly widespread in the public schools than in others.
Indeed the public schools now see themselves as the last stronghold of academic standards, interpreted over a very broad
curriculum.[22] Though the public schools greatly enlarged their
non-academic provision - for the arts, music and so on - other
schools, especially progressive and independent schools did on
average even more.

In other, expressive, areas the patterns are similar. All schools
changed many areas of their pastoral and residential life,
rationalizing rules, developing social service and the like. In all
schools, too, there was a move to more freedom for the pupils,
more freedom of expression, movement, activity and relations.
All schools were providing more privacy for seniors and fewer
dress restrictions, more chances of meeting and working with
the other sex and more access to their homes. In public and
independent schools fagging and beating were declining along
with absurd privileges, structures of authority were being
simplified and rendered less rigid, while alternatives were
provided to compulsory CCF, religion and team games and
more freedom of expression in dress, appearance and life style
allowed. There was, in such schools, a subtle but fundamental
change of atmosphere away from the brutal and rigid relations
between boys of past days to infinitely more flexible and more
sympathetic styles of relationships.[23] Progressive schools show
least change of this kind because the freedom they offered was

already so much greater than that found in other schools, but even here deliberate efforts were being made to break down the 'total' system imposed by rural location, isolation from the locality, from the home and by conformity of values, fashions and social class. Resistance to this tendency of lessening the total control of boarding is concentrated mainly in some minor public schools, about half the integrated schools on our sample and a similar proportion of girls' schools.

If we sum up these internal changes we see that fundamental alterations of aim and structure occurred among state schools and to a lesser degree among progressive and other independent schools. Fewer structural changes occurred among the public schools; here the old aims and structures remained but the spirit in which they are worked is often very different from the past. External forces have most powerfully promoted the instrumental changes. Competition for university entry and professional qualification has led to increased academic stress and a significant broadening of the curriculum in most public schools and in the other schools. Contrary pressures away from high and uniform academic stress has come from public policy with regard to comprehensive education or to meeting the adjustment of children with need and these tendencies have affected state, smaller independent and some progressive schools. Other progressive schools are moving in the academic direction of the public schools in this matter in response to parental and university pressures.

Changes on the expressive side are mainly internal in derivation and come chiefly from restlessness on the part of the pupils or younger staff and, as far as more frequent access to the home is concerned, from parents. The reference point of the boarder increasingly tends to be the adolescent *outside* the boarding school and spurred on by this example and a pervasive (but not uniform), youth culture, the pupils have been themselves opening up their closed societies. Indeed ten years ago in 1963-5, just as this research was beginning, there was much talk at boarding school meetings of 'the sixth-form revolt'. No revolt has occurred. The boarding schools of the early nineteenth century eliminated riots and disaffection by creating the closed, totally controlled school we have inherited,[24] while those of 1960-70 drained off gathering discontent by diminishing, albeit very variably and sometimes gingerly, their total nature. This dynamic is still at work. Progressive schools which were so revolutionary in the 1920s in their expressive freedoms are now becoming a sort of model for other schools, pupils and parents, while some of those which once claimed to be part of the progressive movement such as Rendcomb, Badminton, Bryanston, Dauntseys, Bedales and Leighton Park are now virtually part of the public school system.[25] The movement towards openness occurs most radically in schools which are socially open and heterogeneous in culture and are sensitive to their composition. Such schools are also frequently bridging the gap between boarding and day education by offering a whole dimension of experience in which the merits of both kinds are available to children. As the experiments discussed in the next chapter indicate it could be the mission of boarding schools, which were once the most closed and institutional of educational structures, to pioneer the way into providing a non-institutional and non-school setting for the development of the young. This is an extreme case, but still representing a general trend in boarding away from the total institution.

IV

What other growing points are there and what signs of renewal within this kind of education which in its scale may be on the wane? There are some fairly widespread new developments and others more isolated but none the less significant for the future.

Most obvious during the period of our field work and since the 1970s has been the trend towards coeducational boarding. Impelled by parents who often nowadays want their children kept together for emotional reasons and those of convenience, by the boy and girl boarders themselves who strongly react against cloistered seclusion from the other sex and by the need to keep up demand for places, some boys' schools are taking in girl boarders. (No girls' schools, significantly enough, are taking in boys). About twenty full public schools and a few prep schools are among them. The introduction of girls is, however, smaller than the number of schools concerned would imply. By late 1971 there were only 166 girl boarders among some 35,347 boy boarders in HMC schools.[26] The old established coeducational boarding schools - independent or progressive - which down to the 1960s were viewed with considerable suspicion by traditional boarding school parents are now much sought after by them and are enjoying (at least those of them with facilities comparable to those of good public schools) an unprecedented demand. This is likely to continue not only as attitudes change but as need for boarding among mobile middle-class families increases, accompanied by a desire to keep children of both sexes together.

The consequences of this trend if the numbers of girl boarders increase in public schools could be revolutionary for traditional patterns of boarding education. If the structures, mode of operation and ethos of the style of boarding associated with the public school is not to be altered by changes in the social class of their pupils as recommended by the Public Schools Commission of 1968, important changes may still be wrought by the influx of middle-class fee-paying girls, even the sisters of the boys already there. This is not to contend that coeducation necessarily leads to more open or liberal approaches to residential education. On the contrary coeducational schools are just like the socially integrated ones we have already described: in face of the fundamental problems presented by mixed social or sexual composition, boarding schools, more than others, tend to polarize to extremes along the dimension of control, some being extremely enclosed and rigid, others extremely open and free. We have discussed earlier the different existing styles of coeducational boarding and elsewhere given an analysis of what options single-sex schools have if they admit the opposite sex.[27] But even if the present boys' boarding schools opt for the least fundamental changes, that of creating a divided community segregated by sex, their own style will still undergo severe modification. The presence of girls is likely particularly to affect not just the curriculum and extra-curricular provision but also patterns of authority, corporal punishment, the hierarchy and rituals, modes of relationships, norms of conduct and status among the pupils. Their presence, especially in the more progressive boys' public schools making this change, enhances the movement towards greater freedom especially in dress, privacy and informality of relations. Though it is unlikely that many schools will move to the radical extreme

of coeducation found in some progressive schools, most will
find that the change will gradually lead to alterations of staffing
provision, residential structure and subtle but profound developments in ethos, norms and relationships.

This is but one of the challenges presented by the change
within the families using the boarding system. Not only should
children be kept together but they should be kept in as close as
possible touch with their parents and homes. To some schools
such a change poses a radical threat. Parents not only
increasingly invade the boarding school at weekends but
increasingly want their children home at weekends. To most
boarding schools this is a challenge to the close control, the
sustained protection from contaminating, outside values which
they seek to provide. Most of them have rigidly prescribed in
the past how many weekends parents may visit and limit the
amount of term time exeats pupils may have to the outer
world. In all, however, the tendency is for more access by
parents and more access by the children to home.

A few - chiefly state and progressive schools - have gone
much further, in the belief that the school cannot and should
not replace home and parents and should build a continuum for
the child between his two living environments. Whereas conventional schools exclude parents and visiting for a specified
period when a new child arrives and undergoes the pains of
homesickness, some of this group invite one or both of the
parents to come and stay so that the child can get over
homesickness with the family present. Others have created
flexible patterns of boarding by which those who want can go
home at any weekend and not just at one or a few prescribed
times. There is no evidence from our research that the
community life of such schools suffers fatally or that, given
complete freedom of access to the home, more than a few
children use it at any one time, though these are children who
probably most need such contact. Other schools bring parents
into their life, not just in the sense of raising money or, as in
some state boarding schools, digging swimming pools and the
like. At the Fyfield state boarding school in Essex during a 'flu
epidemic a rota of mothers came and lived in the school over a
considerable period to help with the nursing and domestic work
of their children, and many school activities are run by parents,

some of whom are as familiar about the premises as the teachers. The parents and their other children not only enlarge the texture of the school but themselves gain more insight and understanding of what it is trying to do than they could possibly gather from formal parents' days, prospectuses and tedious lectures from the headmaster.

The change in the attitude of the family to boarding presents schools with the opportunity to diminish one of the very real disadvantages of this form of education and to create a closer working partnership with the home than day schools often seem to manage. This is a challenge which has to be met if boarding is to continue on any scale in this country.

More extensive are the developments linking day and boarding education, bridge-building exercises which provide children with the benefits of both kinds of education. These changes are of three sorts.

Some very few boarding schools which try to match residential provision with the varying needs of their pupils are trying to make a continuum with day education. Thus, just as boarders can go home at weekends or at other times, so day pupils in the school can sleep in when they need to do so.

Less rare and found mainly in the state system are new sorts of boarding annexes attached to day schools. We have noted the tendency for many hostels to die off. The vital ones are usually coeducational, fairly large, containing between sixty and a hundred children and are run on family styles of residence associated with child-care training. They are often filled with children with need for boarding, mainly from families in the armed services living abroad. Situated in large day schools, like the one at Lairthwaite, Cumberland, or Crown Woods in Eltham, London, these relaxed and homely hostels can give a warm and lively focus to a large and possibly impersonal institution and a centre of continuous activity for all pupils at evenings and weekends when day schooling might have ended. Another is opening in the 'progressive' comprehensive school at Countesthorpe in Leicestershire. In other words the necessity of residence is turned into a virtue which is used to enlarge the educational provision for *all* the pupils in the school. Such hostels are in their style and function the opposite extreme of those others - the majority - which remain dismal and isolated communities on the periphery of their day schools.

More radical and possibly more significant for the future are those hostels attached to day schools for children *from the area itself*, not for cases of need from distant counties or lands. There are only two, at the moment, both in the mining town and educational priority area of Conisbrough in Yorkshire, one run by the educational priority team for children from the local primary schools and the other run by Dartington Hall and the local authority for children of secondary age from the one large comprehensive school which serves the whole town.[28] These converted houses provide boarding experience for working-class children in their own home context, alongside their homes, in fact. Boarding is urban not rural, next door to and enmeshed with the family situation, not distant and opposed to it, and integrally related with the day school. Pupils move in and live for varying spells and courses based on the day school or at the centres themselves. Similarly, other children with need to live away from their nearby homes (because mother is having a baby, because of family tensions, death or separation of parents, or of need for quiet privacy before exams) live in the houses sometimes for very long spells. Besides offering positive boarding experience to all, within a recognizable context which minimizes the disadvantages of conventional residence, such annexes meet the needs of many children in distress in ordinary day school situations who may benefit from living outside the family but need to be close to it, to their friends, their neighbours and their teachers. Developments like this could not only lead to a new kind of boarding - urban, working class and local - but also more sensitively meet need for boarding, much of which is known to day school teachers and headmasters but is not met by local authorities because of the expense of removing children to distant boarding schools or child-care establishments or because of the reluctance of families which have need to contemplate moving their children out of their ordinary environment. It is very much in line with developments in the care of children from delinquent or special backgrounds.[29]

This is *not* the pattern now being adopted by most authorities. The third and most extensive development linking boarding and day education in this country since the war has been in short-term boarding provision by the local education

authorities. Residential centres for study, adventure or
expeditions, or residential cruises serving groups of schools are
frequent, as are the hostels in the country attached to one large
day school. Sometimes these hostels are redundant primary
schools, old cottages or, in some cases, large Edwardian houses
near the seaside. To them come children and staff, sometimes
for holiday courses, projects or expeditions and sometimes for
sustained periods of study. Many local authorities anxious to
provide boarding experience see in such hostels, partly financed
by parental contributions, the answer to the dilemma of limited
finance and strict egalitarian provision for every child. With
some such aim in mind the Inner London Education Authority,
in some ways the most important one in the country, has gone
on record with its intention of providing boarding experience
for every child in its care at some point in his or her school
career.

The rapid proliferation of this kind of facility has not been
accompanied by much evaluation of its benefits and disadvantages though in 1971 we undertook a survey of the provision in one county.[30] Short-term boarding provision directly
linked to a day school and used by all pupils periodically can
obviously benefit the day school, especially the large and
impersonal kind. At the short-stay centre staff-pupil relations
clearly improve, relationships among pupils develop and deepen,
commitment to the school and education can increase and these
changes can feed continuously and beneficially back into the
experience of the day school. Given the infrequent and limited
stays by pupils, however, it is doubtful if the other possible
benefits of boarding experience - such as the development of
social sensitivity, enlargement of horizons, of social and personal
skills, appreciation of the family - are communicated and if they
are they do not survive the return to the distant day school.
The fact that these centres are far away in the country provides
the stimulus of change and fresh air but frequently gives the
experience a detached, anomic quality reminiscent of a school
holiday party in which ordinary norms, patterns and relationships are relaxed while away but rapidly revert to their old rigid
selves on return to the ordinary day-to-day context. Equally
such centres do nothing to meet the problems of children in
distress and with need for living away from home who live in the

school's own catchment area; developing a residential provision
for them near the school might provide a whole new dimension
of experience, facility and challenge for day schools which might
also make more real their common claim to be 'community
colleges.' Boarding in the ordinary context of the childrens'
main school might not only be cheaper, enable schools to provide variably for children's needs instead of standard doses of
residence for each, but might also give continuity of experience
between boarding and day experience so that skills and relationships fostered in the one relate immediately and continuously to
the other because they take place in the same context. Such
local urban annexes are quite consistent with the present kind
of country centres run for groups of schools in which the
outward bound, project or holiday kind of residence could still
be provided. Ironically the uniform trend in short-term
boarding often provides not only the minimal educational
returns and possibilities but perpetuates some of the disadvantages (anomic, isolation and irrelevance), which apply to
the standard kind of long-term boarding in England. Far more
variety and experiment is called for, instead of the present very
stereotyped provision and as much could be learnt from Soviet
and Israeli patterns of urban boarding as from the classic rural
form in England.

We reach then the final area of growth in this kind of
education: the area of social integration or integration between
the various sectors of education. Boarding in this country is the
preserve of the upper socio-economic groups and even in
integrated schools, or those with many cases of need, the lower
socio-economic groups are scarcely represented. Since the
Fleming Report of 1944 the question of the social exclusiveness
of boarding schools and that of enlarging their social composition has been a live issue and the whole matter was again considered by the Public Schools Commission of 1966-8. Despite
two enquiries and reports and endless public debate little has
happened in practice to enlarge the social entry into boarding
schools or to link them effectively to the national system of
education. Some of the Flemingite schemes started in the
1940s survive at such schools as Mill Hill, Wycombe Abbey,
St George's, Weybridge, and other public schools have entries
from local authorities such as Rendcomb from Gloucestershire,

Christ's Hospital from the Inner London Education Authority and Llandovery from Welsh authorities. As most such scholarship entries are of bright children it follows, as we know from all selection processes based on measured intelligence in this country, that the pupils selected are substantially middle class in character.[31] What happens to such children on such schemes is very instructive and has been studied in a special report of this research unit. Integration of this kind - except at Llandovery and to some minimal extent at Rendcomb - seldom leads the boarding school into any significant contact with the pupils' home and culture, or with the staff and day schools on which it draws or to any organic relationship with local state day education. No further schemes of this kind are likely in the future: they cost too much, their effects on the pupils involved are dubious, they are ineffective in enlarging the schools socially or in lessening the gap between independent boarding and maintained day education in general.[32]

Though much has been said by boarding school headmasters about the desirability of integration on the part of their schools very few have done anything but talk. In the rare cases where action has ensued some very significant steps forward have been made in the late 1960s which suggests different kinds of growth which could develop later.

In 1965 Marlborough College, the large boys' public school in Wiltshire, embarked on a pilot scheme of integration different from the old Fleming kind. It took twenty-one boys at sixth-form level, accepted minimal academic qualifications for entry, took them all from the nearby town of Swindon and, in an effort to enable them to keep their own identity and relationships with their homes and friends, deliberately made some changes in its own system. The whole scheme was evaluated by research and has been described elsewhere. The experiment showed up markedly some of the real possibilities of boarding of this kind and some of the problems brought to the school, the boys and their families by the scheme and the need for a closer relation with the feeding state schools. Unfortunately, no finance was available for it to continue after the initial entry had left and there was no chance to see if the problems could have been minimized for subsequent entries by still further changes. The lessons of the scheme are, however, crucial if this or any sort of integration is to be attempted again.[33]

Likely to be more enduring are some of the schemes of integration between public schools and the maintained sector. These do not involve local authorities taking up places in boarding schools but an organic link between independent boarding and state day schools as part of the development of large comprehensive consortia within the maintained sector. At Banbury in Oxfordshire three small independent boarding schools, one a public school for girls (Tudor Hall), another for boys (Bloxham), and the third a coeducational Quaker school (Sibford Ferris) have joined a comprehensive consortium based around the state school in Banbury. They teach minority subjects to pupils from the other schools in the consortium and their own boarders go off to the other schools for specified parts of the curriculum. Though there are no changes in the boarding composition of the schools, the scheme is bound to affect their ethos, their 'total' character as well as academic provision. It will be interesting to see if developments do follow on the residential side. This is true too of the other similar scheme by which the boys' public school, Dauntsey's, in Wiltshire, is integrated with the neighbouring West Lavington High School in a reciprocal scheme making one comprehensive unit. Quite apart from other effects this has already led to girls from the high school joining the hitherto single-sex boys' boarding school as full-time day students. It is too early to evaluate such schemes and to consider how far reciprocation will be found at staff and parent level and what sort of social mix may result, and the role that boarding provision may ultimately play within the comprehensive units. The important developments lie in the organic linking with state day education and administration and the identifying with and opening up to the immediate locality which all this implies: both features until now almost entirely alien to the independent residential school.

Based partly on experience of these two kinds of development and on the evident failings of the old Flemingite kind of integration which this research project charted, a third and deliberately more radical kind of bridge building between the independent boarding and state day school has been attempted by the author of this book at Dartington Hall School in the years since 1968. It is fully discussed in the next chapter. Apart from this however the scene in the mid-seventies is virtually barren of initiatives, though a group of prep school heads have put forward an enterprising, parent-financed plan by which a few less well-off children might enter their schools on Flemingite lines.[34] It is noticeable that when Conservative governments are in power in England, content to leave the issue of independence in education alone, the social consciences of independent school headmasters, which are so paraded when Labour governments are in office and scrutinizing the issue of independence, seem to wither away and little is said and nothing is done on the matter. Indeed the gulf between the sectors may have grown wider since the mid-1960s, for public schools increasingly tend to regard themselves as bastions of high academic standards, order and civilized values which, they sometimes imply, are disappearing in the maintained sector of education.

These then are the growing points in boarding now, some of them widespread but most few and some indeed precarious. Within most schools the slow process of renewal is always at work, but there has been signally little rethinking of the nature of residence, its structural relation to day education or of the connection between the independent boarding and state day sectors in this country. What initiatives there have been in these areas, either by individual schools or by local authorities, have scarcely affected the general situation, though they have provided useful indications of what might be done.

12 The research applied: experiments at Dartington 1968-73

This book has inevitably been concerned with generalities, with the broad objective conclusions of our researches. In this penultimate chapter, however, it becomes more particular, detailed and even personal.

One unique and unexpected sequel to the research programme of the period 1964 to 1968 was that it resulted in practical action to implement some findings and conclusions in the following years. During my visits to our sample of English boarding schools I carried out research at the well-known 'progressive' boarding school at Dartington Hall in rural Devon, first for a stay of three weeks at its senior school in 1966 and again for a similar span at its junior department in 1967. Somewhat later that summer I discussed with one of the Dartington Hall Trustees the conclusions of my research at the school seen in the perspective of the whole study of English boarding education. A couple of weeks later most of the trustees arrived suddenly one evening at Cambridge to suggest that I consider becoming head of their school to carry out the ideas which I had put forward in our earlier meeting. Used mainly to university life and teaching, I was taken aback: I had never considered becoming a headmaster, still less of a private boarding school and one of the progressive style at that. The trustees, however, were in earnest and the chance actually to put into practice in sympathetic surroundings some of the ideas which years of research had indicated as desirable was irresistible. I drew up a programme of action which the trustees accepted, the staff at the school endorsed and was later published for all to read.[1] At Christmas of 1968 I took over the headship of the school on the retirement of the previous heads. Two parents withdrew their children immediately.

Five years later I am writing this chapter in the study of the headmaster's house only a month or two before finally giving up the headship of the school. This book is obviously not the place to review objectively all that has been attempted at Dartington in those years. Indeed some of the efforts are not particularly relevant to its theme. Thus the aim to revitalize the school must be one which every incoming headmaster has. Another aim was more particular to the Dartington style of education: to apply the progressive ethic, which had become so rigid an orthodoxy practised in remote boarding schools for the children of wealthy people, to situations more testing of its educational value, flexibility and relevance to the needs of ordinary children in the 1970s. These themes will be treated elsewhere. Here I shall discuss, as frankly and objectively as I can, the effort which Dartington has made to develop the nature of boarding education and the role of the independent boarding school in this country.[2] In all that has been done in these two areas I was guided by the research findings which this book has already summarized and also by the failure of the Public Schools Commission of 1966-8, in whose research activities I had been much involved, either to make practically acceptable proposals for ending the isolation of the independent boarding sector from the mainstream of education or even to use the special powers given to it to initiate experimental schemes of integration between the independent boarding and the state day sectors.

I was also, of course, affected by the needs and nature of the school which had been entrusted to my charge and which I must briefly introduce.[3] In 1926 Dorothy and Leonard Elmhirst bought the derelict estate of Dartington near the sea in south Devon to use as a model for rural revival. They aimed to introduce to the then depressed countryside the modern economy, humane relationships and rich quality of life more associated with the town. Alongside the flourishing farms and varied rural industries which were soon established they developed many educational and cultural enterprises. From 1926 to 1930 the 'school', a small flexible unit of broad social composition, was intimately interwoven with the farms and industries themselves in a way which (to me now) seems more relevant to the present day and more revolutionary in its time than has ever been acknowledged. From 1930, however, the school crystallized into an institution under a charismatic headmaster, William Burnlee Curry. A friend and disciple of Bertrand Russell, he belonged to that group of educators who, deeply influenced by psychology, established a second radical wave of progressive schools in the 1920s.[4] The school he developed at Dartington soon became famous for its apparently democratic government, its fearless coeducation, its warm egalitarian relationships between staff and pupils, its stress on the arts, on self-expression, its provision of single study bedrooms for each pupil of whatever age. Housed in well-equipped buildings provided by the Trust, it developed as a small largely boarding school of around a hundred pupils drawn from fee-paying, well-to-do families living well outside the locality in which it became, unjustly, notorious. Curry was succeeded, from 1957 to 1968, by Hu and Lois Child who rebuilt the school physically, enlarged its size to 230 pupils, restored its economy, introduced more structure and obligation into its life, and developed the curriculum and selectivity of a grammar school.[5] It remained, despite a generous annual endowment from the Trust, mainly for well-off and fee-paying parents from outside the district, with which its links were tenuous. When I arrived late in 1968 the school comprised a small exclusively fee-paying nursery for children who then went on to the small fee-paying junior school for day children; boarders entered the middle school at the age of ten and moved up to the separate senior school at thirteen, usually staying until they were eighteen. Two-thirds of the school were boarders.

The objectives in 1968 were four. First, the school was to be opened up educationally, turned from a grammar school (like most independent boarding schools) into one catering for a broader intellectual span, turned outwards from a rather inward-looking defensive community to one which was more open to outside influences hitherto kept beyond the progressive pale, and rendered a place where pupils could realize themselves intellectually and in other respects more fully than had been the case in a school where informal norms had been antagonistic to certain kinds of achievement through work. Like other boarding schools that we encountered on our researches Dartington was extraordinarily rigid and monolithic in its residential structure and practices: the second aim therefore was to render it more flexible, more adaptable to the needs of young people of different ages, of different parents and families. This was to

be done by enlarging the styles of residence the school offered
to its own children. Also, like all other boarding schools on our
research, Dartington was almost totally cut off from the local
community, the local village, the town of Totnes and, less
understandably, cut off from the estate and branches of
Dartington Hall itself. The third aim then was to reintegrate
the school with the community, which in the years 1926-30 it
had been created to serve. Finally, and again like all other
independent boarding schools, Dartington was severed from the
mainstream of state education in this country; a situation which
we felt damaged the school socially and educationally. We
resolved therefore to try to create a new form of thorough and
realistic two-way integration between this independent progressive school on the one hand and the state educational
system on the other, one which would learn from the failures
and mistakes of past schemes of integration (virtually all of
which had ended by 1968) and one which could prove a possible
model for the future. We also recognized that a small community lost amid the Devon hills offered like all rural boarding
schools, which are the majority, only a limited kind of stimulation to its students. We decided therefore to provide our
students not only with continuous experience of urban life and
problems in this country but vantage points in other societies,
to plant outposts of the school in cultures abroad at which the
students could live and work and from which they might
acquire a new perspective on themselves and their own society.
Such ventures would also diversify the routes by which
students left the process of schooling and entered adult life.

These then were the somewhat grandiose objectives. How far
have they been fulfilled?

II

Of the first group of aims I shall not say much, as they have
little to do with boarding education *per se* though much to do
with the possibilities of change in residential communities
dominated by powerful informal normative systems. In the
effort to revitalize the intellectual life and extend the
intellectual range of the school downwards a major enlargement
and restructuring of its curriculum, its recreational activities,

working practices and staffing took place. Thus more new subjects or interdisciplinary groups of subjects were introduced into the senior school and staff was deliberately recruited with experience from outside the progressive system. To break down the somewhat closed and remarkably uniform system of values in belief, expectations, outlook and even dress found in schools of this kind, the place was deliberately opened up by recruiting students, as we shall discuss below, from a wider social, political and economic range of backgrounds and by carefully introducing elements which had been thought incompatible with the progressive style of life. For example, in a school dominated by agnosticism, where religion had been something banished to the world of superstitious darkness outside, a visiting priest was appointed who lived and worked alongside the students, held communion services in student rooms, received neither support nor opposition from the authorities and produced an extraordinary ferment, outrage and discussion. Likewise to counteract the pronounced individualism generated in students by a progressive style in which small group structures had no part and which resulted in the inability of children to work and learn together in group situations, an effort was made to reconstruct the basic unit of the school along tutorial group lines. At the junior end of the school a warm and supportive atmosphere had long been maintained but an effort was now made to increase both the basic skills learned and group interaction and awareness. To accomplish all this, the entire administrative structure of the school was reshaped to include a much greater participation by staff and students in decision-making and the running of the school. Finally, the financial structure of the school was also completely recast. The endowment, which had always been used to subsidize all fees indiscriminately, was now gradually withdrawn and the fees doubled in consequence from £600 per annum to £1,200 per annum, releasing most of the endowment of £35,000 per annum as a fund to support less well-off children to come to the school and to launch the experimental schemes discussed below.

That these changes and the others mentioned below could receive the support of staff, students, parents and trustees speaks for the flexibility and openness to change of those concerned with progressive education. Whether all the effort in the end achieved its aims is quite another matter. Thus the intention to become academically comprehensive has not been fully realized. The school has not extended its intellectual scope as widely as was hoped, partly because it still draws mainly from upper-middle-class families whose children are all heading for higher education, partly because parents in such groups with less academic children refuse to face the fact, partly because of the inherent difficulties of changing the grammar school style of education, and partly because of the small size of the place. It still cannot really cope with the needs of those less bright, indeed sometimes illiterate, working-class children who throng its corridors as part of its scheme of integration: for these groups special *ad hoc* courses have to be laid on. Long-term boarders on the scheme of integration have now to be of a certain intellectual standing, though the intellectual level for admission to the school for all entrants is considerably lower than it was in 1968. Whether the other aim of decreasing the gap between talent and achievement has been attained is also doubtful. The pervasive values of spontaneity, happiness, freedom and self-expression sometimes militate against those qualities of hard work, self-denial and perspective required to fulfil talents.[6] In so far as examination performance measures intellectual achievement there was a spectacular improvement for the first four years in the school's results at A level, bringing it into line with those of the more celebrated public schools, but these results have recently begun to fluctuate as though the impetus for achievement is on the wane. The restructured tutorial groups introduced to counteract exotic individualism quietly vanished, eroded by the very forces they were designed to limit. More clearly successful has been the effort to introduce into the school heterogeneous values and widely differing cultural styles: the annual injection of large groups of new students from diverse backgrounds at the age of thirteen and also at sixteen, along with the powerful experiences of the integration schemes have sometimes painfully prevented a retreat to the closed and homogeneous culture of the past. The effect has been emphasized by the presence in the senior school of many teachers with backgrounds other than that of progressive or public schools. The senior school is undoubtedly broader, more outward-looking as a consequence and many of the pupils now have what their predecessors always lacked: a background experience of education outside to provide, what was also lacking before, an informed critique of the school's practices and achievements from within.

All the efforts to effect similar changes in the separate and smaller junior and middle schools, however, have failed; similar schemes and ideas have been launched there but they have been sunk without trace along with some of the staff more intimately involved. They have foundered on the quiet and persistent expectations of the informal staff network and of parents (many with children who are disturbed or who have 'failed' in conventional schools) as to the nature of this part of the school. It remains as ever a happy, warm, close and somewhat smothering museum piece, well to the left in education compared with the single-sex prep school but still much to the right of the advanced state primary school which has left it, in its mode of teaching and its view of the curriculum, trailing behind.

One effect of these kinds of change and the dramatically increased fees has been surprising. The school, particularly at the senior end, has never been so over-subscribed: applications for admission more than trebled per annum between 1969 and 1973 and there are now about eight serious applications for every vacant place. Though many other reputable coeducational schools are riding the crest of the wave which we have described earlier in the book, it does seem that some of the changes introduced and still working at Dartington appeal to the students and parents who are deterred by the conventional forms and isolation of boarding in England.

III

A thorough effort has been made to diversify patterns of boarding in order to bring this method of education more in tune with the needs of different children of different ages and from different families. Some but not all of the aims clearly have been realized.

'Flexible' boarding has been introduced with little but benefit to everyone. Pupils go home any weekend if they wish in the belief that if they need home they should have it. Only a few boarders go home regularly, more go occasionally but some not at all. The effect on the weekend life of the school has been variable but probably detrimental: but this is compensated for by the genuine gain to individuals and families. Parents are welcomed at the school during the day or at weekends for as long as they wish. To help this a hostel was opened within the school for parents where they could live alongside the pupils. It was a great success but in the end had to be closed as part of an economy campaign in 1972. Many visiting parents now stay with staff or elsewhere in the school. A special youth hostel with twenty beds, made in the school, for boys and girls has been opened. Here can stay at any time the brothers and sisters or friends of boarders at nominal charges. One girl's sister, for example, comes every weekend. Day pupils of the school can stay overnight whenever they wish and visiting parties from other schools and colleges book and live at the hostel as well. There have been parties from such places as Marlborough public school or Crown Woods comprehensive in London, and each year, waves of boys from various approved schools come to stay, living with girls and boys from the Dartington School. This facility has thus been in many ways an important asset to the whole school.

Thus a completely flexible boarding pattern has been established: boarders go home or not as they wish, day pupils reside if they need or wish, parents, friends and families of boarders can stay when they wish and visiting groups can live at the school for as long as is needed without intruding on its other accommodation or life. Boarders or day pupils can also live in part of the school during the holidays either for work or for special projects. These simple changes have relaxed the strain of boarding, provided regular contact with families and opened up the possibilities of residence to day pupils at the school and outside.

Equally workable has been the change in the age structure of boarders. As we have seen earlier, most schools start boarding at seven or eight with the child moving on to a senior school at thirteen which he leaves only when quitting school altogether. At Dartington the age of boarding was ten, although some day pupils entered the school at the age of three and stayed (as day or boarders) until eighteen. This continuity was in some senses a great asset but it was also a weakness making for the uniformity of values and inward-lookingness found in this and many other schools of a similar kind. It also patently failed to suit the needs of different children and families. By creating a special sixth-form centre with sixty-two extra study bedrooms, leeway was made to recruit as a matter of deliberate policy substantial numbers of pupils annually at the age of thirteen and again at sixteen. Instead of the long-term span of ten to eighteen, therefore, which a valuable core of pupils still undertake, boarding at Dartington could now be for variable spans: from ten to thirteen, or ten to sixteen, or thirteen to sixteen, or sixteen to eighteen, and so on. We found that one-year spans were far too short to be of value to anyone. Boarding can thus be provided to suit the needs, both educational and financial, of the individual and the family. The results for the school community are by no means as fragmented as the variable spans above may make it seem. Admittedly at first the injection of large numbers of outsiders, often from backgrounds utterly different from or hostile to the self-regulated participatory free style of Dartington, caused acute problems of adjustment but, over time, these have been minimized. The newcomers have indeed done much to open the school, to change it and diversify it as well as use its abundant resources more fully than many who had been long-term residents in the past. These variable spans also suit family needs as the increased demand for the school clearly implies.

One further, and to me, most important attempt to diversify the institutional structure of residence was never fully realized. For a school which claimed as part of its principles to suit the individual, the residential system was amazingly uniform, as drearily unifrom as that of schools which never made such slaims: providing houses of identical size, structure and regime for pupils to live in, only differing according to the accidental characters and styles of houseparents.

To suit the needs of different children and also of different stages of development, clearly a whole range of residential and learning situations and atmospheres ought to be provided. Immediately in 1969, by using the vacant headmaster's house and by adding three specially built residential units, a new sixth-form complex was rapidly brought into being containing sixty-two study bedrooms for boys and girls,* dining rooms, a bar, common rooms, launderette, craft rooms, library, garage and repair workshops. The aim here was to allow sixth-form students of both sexes who so wished to live free of the structure of houseparents and staff in a community which was entirely regulated by themselves: a deliberate reversion to the original aims of radical progressive education which had been eroded in the school by the need in the past to provide more structure and obligation especially for the younger pupils. An adult warden was housed nearby and from time to time individual staff live in the centre but in ordinary student rooms and with neither more nor less authority than their neighbours. Only one proviso was imposed on this community by the school: that students should first have experienced the tighter structure and self-disciplined mode of life of the main school. In the first two years of the enterprise, when we had doubled the size of the sixth form to 120, this aim could not be realized and many students new to the school entered the Old Postern sixth-form centre direct from outside. In those years there were serious problems of noise, inability to work, the dossing-down of outsiders and sleeplessness which the students seemed unable to solve for themselves at their meetings and I, as headmaster, was tempted to intervene. In the last three years, however, almost all the residents have moved up from the main school and continuity of personnel and values and objectives has been built up so that the former problems have largely disappeared. The place works as one of the freest and yet most orderly living units for young people of both sexes found at school or university level in this country. Not all the students who are eligible choose to live there, however, as some prefer the greater structure, the adult presence found in the houses back at the main school and continue to live there.

By itself this experiment was obviously inadequate. It was still school, still institution, still large, however genuinely free and self-regulating its life may have been. To provide the students who wanted to get away for a time - or for all the time - from other pupils and staff or from school atmosphere, other smaller ventures were begun. One group of students went

* There is no segregation of boys' and girls' rooms at Dartington.

to live at the little hostel tucked a mile away from the school near the old medieval Hall, occupied by the body of working boys and girls who formed the vocational gardening unit with which we had linked up as described on p 324. The atmosphere, the style, even the food, was very different from that of the school and some pupils, particularly girls, found it refreshing. For others who wished to lead a still more normal life than boarding ever provides, we rented a small ordinary terraced house in a back street of Totnes, the market town some three miles away from the school itself. Though the eight students of both sexes who lived there came to school for lessons and, if they wanted, for their main meals, they lived on their own, shopped and cooked for themselves and did all their own housework. Again the atmosphere and life away from the school suited some admirably for a time, some for most of the time, though the majority of the pupils did not want it at all. No untoward problems arose. Other students who wanted more of a family life moved out to live with nearby staff or parents or others, including a local farmer.

Deriving from the logic of these developments and from the deeper forces at work among idealistic young people faced with privileged living and with an educational system which seemed to consist of the pursuit of qualifications rather than the attainment of wisdom, there came an insistent demand from a substantial minority of the school for yet a further development: the setting up of a sort of commune of staff and pupils who would live together, run their own domestic affairs, cook their own meals, grow some of their own vegetables and foodstuffs, and live more as a mutually interdependent group than is found elsewhere in the school. Linked up with this was the proposal to run a different learning situation for some or all of the group alongside and outside the school itself, one which dispenses with conventional teaching and teachers as well as fragmented lessons. After much debate of an unusual and intense kind, both proposals were defeated by referendum of the whole school, though I personally was in favour of them both.

Not all these developments in atmosphere continue. Living out at the vocational hostel stopped when, as explained soon, our integration scheme with that unit collapsed. For other extrinsic reasons the town house has been given up. The alternative-to-school project is starting in Yorkshire not in Devon.

The aim of providing a whole dimension of living and learning to suit the needs of differing children and ages has therefore not been fully attained. Though still unusually free in its general atmosphere and life, Dartington Hall School still provides within an institutional framework a somewhat varied semi-structure for everyone. It is clear from the responses and behaviour of the pupils that some of them require a much tighter structure for living and learning, while on the other hand another minority would benefit from something altogether different, less structured and less institutional. Nevertheless the developments of the last years have undoubtedly demonstrated how relatively easy and valuable it is to diversify the nature of residence in education which is elsewhere so uniformly and rigidly stereotyped for everyone.

IV

One major aim was to reduce the isolation from the community which Dartington shared along with nearly all the other boarding schools we visited on our research. Indeed at Dartington the isolation was doubly disturbing. The school had not only grown apart from the workshops, industries and other enter-prises of the Trust with which in the years 1926-30 it had been so closely interlinked, but also from the Trust's nearby educational activities. In 1968 there was no contact with the Trust-operated College of Arts for students aged eighteen to twenty-two a mile away and even the Trust's own youth club, only five minutes' walk away, was actually banned to students at that time. With the village of Dartington and the town of Totnes relations were if anything worse than those found in other boarding schools on our travels. A long tradition of hostility had been generated: the rural folk of Devon did not in the 1930s take easily to such practices as mixed nude bathing which then flourished at the school or to the sight of long-haired girls sauntering up the High Street in bare feet eating cornflakes from a bumper-size pack. The students themselves, obsessed by the feeling of difference, of being avant-garde, and in actuality being different in their social class, in their sophisticated urban culture, were drawn into the defensive intense culture of the school and tended to regard the locality as the preserve of backward bumpkins. By 1968 these hostile stereotypes had definitely faded as the youth culture outside began to catch up with that of the progressive school but there was still little contact with local youth, with the nearby comprehensive or primary schools.

To me this situation was deplorable. Here was a school and its young clearly not getting the best out of the great richness of the environment provided by the industries, training units, educational ventures operated by its own governing body or out of the organizational and social variety offered by its own local community. In return the school itself had something unique to offer to all of them. Therefore over the last years a sustained effort has been made to link meaningfully with other groups in the locality. With only a few minor exceptions the result by 1973 was failure. In fact it proved easier to integrate, as we shall see, with a mining community three hundred miles away in Yorkshire or with a peasant village one thousand miles away in Sicily than with our neighbours on the Dartington Hall estate, in the local village or in the town of Totnes. Some account of this failure takes us to the heart of the limitations and the yet unfulfilled potentials of boarding education generally.

It was the extraordinary possibilities of vocational education which had most powerfully tempted me to Dartington in the first place. Here, under the direction of one body of trustees, and close to each other, were on the one hand a collection of educational units - school, college, adult education centre, youth club and so on - and on the other a set of industries, among them farms, forests, building contractors, furniture factory, textile mills, sawmills, plant hiring works, all containing young people on apprenticeships and training. Indeed, and most exciting of all, experimental situations had developed already. Thus a training scheme for horticulture had been set up on the estate focused round the superb gardens at Dartington Hall and a group of a dozen boys and girls aged fifteen and over who had left school were undertaking a two-year course involving paid work, instruction and residence in a small purpose-designed hostel two minutes from the College, ten minutes from the senior school. Still nearer the school was the well-equipped base of a second group of school-leavers, this time fifteen-year-old lads taking a two-year training course to become foresters, paid wages once again but not actually resident. Sadly enough, neither of these groups in 1968 seemed to have any formal links or even much informal contact with any of the educational units round about. They were isolated little enclaves, the potentiality of the situation was unused by them and by everyone else.

I had been deeply impressed on my research travels by schools like the now closed Adcroft Building School in Wiltshire, by the way in which vocational education there had loosened up the nature of schooling and had gathered up the commitment of young people of a wide span of ability who would otherwise have been alienated from education altogether. I was aware also that the extra school year being imposed by law in 1973 on many reluctant youngsters demanded a rethinking of vocational education, one in which, in my belief, payment for a job should have some place. I therefore saw at Dartington the separate elements already existing for an experiment of more than local significance: one in which the industries and educational units could combine to provide a model for others to follow. The long-term aim was to provide a foundation year for potential trainees in their extra school year in which they sampled in turn each of the industries available and carried on with a broader education. At the end of that year they would opt for training in one of the industries concerned or for further education either at Dartington Hall School, the local comprehensive or technical college or elsewhere. The scheme had the merit of keeping options open for the people concerned and saving the great wastage which occurs in vocational schemes from students who join one before knowing fully whether it suits them. A spell of residence would also have been involved in the preliminary year on a short-term basis for all and a longer-term basis for some who needed to live nearer their work. This scheme was endorsed by a group of HMIs and seemed to offer a model for consortia of industries and state schools in other communities to develop further.

Things started well. Within a few months, owing to the

goodwill of both sides, the horticultural students were having their basic teaching done by the school, the school had made its market gardens over to them, half of them had voluntarily gone off to live in the new sixth-form centre and some of the Dartington school students had gone up to live in the garden hostel. Somewhat later the forestry boys also joined the scheme: most of them left their isolated digs and moved in to live in the sixth-form centre with the sixth formers and garden students. Some of the young workers began to take individual courses such as art or English or maths or remedial tuition at the school both in day time and evening. All used the recreational facilities and joined in the student-organized social service programme. There was not much intense social mixing between the diverse elements though some individuals did make close friends particularly of a coeducational kind, and the presence in the sixth-form hostel of a large group of students from the Yorkshire mining town which we had also now linked with helped to bridge social gulfs. Living together, however, clearly enlarged the awareness of everyone. Along with the Yorkshire entry these groups of young workers quietly exploded the homogeneous culture, style, manners and value system of the old school. This in itself produced no serious difficulties and the presence in holidays and termtime alike of twenty or more paid manual workers was an asset rather than a problem.

The problems that occurred arose at the other end. To the gardeners and forestry students life in a free adult society, alongside young people most of whom enjoyed their education and were anxious to continue it after the age of eighteen, was bound to provide a new perspective on themselves, their vocations and their backgrounds. A couple of the young workers started occasionally to be late for work. Others, reflecting the participatory society of the school, began to question the working and hierarchical set-up in their own units. Some, like the school students, began now to swear at their vocational instructors to their faces instead of, as previously, behind their backs. Others, mainly early school leavers from secondary modern schools, now found an interest in further education kindled within them. One lad for example took an art course at Dartington, then left his unit and later trained and became an engineer. Two others, active in the school's social work programme, have since become social workers. In fact the school privately tested the forestry boys, who were all from secondary modern schools, and found that their level of ability was as high as that of many fee-paying entrants to the school. They were also in so many other ways very impressive, rich people. A group of them asked to do some O level courses, if need be in their own time, and we were delighted. But the Forestry Training Committee was not: it did not agree and we had to teach some of the boys surreptitiously. Nevertheless it should be emphasized that the large majority of students in both units went on into the career for which they had been prepared.

As the integration proceeded a curious dichotomy began to emerge: if you were sixteen to eighteen and at the school run by the Dartington Hall Trust you were expected to speak your mind, to share in the government, pursue your interests and develop your talents as widely as possible; if you were sixteen to eighteen and at one of the educational/vocational centres run by the same Trust, you were expected not to question orders or authority, not to participate in decisions, and not to set your sights beyond the limited vocational jobs which you had chosen at secondary modern school without any experience before the age of fifteen. Given this divergence of approach, the scheme of integration could not continue. After a couple of years the gardening group were withdrawn into the isolation of the hostel from which they have not again emerged: and somewhat later the forestry boys were, without regard to their wishes or the school's, withdrawn and scattered in digs nine miles away. Their places have been taken by sixth-form pupils at £1,400 a year. It is a feature which we noticed in other 'progressive' communities that when important decisions concerning finance or long-term policy are taken, the values of participation and human concern which they so publicly profess are suddenly suspended and action ensues which can be as bureaucratic, authoritarian and ruthless as any found in organizations without 'progressive' ideals.

The response of the other industries was the same. Personal explanations of the broader aim of linking the Trust's industries and educational activities to provide a realistic vocational training system received but frosty welcomes from the personnel and economic heads of the various enterprises. At one meeting at which three HMIs spoke warmly in favour of the general scheme it became clear that the current system of day release and wastage was preferable to a broader involvement in education which might produce subversive workers. One major enterprise owned by the Trust even refused to let its young apprentices spend a residential weekend with boys from other industries owned by the Trust for the fear of contamination: 'they might get ideas' it was said.[7] It hardly needs to be added that the Trust's own industries are very different from their educational concerns: there is no participation by workers, no sharing of profits and little organized labour. Despite all the discussion nothing has therefore happened to implement the scheme in general.

To me this was the worst setback in my time at Dartington. It so clearly missed a great opportunity of trying something relevant not only to Dartington but to work and education generally outside, and it so clearly went against the wishes and needs of the young people who had begun to get involved. The failure occurred partly because I was too precipitate. Also there occurred the natural tendency of all institutions to withdraw inwards when contact with others caused them problems. The spectre of wastage, as some students began to opt to go on into education rather than into their assigned jobs, was conceived as a loss not a gain by their employers. It became apparent that the ethos of education and the ethos of work at Dartington were diametrically opposed, and the trustees, having approved the general idea of integrating the two, failed to back that policy when the crunch came and decisions one way or the other were needed. In the long run it is to be hoped that a broader view of education and work and a scheme linking the two can still be tried at Dartington and further initiatives are now afoot in this direction. But in 1973 the situation is exactly back where it was in 1968.

In some other areas in the locality some progress had been made. With the youth club down the road, which had been prohibited by the school to its students before 1968, a joint youth leader was appointed and free access allowed. Nothing much came of this, however, though no particular problems arose. The local village youngsters and the upper-middle-class children of the school had but limited points of contact, for

even their styles of pop music were subtly, but to themselves
irreconcilably, different. The school's own life and rich
recreational provision made the youth club less than tempting.
However the advent of the Yorkshire students at Dartington
kept the link going, for some of these go to the club and have in
fact ramified links in the area with working-class boys and girls,
some of them 'skin-heads', who have free access to the school
and, apart from one attempted rape, have never caused any
particular bother.

With the youth club and the local comprehensive school
Dartington set up a social work organization entirely run by
the students themselves. The aim was not only to provide a
service in the area but also to link local young people in this
worthwhile activity. The social work accomplished has been
impressive, but the social links formed among the workers have
been non-existent.

With the college of arts nearby on the campus, there has been
a joint teaching appointment, some joint staff gatherings and
discussions, more involvement of the college students as teacher
trainees in the junior school, but nothing more despite mutual
goodwill and much further potential.

Between the local school of Totnes and that of Dartington
there has been in the past something of hostility and virtually no
regular contact. Now rebuilt as a large comprehensive school
near the very gates of the Estate, the Totnes school could no
longer be ignored. Indeed considerable efforts have been made
to establish some links so that the students and staff at either
end have their experience of education enlarged and so that each
school can use the facilities that only one possesses. No contact
has been successfully made in boarding areas, the small boarding
hostels at the comprehensive school are run on different
segregated styles of coeducation almost at a polar extreme from
that of Dartington itself. However, joint teaching appointments
have been made and a common programme created for students
in two sixth-form subjects and there have been numerous *ad hoc*
links. It is very doubtful whether these efforts have made any
impact, certainly not as much as the considerable effort that
has to be put into parallel timetabling, special bus services and
so on may make it seem. Perhaps the former hostility has
become lukewarm indifference but there has been no noticeable

feedback of interest and ideas in general between the two schools. Still the link has survived many hazards and again keeps open the possibilities of further development.

At only one point has the policy of local integration been an unequivocal success, and that significantly in day education. In 1968 the nursery school was housed in a corner of the estate and was exclusively for fee-paying children who were contemplating going on into the Dartington main schools later. By 1971 the nursery had been completely rebuilt in purpose-designed buildings right in the middle of the village of Dartington itself and with over two-thirds of its enlarged places open to parents and children without any fees, irrespective of whether they were going on to Dartington or into the state system on leaving. The school is completely integrated in its daily life. It serves the whole community and is jointly run by the Trust and the Devon local education authority. One small achievement then is the creation of a common education for all local children up to the age of five. After that the divisions have proved insurmountable.

As far as the boarding school goes little has been accomplished by these and other undescribed efforts to link with the local community. Perhaps my hopes were always unrealistic. The boarders come from everywhere but Devon: how can they identify with this locality? Their cultural backgrounds and style are so markedly different from those of people round about: what have they in common with them? The school by its community life and recreational richness leaves little to be offered by the small market town nearby. Institutions inevitably, in their effort to establish common values and cater for their inmates, generate powerful inward pulls in order to cohere: how can outward initiatives be sustained? These are the facts which most residential schools face. Nevertheless there is something infinitely sad in their acceptance. Boarders are deprived of a normal community life at home and then are offered only the very artificial kind of the one at school. With what mixed and normal community of people can they identify and gather experience? Perhaps, as the next section discusses, more radical experiments are called for in the very nature of the school. To identify with an outside community perhaps the students should go and live and work in it.

V

By far the most significant experiments at Dartington are those
which attempt to enlarge the limited experience offered to its
pupils by the school to include other cultures in this country
and abroad. In the pursuit of this general end two bases have
been established, in a Yorkshire mining town and in a village in
north-west Sicily. Despite many difficulties, the huge distances
involved, the sharp contrasts of culture encountered (the
Yorkshire town was as remote from the mores of Dartington as
Scopello in Sicily), despite such details as the attentions of the
Mafia, these ventures have been fully developed as real
growing points of the school. Both of them, to my mind, by
their possibilities and problems offer models and lessons for the
future, in the nature of education itself, in that of residential
education in particular and also, more provincially possibly, in
the relation of the independent and state sectors within this
country. A third venture, far more limited and conventional in
its aims, was the linking with a school in Brittany which our
pupils claimed to be misnamed the *Ecole du Gai Savoir*. This
collapsed in hilarious confusion. Here I shall only discuss
integration with Yorkshire and the base in Sicily.

Frankly I was not prepared to become head of a school solely
for the education of the rich. Apart from my own delicate
moral scruples on the matter, the conventional English boarding
school which operates as a sort of closed ghetto for children of
one social, economic and cultural group seemed to me to be
profoundly non-educative, confining instead of enlarging the
experience of young people and their awareness of their society
and its diverse cultures. One precondition of my going to
Dartington therefore was to open up the social structure of the
school. Nor was I prepared to preside over a solely 'independent' school. The gulf between the independent boarding sector
for a minority, on the one hand, and the state day sector for the
majority, on the other, seemed to me, even more after the
researches recorded in this book, a social and educational
calamity. Something had to be done to bridge the gulf, if only
on the basis of individual schools. Finally, it seemed to me that
if a progressive school like Dartington was supposed to be an
educational spearhead, then its adventures should relate to and

derive from the needs of the majority of children. In short, to justify its privileged existence as an independent progressive boarding school, Dartington should enlarge its own structure and become interwoven in a continuous two-way relationship with the mainstream of education in this country.

In 1968 such fulsome principles seemed strangely out of place. The old Flemingite integration by which a few selected, scholarship pupils entered a few public schools was by then discredited and disappearing. The proposals of the Public Schools' Commission of 1966-8, by which large numbers of children with alleged 'need' for boarding were to be channelled through a central agency into boarding schools, had been greeted, rightly in my view, with universal derision. The Commission had neglected its powers of initiating experiments which might have kept the situation open and the issues alive. The one important experiment of the 1960s, the Marlborough-Swindon scheme, which my group had covered by research from start to finish, had been allowed to lapse through lack of funds in 1968 just when its first lessons were beginning to emerge.[8] After the fiasco of the Commission, the issue seemed burnt out: the independent schools forgot integration and went their own way while their critics turned to more urgent issues in day education. Little has been heard of the matter in the last six years.[9]

Yet within six months of the change of headship at Dartington, in the summer of 1969, the first group of boys and girls from the town of Conisbrough in Yorkshire were camping on the playing fields at Dartington, a house was in the process of being bought by the Trust in their home town and a group of pupils from Dartington were living with their families or going to the state school in Conisbrough itself. This rapid progress had nothing to do with subtle magic or excessive money on our part. It happened that the kind of integration proposed made sense to the local education authorities, economic sense, educational sense and egalitarian sense. Though we entered into a relationship with the West Riding local authority in March 1969, shortly afterwards three other authorities, hearing of our intentions, also approached us for a similar connection and we had, reluctantly, to refuse. There were plenty of prospective takers for integration therefore, even in the circumstances of 1969. If other independent schools, which so loudly proclaim that they want greater social width, had put forward realistic proposals on the matter, it is likely that they too would have met a favourable response.

How then did our own ideas differ from what had gone before? Integration in English education had hitherto meant one of two things. The first kind was for the independent boarding school to take children selected according to 'need' who were paid for by public funds. This mode may have enlarged the social composition of the school but it integrated it with nothing outside. The second kind consisted of taking bright selected scholarship children from various areas who were then more or less assimilated into the school as long-term boarders, as in the well-known scheme which linked Hertfordshire and Eton and the other one between Middlesex and Mill Hill School for example. Such schemes failed to enlarge the society of the school as the entrants were too few and mainly aspirant middle-class in origin anyway,[10] and they failed to connect the school with the state system or the community from which the pupils were drawn. The schemes did, however, produce acute problems of adjustment for some of the children concerned. Both these methods loftily assumed that the independent boarding school had inestimable benefits to confer on less fortunate children but nothing to learn from the day educational system, the particular schools, the families, communities and cultures from which they came.

The Dartington integration scheme has worked on principles other than this *noblesse oblige*. For it is essentialy *two way*. It is based on the recognition that the independent boarding and the state day sectors each have strengths to offer which can be interwoven into the educational experience of children. Thus our integration has consisted of two different communities and schools opening themselves to each other at all levels. In practice not only do pupils, staff and parents come down from the state school and working-class town to derive the benefits of the boarding situation and enrich its society without losing their own identity, but the boarders and their staff go back to the day school and the mining community to discover its strengths and experience its way of life. Nor is the experience confined to a selected few as in other schemes. *All* the children at both ends are in some way or another involved and affected, the two schools have become enmeshed and unexpected developments concerning parents, industry and even the nature of education have occurred.

The scheme now works in 1973 like this. Conisbrough is a uniformly working-class mining town on the south Yorkshire coalfield with about 18,000 people, a high rate of male unemployment and social and educational handicaps serious enough for part of it in 1968 to have been designated by the Government as an educational priority area. No greater contrast with the lush rural surroundings, the pure air and rivers, the abundant facilities of Dartington can be imagined, though Conisbrough rapidly proved to have strengths of community, of stability, of warmth of family and recreational life which belied its somewhat ravaged external appearance.[11] It possesses one secondary modern school for about 1100 boys and girls housed, until new buildings scheduled for 1974, in old and overcrowded premises. A few brighter pupils were filtered off to the grammar school in nearby Mexborough but this stopped in 1973 when the Northcliffe High School became comprehensive. In the last twelve years, under an enterprising headmaster, vigorous efforts have been made at the school to counteract the deprivation of its pupils by providing a much broader and more realistic curriculum, opportunities for travel, and by keeping the school open for a wide range of purposes every evening of the week. No one at Dartington, including myself, had been to Conisbrough or met anyone from there before the scheme started and that happened solely because I knew, as a result of the research visits undertaken for this book, the leader of the educational priority team which had just started working in the district. The West Riding authority and its open-minded education officer saw that our proposals involved *all* the children in this underprivileged community and that it consisted of give and take on both sides (not just take on the part of the independent schools as in previous schemes of integration) and therefore gave it their blessing and later even their financial backing. The two schools are 306 miles apart, a six hours' journey by rail or car.

To the senior school at Dartington, with a size of 220 pupils, come annually about twenty long-term boarders from

Northcliffe School. Most of them take a two-year sixth-form
course, though some younger ones stay for three or four years
or more. In the first years no form of selection was applied to
these students, all those who wanted to come did so with the
results described below. In addition to these about another six
boys and girls come, on grounds of need for boarding or for
a break from home, for spells of a term each. All these pupils
live and operate in the school like any boarders from elsewhere.
In addition to them waves of short-stay groups of about eight to
twelve pupils at any one time come to Dartington for courses of
about a month successively throughout the term and holidays,
living in dormitory or room accommodation reserved in the
school alongside the other pupils. These youngsters take special
courses provided by the Dartington staff or their own teachers
or both, but otherwise live as normal boarders. In all there have
been about sixty long-term boarders at Conisbrough since the
scheme started four years ago and about eight hundred short-
term ones. At any one time about fifteen to twenty per cent of
the students in the senior school are from Conisbrough in
Yorkshire and their presence is more pronounced than this
statistic may make it seem. The flow of short-stay visitors helps
the long-term boarders to keep in touch with home and not to
lose their own identity and culture. Some of the short-stay
boarders come down to Dartington during their school life
several times in terms or holidays and later may become termly
or full boarders as the case may be. Most of the children of the
community school of Northcliffe therefore have at least one
chance of a residential spell in their school life at Dartington and,
if the scheme continues, this means that virtually the whole
young adult population of the town will have had such
experience. Teachers travel down regularly with groups and the
parents of boarders follow suit either for meetings or for
holidays at Dartington or elsewhere.

In return Dartington pupils and staff go to Conisbrough,
though in fewer numbers as the school at the southern end is so
much smaller. As the base for this exchange we bought cheaply
from the National Coal Board a large house called The Terrace
which had been standing empty and useless for some time right
in the heart of Conisbrough's shopping centre. It has been
converted to sleep about twenty-five adults and children and

contains common rooms, a quiet room, a library and so on. To this younger students from Dartington go in small groups for periods of three or four weeks at a time during term either to do ordinary lessons at Northcliffe High School or to take special courses run by Dartington or Northcliffe staff. Such courses are undertaken with Northcliffe pupils and indeed pupils from the town move into The Terrace to live with Dartington students during their stay. In other words a second form of residential experience is thus provided for Conisbrough children, inside their own community. As Northcliffe has no sixth form and Dartington has a large one, now 120 out of a senior school of 220, the school at first linked with the sixth-form college at Mexborough, a town adjacent to Conisbrough. But the style and educational aims of the two schools proved incompatible and this aspect of the scheme ended quickly. Out of this failure something infinitely better has emerged, for now each year the whole of the Lower Sixth at Dartington goes up to live in Conisbrough in separate groups of fifteen for an action/study course on the work and community of Conisbrough which is in fact conducted often in the streets, on the allotments, in the trade union centres, down the pit, in the chapels, in the clubs, by local parents, by miners, trade unionists, old age pensioners, local councillors and the like. Teachers are not to be seen. It has proved a great and moving success. In addition to this some senior students go up in the holidays to help run play projects and the like, based at The Terrace, and each year a few Dartington sixth-form leavers give up a whole year to work in Conisbrough, helping at our base and at the local school. Of course The Terrace is also regularly used for special courses run from Dartington on the lines of environmental studies or the history of art and so on. In the one year, 1973, no less than ninety-three boarders from the senior school of 220 lived and studied in Conisbrough for between a week and a month. The figures show that in the course of their years at Dartington many students live in Yorkshire several times for differing purposes and some, who have sunk roots, go up there to stay with families in the holidays as well.

In the long run the most important innovation has been The Terrace itself. For not only does this function as the living base for Dartington/Northcliffe groups and as a centre for the

Dartington head and staff to entertain and keep in touch with
local parents and others, but it has inevitably developed an
independent role of its own. A vigorous parent group meets,
socializes and helps there. Special courses, day or resident, are
run there for local children and students during term and holiday
times. In the evenings and at weekends a range of activities is
provided for local children in a domestic atmosphere, kept
deliberately different from that of the school and youth clubs in
the neighbourhood. The demand has been so overwhelming
that some limitation on entry in the evenings has had to be
imposed. Intense pastoral care is provided for some children and
their families by the staff. From 1973, deriving directly from
the needs and attitudes we have found among some Conisbrough
young people, a pilot scheme is being launched from The
Terrace by which a group of Northcliffe's volunteer students are
released from the need to go to school at all during their final
year and will instead with a group of adults and parents live and
operate as a group which has to earn an income by some
individual or group work to survive. In other words The
Terrace, besides providing diverse residential experience for
working-class children in their own community and a complex
and informal alternative base for community action and care
alongside the formal structure of the school, is also proving
more flexible and relevant as a growing point than the home
centre at Dartington itself. If the residential exchange programme and the long-term boarding at Dartington were ever to
end completely, The Terrace is now in a position to continue as
a viable experimental centre working within the context of the
mainstream of English life and education.

The Terrace, all its activities and all the short-day residential
experience at both ends of the scheme, cost annually about
£12,000 which expense is shared equally between the local
authority and the school at Dartington. The twenty or more
long-term boarders at Dartington cost £20,000 per annum and
this heavy burden is borne exclusively by the Dartington Hall
endowment, though parents contribute according to means.
Such long-term boarders are the costliest and most inegalitarian
aspect of the scheme, but the presence of a sizeable group of
pupils as full ordinary Dartingtonians has undoubtedly helped
generate commitment from the staff of the school to the

scheme, eased the passage of innumerable short-stay residents
during their time in Devon, and given everyone a deeper and
more sustained involvement back into the life of Conisbrough
itself. For example, some of the parents whose children were
long-term boarders and left some years ago are still vigorously
active at The Terrace, helping our own students and other
youngsters in Conisbrough. To cement the links, the chief
education officer of the West Riding has now become one of the
seven trustees who guide the entire set-up of Dartington Hall.

What do all these facts mean in human and educational
terms? Have the aims of integration really been achieved by so
much traffic and rapid growth? What have been the problems
and failures?

To the boarding community at the senior school of
Dartington, the Yorkshire scheme has brought a new variety
and richness: different accents, different codes of behaviour,
different styles of dress, different life expectations, different
intellectual needs, even different preferences in food. As the
Yorkshire long-stay students enter mainly at the age of fifteen
or above, they are already too developed to lose their own
identity easily and that is anyway continually recharged by the
prominent presence of the short-term boarders who never are in
danger of losing theirs. They have injected a healthy strain of
aggression into a school which for too long had been almost
apathetically pacific: there have been fisticuffs for the first
time in a society hitherto so passive and verbal. There have
been boys in naval and military uniform appearing in a school
heavily pacifistic and vegetarian. There has even been a rugby
team founded and the sports standard of the school has
soared. Yorkshire students have also been prominent in the
social work schemes of all kinds, particularly the girls. They
have challenged the whole curriculum of the school. At first,
to avoid the old snare of integration, that of creaming off the
brightest from state schools, we deliberately took anyone who
wanted to come as long-term boarders, irrespective of
intellectual criteria and attainment and found ourselves with
some pupils of university potential and some who could
literally neither read nor write. With this wide span the staff
and school at Dartington, used to bright middle-class children,
manfully tried to cope but in the end the small school could not

become compehensive enough in such a short time to deal
with this intellectual range. It now regretfully has to select long-
term boarders for the specific courses it offers them, mainly of
a CSE, O and A level kind. However all the short-term boarders
are unselected by Dartington and there have been many special
courses organized for deprived youngsters whose social and
educational skills are negligible and whose physical condition
seems sometimes more reminiscent of Calcutta than England in
the 1970s.

The Yorkshire students have challenged much else. Some,
used to a family background of shift work, a life spent out of
home in the streets, pubs and clubs, and therefore expected to
be far more adult and independent at fifteen than their
middle-class boarding contemporaries, found the set routines of
bedtime and mealtimes and the childish behaviour of others
difficult to bear and have forced the school into much greater
flexibility than even it as a progressive school already had. As
the school makes few demands on matters such as dress,
smoking and personal expression, some acute problems which
occurred for example in the Marlborough-Swindon scheme have
not been repeated at Dartington. There have been plenty of
other ones, however. Some of the Yorkshire boys were used to
heavy drinking and also brought with them an alien mode of
predatory sex. A tiny few carried out breaking and entering
expeditions sometimes on an extensive scale. We had to vary
the food provided, to suit Yorkshire taste, more chips, more
meat, fewer foreign or vegetarian menus. All of this has
rendered the school more complex, more interesting, more
normal.

The social mixing among the different groups has been
undoubtedly aided by coeducation, as the heart seems not to
recognize social barriers. Some students from Yorkshire have
associated mainly with other Dartingtonians. Indeed one son of
a miner, a year or two after leaving the school, married the
grand-daughter of a viscount whom he had met at the school,
while the daughter of another miner has now married a member
of the staff. Two other engagements impend and there are
plenty of boy/girl friendships which cross either ends of the
scheme. Most Yorkshire pupils develop ordinary friendships
and operate as normal Dartingtonians but a few, and especially

some girls, tend to keep together and noticeably fail to integrate socially as much as the others. Probably the differences between the girls in the school from Conisbrough, where women are kept in the home, have low status and extraordinarily limited lives, and those from progressive upper-middle-class backgrounds of the Hampstead kind are the most extreme in life style, breadth of experience and future prospects. Some Conisbrough girls have also suffered acute problems of homesickness and distress on leaving their boy-friends behind them. In a school where pupil norms ordain informal dress and the daughter of a millionaire can go around looking like the daughter of a tramp differences in wealth are not externally visible but do emerge in more subtle ways. The school has in fact had to make many quiet gestures and allowances to the students from Conisbrough to enable them to keep going socially.

Given such a verbal, discussion-prone society, all the entrants to Dartington have gained impressively and inevitably in their ability to express themselves, their self-confidence and their adaptability in different social situations. Otherwise the gains to them have been very variable. Many had, like the Swindon boys who went to Marlborough, high academic expectations from Dartington and these, often unrealistic anyway, have not always been fulfilled. Some have done fairly well and gone on to university, teacher training or art colleges and probably more than would have been the case if they had never come to Dartington. There has also been a noticeable trend towards social work careers among the leavers, both girls and boys. Some however have not clearly benefited academically or career-wise, especially some of the less able or actually backward pupils who leave at the age of sixteen or seventeen. They have returned to manual jobs in the pit or elsewhere at Conisbrough and some are, like other youngsters in the town, unemployed. Similarly, the use of the wide cultural provision at Dartington has been very variable. Some have made full use of all that the school offers but fewer than might have been expected and fewer than the Marlborough-Swindon experience would have predicted. Indeed some of the pupils remain very fixed in their academic methods and in their interests and activities: much of the best that Dartington has to offer in fact passes them by. Perhaps they have arrived too late, or are too

strongly shaped by the powerful and narrow culture of
Conisbrough itself, or perhaps in a deep way they feel that to
open up to the interests and activities of another culture would
be a compromise or a betrayal of their identity which they
unconsciously or consciously do not wish to make. Most
remain deeply committed to Conisbrough as a place and to their
homes and families, though it is difficult here to generalize about
the effect that their experience has had on their intimate family
relationships. By no means all the pupils find that the free semi-
structure of the progressive style of education is easy to get used
to. Indeed some of them, almost exclusively boys, used to
authoritarian frameworks, have at first collapsed or gone wild or
developed exaggerated styles of dress and life and abused the
freedom which depends on many subtle self-restraints. Thus one
boy let off over twenty fire extinguishers in his first term but at
the end of his stay qualified and went successfully to college.
Another, among other delinquencies, threw a copper coal-
scuttle at the headmaster, missed him but destroyed a valuable
painting. He is now a demolition worker. Some few have been taken
off the narrow but directed tracks along which their lives were
moving and seem, so far, to have lost direction altogether. But
most of the long-term students, whatever the unprogressive
nature of their background, have taken to the school and its
practices as normal and have been some of the most obviously
successful exponents of free, self-regulated, tolerant and
responsible attitudes in the place.

To the Dartington staff and pupils the scheme has brought
enlargement of awareness of life, of opportunities and of
problems. Almost all are well disposed to the scheme though
sadly but inevitably only a minority of the teaching and housestaff actively participate in it and go regularly to Conisbrough.
By no means all the younger boarders want to go on the visits
and courses in Conisbrough. Perhaps they are frightened by its
reputed violence and hardness, are not interested in a large state
day school or cannot pull themselves away from all the cosy,
busy attractions and preoccupations of boarding school life.
The junior and middle schools have never fully participated in
the scheme on similar grounds and have frozen off approaches
for links from progressive primary schools in the town. To not
a few pupils and staff, however, the Conisbrough connection

has been a revelation. Many of them had never experienced in their own lives the warmth of spirit, the sense of togetherness, the stability of community, the close family life and the concrete political urgency found among people in Conisbrough, which derive from the common struggles, disasters and fellowship of work at the pit. Many had never been in a state secondary school and were surprised to find it as benign in its own way as the progressive school they had known. Indeed the experience has given some students a romantic view of working-class life, one which ignores the genuinely poor housing in parts of Conisbrough, the inward-lookingness of the community, the hardness of attitudes, the subjection of women, the narrowness and increasing commercialism of much of the local culture. What the Dartington students will make of all this experience in their later lives and attitudes cannot be known. Their parents have been generally and warmly supportive as the children are, after all, getting the benefits of both private and state education together.

The impact on Northcliffe School in the town of Conisbrough has clearly been less up till now. The short-term residential experience which so many of the Northcliffe children have at Dartington probably has already produced greater powers of self-expression and greater commitment to the idea of education as well as some extension of horizons for children who, like the boarders at Dartington, were used to one uniform style of life. To a relative few, more continuously associated with the school and the work of The Terrace, the scheme has meant much more width of opportunity, enlargement of outlook and personal support. The educational impact of the scheme might well be slower than in Devon but the cumulative development in Conisbrough and particularly as a result of the activity at The Terrace may, in the long run, prove profound and important. Obviously fewer problems have been caused to Northcliffe than to Dartington: though the association has naturally raised in the northern school such issues as the extent of freedom, the use of Christian names for staff, the relations of parents and school, the question of structures for children as well as details of boy/girl relations and smoking. The 'alternative-to-school project' in Conisbrough is a direct local outcome of the link. Staff at Northcliffe, like those in Devon, have shown general goodwill to the scheme though once again only a few are closely identified with it. Perhaps for Conisbrough the most significant consequence so far has been the evident faith which that community has generated among the Devon strangers at a time when, as the local pits begin to close, the community may have been somewhat in danger of losing faith in itself.

The next stage should be for the Trust to launch an industry in Conisbrough which, besides meeting the demand for skilled male employment in the town and linking experimentally with education, will provide for adult workers a genuine participation in decision and control which is found in the Trust's own educational enterprises at Dartington and now at The Terrace in Conisbrough.

So much then for a brief review of this experiment in integration between the state day and independent boarding sectors of education and the provision of differing kinds of residence for working-class children. I am not contending that this scheme provides *the* model on which the 'public school problem' for example could be solved, though the linking of more such independent schools to educational priority areas might be one answer to several dilemmas. There are clearly very different answers suitable to different schools and situations. This experiment does, however, show the need for more. And it does indicate that, however hostile the general climate of opinion, given goodwill on both sides and a genuine desire to give and learn as well as take from each other, some trial pontoon bridges can be erected so that children can pass over one of the most unnecessary and damaging divides in English education.

VI

One final link with a reality which no boarding school can by itself encompass has also been slowly and somewhat painfully forged in these years. My aim was to provide the school, so well equipped in all other senses, with a reference point in the third world, one even poorer than Conisbrough; to do this not merely by academic contact or by collective charitable effort (such as raising money or sending parcels and the like) but by the students themselves going, living and working for a year or more with the people concerned, to establish some identity

with them if nothing more useful. Apart from anything that
the students might contribute to others, it was hoped that such
a venture would feed back to the school a sense of this outer
world, and that the training programme by which the students
would be prepared in their time at school would also enlarge
the curriculum, give a sense of practical purpose to study and
preparation, and even provide a model for so many schemes
of voluntary work overseas for which students are seldom
thoroughly prepared beforehand. Once again, as with the
integration scheme in England, the aim was to connect deeply
with one definite, recognizable, human group in another
economic and cultural setting.

After following various false trails we ended up in 1969,
through the agencies of a member of staff who had gone out
exploring for half a year, at the .iny village of Scopello, perched
on the edge of the Mediterranean in the north-west corner of
Sicily. Here the immemorial classic peasant culture was in
decay, the village largely deserted through emigration, the fields
increasingly abandoned, the survivors left living in a sort of
ghostly poverty which contrasted grotesquely with the ostenta-
tion and vulgar luxury of the villages and marinas for wealthy
Italians which had crept up the coastline to the nearby,
shuttered and sinister Mafia town of Castellamare. It was
decided to build our group on the welcome and the support
which the staff member and his wife, themselves Catholics, had
generated by living among the local people, from the poorest of
the poor (the shepherds), the gnarled peasant farmers, the priest
banished to this remote spot for being too avant garde, to the
local Marchese, benevolent but detached.

Despite many vicissitudes - the expulsion of the group by the
police in one year, an assault on a member of staff by some
marauding youths in another, a threat to kill me by the Mafia,
the unexpected reluctance of the Dartington Hall Trustees
positively to help the venture with money - five years later it
continues, though in a different form from that which had been
envisaged at the outset and with different effects.

The students, including some boys and girls who come from
Conisbrough, are prepared in their final year at school and in
the holidays. They undertake intensive Italian and Sicilian and
courses on the history and culture of an island which has had

imposed on it most layers of European civilization: those of ancient Greece, Rome, the Normans, the Moslems, Spain and France. They discuss the values and constraints which they will have to accept in the peasant culture they will soon be living in. They all learn how to cook with the simplest fare that they may expect to find or grow out there, rice, pasta, greenstuff, some eggs, no meat, homemade bread and wine. They all do hard physical farmwork. Each of them specializes in one or other of the crafts, from woodwork to pottery or macramé. They teach and work with young children in primary schools around Dartington, in special schools, and in running play ventures at the Yorkshire base. They live together in a simple wooden cabin built by themselves.

During their year or more in Sicily they live in two rented houses in the village, identical with those of other villagers, with no glass windows, leaking roofs and with one lavatory sited (though screened) in the main living room. Though their parents and the school's fund-raising efforts help towards the basic costs, the group lives on the bare minimum: diet is limited, work is hard and luxuries nonexistent.

Over the years the focus of activity in Sicily has changed with circumstances. At first the group lived in Scopello, worked in its own fields (reclaimed from abandoned ones), helped in Danilo Dolci's craft centre, taught in local schools and also worked in a slum school in the teeming markets of Palermo. One boy lived there for two years, writing, designing and reproducing his own manual to help teach the illiterate market boys how to read their own language. The girls lived and worked there too, braving the predatory males with amazing fortitude. In 1972, however, such work had to stop for the time being and the group were asked to leave by the police as the result of a drive against foreigners of all kinds. They were allowed back in Sicily some months later, however. As this social work side declined work in the crafts at Scopello increased. Danilo Dolci, the great Sicilian reformer, himself realizes that self-expression through the arts has revolutionary and political implications in a society in which everyone is expected to do exactly as told by someone one degree higher than himself in the hierarchy. In the primary schools, for example, children are expected to copy identical likenesses of

Mickey Mouse in an exercise called 'art'. The craft centre run
by the students in the village, serviced by a brick-built kiln in
the open air powered by an old vacuum-cleaner, now recruits
numbers of young people from the region. The group also
not only tends its own fields but works in those of all the other
peasants for nothing. Out of this practical gesture, out of the
presence of the group in the village with no material gain of its
own in view, out of the reconciling and negotiating work of the
group leader, the peasants in the village, who have never until
now been able to combine for any positive purpose, have
formed an agricultural co-operative, acquired government
grants, bought a tractor in common, and are working together
in amity - a state which five years ago seemed impossible. They
are now talking of setting up a craft co-operative as well. Thus if
the Dartington presence were to end tomorrow, and no one
knows when the next police swoop may be or if its funds will
run out, the local Scopello community will have moved clearly
ahead socially and economically as a result of the group having
been there.

To the students the experience has been sometimes overwhelming. Some of them, who were lazy, apathetic or
unfocused at school, have now become practical, hard working
and purposeful. In some girls it has produced an emotional
ferment and even some definite disturbance. All have perceptibly
matured. Faced with such a life, with hard physical work in
stony soil, with primitive housing and food, with no recreations
other than those devised from their own resources, with no
privacy in a situation from which there is no easy escape, with
the threat of police and Mafia activity, in a place where every
family has a tale of violence to tell, how could anyone not
mature? It is all rather different from an English boarding
school.

Not all the aims have been realized. The group has not yet
grown beyond the number of twelve each year for economic
reasons. There has so far been little feedback to the school's
ordinary life. As with the Yorkshire scheme though some
students and staff are enthusiastic the majority have been
mainly indifferent. Most disconcerting of all, the Trust has not
found it possible to provide a positive grant to the scheme apart
from what the school provides and around £3,500 per annum

has to be found from the parents or by fund-raising, a large drain on the resources of a small school with many other commitments. This monetary problem has sometimes almost displaced the positive goals of the scheme and some demoralization has inevitably occurred. No other department of the Trust, neither the forestry nor the gardening groups nor even the college of arts, has contributed students to the scheme. Even in Sicily the economic circumstances have changed remarkably in a few years and Conisbrough now seems more of a third world than Scopello itself.

Nevertheless, despite all the adversities, the scheme has continued, endlessly changing and developing, founded on the sympathetic personality of its leader out there, on the eagerness of some students for the experience and on the enthusiasm of some adults at Dartington. Although its full potential still remains to be realized the scheme seems to have helped the people of Scopello towards a greater togetherness, has undoubtedly deeply affected for good around sixty young people in a few years from England, has, however tenuously, made the rest of the school community personally aware of a situation outside their own little experience and has, educationally, opened out yet another area in which real work and residence unite in a more meaningful form.

VII

I make no apology for such a detailed personal chapter in a book which otherwise attempts to be so general and objective. This experience at Dartington focuses more sharply for the reader both the possibilities and the limitations of change in one of the most flexible and open of contemporary boarding situations. Of course much that I originally hoped to do was never started, checked by the fluctuations in the Trust's income in the early 1970s, by changes in its directorate, and possibly by its realization that radical change is a dangerously open process which never ends. Not a few of the changes that were introduced have had little or no effect, because of unforeseen economies, because of misconceptions at the start, because of general defects on my part or because of the powerful resistance of custom or of plain inanition. In the progressive style of boarding informal norms tend to be more homogeneous and strong than in some other kinds of schools. In some basic areas, those of developing fundamental skills or of self-disciplined achievement, I doubt whether the effort has had more than marginal effect. In other ones, in which the charismatic leader which such schools demand and devour cannot continuously be present, nothing very much has happened. Thus the junior and middle schools have quietly accepted but also quietly ignored almost every innovation and they remain - for better or worse - almost exactly as they were when I took office. Only those changes which introduced new people and values and dramatic new structures, such as the nursery school, and the link with Yorkshire, and the Sicily scheme, have had some clear innovating impact and even this should not be exaggerated. The demand at Dartington is now for consolidation, for an end to outward movement and change, for a pulling together towards common values and community feeling. And this may indeed be necessary.

The experience of Dartington does show that many of the basic changes which boarding schools talk about - such as flexible and coeducational residence, greater self-directed freedom for youngsters, diversifications of atmosphere, greater social width - can be accomplished without disruption and with positive gain in many ways. It shows that remote and isolated centres of one class culture can link and develop organic relations with other cultures for the benefit of all. It shows - in its failures as well as in its successes - that residence can be enlarged in its nature and open to groups who do not normally experience it. It has also unexpectedly opened up much more fundamental educational questions - whether schooling, as we know it, however free, however self-disciplined, however diversified in structure, however enlarging in itself, is the only sensible way of allowing the young to grow, learn and develop; and how best to relate the human need for work with that of learning. The Dartington experience has opened up these questions in acute forms but has not of itself provided any coherent or convincing answers. To seek the answers, along with other people exploring in other situations, one has possibly to search, live and work with young people in the Conisbroughs or Scopellos of this world.

13 Conclusion: has boarding a future?

This book has indicated that boarding education can produce some effects on children less likely to be promoted by day schooling. Some of these effects may be thought beneficial, others are definitely damaging. But this research has shown, also, that many of the disadvantages usually claimed to be inherent in boarding itself are in fact but aspects of one particular style of it. There are several established styles of boarding and yet others now being developed in this country and elsewhere. Though most of them produce similar beneficial results and all share the inherent disadvantages in some the disadvantages are reduced to a minimum while in the others they are magnified, indeed, exaggerated. It is unfortunate that the most widely known style - that associated with early boarding and the public school - is one of the latter kind, in which, however great the benefits, some of the disadvantages are clearly also at a maximum. Any discussion or policy making should bear in mind that, for the different groups of young people or situations in question, *various* styles of boarding exist or can be created which transmit the strengths but minimize the weaknesses of this method of education.

The most obvious question which faces the parents of a child or the constructors of policy is this: are the strengths of boarding worth the cost? Long-term boarding in one of the established English schools is expensive and increasingly so: expensive because of the initial capital outlay and maintenance required for a residential community, expensive in the quantities of domestic and ancillary staff needed and expensive in its employment of teaching staff in a ratio to pupils more favourable than that found in day schools of the same kind whether they are state, progressive, public or independent.

It is most unlikely that the strengths of long-term boarding will ever be thought worth the considerable cost by those who create policy in the national system of education. Boarding provision for ordinary children, as distinct from those with special needs, can never expect to have a claim on public funds when - as will always be the case - there are far more basic and urgent priorities within day education. We have seen that what experimental provision there has been created in the past by local authorities is now diminishing. In the future boarding for ordinary children provided by the State will be of the short term variety linked to day schools and, according to how it is provided as we saw in Chapter 11, some of the strengths of long-term residence may be provided for many children. The LEAs still have responsibility for children with need to live away from home. Few, at present, face this responsibility seriously and there is now overwhelming evidence that there are far more such children with need for some care or living outside their homes than are being provided for.[1] The local authorities at the moment only support the most obvious cases of need or those with the most pressing or articulate parents. The majority of these children are supported in independent schools. Not only, as we have seen, are such schools not always likely to help the adjustment of children with special need, but they are also sometimes expensive in their own right. The LEAs could do far more to meet the cases of need they ignore at their doorstop, much more cheaply and with still greater sensitivity to the educational and emotional requirements of such children and their families, if they sought to combine more often the short-term provision they make for ordinary children with long-term provision for children with some abnormalities of background. The provision of such centres adjacent to large day schools would render short-term experience more varied and meaning-ful, lower running costs by intensive use, and provide a situation flexibly and sensitively to meet local needs. It would also offer many other educational possibilities. There are few signs that LEAs are moving in such a direction at the moment. As boarding is so small a part of their functions, no coherent or imaginative policies are developed for the whole as in the Soviet Union or Israel. There is no positive central policy or machinery apart from suggestions on administrative practice, and whenever special enquiries are made they are inevitably mesmerized by the issue of the public schools. The central inspectorate, confining itself to basic issues of building and staffing, has failed to provide any initiative or positive critique of what has been done. The future here then is likely to be a mixture of sporadic growth of provision, most of it stereotyped, some rarely imaginative and none co-ordinated or evaluated. Nevertheless the most exciting and extensive development of the method in future will be essentially in short-term boarding within the state sector of education.

Parents who consider paying for boarding education on purely educational grounds - admittedly a minority of those interested - are also increasingly deterred by rising costs. Sometimes, too, available day schools begin to offer their children many of the advantages of boarding as curricula widen, extra-curricular activities enlarge, third (evening) sessions and short-term annexes open up and staff-pupil relations improve. Of course, many state schools are not like this and do not confer any of the advantages of boarding. Parents living in their catchment areas tend to choose independent day schools, which are booming, or shorter spells of boarding. In the latter connection, there is now quite a trend for parents who may have chosen boarding at seven in the past to choose it now at thirteen in order to avoid the local secondary school or even at sixteen for two years in the sixth form to give the student greater enlargement, independence, responsibility and preparation for college life than some state day schools would confer. It is likely that the 'rational choice' type of parent will opt for shorter spells of boarding to reduce his financial burden. Later entry without prior socialization into boarding and shorter stays present the schools with considerable problems and may force them to be more open in style and less uniform in values than hitherto.

But, as we know, most parents do not choose boarding mainly on the rational grounds of its educational merits compared with day schooling. It is chosen on extrinsic grounds: because it confers social attributes or increased life chances or because the family situation or pattern of life necessitates the child's removal to a boarding environment. These two reasons are often mixed up with the rational choice kind. It is likely in the future that boarders will, however, fall into the two groups, those with need and those with parents who are buying social advantage.

As long as the association of certain kinds of boarding with various kinds of elite continues there is no likelihood of any dramatic decline in demand for such schools. In them costs have risen even more than elsewhere but, such are the benefits they are considered to bestow, parents are still prepared to pay and eager to enter their sons. There seems little likelihood that the functions of such schools will alter rapidly. The failure of the Labour Government of 1964-70, which entered into office pledged to alter the public school system so as to eliminate its social divisiveness, to take action beyond setting up a commission whose report it subsequently ignored is indicative. It is improbable that any effective political action will occur to alter the allocative role of this sort of boarding: it will therefore continue to command a market whatever the price it charges. Changes will occur from within the schools and there may be over the years some decline in high status boarding schools as independent day schools prosper and assume a more secure position in the process of upward social allocation.

Nor will the other kind of boarding decrease: the meeting of need for schooling away from home. This administrative function has always been a major one for residential schools. Already over 35,500 children or nearly a quarter of all boarders are assisted on grounds of need by public authorities. There are many others with need entirely paid for by their parents. In the future this function is likely to grow larger and more explicit. This is not to predict a steady rise in broken or difficult homes so much as a greater physical mobility among more families in the upper and middle income groups with a consequent need to give their children a settled education. As the proportion of children with explicit need forms an ever larger percentage of the whole the schools may be forced by parental demands and the problems posed by such children to readjust their aims and methods away from abstract educational ideals or upward social allocation towards the more practical ones of providing a social service suitable for those who, but for abnormalities of background, would not have chosen to be boarders at all.

Much of the future of long-term boarding, therefore, lies within the schools in the way they adapt to changing functions, changing patterns of family relations and attitudes and changing reference points on the part of their pupils. Pressures from the family are towards coeducation, shorter boarding spans for their children, more access to home and parents. Pressures from the pupils are towards a less uniform system of cultural values, towards more freedom of expression, recognition of the adolescent role, more real participation in decisions, more informality of relations and less hierarchy, fewer privileges and rituals. Slowly the schools will lose much of their deliberate closedness and have to relax the total control of the past, and what totality remains will derive from accidental features of location and organizational convenience rather than from educational policy. For schools which are now so effective in transmitting both skills and values by closing and tightly controlling their societies, this openness presents a fundamental challenge. Will their effectiveness be impaired if they open their doors to diverse values, styles of life and freedoms of expression, movement and activity? The few schools which at present do this should offer encouragement to the others, for where schools are run as open societies on the lines mentioned above their effectiveness in the transmission of basic educational aims is ensured by the extensive and deep pupil commitment which our researches found to result. But such changes involve a whole-hearted shift of aims which schools may find difficult to achieve. Over this particular development, as over so much else in boarding education, there hangs therefore a large question mark.

It is difficult not to conclude this book and our study of boarding education on a somewhat pessimistic note. Here is an intensive method of education which, though our researches show its impact to be less than often claimed, can be more effective than day schooling in achieving some kinds of educational goals. In the transmission of some instrumental skills, intellectual, organizational and social, in the development of some expressive values, cultural, social and personal, in the provision of a caring, pastoral environment, it can undoubtedly help some or most young people to develop more fully than can alternative methods at present in use. Its inherent disadvantages can be minimized for different populations by the adoption of alternative styles of approach and lengths of stay. The paradox of boarding in England is that its benefits are conferred on the whole on those who may be considered least to need them, on children whose backgrounds already give them distinct educational and social advantages. This is not to say that such children, many of whom need to live away from home, should not have the right to this kind of education. It is, however, to say that in our society, unlike that for example of Israel or the Soviet Union, there has been - despite the odd development here and the odd experiment there - no systematic effort to use this method for the benefit of those without advantages or who are indeed actually disadvantaged. For the majority of children some form of boarding education only becomes likely when they reach the social extremity of being taken into care or into custody and that is often too late. But for its historical connection with the allocative process, boarding in England would be an interesting irrelevance, socially and educationally. Until its possibilities are used in some intelligible way to contribute to the whole national pattern of education its potential will remain unrealized.

Notes

Chapter 1

1   I am indebted to my former colleague Dr M. Wober and his unpublished paper 'Partial analogues of the English boarding school in African tribal cultures'.

2   I. Kopytoff, 'The Suku of South Western Congo', in J. L. Gibbs (ed.) *Peoples of Africa* (1965). K. L. Little, *The Mende of Sierra Leone* (1951). A. H. J. Prinz, 'The Swahili-speaking people of Zanzibar and the East African Coast', in *Ethnographic Survey of Africa* (1961). I. Schapera, *A Handbook of Tswana Law and Custom* (1938). G. Schwab, 'Tribes of the Liberian Hinterland', in D. G. Scanlon (ed.) *Traditions of African Education*, 1964. C. M. Turnbull, 'Initiation among the Bambuti Pygmies of the Central Hari', *Jnl. Roy. Anthropological Inst.*, 1957, pp. 87, 191-216. A. Van Gennep, *The Rites of Passage*, 1960. G. Wagner, *The Bantu of North Kavirondo*, 1949.

3   M. H. Watkins, 'The West African Bush School', *American Jnl. Sociology*, XLVIII, 6 (1943), pp 1666-75.

4   J. S. Bentwich, *Education in Israel* (1965). G. Loveluck, *Secondary Education in Israel* (1966). On Israeli boarding and the Youth Aliyah, I am indebted for help to Dr Yochanan Ginat, its director. See also the publications of the *Fédération Internationale des Communautés d'Enfants, Documents*, nos 1 and 5, and *Etudes Pedagogiques*, nos 3 and 7.

5   N. Grant, *Soviet Education* (1965). M. Kaser, *Memorandum on Soviet Boarding Schools*, submitted to the Public Schools Commission, 1967 (unpublished). Some members of the former Plowden Committee also reported privately to me on their visit to Soviet boarding schools.

6   E. Thrane, *Education and Culture in Denmark* (1958), p. 28.

7   *Spain Today*, 18 October 1965.

8   W. Fraser, *Residential Education* (1968), pp. 24-48, 80-2. Private information to me from government departments and religious orders in Greece, Italy and Germany. J. Dancy, *The Public Schools and the Future* (1966 edition), pp. 187-92.

9   J. Porter, *The Vertical Mosaic* (1965), pp. 284-5.

10 See e.g. A. Foot, *The Doon School Book* (1945).

11 The case for the link between private boarding and the power elite is put by E. D. Baltzell, *Philadelphia Gentleman* (1958); V. Packard, *The Status Seekers* (1959), ch. 16, C. Wright Mills, *The Power Elite* (1956), pp.63-6. An opposing case has however been put by J. McLachlan, *American Boarding Schools: a historical study* (1970), pp. 8-13.

12 This figure, given by the Public Schools Commission, is exaggerated as it contains schools which are overwhelmingly single sex except for a few of the other sex. The number of boarding schools where the number of boys and girls are roughly equal are twenty-six secondary and six primary.

13 Public Schools Commission, *First Report*, vol. 1, ch. 3. G. Kalton, *The Public Schools* (1966), ch. 6. *Higher Education* (The Robbins Report, 1963). Appendix 2B, pp. 5 and 59. R. K. Kelsall, *Higher Civil Servants in Great Britain* (1955). T. H. J. Bishop and R. Wilkinson, *Winchester and the Public School Elite* (1967). J. Wakeford, *The Cloistered Elite* (1969), p. 221.

14 See below passim. R. Lambert, J. Hipkin, S. Stagg, *New Wine in Old Bottles* (1969), passim. I. Weinberg, *The English Public Schools* (1967), passim. Wakeford, *The Cloistered Elite*, passim.

15 In 1967, the last date at which accurate statistics are available, 18,573 boarders were supported by local or central government funds in independent schools on grounds of 'need'. Of course there are many children in public schools who have 'need' for residence who are not so assisted. In 1972 the HMC itself claimed that thirty-two per cent of the boarders in their schools have such a need, as defined in R. Lambert, *The State and Boarding Education* (1966) (*Daily Telegraph*, 21 June 1972). This very much confirms our own data gathered from pupils in our extensive and intensive surveys in the schools and the estimates given by head and house masters.

16 E. C. Mack, *Public Schools and British Opinion*, (1938 and 1941) 2 vols. T. W. Bamford, *The Rise of the Public Schools* (1967). D. Newsome, *Godliness and Good Learning* (1961).

17 R. Lambert, *The State and Boarding*, passim. Public Schools Commission, *First Report*, ch. 6.

18 See J. Underwood, in R. Lambert (ed.), *The Place of the State in Boarding Education* (Conference report, Cambridge 1964). See also family survey below, Chapter 10. R. Lambert, *State and Boarding*, p. 37ff. R. Lambert, *The Demand of Boarding* (Cambridge 1965) passim. R. Lambert and R. Woolfe, 'Need and Demand for Boarding

Education', in *First Report* of the Public Schools Commission, vol. 2, p. 241ff. R. Woolfe, *Away to School* (1974).

19 Data privately supplied to me by the heads of all the mainly boarding schools in the maintained sector. In fourteen of the twenty schools about fifty per cent of the pupils are 'need' cases. In only one of the rest does the proportion of need exceed seventy-five per cent of the pupils.

Chapter 2

1 Hu and Lois Child, *The Independent Progressive School* (1962).
2 See below Chapter 11.
3 These are only local authority definitions. If 'need' is defined more broadly (as in R. Lambert, *The State and Boarding Education* (1966)) then the numbers with need in all schools would increase substantially. Thus, using such broad criteria, the HMC in 1972 estimated that its schools contain thirty-two per cent of children with 'need'.

Chapter 3

1 See above Table 2:4.
2 Of the schools on the Governing Bodies' Association which are boarding, only twenty-three of 195 are non- or inter-denominational. Of day schools on the GBA, thirty-three of ninety are non- or inter-denominational.
3 W. A. C. Stewart, *The Educational Innovators* (1968). R. Skidelsky, *English Progressive Schools* (1970).
4 Both of them originally advertised themselves in handbooks containing only 'progressive' schools.
5 Evidence from headmasters' interviews (particularly on forces promoting or obstructing change) and those from governors, and analysis of governing bodies. Questionnaires from pupils or kin in their schools.
6 Evidence from interviews with headmasters and housestaff, parents, notes of observation, magazines, etc.
7 Evidence as in previous footnote.
8 See above Table 2:13.
9 For the development of the HMC see T. Bamford, *The Rise of the Public Schools* (1967). For its activities see its quarterly journal *Conference*. The Methodist Report on the future of its schools was issued in 1972.

10 *Report of the Working Party on Assistance with the Cost of Boarding Education* (1960). Earlier reports of 1947 helped define the criteria of 'need' on which state supported boarding is based.

11 Kalton, *The Public Schools*, p. 47.

12 Kalton, *Public Schools*, p 96; Public Schools Commission, *First Report*, vol. 1, pp. 25, 53; vol. 2, p. 107.

13 J. Dancy, *The Public Schools and the future* (reprinted 1966), pp 56-60, judges the schools' excellence by Oxbridge awards, a criterion we found used at many speech days, in school magazines, and in systems of promotion and status.

14 Public Schools Commission, *First Report*, vol. 1, pp 58-61. In 1947 fifty-five per cent of the top ranks of the services came from public schools. The close connection they have with other professions and careers was shown in the unpublished evidence to the Public Schools Commission. Some extracts are given in *First Report*, vol. 2, pp. 131-240.

15 Figures given in *Times Educational Supplement*, 23 June 1972. See also *Report of the Executive Committee of the Industrial Fund for the advancement of scientific education in schools* (May 1957). Public Schools Commision, *First Report*, vol. 1, p. 158; Kalton, *Public Schools*, p. 141.

16 Evidence from M. Punch in M. Ash (ed.), *The Living Experiment* (1974). See also his thesis on the follow-up study of alumni from Dartington elsewhere, at the Library of the University of Cambridge, 1972.

17 Data from staff interviews and pupil questionnaires.

18 Staff interviews. See also Kalton, *Public Schools*, p. 53. Public Schools Commission, *First Report*, vol. 2, p. 118. This latter evidence does not distinguish HMC schools from the others. The public schools are now tending to draw staff from wider backgrounds.

19 Evidence as in previous footnote.

20 Data from staff interviews, role questionnaires, notes of observation.

21 See the evidence below in Chapter 10 from the parents' survey. Also data from analysis of occupations and education of parents of pupils on the intensive sample; data of a similar kind from questionnaires on the extensive sample, and interviews with heads and housestaff in such schools.

22 Data from parents' interviews, headmasters' interviews, Public Schools Commission evidence. H. Glennester and G. Wilson, *Paying for private schools* (1970).

23 Data from parents' interviews (Chapter 10); intensive and extensive samples, questions on education of parents.
24 Evidence from family survey, headmasters' interviews, M. Punch, in Ash, *The Living Experiment*.
25 See Chapter 10.
26 M. Punch, in Ash, *The Living Experiment*, private information.
27 See Chapter 10.
28 Chapter 10, M. Punch, private information.
29 See Chapter 10.
30 Chapter 10.
31 Chapter 10.

Chapter 4

1 See R. Lambert, S. Millham and R. Bullock, *A Manual to the Sociology of the School* (1970) and S. Millham, R. Bullock and P. Cherrett, 'An analytic framework for the comparative study of residential institutions' in J. Tizard, R. Clarke and I. Sinclair (eds), *Varieties of Residential Experience* (1974).
2 See, for example, the classic collection of articles published in 1961, A. H. Halsey, J. Floud and C. A. Anderson, *Education, Economy and Society*.
3 See, for example, the articles by B. Bernstein, G. M. Esland and N. Keddie in M. F. D. Young (ed.), *Knowledge and Control* (1971), and the Open University reader, *School and Society: A Sociological Reader* (1971).
4 See A. Etzioni, *A Comparative Analysis of Complex Organisations* (1961); D. Silverman, *The Theory of Organisations* (1970), and C. Perrow, *Organisational Analysis* (1970).
5 For the classic account of total institutions see E. Goffman, *Asylums* (1961).
6 *Ibid.*; among the most important in the fields of prisons, hospitals and schools are: G. Sykes, *Society of Captives* (1958); R. Giallombardo, *Society of Woman* (1966); D. A. Ward and G. G. Kassebaum, *Women's Prison* (1965); T. and P. Morris, *Pentonville* (1963); A. R. Edwards, 'Inmate adaptations and socialization in the prison', *Sociology* vol. V, pp. 213-26 (1970); S. Wheeler, 'Socialization in correctional communities', *American Sociological Review* vol. 26, pp 697-712 (1961); Stanton and M. S. Schwarz, *The Mental Hospital* (1954); H. S. Becker, *The Boys in White: Student Culture in Medical School*

(1961); H. Polsky, *Cottage Six* (1962), and *The Dynamics of Residential Treatment* (1968); J. Coleman, *The Adolescent Society* (1961); D. Street, C. Vinter and C. Perrow, *Organisations for Treatment* (1966); D. Hargreaves, *Social Relations in a Secondary School* (1967); C. Lacey, *Hightown Grammar* (1970), and articles by Becker, Hughes, Becker and Geer and by Werthman in *School and Society: A Sociological Reader*.

7 For further discussion see S. Millham, R. Bullock and P. Cherrett, 'Social control in organisations' *British Journal of Sociology* (1972), vol. 23, pp. 406-21.

8 See R. Lambert, S. Millham and R. Bullock, 'The informal social system', in R. K. Brown (ed), *Knowledge, Education and Cultural Change* (1973).

9 See G. Sykes, *Society of Captives*, and H. S. Becker, *The Bo‧ ‚ in White*.

10 For a discussion of these issues see A. V. Cicourel, *Cognitive Sociology* (1973); D. Silverman, *The Theory of Organisations*; P. Filmer, M. Phillipson, D. Silverman and D. Walsh, *New Directions in Sociological Theory* (1972) and H. Garfinkel, *Studies in Ethnomethodology* (1967).

Chapter 5

1 For a full discussion of the concept of goals and the methods of studying them see R. Lambert, S. Millham and R. Bullock, *A Manual to the Sociology of the School* (1970). For a more theoretical analysis see A. Etzioni, *A Comparative Analysis of Complex Organisations* (1961), and for an evaluation of this approach to the study of organizations, see D. Silverman, *The Theory of Organisations* (1970).

2 For definitions and discussions of these terms see R. Lambert *et al.*, *A Manual to the Sociology of the School*, and the paper by S. Millham, R. Bullock and P. Cherrett, 'A conceptual scheme for the comparative analysis of residential institutions' in R. V. G. Clarke, I. Sinclair and J. Tizard (eds.) *Varieties of Residential Experience* (Routledge and Kegan Paul 1974).

3 For a discussion of this theoretical issue see: Silverman, *The Theory of Organisations*, and S. L. Millham *et al.*, in *Varieties of Residential Experience*.

Chapter 6

1 The earlier literature is admirably summarized in E. Mack, *The Public Schools and British Opinion 1780-1941,* (1938 and 1941), 2 vols. Since then the spate of literature continues unabated. Among the partisan books championing the public schools have been Spencer Leeson, *The Public Schools Question* (1948); J. Wolfenden, *The Public Schools Today* (1948); G. Snow, *The Public School in the New Age* (1959). A serious justification of the role of elitist education for specific families can be found in T. S. Eliot, *Notes Towards a Definition of Culture* (1948), pp. 35-49. The more recent advocates of the public schools are more self-critical, restrained and open-minded e.g. John Wilson, *Public Schools and Private Practice* (1962), and especially John Dancy, *The Public Schools and the Future* (1966 edn). T. E. B. Howarth, *Culture, Anarchy and the Public School* (1969) is in an older vein. The schools are still attacked in political literature and in novels, e.g. those by David Benedictus and Simon Raven. The schools themselves have produced more factual accounts of themselves than in the past, e.g. in the series of books written 'by the boys' on Charterhouse (1964), Marlborough (1963) and Tonbridge (1964), or in J. McConnell, *Eton, How it Works* (1967). More objective studies of the schools have been published by R. Wilkinson, *The Prefects* (1964); I. Weinberg, *The English Public Schools* (1967); J. Wakeford, *The Cloistered Elite* (1969); G. Kalton, *The Public Schools* (1966); R. Lambert, *The Hothouse Society* (1968), and the Reports of the Public Schools Commission, and the Bloxham Research Unit. A brief review of the present position with several diverse contributions is in H. Anderson (ed), *Education in the Seventies* (1970), ch. 8.

2 See Chapter 2.

3 See also R. Lambert *et al., New Wine in Old Bottles,* and J. Wakeford, *The Cloistered Elite.*

4 See e.g. L. C. Taylor (ed), *Education at Sevenoaks* (1965), the magazine of the HMC *Conference* and a survey undertaken for the HMC on subjects and teaching published in a supplement to *Conference* in 1968.

5 Public Schools Commission, *First Report,* vol. 4, pp. 72-7.

6 Despite the opportunities provided by the residential setting in almost every boarding school we visited the curriculum and pedagogic style were similar to those found in orthodox secondary day schools.

Bernstein would describe the schools as having a closed pedagogy which, using Esland's concepts, is dominated by psychometric considerations.

7　B. Bernstein, 'On the classification and framing of knowledge' in M. F. D. Young (ed), *Knowledge and Control* (1971); B. Bernstein, 'Open schools, open society', *New Society,* 14. Sept. 1967; B. Bernstein, 'Ritual in Education', *Philosophical Transactions of the Royal Society of London* (1966); G. M. Esland, 'Teaching and learning in the organisation of knowledge' in M. F. D. Young (ed) *Knowledge and Control*; G. M. Esland, *Pedagogy and the Teacher's Presentation of Self*, Open University School and Society Course Unit 5. See also H. R. Kohl, *The Open Classroom* (1970). Because in public schools the academic sub-system is one of many and as it may not be viewed, formally or informally, as the most important, the orthodox curriculum and system of setting does not produce the rejection and withdrawal responses found among low stream pupils in day schools by Hargreaves, *Social Relations in a Secondary School* (1967), and Lacey, *Hightown Grammar* (1970).

8　*Times Educational Supplement*, 23 June 1972.

9　*TES*, 23 June 1972. See also R. Richardson and J. Chapman, *Images of life* (1973), which represents the findings of the Bloxham Research Project, summarized in three discussion papers *Changes and Chances*, *No and Yes, Trust in School.* Many of the changes in the text are based on data from *Conference*, the journal of the HMC.

10　See R. Lambert, Introduction to Kalton, and *The Hothouse Society*, chs 5 and 6; J. Wakeford, passim.

11　I. Weinberg, *The English Public Schools*, ch. 4.

12　Interviews with matrons and observation.

13　This is substantiated by our own findings on pastoral relations between boys and staff. See also the Bloxham Reports, passim and R. Lambert, 'Religious education in the boarding school' in P. Jebb (ed), *Religious Education* (1966). *Report on Public School Religion*, Bloxham (1967).

14　At one public school the housemasters' wives or some women staff (connected with art) seem to run informal *salons* or therapeutic sessions for different groups of boys.

15　See the discussion in Chapter 4, p. 73, and references there given. See also I. Weinberg, ch. 5, and J. Wakeford, *The Cloistered Elite*, pp. 39-42 and passim.

16　The classic account of the characteristics of total institutions can be found in E. Goffman, *Asylums* (1961). J. Tizard *et al.*, *Patterns of Residential Care* (1971), and P. Morris, *Put Away* (1969), have both developed measures of these features and applied them to residential institutions.

17   Pp 43-7.

18   The prep schools suffer even more than public schools from an adverse public image and parodies in novels by Waugh and others. Very few objective studies of them have been published, of which P. Masters, *Prep Schools Today* (1966), is most useful. See also IAPS, *Evidence submitted to the Public Schools Commission*, 1967; IAPS, *Choice: a survey of opinions of parents with sons at IAPS schools*, 1967.

This section reports on some of the findings of our research project into prep schools.

19   Masters, *Prep Schools Today*, ch. 11.

20   Plowden Report, vol. I, *Children and their primary schools*, para. 506. See vol. I, ch. 16 and vol. II, appendix XI for a discussion of the teaching methods based on this idea.

21   See *Foundations and reconsideration of teaching in preparatory schools*, IAPS (1959), and *Prospect, the purpose and practice of teaching in prep schools*, IAPS (1965); IAPS, *Evidence to the Public Schools Commision*, pp. 15-20; Masters, *Prep Schools Today*, ch. 7.

22   Masters, *Prep Schools Today*, pp 94-6, IAPS, *Evidence*, p 13.

23   Masters, p. 67. Research evidence.

24   Data from our surveys of staff in prep schools.

25   For progressive schools see W. A. C. Stewart, *The Educational Innovators*, (1968), 2 vols.; R. Skidelsky, *English Progressive Schools*, (1969); M. Ash (ed), *Who are the Progressive Now?* (1969), H. and D. Child, *The Independent Progressive School* (1962); M. Ash (ed), *The Living Question* (1974).

26   See the discussions of these three kinds of coeducation in *Child in Care*, (1971) vol. 2, nos. 2 and 3; R. Bullock, 'The coeducational boarding schools', *Where* (1967), no. 33.

27   The section is based on our research data and the evidence submitted by the Friends Educational Council to the Public Schools Commission.

28   The discontent in some sixth forms in Quaker schools was pronounced. It is reflected in the findings of the Bloxham Research project whose schools were mainly Quaker. The sixth formers in these coeducational schools exhibited more dissatisfied responses than from the integrated kind on our sample or in coeducational day schools.

29   For the 'radical' schools see M. Punch in Ash, *The Living Experiment*,

and his thesis of 1972 in the Cambridge University Library. See also
A. Neill, *Summerhill* (1961), and *Neill, Neill, Orange Peel* (1973);
W. B. Curry, *Education for Sanity* (1947); B. Russell, *Autobiography*,
vol. 2, pp. 152-4, 190-1. See also the journal *New Era* which is the
mouthpiece of the movement and the Coeducational Conference
Newsletter.

30 See the children's responses to goals in Table 4, Appendix IV.

31 There is virtually no literature on these schools, what follows is based
on our research.

There are several books about small schools catering for disturbed
and deprived children and although they are not comparable to the
schools surveyed in this section, they do indicate something of the
ethos of the small, non-academic boarding school. See, for example,
F. G. Lennhof, *Exceptional Children* (1960); M. Burn, *Mr. Lyward's
Answer* (1956); D. Wills, *Spare the Child* (1971).

Chapter 7

1 There are virtually no books on schools of this kind except historical
accounts of certain individual schools which we do not quote from as
they will identify schools in the text, which we promised would not
happen. The section is mainly based on our own research data.

2 Goffman, *Asylums*, pp. 20-8.

3 *New Wine in Old Bottles*, pp. 27-64.

4 See below, Appendix V, Table IV; *The Hothouse Society*, pp 33-7;
New Wine in Old Bottles, pp. 80-1.

5 See below Appendix V, Table IV.

6 See R. Lambert, 'State Boarding', *New Society* (1966), no. 161;
Report of the Place of Boarding in State Education (1966), pp. 9-11,
15-26, 52-68; R. Lambert, *The State and Boarding Education* (1966);
Public Schools Commission, *First Report*, vol. 1, p. 58; R. Lambert,
introduction to Kalton, *Public Schools*, passim; J. Dancy, *The Public
Schools and the Future*, pp. 170-4.

7 Research data, staff questionnaires.

8 See Chapter 10, school B.

9 Chapter 10.

10 See Chapter 11.

11 We visited six in the research period and another twelve since 1968.

12 HMSO *Educational Priority*, vol. 1, pp. 119-29.

13 These schools approach the model of the negative total institution as

analysed in Goffman, *Asylums*.

14   Pp. 27-64, 80-1.

15   The first meeting for representatives from all kinds of boarding was
      in 1965, organized by the author. The Boarding Schools Association
      was set up as a consequence. It is noticeable that the public schools
      are less prominent in its affairs than other groups of boarding schools.

16   The Public Schools Commission did not explore boarding provision
      outside the public schools system. Its recommendations about the
      meeting of boarding need were bound to be defective as it had not
      reviewed all the patterns by which need was being or could be met.

Chapter 8

1   Though there has been much research on residential education, it has
     nearly all been concerned with special education and its results
     cannot be applied to schools for normal children. There has been
     virtually no research into the effects of boarding for such children.
     One early attempt was by B. M. Spinley, *The Deprived and
     Privileged* (1953).

2   Perhaps the most recent and considered claims for boarding of the
     public school kind are to be found in J. Wilson, *Public Schools and
     Private Practice* pp. 109-14 and in J. Dancy, *The Public Schools and
     the Future*, chs 2-4 inclusive. The claims made in G. Snow, *The
     Public Schools in the New Age* (1959) are manifestly absurd. ·The
     Public Schools Commission summarized the arguments for and against
     boarding: *First Report*, vol. 1, pp 90-1.

3   M. J. Power, M. R. Alderson, C. M. Phillipson, E. Shoenberg and
     J. N. Morris, 'Delinquent schools', *New Society*, 19 October 1967,
     pp. 542-3. M. J. Power, R.T. Benn, J. N. Morris, 'Neighbourhood,
     school and juveniles before the court', *British Journal of
     Criminology*, vol. 12, no. 2, pp. 111-32. See also D. E. Frease, 'The
     schools, self-concept and juvenile delinquency', *British Journal of
     Criminology*, vol. 12, no. 2, pp. 133-46.

4   E.g. Dancy, *The Public Schools and the Future*, ch. 2. Wilson, *Public
     Schools and Private Practice*.

5   See, e.g., the critique of Kalton's data by R. R. Dale in his evidence to
     the Public Schools Commission, republished in the *British Journal of
     Educational Psychology* (1967). In another paper, an educational
     psychologist has shown that eminent members of the British medical

profession who have been to public schools tend to specialize on living rather than dead bodies, on the head rather than on the lower trunk, on male bodies rather than female bodies and on the body's surface rather than its inside. See L. Hudson and B. Jacot, 'Education and eminence in British medicine', *British Medical Journal* (1971), vol. 4, pp. 162-3.

6 See also Kalton, Table 3:7.

7 This evidence diametrically contradicts the statement by Wilson, ('the home does not provide such an effective atmosphere for hard work as a boarding school does'), *Public Schools and Private Practice*, p.110.

8 Wilson, p. 110.

9 Wilson, p. 63, 64.

10 *New Wine in Old Bottles*, p 158.

11 See also evidence in Bloxham Research Project, *Trust in School* (1972), p. 24, table five.

12 R. Lambert, S. Millham and R. Bullock, 'The informal social system' in R. K. Brown (ed.), *Knowledge, Education and Cultural Change: papers in the sociology of education* (1973). See also S. Millham, R. Bullock and P. Cherrett, 'Social control in organisations', *British Journal of Sociology* (1972), vol. 23, no. 4, pp. 406-21.

13 See E. Goffman, *Asylums*; D. Clemmer, *The Prison Community* (1958); T. and P. Morris, *Pentonville – a Sociological Study of an English Prison* (1963) and D. Street, R. D. Vinter and C. Perrow, *Organisations for Treatment* (1966).

14 R. Lambert, S. Millham and R. Bullock in Brown (ed.) *Knowledge, Education and Cultural Change*.

15 See also J. Wakeford, *The Cloistered Elite*, pp. 128-59.

16 Wakeford, p. 107.

17 The evidence produced by the Bloxham Research Project, *Trust in School* (1972), p. 21, is rather different. It should be remembered that their questions involved only a general agreement or otherwise with a statement about the helpfulness of staff, whereas ours asked pupils concretely who they would go to with three specific types of problem. None of our experience would indicate the concrete turning to staff with personal, familial or even work problems in comprehensive schools on the scale implied in their figures of assent to general propositions. Also the coeducational boarding schools they investigated are all of the 'divided' kind, marked by lower recourse to staff than in 'integrated' or 'mixed' styles of coeducation.

18 Pp. 65-72.

Chapter 9

1 R. Lambert *et al., New Wine in Old Bottles,* pp. 143-4.
2 The evidence presented in the Public Schools Commission, *First Report,* vol. 2, p. 69, table 30A is misleading as it gives the percentage of schools with differing size bedrooms or dormitories. Reworked, we find that in public and state boarding schools, pupils sleep in the accommodation:

	Percentage of pupils sleeping in	
	Public schools	*State schools*
Single Rooms	12	1
Double	2	1
3-6	14	18
7-12	31	33
13-16	16	10
17-20	8	11
20+	17	27
N =	38,038	3,996

3 See D. Miller, *The Age Between* (1969), and B. F. Atherton, 'Coeducational and single-sex schooling and happiness of marriage', *Educational Research* (1973), vol. XV, no. 3, pp. 221-6. There are, however, serious methodological weaknesses in the latter.
4 E.g. the Bloxham research project's findings, from *one* style of coeducational boarding cannot be generalized to all kinds of coeducation.
5 But it must be remembered that many of the frustrated or rebellious girls in single-sex schools have left before the sixth form, which tends to be full of those who have happily adapted to the school. Only fifty-seven per cent of the girls who start at single-sex public schools are still there by the time they are seventeen (Public Schools Commission, *First Report,* vol. 1, p 69). This accounts for the high level of satisfaction and commitment found among those who remain by the Bloxham project and by Dr Wober in their research.
6 See the reports of R. R. Dale on coeducation in the three volumes, *Mixed or Single-Sex School* and B. F. Atherton, 'Coeducational and single-sex schooling and happiness of marriage', *Educational Research,* vol. 15, No. 3, 1973, pp 221-6. The sampling method of this survey leaves much to be desired.
7 M. Punch in Ash, *The Living Experiment.*

Chapter 10

1 See Public Schools Commission, *First Report*, vol. 2, appendix 9. See also R. Lambert, *Demand for Boarding*; R. Woolfe, *Away to School* (1964).
2 For a survey of the large literature on these issues see R. Dinnage and M. L. Kellmer Pringle, *Residential Child Care Facts and Fallacies* (1967), pp. 6-18. Some of the early work by opponents of institutional care is summed up in J. Bowlby, *Child care and the growth of love* (1965 edn). See also T. Ferguson, *Children in care - and after* (1966).
3 Figures from Public Schools Commission, *First Report*, vol. 2, appendix 6, table 4. Our evidence and more recent testimony indicate that public schools are tending to become more heavily regional in composition (*Times Educational Supplement*, 23 June 1972).
4 See supporting evidence Public Schools Commission, *First Report*, vol. 2, appendix 6, tables 33 and 34.
5 Further sampling data are found in Appendix II.
6 For details of comparable pupils in integration schemes, see Lambert *et al.*, *New Wine in Old Bottles*, pp. 104-5, 134.
7 Data on which this section is based will be found in Table 3, Appendix IV.
8 Bloxham Project Research Unit, *No and Yes* (Spring 1972), p. 31

Chapter 11

1 Figures from *Times Educational Supplement*, 23 June 1972. These were substantiated by much evidence in our research with head-masters. The HMC Conference of 1971 provided further public evidence.
2 The responses of boys in the minor independent schools showed the largest and most consistent gaps between what they felt the schools should be achieving and what they perceived them to be achieving in practice.
3 Two HMC schools have closed recently: Beaumont and Sebright. Some of the independent schools on our sample of sixty-six have also closed.
4 Even the public schools are now prepared to admit that thirty-two per cent of their pupils have some need for boarding. See the Chairman of the HMC, *Daily Telegraph*, 21 June 1972.

5 Figures published by the IAPS in 1973. The reasons for the increase in junior boarding so claimed are not yet clear, whether they reflect a 'bulge' in population, an increase in need boarding or what. It is clear, however, that demand for day places grows faster than that for boarding ones.

6 Howard Glennester and Gail Wilson, *Paying for private schools* (1970). Since then they have increased by nearly another seventy to a hundred per cent.

7 This was clearly the case with even the established public school parents in our family survey.

8 For evidence on these features see the Public Schools Commission, *First Report*, vol. 1, chapter 4, *passim*.

9 Wober, *Girls Boarding, passim.* The thesis that single-sex boarding causes more difficulty in the growth of personality and identity to girls than boys was developed by Dr Derek Miller of the Tavistock Clinic at the Boarding Schools Association Conference in 1967. See *Transcript*.

10 Extensive data from the schools we visited with relatively few boarders confirm this.

11 *TES*, 23 June 1972.

12 Adcroft, Horsley's Green and Whalley schools, all LEA maintained schools, have closed. The Liverpool Corporation has opened a short-stay boarding school at Collomendy.

13 Our own research data, those of R. Woolfe and the figures released by HMC and IAPS all confirm this.

14 *New Wine in Old Bottles, passim.*

15 *State and boarding education, passim.* Public Schools Commission, *First Report*, vol. 1, ch. 7; vol. 2, appendix 14. R. Woolfe, *Away to School, passim.*

16 In 1973 the average cost of a place for an adolescent boy at an approved school was £2,000 p.a.

17 *First Report*, vol. 1, p. 187.

18 Many of the schools set up in the 1920s collapsed in the thirties or before the war. See W. A. C. Stewart, *The Educational Innovators*, vol. 2. One progressive school has been established in Ireland since the war and, of course, more recently in the 1970s a wave of day 'free' schools, catering for a very different sort of population in twilight urban areas but imbued with ideas remarkably akin to the 'radical' progressives of the 1920s.

19 Private evidence and from the meetings of the Coeducational

Conference at Dartington in 1969 and 1971.

20 Definitions of these terms are given in Lambert, Bullock and Millham, *Manual*, p. 166.

21 Our exploration of changes in the interviews was exhaustive and was double checked by the use of documents, children's writings and magazines.

22 HMC Conference of 1973.

23 See e.g. 'Survival of the public schools', *TES*, 23 June 1972, for confirmation of a trend which was clearly on the way in our research period and can be studied more fully in the quarterly issues of the HMC journal *Conference*.

24 See Newsome, *Godliness and Good Learning* and T. Bamford, *History of the Public Schools, passim*.

25 All these schools were on the original list of independent schools in the 1930s. (See M. Punch, doctoral thesis on 'The effects of progressive education at Dartington', University of Cambridge, 1972). Dauntsey's, Rendcomb, Bryanston and Leighton Park are now all members of the HMC.

26 There were only 193 full-time day girls at HMC schools in 1971. The much trumpeted admission of girls has clearly been a very slow and careful process.

27 Millham, Bullock and Cherrett, 'Styles of Coeducational Boarding', *Child in Care* (1971), vol. 2, nos. 2 and 3.

28 See the account of the West Riding EPAs Red House in A. H. Halsey (ed.), *Educational Priority* (1972), p. 119.

29 A. Clegg, B. Megson, *Children in Distress*; Lambert, *State and Boarding*, Woolfe, *Away to School*; Evidence submitted to the Public Schools Commission from the Home Office Child Care Department. Reports of the Home Office Development Group of 'Community Homes', 1968-71.

30 W. H. D. Ames and the Dartington Research Unit, *A survey of short-term residential centres . . . in Devon* (1971), County Hall, Exeter.

31 See Douglas and Ross, *The Home and School*, and *All our future, passim*, among many other confirmations of this fact.

32 Lambert *et al.*, *New Wine in Old Bottles*, especially papers one and two.

33 Lambert *et al.*, paper three.

34 Group of IAPS heads, 1972. The aim is that all parents in the schools concerned will pay fees beyond the economic cost of a place and from this surplus a fund will be set up to support less well-off

entrants. The scheme is speculative at this time.

Chapter 12

1 'What Dartington will do', *New Society*, No. 371, January 1969.
2 See 'Alternatives to School', W. B. Curry Memorial Lecture, University of Exeter (1971), and my chapter in M, Ash (ed.) *The living question: studies in the history of Dartington Hall School* (1974).
3 As note 2. Also V. Bonham Carter, *Dartington Hall* (1958), and W. A. C. Stewart, *The Educational Innovators* (1968), vol. 2, ch. 7.
4 As note 3. See his book, *Education for Sanity* (1947). Also the chapter on him by M. Punch and S. Isaacs in M. Ash (ed.) *The Living Question*.
5 See their description in H. A. L. Child (ed.), *The Independent Progressive School* (1962).
6 See M. Punch in M. Ash (ed.) *The Living Question*.
7 Verbatim notes of this meeting in the author's possession.
8 See Lambert et al., *New Wine in Old Bottles*. Its lapse was not the wish of the then authorities at Marlborough who had been extra-ordinarily open-minded and sympathetic about the whole scheme.
9 See *The Times*, 28 May 1972, in which a spokesman of the public schools (Dr J. Rae) gloomily sees little possibility of contact between them and the state system.
10 See J. Hipkin in *New Wine in Old Bottles*.
11 See the Report of the West Riding Educational Priority Area team, 1972, for an account of the area. It is very similar to that described in R. Henriques, N. Dennis and D. Slaughter, *Coal is our life* (1956). For a perceptive, but somewhat romanticized, view of a similar community, see B. Jackson, *Working class community* (1968).

Chapter 13

1 See Public Schools Commission, *First Report*; Lambert, *State and Boarding*; Woolfe, *Away to School*; Clegg, *Children in Distress*. Most of the evidence submitted to the Public Schools Commission also supported this view, e.g. that of the British Medical Association, Inner London Education Authority, Association of Child Care Officers, Workers Education Association, Gloucestershire County Council, Ministry of Defence, Association of Municipal Corporations, National Association of Divisional Executives for Education. This

was also the one point on which the evidence from the Conservative and the Communist parties was in agreement.

Appendix I

Publications resulting from the Research

BOOKS

Lambert, R., *The State and Boarding Education* (Methuen 1966).
Lambert, R. with Millham, S., *The Hothouse Society* (Weidenfield and Nicolson 1968).
Lambert, R., Hipkin, J. and Stagg, S., *New Wine in Old Bottles?*, Occasional Papers in Social Administration (Bell 1969).
Lambert, R., Millham, S. and Bullock, R., *A Manual to the Sociology of the School* (Weidenfeld and Nicolson 1970).
Wober, M., *English Girls' Boarding Schools* (Allen Lane 1971).
Woolfe, R., *Away to School* (Janus Books 1974).

SECTIONS OF BOOKS

Lambert, R., 'The Public Schools: a sociological introduction' in Kalton, G., *The Public Schools* (Longmans 1966).
Lambert, R., 'Religion in the Boarding School' in Jebb, P. (ed.) *Religious Education* (Darton Longman and Todd 1966).
Lambert, R., 'The future of boarding in modern society' in Ash, M. (ed.) *Who are the Progressives Now?* (Routledge and Kegan Paul 1968).
Lambert, R. and Woolfe, R., 'Need and demand for boarding education' in Public Schools Commission, *First Report*, vol. 2, appendix 9.
Lambert, R., Millham, S. and Bullock, R., 'The Informal Social System' in Brown, R.K. (ed.) *Knowledge, Education and Cultural Change: papers in the Sociology of Education* (Tavistock 1973).
Lambert, R., 'The Progressive School: museum or laboratory?' in Ash, M. (ed), *The Living Question: 50 years of Radical Education at Dartington* (Watts and Son 1974).
Millham, S., Bullock, R. and Cherrett, P., 'Dartington in the context of other schools' in Ash, M. (ed), *The Living Question* (Watts and Son 1974).
Millham, S., Bullock, R. and Cherrett, P., 'A conceptual scheme for the comparative analysis of residential institutions' and 'Socialization in residential communities' in Tizard, J., Clarke, R., Sinclair, I. (eds), *Varieties of Residential Experience* (Routledge and Kegan Paul 1974).

PAMPHLETS OR ARTICLES

Boarding Schools Association, *Different Approaches to Boarding* (Kings

College Research Centre 1966).

Bullock, R., 'The Coeducational Boarding Schools', *Where*? (1967), No. 33.

Hipkin, J., 'Outsiders in the Public Schools', *New Society* (1968), No. 303.

Lambert, R., *The Demand for Boarding* (Cambridge County Council 1966).

Lambert, R., 'State Boarding', *New Society* (1966), No. 161.

Lambert, R., 'State boarding a choice for all', *Where*? (1969), No. 21.

Lambert, R., 'What Dartington will do', *New Society* (1969), No. 371.

Lambert, R., *Alternatives to School*, W. B. Curry Memorial Lecture (Exeter University 1971).

Millham, S. and Bullock, R., 'When a child goes to school', *Where*? (Jan. 1969).

Millham, S., Bullock, R. and Cherrett, P., 'Styles of Coeducational Boarding' and 'Coeducation in Approved Schools', *Child in Care*, Journal of the Res. Child Care Association (1971), vol. 2, nos. 2 and 3.

Millham, S., Bullock, R. and Cherrett, P., 'Social Control in Organisations', *British Journal of Sociology* (1972), XXIII, no. 4, pp 406-21.

Millham, S., Bullock, R. and Cherrett, P., 'Some findings of the first stage of research into approved schools', *Community Schools Gazette* (Dec. 1971), pp 502-17.

Millham, S., 'The residential care of adolescents', *Proceedings of the Sixth Conference, Association for the Psychiatric Study of Adolescents* (1971).

Millham, S., 'Research in approved schools', *Approved Schools Gazette* (June 1969), pp 123-7.

Wober, M., 'The meaning of convergence and divergence, with data from girls' secondary schools', *Educational Review XXIII* (1970), pp 33-49.

Woolfe, R., 'A role for boarding education in the context of the social services', *Social and Economic Administration* (1968), vol. 2.

UNPUBLISHED MATERIAL

Millham, S., Bullock, R. and Cherrett, P., 'A comparative study of eighteen approved schools which explores their stylistic variety and the commitment of boys and staff', Report to the Home Office and Department of Health and Social Security, 1972. To be published by Chaucer Books.

Millham, S., Bullock, R. and Cherrett, P., 'Some Effects of Approved School Training', Report to the Department of Health and Social Security, 1973. To be published by Chaucer Books.

Punch, M., 'The Concept of Totality', Research Report (Kings College Research Centre 1967).

Punch, M., 'A comparative analysis of three boarding schools as complex organisations', unpublished MA thesis (University of Essex 1966).

Appendix II
A note on methods

Social inquirers are seldom able to carry out the ideal design of research they may have in mind. In the case of the boarding school inquiry this was emphatically the case. No internal or external survey of boarding schools by sociological methods had been attempted before 1964. Unlike many state schools which are used to educational inspectors and research workers virtually no boarding schools had ever participated in research, let alone had sociologists active in their midst. Moreover, as the educational issue of boarding was inextricably bound up with the policial issue of the fate of independent education, research - especially that sponsored by the central Government - could be conceived by the schools as a threat to their existence. No wonder then that the neat and coherent research programme met some vicissitudes.

More wonder was it that so much of the programme was in fact accomplished. In the end only two schools refused to co-operate and remarkably few obstacles were put in the way of our activities inside the schools. The initial hostility of the schools was overcome by making it clear that the research group was independent of political affiliation, of Government policy and even, later, of the Public Schools Commission, with whose methods, treatment of its terms of reference, of the evidence presented to it and conclusions, we failed to sympathize. More-over by working in some schools (the intensive sample), strategically chosen, our methods and aims became generally known and accepted. Finally, throughout the research we made it publicly clear that we were concerned with boarding education as a method, not with the independent and public school problem as such, and arranged meetings and issued publications which referred, for example, to the hitherto unknown state boarding sector to make clear our concern with a general educational rather than a local political issue. This, in turn, inevitably made some people think that we favoured boarding as a method, even more so as our researches tended to show that more children with 'need' for residence away from home existed than was recognized by public policy. When, in the end, our researches indicated that conventional boarding schools (or any boarding schools) might *not* be the best method of meeting 'need', and when in *The Hothouse Society* (published in 1968) a very rounded view of the whole boarding scene was presented, we were denounced by some pro-boarding fanatics, who had previously regarded us as allies, as traitors within their midst, while enemies of the public schools, who had previously viewed us with suspicion, now hastened to our defence. That this research could be finished at all, given the heated public controversies of 1964-8, is something of a miracle. That the ideal programme was not always realized is not surprising.

The extensive and intensive samples

From the start the original aims were curtailed by the request of the body making our research grant to exclude preparatory and girls' boarding schools and all those not recognized as efficient by the Department of Education. This was a severe limitation which the later studies of girls at prep schools could not repair. The absence of non-recognized schools from our programme meant that boarding was being surveyed in schools only above a certain physical and educational standard: by its best exemplars and not by a fair balance including the worst. (Though we may have never gained access to them.)

We drew our sample from schools on the Department's lists 70 and 73 for Independent and Direct Grant Schools, published in 1960, adding a list of our own (none was publicly available) of boarding schools maintained by local authorities. Schools were then excluded which did not contain boys, did not provide courses for pupils of secondary age (11-15, 13-18 years), and had fewer than fifty per cent of their pupils as boarders. There were at this stage 198 independent schools left on the list.* These were then stratified at two levels, first into four groups

---

* The slight difference between the 198 independent boys' and coeducational schools which were boarding secondary and recognized on our list, and the number given in Table 1:2 in the text is due to changes in composition, size and structure of the schools and the recognition of schools between 1960 and 1967.

according to the size of the fees and then subdivided into seven groups according to the number of pupils. The nineteen state schools were stratified too by size. Since we wished to give more than proportionate representation to schools the educational interest of which outweighed their numerical importance, we then classified the stratified schools according to their presence on the HMC list, the list of 'progressive' schools found in Hu and Lois Child's book of 1962, and the maintained schools list. We then took a random sample of 1 in 3 HMC schools, 1 in 3 of the progressive groups, 1 in 1·5 of the state schools and 1 in 5 of all the other independent or integrated ones. This left us with sixty-eight schools, of which two refused to co-operate and so our general sample ended at sixty-six schools, the names of which are given in Appendix III. Later we studied three other boarding schools and several boarding hostels but statistical results from these are not used in the book.

The intensive sample had been carefully planned to include schools matched from the general sample on various criteria but this was frustrated by the refusal of some schools so chosen to submit to intensive investigation. In the end we studied five public schools in one region: two major expensive and large ones, exclusively boarding; two middle size public schools of the middle price range but with over a third of their number as day boys; one with a direct grant entry; the fifth minor public school with few day pupils; two state boarding schools, one for boys and long established on public school lines, one co-educational.

Methods in schools

The group of schools to be explored intensively were visited first and methods piloted beforehand at a direct grant boarding/day school. The length of stay in the intensive sample was usually half a term, though in two cases it was substantially longer and in three other cases visits for research were repeated on several occasions. In these schools the researcher lived usually in the boarding houses (*not* in the headmaster's house as an honoured guest). He sometimes took odd classes or even an actual course in the school as a teacher but was careful not to take up an ordinary disciplinary adult role. The researcher always explained his purpose and the research to staff and pupils and he rapidly became known as 'a researcher from Cambridge University' with all the difficulties of identification and attempted manipulations that an effort to sustain such an independent role produces. The researcher went through all the life of the school and was enabled to observe much of the under-life at both pupil and staff level. He kept detailed and systematic notes of observation and used a wide range of documents provided by staff, pupils and domestics, and observed on boards and the like. In this book as it now appears we have, for reasons of space, quoted virtually no documentary material gathered on our stays or quoted from our notes of observation.* Our judgement and perceptions have however been very much formed by the experience of living, participating but striving to be an independent observer, in the schools. A fuller account of the methods used is found in *A Manual to the Sociology of the School*, part three.

In the other schools, which we call the extensive sample, the spells of residence were shorter, most being around two weeks, though again in some cases the schools were visited later on several occasions. Also several members of the research team visited some of the schools together. In the case of large schools three researchers might be there together for a fortnight or more. Once again the researchers lived in the school day and night, if possible in the boarding units, went through as many aspects of its life as possible, as well as collecting documentary data according to a standard procedure for all schools, conducting interviews and supervising questionnaires. Again an account of the methods used on the extensive survey is given in the *Manual*, part three.

Material used in this book

The material used in this book comes mainly from questionnaires used in the extensive and intensive sample of schools and somewhat less from interviews.

* As one of the seven schools refused to let us use questionnaire methods for statistical purposes our intensive sample is therefore six.

(i) Questionnaries

We piloted questions to elicit information concerning our hypotheses (*Manual*, pp 234-41) at a boarding direct grant school before starting work on the intensive sample of schools. After working in each for a couple of months it was hoped that enough goodwill and confidence would have been established in the research (and the researchers) for the senior pupils to complete, in confidence, a searching and exhaustive question-naire. In six of the schools this was done; in the seventh, a minor public school, objections raised by the school authorities made it impossible.

We had hoped to sample from among the pupils aged sixteen to eighteen who were in the sixth forms of the schools, and in the fifth form or extra year at the secondary modern state schools. Sampling, however, proved out of the question. Not only did the pupils and staff regard the idea as tantamount to selecting a possibly biased group of responses, but the teachers simply were not prepared in any school to have their classes depleted for a whole half-day by the absence of the pupils in our sample. Equally, pupils not on the proposed sample felt indignantly that *they* were being eliminated from the research. All this was unexpected and so we had no alternative but to let the whole age group concerned answer the questionnaire. This was done for a three to four hour continuous session in each school, usually with the pupils gathered together in one examina-tion hall: the researcher(s) supervised the process (the staff had the time off) and introduced the questionnaires, helping individuals with any difficulties of interpretation. Over ninety-seven per cent of the sixth forms completed the questionnaires, though a few failed to answer certain questions.

This survey was thus a census quantitatively far in excess of what was needed for purposes of statistical validation. Again we had hoped to sample from the completed questionnaires but, once again, in some schools the staff and pupils objected to any form of identification being allowed on the questionnaire: this meant that in these schools any truly *random* sampling could not be attempted as the sample taken might have been weighted in terms of one age group, a few boarding houses, and the like. In the end then we coded and analysed all the questionnaires and the results given in the text are from 1238 pupils.

Pupils answering questionnaires

School	Boarders	Day	Percentage of all eligible
A	239		99
B	441		97
C	189	85	99
D	67	36	100
E	97		100
F	84		100
	1117	121	

The questionnaire given to these pupils is given in the *Manual*, pp. 254-90.

In the extensive sample of boarding schools we did not apply the same questionnaire but a selected version of it, to test certain hypotheses, and some specially devised tests and questions. In these schools again we found it practically impossible to remove a random sample of pupils for testing and instead we gave the same groups of tests and questions to pupils of different age groups in each of the schools which permitted it. These standard questionnaires were set by us personally in classroom or exam conditions to pupils in the first year (eleven- to twelve-year-olds) in state schools, fourth years (or fifteen-year-olds), fifth years (or sixteen-year-olds), the lower sixth and upper sixth in all the schools which permitted it. The questions actually set are printed in the *Manual*, pp. 292-6. In all, 10, 181 children completed such tests, 53·1 per cent of the total numbers in the schools. In the year groups in question over eighty-seven per cent of the pupils answered the questions, except for one school where the percentage was seventy-five. It was not always practicable or permitted to set all the questions in each of the fifty-nine schools and we therefore give in the text of the book the number of pupils and the number of schools from which the answers come when using material from this survey. We used sub-samples of schools in our earlier interim reports such as *New Wine in Old Bottles*, paper one. Not all the large amount of material which we had been compelled to collect because of the impracticability of randomly selecting pupils has been coded and used.

(ii) Scales
In all schools standard scales which attempt to measure the level of control, both institutional and expressive, were applied. They are published and discussed in the *Manual*, pp 317-29. In each case the researcher or group of researchers has arbitrarily to assign a score for certain features and practices in the school. These scores were assigned only after careful crosschecking with groups of staff and pupils, as well as the researchers' own observations, to ascertain the actual situation in the schools. A modified and improved version of these scales has been used valuably in our later researches into approved schools.

(iii) Interviews
With some individuals we adopted the technique of focused interviews in depth and others we asked to complete a brief questionnaire covering certain issues. All the sixty-six *headmasters* answered our questions, though sixty-two of them also went through the whole focused interview in depth lasting three hours and also completed the standard goals questions and attitude tests printed in the *Manual*, pp 256-7, 284-7, 298-305. We quote relatively little statistical material from these interviews but they were in general an invaluable source for our analyses of the differences between the schools. We also interviewed a random sample of *housestaff*: one in four of the housemasters in the public schools and one in two and a half of those in other schools (some schools have no housemaster role as such). In all sixty-nine interviews were completed. Again there were focused interviews in depth (printed in the *Manual*, pp 306-10) accompanied by the standard goals and attitude questionnaires. Some statistical use is made of them in the book but in general they provided rich material for an analysis of the style, structure and working of the different schools. Brief interviews concerning school organization were held with every *deputy head* or *senior master*, concerning school leavers with the *careers masters* in forty-six schools, concerning the schools' economy and physical state with twenty-seven *bursars*. We also explored the female and medical role by interviewing one in four of the *matrons* in schools with them (thirty-six interviews) and with one in seven of the *doctors* who proved both elusive (and with a few notable exceptions) guarded and unresponsive

(twelve interviews). A special focused interview was completed with twenty-seven *chaplains* in the schools. With other *teaching staff*, apart from much talk, our inquiries were confined to brief factual data and the completion of the goals and attitude questionnaires and role sheets (*Manual*, pp 313-4) by one in six of the staff (403 of them). Altogether, 752 members of staff in the sixty-six schools contributed in the above ways to the research. In its final shortened version the book publishes only a little of the statistical material so gathered but clearly is heavily dependent for its descriptions and analysis on all this data.

Interviews with *pupils* were confined to a standardized interview in depth with the head boy of each school (*Manual*, pp 310-2), organizational interviews with the head of one in three of the houses (fifty-two interviews). We also interviewed in an unstructured way numerous individuals for particular purposes, as well as discussing and questioning groups of pupils for similar purposes: all in a non-random way. We have records of 711 of these kinds of interviews.

(iv) Factual and documentary data
Factual data on a range of basic features (staff-pupil ratios etc.) were gathered and completed for each school (see *Manual* pp 1-37). We also obviously used the prospectuses, published sets of rules, handbooks, school magazines and the like. We had access to minute books of housemasters' meetings and of innumerable committees, and to the private books written by heads of house to their successors (of which we were allowed to read twenty-seven from eleven schools) and many confidential memoranda on many matters. Great use was made of the notice boards in the schools as well.

(v) Diaries
We encouraged pupils to keep a detailed record of a week while we were there and 410 did so. Many wrote for us or to us in other ways. We used much of the documentary and diary material relating to the children in *The Hothouse Society*.

(vi) Evidence to the Public Schools Commission
We were also allowed to read all the evidence submitted to the

Public Schools Commission but, as much of this is confidential, quote only from those pieces of evidence which have been published or are purely statistical.

The comparison schools

To enable some comparisons to be made with the data collected on the extensive and intensive sample we tried to construct a group of schools similar to them in all but the fact that they were mainly day schools. Again the effort was not exact as some of the schools we chose would not admit research of the kind we wanted to do. In the end we worked in four schools. One was an independent public day school for boys, of similar standing, size, social class composition and organization to two on the intensive boarding sample. Two were bilateral or grammar schools, both becoming comprehensive and with a public school tone: one had a boarding side to it. They were similar to the direct grant and state bilateral schools on the extensive sample, except that both were coeducational. The fourth school was a secondary modern boys' school.

The data from these schools offered at least roughly comparable material to that from the boarding schools but no more. In the schools we asked the sixth forms and the fifth form in the secondary modern to complete a questionnaire supervised by us and covering in identical terms about a third of the crucial questions asked of the pupils in our intensive sample: 310 pupils did so, ninety-eight per cent of those eligible.* We also set a very brief questionnaire covering some of the questions set to the junior pupils in the extensive sample to junior pupils in these schools, with again a ninety-seven per cent response.

Comparison schools and boys by forms

	Sixth	Fifth	Third and fourth
Public	80*	146	306
Bilateral/comprehensive (day boys only)	90	155	343
Grammar/comprehensive	52	152	337
Secondary modern		88	83

* Upper sixth only.

* Only pupils in the upper sixth of the public school answered our questionnaire.

In this book we make general comparisons between the data from the 310 day boys in the senior forms of these schools and those from the extensive and intensive samples of schools: this is obviously not a scientifically 'controlled' comparison. Ninety-eight per cent of the girls in the two coeducational sixth forms also answered the questionnaire: there were 147 of them but their answers were only used in our discussion of pastoral care in day situations.

The preparatory school survey

Some use is made of the preparatory school study undertaken at the initiative of the Public Schools Commission between 1966 and 1968, and a brief account of the research is given here.

Schools were selected from those in membership of the Incorporated Association of Preparatory Schools, and a sampling frame constructed using for variables region, proportion of boarders, size and the level of fees. For administrative reasons the sample to be studied was fixed at twenty-five. In order to have a representative sample in terms of the four variables we then chose schools in each of six regions, not on a random number, since this did not result in a representative sample, but by the codes used in the sampling frame. That is, the schools were chosen by looking only at the codes to get a balance and not by the names of the schools in order to avoid bias. In addition to the twenty-five thus chosen and used for statistical purposes, some other schools were visited out of special interest, such as the two coeducational prep schools feeding two 'progressive' schools, the only state boarding primary school, two very famous boys' prep schools which did not turn up on the sample and two others well known for experiment. No statistical results were used from these schools. In addition a group of day preparatory and primary schools was selected to be close in situation, size, sex composition and social class to some of the preparatory schools on the sample and work was done in them.

The girls' school study

The research on girls' boarding schools has been published in

Mallory Wober's book *The English Girls' Boarding School* to which reference should be made for sampling data.

The family study

For financial reasons this study had to be limited and to enable comparisons to be made with the boy boarders we decided to survey parents in three schools on the intensive survey which were likely to give us access to records and backing in approaching parents. These were one large famous public school, a bilateral state boarding school with a public school ethos and a state coeducational boarding secondary modern school.

We piloted methods at first with thirty-five parents from the public school contacted on a personal basis and not eligible for our random sample.

We then took all the parents in the public school with sons who had been there four years or more and excluded those living in Scotland or abroad. We then stratified the rest by eight regions and from the families took a one in four sample, which resulted in fifty-seven interviews. One couple refused to be interviewed but fifty couples, two widows, one widower, two fathers only and two mothers only were interviewed, 107 people in all.

From the state bilateral school we took parents living in England and Wales whose sons were in the fifth and sixth forms and took a one in three sample. Regional stratification was unnecessary as most lived in one county. Twenty-two families were eligible, one refused, and interviews were completed with sixteen couples, two widows, one mother only, and two mothers separated or divorced, thirty-seven parents in all.

At the state secondary modern school we took a one in two sample of parents resident in England and Wales (chiefly in one county) whose sons were in the fifth form. Nineteen accepted and so we interviewed sixteen couples, one widow, one widower, and one divorced father, thirty-five parents in all.

A structured interview in depth was completed with 179 parents. The interview was mainly done at the family home but in quite a few cases the mother was interviewed at home during the day and the father separately at work. Most of the fathers and mothers sat in on at least part of each other's interview. Standard separate schedules were used for each, that for the mother was longer. The interviews together lasted for three to four hours. Standard data were collected from the parents on their own backgrounds, their child-rearing practices, their children's education, their careers, social/political attitudes, their attitude to schools' goals, their social lives. Systematic data were also collected about all their children and the educational career of the boy in question, the choice of schools, their choice of boarding, relations and attitudes to their son's school over time, effects on their son, reactions to boarding by the parents, family and boy, holiday behaviour, current relations with the family and changes over the past. In all, eighty-eight questions were asked, some open, some closed and precoded. Copies of the questionnaire can be seen at the Dartington Research Office.

Appendix III
List of schools on the general sample

Friends' School, Ackworth, Yorks.
Adcroft, Wilts.
Apley Park, Shropshire.
Bearwood College, Berks.
St Bees, Cumberland.
Bedales, Hants.
Bembridge, Isle of Wight.
Bloxham, Oxon.
Bradfield College, Berks.
Bryanston, Dorset.
Brymore, Somerset.
Canford, Dorset.
Carmel College, Berks.
Christ's Hospital, Sussex.
St Christopher's, Herts.
Clifton College, Bristol.
City of Coventry, Shropshire.
Cranleigh, Surrey.
Crediton, Devon.
Crewkerne, Somerset.
Culford, Suffolk.
Dartington Hall, Devon.
Downside, Somerset.
Eccles Hall, Norfolk.
Eton College, Berks.
St Edward's, Oxford.
Elmbridge, Surrey.
Fyfield, Essex.
Gosfield, Essex.
Grenville College, Devon.
HMS Conway, Anglesey.
Royal Hospital School, Holbrook,

Suffolk.
Horsley's Green, Bucks.
Kennylands, Berks.
Kent College, Kent.
Keswick, Cumberland.
King Edward's, Witley, Surrey.
King's College, Taunton, Somerset.
Langley, Norfolk.
St Lawrence, Ramsgate, Kent.
Leighton Park, Berks.
Leys, Cambridge.
Marlborough, Wilts.
Mili Hill, Middlesex.
Milton Abbey, Dorset.
Ottershaw, Surrey.
St Peter's, Formby, Liverpool.
St Peter's, York.
Ratcliffe College, Leicester.
Rendcomb College, Gloucs.
Rishworth, Yorks.
Rossall, Lancs.
Friends' School, Saffron Walden, Essex.
Sheephatch, Surrey.
Sherborne, Dorset.
Sibford Ferris, Oxon.
Stanbridge Earls, Hants.
Old Swinford Hospital, Stourbridge, Worcs.
Tonbridge School, Kent.
Royal Wanstead, Essex.
Wellington School, Somerset.

Wennington, Yorks.
West Buckland, Devon.
Winchester, Hants.
Royal Wolverhampton, Staffs.
Woolverstone Hall, Suffolk.

Appendix IV Statistics

TABLE 1 Content analysis of stated goals of headmasters and housestaff in depth interviews
Coll/Ind. means collectively or individually oriented;
Instr/Expr/Org. means instrumental, expressive or organizational;
I/E means instrumental with expressive tendencies;
E/I means the reverse.

Goals	Coll/ Ind.	Instr/ Expr/ Org.	Public		Independent		Ind/Integrated		Maintained		Progressive	
			HMs (22)	Hse (33)	HMs (7)	Hse (4)	HMs (11)	Hse (14)	HMs (15)	Hse (14)	HMs (7)	Hse (10)
O/A level results	C	I	3	22	4	2	9	5	2	6		2
Preparation for democracy	C	I/E	1	2	1		2	2	2		2	2
Education to ability	I	I/E	4	3	3	2	3	7	7	8	5	2
Preparation for jobs	I	I	3	3	1	1	5	4	7	8		2
Physical development	I	I/E	1	2		1		2	1	1		
Preparation for life	C	I/E	3	8	3	1		5	6	3		5
Independence	I	I/E	12	19	2	1	2	5	5	10	1	7
Sense of purpose	I	E/I	0	6								
Tolerance	C	E/I	13	26	4	1	3	7	2	3	1	6
Sense of service	C	E/I	17	24	3	1			2	1	2	4
Community spirit	C	E/I	16	29	2	2	3	4	3	3	1	1
Manners	C	E/I	10	12	2	1	3	4	2	2		1
Self-discipline	I	E/I	7	8						1		4
Individuality	I	I/E	5	3			6	2	12	4	4	4
Critical awareness/open mind	I	I/E	3	6		1			2	2	5	7
Free atmosphere	I	E/I	0	0	3		5		1		6	6
Intellectual development	I	E/I	13	19	3		6	13	9	11	6	6
Meeting needs	I	E/I	2	3	3		6	13	9	11	2	3

	C	E/I									
Gentleman	C	E/I	0	6			2				2
Values which are anti-commercial	C	E/I									2
Self-awareness	I	E/I	1	2	3	1		5	1	2	2
Self-confidence	I	E/I	2	0	3	0	1	6	1	2	3
Moral awareness	C	E	12	22	4		5	9	5	3	2
Sense of responsibility	C	E	12	16	4	1	5	2	3	1	5
Creative expression	I	E	2	6	2	1	2	3	3	2	6
Personality development	I	E	2	4	1	1	2	3	2	4	7
Happiness	I	E	2	2		1	3	2	9	6	5
Frankness	I	E	1	4			2	3	1	3	1
Warmth	I	E	0	1			2	3	1	1	
Emotional development	I	E	0	0			3	5	3	1	7
Sense of sportsmanship	C	E/I	10	11			3	5	7	7	8
Christian faith and practice, religious, spiritual values	C	E	17	16	3	2	5	5	3	2	4	3
Homely atmosphere	I	E	0	0		2	2	9	7	9	1	1
Discipline, order, reputation of school	C	O	0	9	1		2	10	1	3	
Cultural interests	I	E	13	10	1	2	2	9	9	2	6	4
Sense of 'standards'	C	E/I	6	5							
Leadership	C	E/I	5	12	4		2	2			
Loyalty	C	E/I	7	8	2			1			
Spartan atmosphere	C	E/I	1	0							
Vitality	I	E	2	4	1	2	2	6	6	1	5	2

TABLE 2

Parents' ratings of school goals (in percentages)
School A is the public school, B and C are state schools

	Tries			Should try			Succeeds		
Expressive Goals	A	B	C	A	B	C	A	B	C
Make life like home	29	37	69	32	45	74	24	33	76
Put into practice Christian values	87	69	86	94	79	86	76	61	84
Foster sportsmanship	86	85	90	87	89	90	83	81	85
Promote cultural interests	82	74	79	91	95	90	80	71	80
Tell right from wrong	90	79	86	97	97	95	81	76	87
Foster creative talents	80	71	79	90	87	94	74	65	78
Expressive/instrumental									
Promote individuality	78	86	82	91	94	97	75	83	76
Promote leadership	83	66	73	86	79	74	74	58	69
Promote critical faculties	85	72	82	84	87	87	69	68	79
Promote respect for others	85	72	87	95	95	95	78	66	89
Instrumental/expressive									
Develop physically	75	86	88	85	86	92	73	86	88
Train in managing others	82	77	76	91	85	86	80	72	75
Instrumental									
Give education best suited to ability	83	87	84	96	99	94	74	85	81
Prepare for democracy	85	78	82	89	85	90	77	76	72
Get good GCE results	90	86	78	92	90	90	81	80	74
Prepare for a suitable job or career	68	79	81	88	92	93	66	71	76
Organizational									
Make school run efficiently	90	85	96	96	91	96	80	89	94
Maintain firm discipline	70	76	85	83	85	93	67	69	91
Keep pupils occupied	73	86	93	76	79	91	76	81	96
Keep up a good reputation	80	79	95	82	85	94	85	88	95

(N = 64 32 23)

Scores are based on a five point rating and percentage = $\dfrac{\text{Total ratings}}{\text{Total possible ratings}}$

TABLE 3

Parents' replies to questions on attitudes to social issues (in percentages)
Agree or strongly agree with statements

	Parents			Boys		
	A	B	C	A	B	C
There is a life after death	59	33	53	49	41	42
Religion is the basis of all true morality	73	61	80	54	35	40
Christianity is the highest form of religion	69	36	53	43	32	37
Coloured people are inferior to others	9	0	9	10	11	10
It is wrong to have sexual relations before marriage	59	49	74	35	18	43
There is nothing wrong with family life in this country	32	51	68	47	56	60
Hanging should be abolished	45	33	24	43	36	33
Teenagers in general have too much money	80	73	91	46	35	19
Women are best kept in the home	26	24	9	20	12	13
Intellectuals cannot be trusted	11	9	12	15	13	14
Most modern art is unintelligible	57	58	74	42	40	42
Most pop music is worthless	36	39	59	31	20	13
Television is a menace	17	46	26	26	27	11
Most modern drama is sordid	36	55	50	18	24	42
The best relaxation is still a good book	64	64	62	58	48	52
You can't really read poetry for pleasure	18	18	29	30	50	59
The welfare state is making people soft	74	67	59	43	34	23
There's not much wrong with this country	29	42	65	19	26	36
Nationalization is better than free enterprise	5	12	12	11	10	20
Schools should be run democratically	59	73	74	41	50	33
Games do mould character	75	64	82	55	69	53
(N =	102	33	34	440	97	84)

TABLE 4

Pupils' goal ratings

Sixth-form boarders' evaluations of the degree to which their schools try, should try towards, and succeed in attaining goals (in percentages)

	Public schools			Independent Non-integrated		
Expressive	*Does*	*Should*	*Succeeds*	*Does*	*Should*	*Succeeds*
Make life here something like that at home	29·1	52·7	21·9	29·4	51·2	23·1
Put into practice Christian values	77·5	64·1	42·3	79·0	62·3	37·7
Foster a sense of sportsmanship	69·8	72·2	57·5	71·1	80·7	55·0
Develop our cultural interests	66·4	82·6	51·2	60·2	61·5	47·3
Enable us to recognize what is right and wrong	76·1	86·4	62·1	73·4	88·8	58·1
Develop our creative talents	61·4	85·5	51·9	63·1	81·7	53·0
Expressive-instrumental						
Cultivate each person's individuality	58·5	85·8	51·2	55·4	82·9	51·4
Train leaders for the future	59·9	72·2	49·5	53·1	78·1	39·9
Develop our critical faculties	60·2	80·7	54·2	47·5	79·9	51·0
Teach people to respect each other	64·1	83·6	52·0	60·1	87·2	49·6
Instrumental						
Give everyone the education best suited to his ability	73·3	94·4	64·2	64·9	91·7	55·1
Prepare us for a democratic society	54·4	72·6	46·8	58·5	75·0	47·5
Get good O and A level results	88·6	92·7	72·4	80·0	90·7	59·5
Prepare us for a suitable job or career	68·5	89·6	60·5	60·6	85·3	52·4
Instrumental-expressive						
Develop each of us physically	67·8	72·0	55·3	65·6	77·1	54·4
Provide experience in managing people	71·7	79·5	60·1	58·4	76·3	54·0
Organizational						
Keep the school running efficiently	86·1	88·7	70·7	80·3	89·7	54·5
Maintain firm discipline	78·1	65·0	60·3	70·1	65·9	52·4
Keep us occupied most of the time	68·0	63·5	59·6	63·4	60·9	56·6
Keep a good reputation outside	90·2	79·1	67·5	89·6	82·8	67·2
Schools =	18			6		
N =	2952			307		

Independent Integrated			State schools			Progressive schools		
Does	Should	Succeeds	Does	Should	Succeeds	Does	Should	Succeeds
29·7	63·5	24·5	42·7	63·3	35·1	47·1	52·3	40·2
75·0	51·9	32·1	54·1	49·9	27·8	58·9	44·3	34·2
75·7	80·0	62·0	57·2	69·0	53·1	54·2	54·7	37·2
57·1	81·6	42·0	68·2	76·3	57·0	68·9	83·9	53·6
78·9	85·2	63·1	69·1	85·2	58·1	80·3	89·3	67·1
53·0	76·9	44·0	60·0	82·4	53·9	72·3	87·8	62·9
48·7	80·5	45·1	50·4	86·1	52·8	71·9	88·6	65·8
57·8	77·8	48·3	44·3	63·6	42·7	35·9	47·8	33·4
51·0	77·8	43·1	51·5	75·5	54·0	62·8	75·9	56·2
62·2	80·6	45·0	59·4	79·9	49·9	70·7	89·4	50·9
65·2	87·3	60·0	67·6	94·1	61·1	76·4	93·5	66·1
52·0	62·9	48·1	53·3	64·5	45·2	71·0	78·4	61·4
83·3	91·2	70·6	89·8	91·8	79·5	75·4	76·6	64·1
65·5	88·8	54·4	64·5	87·2	56·4	53·9	79·2	52·0
69·5	75·1	58·6	63·6	62·2	48·3	56·8	59·7	41·1
62·1	77·3	56·9	55·8	70·0	52·5	60·5	69·9	58·1
80·0	82·6	60·6	73·9	82·5	60·2	83·6	89·8	60·8
78·3	67·6	53·7	68·5	63·1	52·6	51·4	50·0	41·2
75·7	61·5	61·0	63·3	61·7	53·1	61·8	57·8	52·1
92·1	78·5	67·8	85·5	76·9	62·8	80·5	62·1	49·2
11			12			7		
511			334			286		

Bibliography

P. M. Abell, 'Measurement in Sociology' *Sociology*, II, 1968, pp. 1-20.

P. Ackerman, 'A staff group in a women's prison' *International Journal of Group Psychology*, XXII, 1972, pp. 364-74.

R. S. Adams, 'Analysing the teacher's role' *Educational Research*, XII, 1970, pp. 121-7.

M. Albrow, 'The influence of accommodation upon 64 Reading University students' *British Journal of Sociology*, XVII, 1966, pp. 403-18.

M. Albrow, *Bureaucracy* (London: Macmillan, 1970).

E. A. Allen, 'Attitudes of children and adolescents in school' *Educational Research*, III, 1960, pp. 65-80.

W. Ames and the Dartington Social Research Unit, *A Survey of Short-term Residential Centres and other out of School Facilities in the County of Devon* (Devon County Council, 1972).

H. Anderson et al (eds), *Education in the Seventies* (London: Heinemann, 1970).

M. A. Ash, *Who are the Progressive Now?* (London: Routledge, 1969).

A. E. Ashworth and W. M. Walker, 'Social structure and homosexuality: a theoretical reappraisal' *British Journal of Sociology*, XXIII, 1972, pp. 146-58.

B. F. Atherton, 'Coeducational and single-sex schooling and happiness of marriage' *Educational Research*, XV, 1973, pp. 221-6.

R. Balbernie, *Residential Work with Children* (Oxford: Pergamon, 1966).

E. D. Baltzell, *Philadelphia Gentlemen* (New York: Free Press, (1958).

M. Banton, *Roles - an introduction to the study of social relations*, (London: Tavistock, 1965).

T. W. Bamford, *The Rise of the Public Schools* (London: Nelson, 1967).

D. Barnes and J. Britton, *Language, the Learner and the School* (Harmondsworth: Penguin, 1969).

R. G. Barker and P. V. Crump, *Big School, Small School* (Palo Alto., California: Stanford University Press, 1963).

J. C. Barker-Lunn, *Streaming in the Primary School* (Slough: N.F.E.R., 1970).

R. Barton, *Institutional Neurosis* (Bristol: J. Wright, 1959).

H. S. Becker, 'Social class variations in the teacher-pupil relationship' *Journal of Educational Psychology*, XXV, 1952, pp. 451-65.

H. S. Becker, 'The teacher in the authority system of the public school' *Journal of Educational Sociology*, XXVII, 1953, pp. 128-41.

H. S. Becker, 'Problems of inference and proof in participant observation' *American Sociological Review*, XXIII, 1958, p. 652.

H. S. Becker, *The Boys in White; student culture in medical school* (Chicago: University Press, 1961).

H. S. Becker, 'Schools and systems of stratification' in Floud, Halsey and Anderson, *Education, Economy and Society: a reader in the sociology of education*, pp. 93-104.

H. S. Becker and B. Geer, 'Participant observation and interviewing: a comparison' *Human Organisation*, XVI, 1957, pp. 28-32; with critique by M. Throw pp. 33-5.

H. S. Becker, 'Latent culture' *Administrative Science Quarterly*, V, 1960, pp. 304-13.

C. Beedell, *Residential Life with Children* (London: Routledge, 1970).

C. Benn and B. Simon, *Half Way There - Report on the British Comprehensive School Reform*, (London: McGraw Hill, 1970).

J. S. Bentwich, *Education in Israel* (London: Routledge, 1965).

B. Berger, 'Adolescence and beyond' *Social Problems*, X, 1963, pp. 394-408.

B. B. Berk, 'Organisational goals and inmate organisation' *American Journal of Sociology*, LXXI, 1966, pp. 522-34.

G. Bernbaum, 'Educational expansion and the teacher's role' *Universities' Quarterly*, XXI, 1967, pp. 152-66.

G. Bernbaum, *Social Change and the Schools* (London: Routledge, 1967).

B. Bernstein, 'Ritual in education' *Philosophical Transactions of the Royal Society of London*, CCLI, 1967, pp.429-36.

B. Bernstein, 'Open Schools, Open society?' *New Society*, 14 September 1967, pp. 351-3.

B. Bernstein, 'Education cannot compensate for society' *New Society*, 26 February 1970, pp. 344-7.

B. Bernstein, *Class, Codes and Control* (2 vols) (London: Routledge 1971 and 1973).

B. Bernstein, 'On the classification and framing of educational knowledge' in R. K. Brown *Knowledge, Education and Cultural Change* pp.363-92.

B. *Bettelheim*, *The Informed Heart* (London: Thames and Hudson, 1961).

B. *Bettelheim*, *Love is Not Enough* (New York: Free Press, 1950).

B. L. *Bible and J. D. McComas*, 'Role consensus and teacher effectiviness' *Social Forces*, XLII, 1963, pp. 225-33.

B. J. *Biddle*, *The Present Status of Role Theory: studies in the role of the Public School teacher* (Missouri, 1961).

B. J. *Biddle and E. J. Thomas*, *Role Theory, Concepts and Research* (Chichester, Sussex: Wiley, 1966).

C. E. *Bidwell*, 'Some effects of administrative behaviour, a study in role theory' *Administrative Science Quarterly*, II, 1957, pp. 161-81.

T. J. H. *Bishop and R. Wilkinson*, *Winchester and the Public School Elite* (London: Faber, 1967).

P. M. *Blau*, *The Dynamics of Bureaucracy* (Chicago: University Press, 1963).

P. M. *Blau and W. R. Scott*, *Formal Organisations, a Comparative Approach* (London: Routledge, 1963).

P. M. *Blau and R. A. Schoenherr*, *The Structure of Organisations* (New York: Basic Books, 1971).

W. A. L. *Blyth*, 'Sociometry, prefects and peaceful coexistence in a junior school' *Sociological Review*, VI, 1958, pp. 5-24.

W. A. L. *Blyth*, 'The sociometric study of children's groups in English schools' *British Journal of Educational Studies*, VIII, 1960, pp 127-47.

W. A. L. *Blyth*, *English Primary Education, a sociological description* (2 vols.) (London: Routledge, 1965).

F. *Bodman, M. Mackinlay and K. Sykes*, 'The social adaptation of institution children' *Lancet*, CCLVIII, 1950, pp. 173-6.

V. *Bonham-Carter*, *Dartington Hall* (London: Phoenix House, 1958).

T. B. *Bottomore*, *Elites and Society* (London: Watts, 1964).

A. E. *Bottoms and F. H. McClintock*, *Criminals Coming of Age* (London: Heinemann, 1973).

J. *Bowlby*, *Child Care and the Growth of Love* (Harmondsworth: Penguin, 1965).

R. *Boyson (ed.)*, *Education: Threatened Standards* (Enfield: Churchill, 1972).

K. *Brill and R. Thomas*, *Children in Homes* (London: Gollancz, 1964).

J. *Brothers and S. Hatch*, *Residence and Student Life* (London: Tavistock, 1971).

Bibliography/397

G. W. *Brown and A. Wing*, 'A comparative and clinical social survey of three mental hospitals' *Sociological Review Monograph*, V, 1962.

R. K. *Brown (ed.)*, *Knowledge, Education and Cultural Change* (London: Tavistock, 1973).

N. J. *Bull*, *Moral Judgement from Childhood to Adolescence* (London: Routledge, 1969).

R. *Bullock*, 'The coeducational boarding schools' *Where*, XXXIII, 1967, pp. 9-13.

M. *Burn*, *Mr Lyward's Answer* (London: Hamish Hamilton, 1956).

T. *Burns*, 'The comparative study of organisations' in V. H. Vroom, *Methods of Organisational Research* (New Jersey: Prentice Hall, 1969).

H. J. *Butcher*, *Educational Research in Britain* (3 vols) (University of London Press, 1968, 1970 and 1974).

J. *Carlebach*, *Caring for Children in Trouble* (London: Routledge, 1970).

R. O. *Carlson*, 'Succession and performance among school superintendants' *Administrative Science Quarterly*, VI, 1961, pp. 210-27.

D. S. *Cartwright and R. J. Robertson*, 'Membership in cliques and achievement' *American Journal of Sociology*, LXVI, 1961, pp. 441-5.

M. *Castle*, 'Institutional and non-institutional children at school' *Human Relations*, VII, 1954, pp. 349-66.

W. *Caudill*, *The Psychiatric Hospital as a Small Society* (Harvard, 1958).

Charterhouse ('by the boys') (London: Keith Mason, 1964).

A. W. *Chickering et al.*, 'Institutional differences and student development' *Journal of Educational Psychology*, LX, 1969, pp. 315-26.

A. V. *Cicourel*, *Method and Measurement in Sociology* (Glencoe: Free Press, 1964).

A. V. *Cicourel*, *Cognitive Sociology* (Harmondsworth: Penguin, 1973).

A. V. *Cicourel and J. I. Kitsuse*, 'The social organisation of the high school and deviant adolescent careers' in E. Rubington and M. Weinberg (eds) *Deviance: The Interactionist Perspective* (New York: Macmillan, 1968).

B. R. *Clark*, 'Organisational adaptation and precarious values' *American Sociological Review*, XXI, 1956 pp. 327-36.

R. V. G. *Clarke*, *Absconding from Approved Schools* (London:

HMSO, 1971).

A. B. *Clegg and B. Megson*, *Children in Distress* (Harmondsworth: Penguin, 1967).

D. *Clemmer*, *The Prison Community* (New York: Holt, Rinehart and Winston, 1958).

R. A. *Cloward*, 'Illegitimate means, anomic and deviant behaviour' *American Sociological Review*, XXIV, 1959, pp. 164-76.

R. A. *Cloward*, 'Social control in prison' in *Theoretical Studies in the Social Organisation of the Prison*, New York Social Science Research Council, 1960, pp. 20-48.

A. L. *Cohen*, *Delinquent Boys - the culture of the gang* (London: Routledge, 1967).

L. *Cohen*, 'Problems of home-school cooperation: the headteacher's point of view' *Sociological Review*, XVIII, 1970, pp. 393-406.

L. *Cohen*, 'Role and headteachers' role conceptions' *Educational Research*, XIV, 1971, pp. 35-9.

S. *Cohen and L. Taylor*, *Psychological Survival: the experience of long-term imprisonment* (Harmondsworth: Penguin, 1972).

J. S. *Coleman*, 'The adolescent sub-culture and academic achievement' *American Journal of Sociology*, LXV, 1960, pp. 337-47.

J. S. *Coleman*, 'Academic achievement and the structure of competition' in Floud, Halsey and Anderson, *Education, Economy and Society*.

J. S. *Coleman*, *The Adolescent Society* (New York: Free Press, 1961).

J. S. *Coleman*, 'The concept of equal educational opportunity' *Harvard Educational Review*, XXXVIII, 1968, pp. 7-22.

J. *Cook-Gumperz*, *Social Control and Socialization: a study of class differences in the language of maternal control* (London: Routledge, 1973).

D. *Cornish*, 'Some evaluations of institutional programmes' *Community Schools' Gazette*, LXVI, 1973, pp. 702-9.

R. G. *Corwin*, *Sociology of Education* (New York: Appleton, Century Crofts, 1963).

B. R. *Cosin, I. R. Dale, G. M. Esland and D. F. Swift (eds)*, *School and Society* (London: Routledge, 1971).

C. B. *Cox and A. E. Dyson*, *Black Papers on Education* (3 vols) (London: Critical Quarterly Society, 1970, 1971).

M. *Craft, J. Raynor and L. Cohen*, *Linking Home and School* (London: Longmans, 1967).

M. *Craft (ed.)*, *Family, Class and Education* (London: Longmans, 1970).

H. *Craig*, 'The teacher's function' *Journal of Educational Sociology*, XXXIV, 1960.

E. *Crellin, M. L. Kellmer-Pringle and P. West*, *Born Illegitimate: social and educational implications* (Slough: NFER, 1971).

D. *Cressey*, *The Prison: studies in institutional organisation and change* (New York: Holt, Rinehart and Winston, 1961).

W. B. *Curry*, *Education for Sanity* (London: Heinemann, 1947).

H. O. *Dahlke*, *Values in Culture and Classroom: a study in the sociology of the school* (New York: Harper, 1958).

R. R. *Dale*, 'Review of Kalton's data' *British Journal of Educational Psychology*, 1967.

R. R. *Dale*, *Mixed or Single Sex School* (3 vols) (London: Routledge, 1969, 1971 and 1973).

R. R. *Dale and S. Griffith*, *Down Stream: Failure in the Grammar School* (London: Routledge, 1965).

J. C. *Dancy*, *Public Schools and the Future* (London: Faber, 1963).

J. C. *Daniels*, 'The effects of streaming in the Primary school' *British Journal of Educational Psychology*, XXXI, 1961, pp. 69-78 and 119-27.

B. *Davies*, 'On the contribution of organisational analysis to the study of educational institutions' in R. K. Brown (ed.), *Knowledge, Education and Cultural Change* pp. 249-296.

H. *Davies*, *Culture and the Grammar School* (London: Routledge, 1965).

I. *Davies*, 'Knowledge, Education and Power' in R. K. Brown (ed.), *Knowledge, Education and Cultural Change* pp. 317-38.

J. A. M. *Davis*, 'Secondary schools as communities' *Educational Review*, IX, 1957, pp. 179-89.

D. G. *Dean*, 'Alienation, its meaning and measurement' *American Sociological Review*, XXVI, 1961, pp. 753-8.

J. P. *Dean*, 'Participant observation and interviewing' in J. T. Doby, *Introduction to Social Research* (Harrisburg: Stackpole, 1954).

N. *Dennis, R. Henriques and C. Slaughter*, *Coal is our Life* (London: Tavistock, 1956).

R. *Dinnage and M. L. Kellmer-Pringle*, *Residential Care: Facts and Fallacies* (London: Longmans, 1967).

S. M. *Dornbusch*, 'The military academy as an assimilation unit' *Social Forces*, XXXIII, 1955, pp. 361-321.

J. W. B. Douglas, *The Home and School* (London: MacGibbon and Kee, 1964).

R. Dreeben, *On What is Learned in School* (Reading: Addison-Wesley, 1969).

R. Dubin, 'Deviant behaviour and social structure: continuities in social theory' *American Sociological Review*, XXIV, 1959, pp. 147-64.

R. Dupan and S. Roth, 'The psychologic development of a group of children brought up in a hospital-type residential nursery' *Journal of Pediatrics*, XLVII, 1955, pp. 124-9.

A. R. Edwards, 'Inmate adaptations and socialisation in the prison' *Sociology*, V, 1971, pp. 213-26.

T. Edwards and D. Webb, 'Freedom and responsibility in the Sixth form' *Educational Research*, XIV, 1971, pp 46-50.

S. J. Eggleston, *The Social Context of the School* (London: Routledge, 1967).

S. J. Eggleston, 'Decision-making on the school curriculum: a conflict model' *Sociology*, VII, 1973, pp. 377-94.

N. Elias, 'Problems of involvement and detachment' *British Journal of Sociology*, VII, 1956, pp. 226-52.

C. D. Elliot and P. D. Pumfrey, 'The effects of non-directive play therapy on some maladjusted boys' *Educational Research*, XIV, 1972, pp. 157-61.

F. Ellkin, 'The soldier's language' *American Journal of Sociology*, LI, 1946, pp. 414-22.

F. E. Emery, *Freedom and Justice within Walls: the Bristol Prison Experiment* (London: Tavistock, 1970).

N. J. Entwistle and J. D. Nisbet, *Educational Research in Action* (University of London Press, 1973).

G. M. Esland, *Pedagogy and the Teacher's Presentation of Self* (Bletchley: The Open University, 1972).

A. Etzioni, *A Comparative Analysis of Complex Organisations: on power, involvement and their correlates* (New York: Free Press, 1961).

A. Etzioni (ed.), *Complex Organisations: a sociological reader* (New York: Holt, Rinehart and Winston, 1961).

K. M. Evans, *Sociometry and Education* (London: Routledge, 1962).

K. M. Evans, 'Sociometry in schools: (i) techniques (ii) application *Educational Research*, VI, 1964, pp. 50-8 and 121-8.

J. Evetts, 'Equality of opportunity: a recent history of the concept'

British Journal of Sociology, XXI, 1970, pp. 425-30.

R. *Farley*, *Secondary Modern Discipline* (London: A. and C. Black, 1960).

Fédération Internationale des Commaimintés d'Enfants, *Documents, Etudes Padagogiques*.

T. *Ferguson*, *Child in Care - and After* (University of London Press, 1966).

L. *Festinger and D. Katz*, *Research Methods in the Behavioural Sciences* (New York: Holt, Rinehart and Winston, 1953).

J. H. *Fichter*, *Parochial School* (Notre Dame: University Press, 1958).

P. *Filmer, M. Phillipson, D. Silverman and D. Walsh*, *New Directions in Sociological Theory* (London: Collier MacMillan, 1972).

D. S. *Finlayson*, 'The goal structure of teachers in comprehensive schools' *Educational Research*, XV, 1973, pp. 188-93.

C. E. *Fishbourn*, 'Teacher role perception in the secondary school' *Journal of Teacher Education*, XIII, 1962.

S. *Fisher*, 'Stigma and deviant careers in schools' *Social Problems*, XX, 1972, pp. 78-84.

J. *Floud*, 'Teaching in the affluent society' *British Journal of Sociology*, XIII, 1962, pp. 299-308.

J. *Floud, A. H. Halsey and C. A. Anderson*, *Education, Economy and Society: a reader in the sociology of education* (New York: Free Press, 1961).

A. *Foot*, *The Doon School Book* (1945).

C. A. *Ford*, 'Homosexual practices of institutionalised females' *Journal of Abnormal and Social Psychology*, XXIII, 1929, pp. 442-8.

W. M. *Frazer*, *Residential Education* (Oxford: Pergamon, 1968).

D. E. *Frease*, 'The schools, self-concept and juvenile delinquency' *British Journal of Criminology*, XII, 1972, pp. 133-46.

M. F. *Friedell*, 'Organisations as semi-lattices' *American Sociological Review*, XXXII, 1967, pp. 46-53.

N. L. *Gage (ed.)*, *Handbook of Research on Teaching* (Chicago: Rand McNally, 1963).

D. E. M. *Gardner and J. E. Gross*, *The Role of the Teacher in the Infant and Nursery School* (Oxford: Pergamon, 1965).

H. *Garfinkel*, *Studies in Ethnomethodology* (New Jersey: Prentice Hall, 1967).

B. J. *Georgopolous and A. S. Tannebaum*, 'The distribution of control in organisations', *Social Forces*, XXXVI, 1958, pp.44-50.

J. W. Getzels, 'A psycho-sociological framework for the study of educational administration' *Harvard Education Review*, XXII, 1952.

J. W. Getzels and E. G. Guba, 'Role, role conflict and effectiveness: an empirical study' *American Sociological Review*, XIX, 1954, pp. 164-75.

J. W. Getzels and E. G. Guba, 'The structure of roles and role conflict in the teaching situation' *Journal of Educational Sociology*, XXIX, 1955.

R. Giallombardo, *Society of Women* (New York: Wiley, 1966).

D. R. Gibson, 'Professional socialization: the effects of a college course upon role conceptions of students in teacher training' *Educational Research*, XIV, 1972, pp. 213-18.

A. Giddens, 'Aspects of the social structure of a university hall of residence' *Sociological Review*, VIII, 1960, pp. 97-108.

H. Glennester and G. Wilson, *Paying for Private Schools* (London: Allen Lane, 1970).

E. Goffman, *The Presentation of Self in Everyday Life* (New York: Doubleday, 1959).

E. Goffman, *Asylums* (New York: Doubleday, 1959).

E. J. Goodacre, *Teachers and their Pupils' Home Background* (Slough: NFER, 1968).

W. J. Goode, 'A theory of role strain' *American Sociological Review*, XXV, 1960, pp. 483-96.

C. W. Gordon, *The Social System of the High School* (Glencoe: Free Press, 1957).

D. Graham, *Moral Learning and Development* (London: Batsford, 1972).

A. Graubard, *Radical Reform in the Free School Movement* (New York: Random House, 1972).

B. F. Green, 'Attitude Analysis' in G. Lindsey (ed.) *Handbook of Social Psychology* Vol. 1 (Reading: Addison-Wesley, 1954).

N. Gross, *Who Runs our Schools?* (New York: Wiley, 1958).

N. Gross and R. Herriot, *Staff Leadership in Public Schools* (New York: Wiley, 1965).

N. Gross, W. S. Mason and A. W. MacEachern, *Explorations in Role Analysis* (New York: Wiley, 1958).

N. Gross, J. B. Giacquinta and M. Bernstein, *Implementing Organisational Innovations: a sociological analysis of planned organisational change* (New York: Basic Books, 1971).

O. Grusky, 'Role conflict in organisations: a study of prison camp officials' *Administrative Quarterly*, IV, 1959, pp. 452-72.

O. *Grusky*, 'Organisational goals and behaviour of informal leaders' *American Journal of Sociology*, LXV, 1959, pp. 59-67.

R. *Gulliford*, *Special Education Needs* (London: Routledge, 1970).

A. W. *Halpin*, *The Leadership Behaviour of School Superintendants*, (Ohio State University, 1956).

A. W. *Halpin and D. G. Croft*, *The Organisational Climate of Schools* (Washington D.C.: U.S.O.E. Department of Health, Education and Welfare).

E. *Halsall*, *Inside the Comprehensive School* (Oxford: Pergamon, 1970).

A. H. *Halsey (ed.)*, *Educational Priority* (London: HMSO, 1972).

D. A. *Hansen and J. E. Gerstl (eds)*, *On Education - Sociological Perspectives* (New York: Wiley, 1967).

D. H. *Hargreaves*, *Social Relations in a Secondary School* (London: Routledge, 1967).

D. H. *Hargreaves*, *Interpersonal Relations and Education* (London: Routledge, 1972).

I. *Harper*, 'The role of the fringer in a state prison for women' *Social Forces*, XXXI, 1952, pp. 53-60.

K. *Heal, I. Sinclair and J. Troop*, 'Development of a social climate questionnaire for use in approved schools and community homes' *British Journal of Sociology*, XXIV, 1973, pp. 222-35.

M. E. *Highfield and A. Pinsent*, *A Survey of Rewards and Punishments in Schools* (London: Newnes, 1952).

S. *Hilsum and B. S. Cane*, *The Teacher's Day* (Slough: N.F.E.R., 1971).

J. *Hipkin*, 'Outsiders in the public schools' *New Society*, No. 303, 1968.

HMC, *Conference* - journal of the Head Masters' Conference.

HMSO, *Report of the Working Party on Assistance with the Cost of Boarding Education* (1960).

HMSO, *Committee on Public Schools* (the Fleming Report) 1944.

HMSO, *Committee on Higher Education* (the Robbins Report) 1963.

HMSO, *Public Schools Commission* First Report 1968, Second Report 1970.

HMSO, *Children and their Primary Schools* (The Plowden Report), 1967.

A. B. *Hollingshead*, *Elmtown's Youth* (Glencoe: Free Press, 1962).

J. *Holt*, *The Underachieving School* (Harmondsworth: Penguin, 1971).

J. Holt, *Why Children Fail* (Harmondsworth: Penguin, 1969).

E. Hopper *(ed.)*, *Readings in the Theory of Educational Systems* (London: Hutchinson, 1971).

T. E. B. Howarth, *Culture, Anarchy and the Public School* (London: Cassell, 1969).

E. Hoyle, 'Organisational analysis in the field of education' *Educational Research*, VII, 1965, pp. 97-114.

E. Hoyle, *The Role of the Teacher* (London: Routledge, 1969).

L. Hudson and B. Jacot, 'Education and eminence in British Medicine' *British Medical Journal*, IV, 1971, pp. 162-3.

E. C. Hughes and H. S. Becker, 'Student culture and academic effort' *Harvard Educational Review*, XXVIII, 1958, pp. 70-80.

P. M. Hughes, *Guidance and Counselling in Schools* (Oxford: Pergamon, 1971).

H. Hyman, *Survey Design and Analysis* (New York: Free Press, 1955).

H. Hyman, *Interviewing in Social Research* (Chicago University Press, 1954).

IAPS, *Choice: a survey of opinions of parents with sons as IAPS schools* (1967).

IAPS, *Evidence Submitted to the Public Schools' Commission* (1967).

IAPS, *Foundations: a reconsideration of teaching in preparatory schools* (1959).

IAPS, *Prospect: the purpose and practice of teaching in preparatory schools* (1965).

B. Jackson, *Streaming: and education system in miniature* (London: Routledge, 1964).

B. Jackson, *Working Class Community* (London: Routledge, 1968).

B. Jackson and D. Marsden, *Education and the Working Class* (London: Routledge, 1962).

P. Jacob, *Changing Values in College* (New York: Harper and Row, 1957).

P. Jebb *(ed.)*, *Religious Education* (London: Dartman, Longman and Todd, 1968).

G. E. Jensen, 'The school as a social system' *Education Research Bulletin*, XXXIII, 1954.

I. Johanneson, 'School differentiation and the social adjustment of the pupils' *Educational Research*, IV, 1962, pp. 133-9.

D. W. Johnson, *The Social Psychology of Education* (New York: Holt, Rinehart and Winston, 1971).

H. Jones, 'Approved schools - a theoretical model' *Sociological Review Monograph*, IX, 1965, pp. 99-110.

H. Jones, 'Approved schools and attitude change' *British Journal of Criminology*, XIII, 1973, pp. 148-56.

G. Kalton, *The Public Schools* (London: Longmans, 1966).

M. Kaser, *Memorandum on Soviet Boarding Schools* (Unpublished) 1967.

N. Keddie (ed.), *Tinker, Taylor* (Harmondsworth: Penguin, 1973).

J. Kelly, *Organisational Behaviour* (Illinois: Homewood, 1969).

M. Kellmer-Pringle, 'Differences between schools for the maladjusted and ordinary boarding schools' *British Journal of Educational Psychology*, XXXVII, 1956, pp. 29-36.

R. K. Kelsall, *Higher Civil Servants in Britain from 1870 to the Present Day* (London: Routledge, 1955).

R. K. and H. M. Kelsall, *Social Disadvantage and Educational Opportunity* (London: Holt, Rinehart and Winston, 1971).

J. F. Kerr (ed.), *Changing the Curriculum* (University of London Press, 1968).

R. King, *Education* (London: Longmans, 1969).

R. King, *Values and Involvement in a Grammar School* (London: Routledge, 1969).

R. King, *School Organisation and Pupil Involvement* (London: Routledge, 1973).

R. D. King and N. Raynes, 'An operational measure of management in residential institutions' *Social Science and Medicine*, II, 1968, pp. 41-53.

R. D. King, N. V. Raynes and J. Tizard, *Patterns of Residential Care* (London: Routledge, 1971).

H. R. Kohl, *The Open Classroom* (London: Methuen, 1970).

W. F. Koontz, 'A study of achievement as a function of homogeneous grouping' *Journal of Experimental Education*, XXX, 1962, pp.249-54.

I. Kopytoff, 'The Suku of South Western Congo' in J. L. Gibbs (ed.) *Peoples of Africa* (1965).

S. Kosofsky and A. Ellis, 'Illegal communications among institutionalised female delinquents' *Journal of Social Psychology*, XLVIII, 1958, pp. 155-60.

C. Lacey, *Hightown Grammar* (University of Manchester Press, 1970).

R. Lambert, *The State and Boarding Education* (London: Methuen, 1966).

R. Lambert, *The Demand for Boarding* (Cambridge County Council, 1966).

R. Lambert, 'State Boarding' *New Society*, No. 161, 1966.

R. Lambert, *Different Approaches to Boarding* (Cambridge: King's College Research Centre, 1966).

R. Lambert, 'State boarding a choice for all' *Where*, No. 21, 1969.

R. Lambert, 'What Dartington will do' *New Society*, No. 371, 1969.

R. Lambert, *Alternatives to School* (Exeter: University Press, 1971).

R. Lambert, 'The Public Schools: a sociological introduction' in G. Kalton, *The Public Schools*.

R. Lambert, 'Religion in the boarding school' in P. Jebb (ed.) *Religious Education*.

R. Lambert, 'The future of boarding in modern society' in M. Ash, *Who are the Progressives Now?*

R. Lambert and S. Millham, *The Hothouse Society* (London: Weidenfeld and Nicolson, 1968).

R. Lambert and R. Woolfe, 'Need and demand for boarding education' in *Public Schools Commission*, First Report, Vol. 2, Appendix 9.

R. Lambert, J. Hipkin and S. Stagg, *New Wine in Old Bottles?* (London: Bell, 1969).

R. Lambert, S. Millham and R. Bullock, *A Manual to the Sociology of the School* (London: Weidenfeld and Nicolson, 1970).

R. Lambert, S. Millham and R. Bullock, 'The informal social system' in R. K. Brown (ed.) *Knowledge, Education and Cultural Change*.

D. Lawrence, 'The effects of counselling on retarded readers' *Educational Research*, XIII, 1971, pp. 119-24.

D. Lawton, *Social Class, Language and Education* (London: Routledge, 1967).

D. Lawton, *Social Change, Educational Theory and Curriculum Planning* (University of London Press, 1973).

P. F. Lazarsfeld, 'Evidence and inference in social research' in D. Lerner, *Evidence and Inference* (New York: Free Press, 1959).

S. Leeson, *The Public Schools Question* (London: Longmans, 1948).

F. G. Lennhof, *Exceptional Children* (London: Allen and Unwin, 1960).

D. J. Levinson, 'Role personality and social structure in the organisational setting' *Journal of Abnormal and Social Psychology*, LVIII, 1959, pp. 170-80.

A. *Lewis*, 'The self-concepts of adolescent educationally subnormal boys' *Educational Research*, XV, 1972, pp. 16-20.

D. G. *Lewis*, 'Subject choice in the Sixth form: a critical view of research' *Educational Research*, XV, 1972, pp. 21-7.

K. L. *Little*, *The Mende of Sierra Leone* (London: Routledge, 1951).

G. *Loveluck*, *Secondary Education in Israel* (1966).

R. *Lynn*, 'The relation between educational achievement and school size' *British Journal of Sociology*, X, 1959, pp. 129-6.

H. *Lytton and M. Craft (eds)*, *Guidance and Counselling in Schools* (London: Edward Arnold, 1969).

J. D. R. *MacConnell*, *Eton: How it Works* (London: Faber, 1967).

E. L. *Mack*, *The Public School and British Opinion* (Columbia University Press, 1941).

J. *McLachlan*, *American Boarding Schools: an historical study* (New York: Scribner's, 1970).

Marlborough ('by the boys') (London: Keith Mason, 1963).

B. *Martin*, 'Progressive Education versus the working class' *Critical Quarterly*, 1972, pp.297-320.

P. L. *Masters*, *Preparatory Schools Today* (London: A. and C. Black, 1966).

T. *Mathiesen*, 'The sociology of prisons: problems for future research' *British Journal of Sociology*, XVII, 1966, pp. 360-77.

P. R. *May*, *Moral Education in School* (London: Methuen, 1971).

R. *Mayntz*, 'The study of organisations: a trend report and bibliography' *Current Sociology*, XIII, No. 3, 1964 (whole issue).

J. B. *Mays, W. Quine and K. Pickett*, *School of Tomorrow* (London: Longmans, 1968).

L. M. *McCorkle and P. Korn*, 'Resocialisation within walls' *Annals of American Adademy of Political Science*, CCXCIII, 1954, pp. 88-98.

L. *McDill, M. S. McDill and J. T. Sprehe*, *Strategies for Success in Comprehensive Schools: an appraisal of evaluation research* (London: Hopkins, 1969).

J. McG. *McMaster*, *Toward an Educational Theory for the Mentally Handicapped* (London: Edward Arnold, 1973).

I. E. P. *Menzies*, 'A case study in the functioning of social systems as a defence against anxiety' *Tavistock Pamphlet No. 3* (London, 1963).

R. K. *Merton*, 'The role set: problems in sociological theory' *British Journal of Sociology*, VIII, 1957, pp. 106-20.

R. K. *Merton*, *Social Theory and Social Structure* (Glencoe: Free Press, 1957).

R. K. Merton, M. Fiske and P. Kendall, *The Focussed Interview* (New York: Free Press, 1956).

R. K. Merton, A. P. Gray, B. Hockey and H. C. Selvin, *Reader in Bureaucracy*, (Glencoe: Free Press, 1952).

J. A. Michael, 'High school climate and plans for entering college' *Public Opinion Quarterly*, XXV, 1961, pp.585-95.

E. Midwinter, *Projections* (London: Ward Lock, 1971).

E. Midwinter, *Social Environment and the Urban School* (London: Ward Lock, 1971).

E. Midwinter, *Patterns of Community Education* (London: Ward Lock, 1972).

D. Miller, *The Age Between* (London: Cornmarket and Hutchinson, 1969).

S. Millham and R. Bullock, 'When a child goes to school' *Where* January 1969).

S. Millham, R. Bullock and P. Cherrett, 'Research in approved schools' *Approved Schools' Gazette*, June 1969, pp. 123-7.

S. Millham, R. Bullock and P. Cherrett, 'Styles of coeducational boarding' and 'Coeducation in approved schools' *Child in Care*, XII, 1971.

S. Millham, R. Bullock and P. Cherrett, 'Some findings of the first stage of research into approved schools' *Community Schools' Gazette*, December 1971, pp. 502-17.

S. Millham, 'The residential care of adolescents', *Proceedings of the Sixth Conference*, Association for the Psychiatric Study of Adolescents, 1971.

S. Millham, R. Bullock and P. Cherrett, 'Social control in organisations' *British Journal of Sociology*, XXIII, 1972, pp. 406-21.

S. Millham, R. Bullock and P. Cherrett, 'Can we legislate for care?' *Special Education*, LXII, 1973, pp. 10-13.

S. Millham, R. Bullock and P. Cherrett, 'Analytic framework for the comparative study of residential institutions' and 'Socialization in residential institutions' in J. Tizard et al. (ed.) *Varieties of Residential Experience*, (London: Routledge, 1974).

S. Millham, R. Bullock and P. Cherrett, *Approved Schools and Their Effects* (London: Chaucer, 1974).

C. W. Mills, *The Power Elite* (New York: Oxford University Press, 1956).

W. S. More, 'The personality of residential staff' *Residential Social Work*, XIII, 1973, pp. 70-2.

J. L. Moreno, *The Sociometry Reader* (Glencoe: Free Press, 1960).

B. Morris, 'Reflections on role analysis' *British Journal of Sociology*, XXII, 1971, pp. 395-409.

P. Morris, *Put Away: a sociological study of institutions for the mentally retarded* (London: Routledge, 1969).

R. N. Morris, *The Sixth Form and College Entrance* (London: Routledge, 1969).

T. and P. Morris, *Pentonville - a sociological study of an English Prison* (London: Routledge, 1963).

I. Morrish, *The Sociology of Education* (London: Allen and Unwin, 1972).

A. Morrison and D. McIntyre, *Schools and Socialization* (Harmondsworth: Penguin, 1970).

A. Morrison and D. McIntyre (eds), *Social Psychology of Teaching* (Harmondsworth: Penguin, 1972).

C. A. Moser, *Survey Methods in Social Investigation* (London: Heinemann, 1958).

M. Mouzelis, *Organisation and Bureaucracy* (London: Routledge, 1967).

P. W. Musgrave, *Sociology, History and Education* (London: Methuen, 1970).

P. W. Musgrave, *Sociology of Education* (London: Methuen, 1965).

P. W. Musgrave, *The School as an Organisation* (London: Macmillan, 1968).

F. Musgrove, *Family, Education and Society* (London: Routledge, 1966).

F. Musgrove, *Patterns of Power and Authority in English Education* (London: Methuen, 1970).

F. Musgrove and P. W. Taylor, *Society and the Teacher's Role* (London: Routledge, 1969).

R. Nash, 'Clique formations among primary and secondary school children' *British Journal of Sociology*, XXIV, 1973, pp. 303-11.

A. S. Neill, *Summerhill* (London: Gollancz, 1962).

A. S. Neill, *Neill! Neill! Orange Peel!* (London: Weidenfeld and Nicolson, 1973).

J. L. Nelson and F. P. Besag, *Sociological Perspectives in Education: Models of Analysis* (New York: Pitman, 1970).

T. M. Newcomb, *Personality and Social Change: attitude formation in a student community* (New York: Holt, Rinehart and Winston, 1943).

T. Newcomb, 'Student peer group influence' in N. Sanford, *College and Character*.

410/Bibliography

T. M. Newcomb, K. E. Koenig, R. Flacks and D. P. Warwick, *Persistence and Change: Bennington College and its Students after Twenty Five Years* (New York: Wiley, 1967).

New Era - journal of the New Education Fellowship.

D. Newsome, *Godliness and Good Learning* (London: Murray, 1961).

J. D. Nisbet, J. Welsh and N. J. Entwistle, 'Age of transfer to secondary education: a postscript' *British Journal of Educational Psychology*, XLII, 1972.

K. Ollerenshaw, *The Girls' School* (London: Faber, 1967).

A. N. Oppenheim, 'Social status and clique formation among grammar-school boys' *British Journal of Sociology*, VI, 1955, pp. 228-45.

A. N. Oppenheim, *Questionnaire Design and Attitude Measurement* (London: Heinemann, 1966).

C. D. Orth, *Social Structure and Learning Climate* (London: Routledge, 1962).

C. E. Osgood, G. J. Suci and P. H. Tannebaum, *The Measurement of Meaning* (Urbana: University Press, 1957).

V. Packard, *The Status Seekers* (London: Longmans, 1960).

T. Parsons, 'Suggestions for a sociological model of the theory of organisations' *Administrative Science Quarterly* I, 1956, pp. 63-85 and pp. 225-39.

T. Parsons, 'The school class as a social system' in Floud, *Education, Economy and Society* pp. 434-55.

T. Parsons, 'Sociological approach to the theory of organisations' in A. Etzioni (ed.), *Complex Organisations: a sociological reader*.

T. Parsons, *The Social System* (New York: Free Press, 1951).

T. Parsons and E. A. Shils, *Toward a General Theory of Action* (Harvard University Press, 1952).

J. Partridge, *Life in a Secondary Modern School* (London: Gollancz, 1966).

A. Passow, M. Goldberg and J. Justman, *The Effects of Ability Grouping* (Columbia College Press, 1966).

J. Patrick, *A Glasgow Gang Observed* (London: Eyre Methuen, 1973).

G. F. Peaker, *The Plowden Children 4 Years Later* (Slough: N.F.E.R., 1971).

L. I. Pearlin, 'Sources of resistance to change in a mental hospital' *American Journal of Sociology*, LXVII, 1962, pp. 325-34.

R. F. Peck, 'Predicting principal's ratings of teacher performance from personality data' *Journal of Educational Psychology*, L, 1959.

R. Pedley, *The Comprehensive School* (Harmondsworth: Penguin, 1969).

C. Perrow, 'Hospitals: technology, structure and goals' in J. G. March

Handbook of Organisations (Chicago: Rand, McNally, 1965).

C. *Perrow*, *Organisational Analysis: a sociological view* (London: Tavistock, 1970).

D. A. *Pidgeon*, 'School type differences in ability and attainment' *Educational Research*, I, 1958, pp. 62-71.

K. *Polk and W. Pink*, 'Youth culture and the school: a replication' *British Journal of Sociology*, XXII, 1971, pp. 160-71.

H. W. *Polsky*, *Cottage Six* (New York: Wiley, 1962).

H. W. *Polsky*, *The Dynamics of Residential Treatment* (N. Carolina University Press, 1968).

J. *Porter*, *The Vertical Mosaic: an analysis of social class and power in Canada*, (Toronto University Press, 1965).

F. W. *Posselt*, 'Coeducation in approved/community schools' *Community Schools Gazette*, LXVI and LXVII, 1973, pp. 689-96. and 19-25.

C. *Poster*, *The School as a Community* (London: Macmillan, 1971).

M. J, *Power*, *M. R. Alderson, C. M. Phillipson, E. Shoenberg and J. N. Morris*, 'Delinquent schools' *New Society*, 19 October 1967 pp. 542-3.

M. J. *Power, R. T. Benn and J. N. Morris*, 'Neighbourhood, school and juveniles before the court' *British Journal of Criminology*, XII, 1972, pp.111-32.

A. H. J. *Prinz*, 'The Swahili speaking people of Zanzibar and the East African Coast', in *Ethnographic Survey of Africa* (International African Institute, 1950).

D. *Pugh, D. J. Hickson and C. R. Hinings*, *Writers on Organisations* (London: Hutchinson, 1964).

D. *Pugh, D. J. Hickson and C. R. Hinings*, 'A conceptual scheme for organisational analysis' *Administrative Science Quarterly*, VIII, 1963, pp. 289-315.

M. *Punch*, *A Comparative Study of Three Boarding Schools* (M.A. Thesis) (University of Essex, 1966).

M. *Punch*, *Dartington Hall*, (PhD Thesis) (University of Cambridge 1972).

M. *Punch*, 'W. B. Curry, a reassessment' *New Era*, VIII, 1972.

J. *Purvis*, 'School teaching as a professional career' *British Journal of Sociology*, XXIV, 1973, pp.43-57.

H. *Richardson*, *Adolescent Girls in Approved School* (London: Routledge, 1969).

R. *Richardson and J. Chapman*, *Images of Life* (London: S.C.M. Press, 1973).

W. K. Richmond, The Teaching Revolution (London: Methuen, 1967).

W. K. Richmond, The School Curriculum (London: Methuen, 1970).

W. K. Richmond, The Free School (London: Methuen, 1973).

L. Ridgway and I. Lawton, Family Grouping in the Infants' School (London: Ward Lock, 1965).

G. Rose, Schools for Young Offenders (London: Tavistock, 1967).

V. Rosenshine, Teaching Behaviours and Student Achievement (Slough: N.F.E.R., 1971).

P. Rosenthal and L. Jacobson, Pygmalion in the Classroom (New York: Holt, Rinehart and Winston, 1968).

J. W. Ross, W. J. Bunton, P. Erinson and T. S. Robertson, A Critical Appraisal of Comprehensive Education (Slough: N.F.E.R., 1972).

B. Russell, On Education especially in Early Childhood (London: Allen and Unwin, 1926).

D. A. Sanford, 'An operant analysis of control procedures in a New Zealand Borstal' British Journal of Criminology, XIII, 1973, pp. 262-8.

N. Sanford, College and Character (New York: Wiley, 1964).

N. Sanford, The American College: a psychological and social interpretation of the higher learning (New York: Wiley, 1962).

I. Scapera, A Handbook of Tswana Law and Custom (1938).

Schools Council, Young School Leavers Enquiry No. 1 (London: HMSO, 1968).

G. Schwab, 'Tribes of the Liberian hinterland' in D. G. Scanlon (ed.), Traditions of African Education (1969).

M. S. Schwarz, 'The uses of sociology in the Mental Hospital' Social Problems, X, 1963, pp. 219-27.

M. S. Schwarz, 'Social research in the mental hospital' in A. M. Rose Mental Health and Mental Disorder (London: Routledge, 1956) pp. 190-202.

M. Seeman, Social Status and Leadership: the case of the school executive (Ohio University Press, 1960).

C. Selltiz, M. Jahoda, M. Deutsch and S. W. Cook, Research Methods in Social Relations (London: Methuen, 1965).

P. C. Sexton, The American School; a sociological analysis (Englewood Cliffs: Prentice Hall, 1967).

A. Sharrock, Home - school Relationships: their importance in Education (London: Macmillan, 1970).

A. Shepherd, 'Married women teachers - role perceptions and career patterns' Educational Research, XIII, 1971, pp. 191-7.

M. Shipman, 'Education and college culture' British Journal of

Sociology, XVIII, 1967, pp. 425-34.

M. *Shipman*, *The Sociology of the School* (London: Longmans, 1968).

M. *Shipman*, *Curriculum Innovation - a case study of a development project* (London: Routledge, 1972).

C. *Shrag*, 'Leadership among prison inmates' *American Sociological Review*, 1954, pp. 37-42.

H. *Silver (ed.)*, *Equal Opportunity in Education* (London: Methuen, 1973).

D. *Silverman*, *The Theory of Organisations* (London: Heinemann, 1970).

J. *Simmonds*, 'The use of group methods in community schools' *Community Schools Gazette*, LXVI, 1973, pp. 514-22.

A. *Simon and L. O. Ward*, 'Age, sex, history grades and moral judgement in comprehensive school pupils' *Educational Research*, XIV, 1972, pp. 191-4.

R. *L. Simpson*, 'Vertical and horizontal communication in formal organisations' *Administrative Science Quarterly*, IV, 1959, pp. 188-96.

R. *L. Simpson and W. H. Gulley*, 'Goals, environmental pressures and organisational characteristics' *American Sociological Review*, XXVII, 1962, pp 344-51.

I. *Sinclair*, *Hostels for Probationers* (London: HMSO, 1971).

I. *Sinclair and R. Clarke*, 'Acting out behaviour and its significance for the residential treatment of delinquents' *Journal of Child Psychology and Psychiatry*, XIV, 1973, pp. 283-91.

G. *M. Sykes and S. L. Messinger*, 'The inmate social system' in Grosser et al., *Theoretical Studies in the Social Organisation of the Prison* (New York: Social Science Research Council, 1960), pp. 5-19.

H. *J. Taylor*, *School Counselling* (London: Macmillan, 1971).

I. *Taylor*, 'Sociological approaches to juvenile institutions' *Approved Schools Gazette*, LXII, 1968, pp. 487-92.

L. *C. Taylor*, *Education at Sevenoaks* (London: Constable, 1965).

P. *Taylor*, 'Children's evaluations of the good teacher' *British Journal of Educational Psychology*, XXXII, 1962, pp. 258-66.

W. *Taylor*, *The Secondary Modern School* (London: Faber, 1963).

W. *Taylor*, 'Student culture and residence' *Universities Quarterly*, XIX, 1965, pp. 331-44.

W. *Taylor*, *Society and the Education of Teachers* (London: Faber, 1969).

T. *G. Tennent*, 'School non-attendance and delinquency' *Educational Research*, XIII, 1971, pp. 185-90.

J. *D. Thompson and W. McEwen*, 'Organisational goals and environment: goal setting as an interactional process' *American Sociological Review,* XXIII, 1958, pp. 23-31.

E. *Thrane, Education and Culture in Denmark* (1958).

Tonbridge ('by the boys') Keith Mason, 1964.

D. *Toomey,* 'Home centred working-class parents' attitudes towards their sons' education and careers' *Sociology,* III, 1969, pp. 299-319.

H. E. R. *Townsend, Immigrant Pupils in England: the L.E.A. Response* (Slough: N.F.E.R., 1971).

C. M. *Turnbull,* 'Initiation among the Bambuti pygmies of the central hari' *Journal of the Royal Anthropological Institute,* 1957, pp. 191-216.

C. M. *Turner,* 'An organisational analysis of a secondary modern school' *Sociological Review,* XVII, 1969, pp. 67-86.

N. S. *Tutt, Care or Containment: Community Homes and the Treatment of Delinquency* (London: Longmans, 1974).

J. P. *Twyman and B. J. Biddle,* 'Role conflict of public school teachers' *Journal of Psychology,* LV, 1963, pp 183-98.

A. *van Gennep, Les Rites de Passage* (Paris: Nourry, 1909).

R. *Skidelsky, English Progressive Schools* (Harmondsworth: Penguin, 1970).

G. *Snow, The Public Schools in the New Age* (London: Bles, 1959).

S. *Soles,* 'Teacher role expectations and the internal organisation of secondary schools' *Journal of Educational Research,* LVII, 1964, pp. 227-38.

M. *Spinley, The Deprived and Privileged* (London: Routledge, 1953).

M. E. *Spiro, Children of the Kibbutz* (Harvard University Press, 1958).

J. C. *Stanley (ed.), Compensatory Education for Children Aged 2-8* (London: Hopkins, 1973).

A. H. *Stanton and M. Schwarz, The Mental Hospital* (New York: Basic Books, 1954).

J. *Starr,* 'Attitudes to corporal punishment among student teachers' *Educational Research,* XII, 1969, pp. 51-5.

F. M. *Stevens, Living Tradition: the social and educational assumptions of the Grammar school* (London: Hutchinson, 1960).

W. A. C. *Stewart, The Educational Innovators* (2 vols) (London: Macmillan, 1968).

D. *Street, R. D. Vinter and C. Perrow, Organisations for Treatment* (New York: Free Press, 1966).

D. H. *Stott, Studies of Troublesome Children* (London: Tavistock, 1965).

S. *Stouffer,* 'An analysis of conflicting social norms' *American*

Sociological Review, XIV, 1949, pp. 707-17.

A. L. *Strauss*, *Psychiatric Ideologies and Institutions* (New York: Free Press, 1964).

B. *Sugarman*, 'Youth culture, academic achievement and conformity' *British Journal of Sociology*, XVIII, 1967, pp. 151-64.

B. *Sugarman*, 'Social class and values as related to achievement and conduct in school' *Sociological Review*, XIV, 1966, pp. 287-301.

B. *Sugarman*, *The School and Moral Development* (London: Croom Helm, 1973).

M. B. *Sutherland*, 'Coeducation and school attainment' *British Journal of Educational Psychology*, XXXI, 1961, pp. 158-69.

N. E. *Svenson*, 'Ability grouping and scholastic achievement' *Educational Research*, V, 1962, pp. 53-6.

D. F. *Swift*, 'Social class and educational adaptation' in H. J. Butcher, *Educational Research in Britain*.

G. M. *Sykes*, *Society of Captives* (Princeton University Press, 1958).

A. J. *Vidich*, 'Participant observation and the collection and interpretation of data' *American Journal of Sociology*, LX, 1955, pp. 355.

G. *Wagner*, *The Bantu of N. Kavirondo* (Oxford University Press, 1949).

J. *Wakeford*, *The Cloistered Elite* (London: Macmillan, 1969).

W. D. *Wall*, *Adolescents in School and Society* (Slough: N.F.E.R., 1968).

W. *Waller*, *The Sociology of Teaching* (New York: Wiley, 1932).

J. *Walton (ed.)*, *Curriculum Organisation and Design* (London: Ward Lock, 1971).

D. A. *Ward and G. G. Kassebaum*, 'Lesbian liaisons' *Transactions*, I, 1964.

D. A. *Ward and G. G. Kassebaum*, 'Homosexuality: a mode of adaptation in a prison for women' *Social Problems*, XII, 1964, pp. 159-77.

D. A. *Ward and G. G. Kassebaum*, *Women's Prison* (London: Weidenfeld and Nicolson, 1965).

C. *Washbourne*, 'The teacher in the authority system' *Journal of Educational Sociology*, XXX, 1957.

M. H. *Watkins*, 'The West African bush school' *American Journal of Sociology*, XLVIII, 1943, pp. 1666-75.

J. *Webb*, 'The sociology of a school' *British Journal of Sociology*, XIII, 1962, pp. 264-72.

N. *Wein*, 'The education of disadvantaged children' *Educational Research*, XIII, 1970, pp. 12-19.

I. *Weinberg*, *The English Public School: the sociology of elite education*

416/Bibliography

(New York: Atherton, 1967).

C. F. Wellford, 'Contact and commitment in a correctional community' *British Journal of Criminology*, XIII, 1973, pp. 108-20.

C. Werthman, 'Delinquents in schools' *Berkeley Journal of Sociology*, VIII, 1963, pp. 39-60.

D. J. West and D. Farrington, *Who Becomes Delinquent?* (London: Heinemann, 1974).

L. J. Westwood, 'The role of the teacher' *Educational Research*, IX, 1966, pp. 21-37 and X, 1967, pp. 122-34.

S. Wheeler, 'Socialization in correctional communities' *American Sociological Review*, XXVI, 1961, pp. 697-712.

S. Whiteley et al, *Dealing with Deviants* (London: Hogarth, 1972).

W. F. Whyte, *Street Corner Society* (Chicago University Press, 1953).

R. Wilkinson, *The Prefects* (Oxford University Press, 1964).

R. C. Williams, 'The effects of school change on Service children' *Torch*, 1965.

C. J. Willig, 'Social implications of streaming in the junior school' *Educational Research*, V, 1962, pp. 151-4.

D. Wills, *Spare the Child* (Harmondsworth: Penguin, 1971).

B. Wilson, 'The teacher's role' *British Journal of Sociology*, XIII, 1962, pp. 15-32.

J. Wilson, *Public Schools and Private Practice* (London: Allen and Unwin, 1962).

J. Wilson, 'Three myths of educational research' *Educational Research*, XVI, 1973, pp. 17-19.

J. Wilson, N. Jackson and B. Sugarman, *Moral Education* (Harmondsworth: Penguin, 1967).

J. Wing, 'Institutionalism in mental hospitals' *British Journal of Social and Clinical Psychology*, I, 1962, pp. 38-51.

R. W. Winslow, 'Status management in the adolescent social system' *British Journal of Sociology*, XIX, 1968, pp. 143-59.

S. Wiseman, 'The educational obstacle: factors that hinder pupil progress' *Educational Research*, XV, 1973, pp. 87-93.

J. Withall, 'Assessment of the social emotional climates and experiences by a group of seventh grades as they moved from class to class' *Educational Psychology Measurement*, XII, 1952.

R. W. Witkin, 'Social class influence on the amount and type of positive evaluation of school lessons' *Sociology*, V, 1971, pp. 169-89.

M. Wober, *English Girls' Boarding Schools* (London: Allen Lane, 1971).

M. Wober, 'The meaning of convergence and divergence with data from girls' secondary schools' *Educational Review*, XXIII, 1970, pp. 33-49.

J. Wolfenden, *The Public Schools Today* (University of London Press, 1948).

R. Woolfe, 'A role for boarding education in the context of the social services' *Social and Economic Administration*, II, 1968.

A. D. Wooster and G. Harris, 'Concept of self and others in highly mobile servide boys' *Educational Research*, XIV, 1972, pp. 195-9.

A. Yates and D. A. Pidgeon, 'The effects of streaming' *Educational Research*, II, 1959, pp. 65-9.

D. A. Young and W. Brandis, 'Two types of streaming and their possible application in comprehensive school' *Bulletin*, XI, 1965.

M. Young and P. McGeeney, *Learning Begins at Home* (London: Routledge, 1968).

M. F. D. Young (ed.), *Knowledge and Control* (London: Collier Macmillan, 1971).

M. N. Zald, 'Organisational control structures in five correctional institutions' *American Journal of Sociology*, LXVIII, 1963, pp. 335-45

H. Zetterberg, *On Theory and Verification in Sociology* (New York: Bedminster, 1954).

Index